Bel ang

Bounded Rationality and Policy Diffusion

Bounded Rationality and Policy Diffusion

SOCIAL SECTOR REFORM IN LATIN AMERICA

Kurt Weyland

PRINCETON UNIVERSITY PRESS

PRINCETON AND OXFORD

Copyright © 2006 by Princeton University Press

Published by Princeton University Press, 41 William Street, Princeton, New Jersey 08540

In the United Kingdom: Princeton University Press, 3 Market Place, Woodstock, Oxfordshire OX20 1SY

Library of Congress Cataloging-in-Publication Data
Weyland, Kurt Gerhard.
  Bounded rationality and policy diffusion : social sector reform in Latin America / Kurt Weyland.
    p. cm.
  Includes bibliographical references and index.
  ISBN-13: 978-0-691-12974-7 (hardcover : alk. paper)
  ISBN-13: 978-0-691-13471-0 (paperback : alk. paper)
1. Latin America—Social policy—Case studies.   2. Decision making—Latin America—Case studies.   3. Policy sciences.   I. Title.
HN110.5.A8W44   2007
361.6′1098—dc22

                                                                        2006102734

British Library Cataloging-in-Publication Data is available

This book has been composed in Sabon.

Printed on acid-free paper. ∞

press.princeton.edu

Printed in the United States of America

10 9 8 7 6 5 4 3 2 1

Contents

Preface

BOOKS RAISE as many questions as they answer. In analyzing some aspects of the incredibly complex world of politics, even substantial-sized volumes inevitably neglect others. In this vein, my 2002 study of market reforms in Latin America focused on political choices in their domestic context and did not examine how decision-makers learned from the experiences of other countries. But of course, there was constant cross-national interaction before and during the wavelike enactment of structural adjustment. For instance, the theory of inertial inflation elaborated by Brazilian economists helped inspire Argentina's Plan Austral, and the initial success of that stabilization program in turn provided a stimulus for Brazil's Plano Cruzado. And in the 1990s, Brazil deliberately avoided the rigidities created by Argentina's convertibility scheme.

Latin American decision-makers frequently learn from experiences beyond their borders. This exchange of information, which is particularly intense inside the region, takes place among chief executives, among party politicians, and especially among technical experts. In designing reform projects, policy-makers commonly consider experiments conducted in their neighborhood. As a result, new policy models developed in one country can sweep across the region in a wave of diffusion. But political science is only beginning to analyze the cross-national spread of innovations systematically. While some scholars have studied the "teaching" of reform models and principles by international organizations, the reception of foreign inputs, that is, learning by domestic policy-makers, has attracted insufficient attention. My study helps to fill this gap by investigating, through in-depth field research, the diffusion of social policy reforms in five Latin American countries. In this way, I hope to shed light on the causal mechanisms that drive the spread of innovations and to contribute to broader theoretical debates in political science, as chapters 1 and 2 explain.

Like so much in life, this book had a serendipitous origin. In 1999, Allison Garland and Joe Tulchin of the Woodrow Wilson Center asked me to help organize a conference in their social policy series. Aware of the omission in the market reform book that I was writing at that time, I took advantage of this opportunity and proposed the topic of diffusion. To stimulate "data creation," we deliberately invited Latin American experts who had participated in important reform projects and asked them to analyze the influence of foreign models on their thinking

viii • Preface

and decision making (Weyland 2004a). The rich experiences of these impressive specialists suggested the core ideas for the present book. Since their chapters and a number of other studies I knew at the time (especially Brooks n.d.; Kaufman and Nelson 2004a, 2004b; Kay 1998; Madrid 2003b) covered pension and health reform in the major Latin American countries, I concentrated my own field research on understudied cases, namely, Bolivia, Costa Rica, El Salvador, and Peru. My initial goal was to draw on this primary and secondary research to cover reform diffusion in Latin America as a whole. But my interest in cognitive processes required specialized, focused inquiries, such as interview questions about options not considered or pursued. Because other scholars examined mainly political-economy factors, their excellent analyses did not yield sufficient evidence on these issues. Therefore, I had to focus the present book on the five nations in which I myself conducted interviews with many leading decision-makers.

In carrying out a research project, one incurs many debts. I am especially grateful to the numerous experts and policy-makers who shared their amazing experiences in often long interviews. They provided insights on the inner workings of the decision-making process that are indispensable for my study. Nothing I say in this book, especially my emphasis on cognitive heuristics that can distort judgments, is meant in any way to criticize their efforts, often conducted under very challenging circumstances. As cognitive psychology stresses, inferential shortcuts shape human decision making in general; they are inherent strategies of the mind, not the product of individual failings.

Among the many scholars who contributed to this project, a few stand out. Rose McDermott again was extremely generous in guiding me through the psychology literature; on many occasions, she broadened my bounds of rationality by making readings "available" that I would otherwise have neglected. She also checked my application of psychological concepts to political science but is in no way responsible for any remaining problems. As for my market reform book, Andrew Stein used his superhuman capacity for information processing (where are his bounds of rationality?) to send me innumerable important documents, reports, and data. At the University of Texas, I am uniquely privileged in having a leading pension reform expert down the hallway. Raúl Madrid has always been available to discuss ideas, share documents from his fabulous archive, and push me to be clearer in my reasoning and writing. He has made a fundamental contribution to the present project. Moreover, the Latin American faculty study group at UT, which also includes Henry Dietz, Larry Graham, Ken Greene, Juliet Hooker, and Wendy Hunter, offered excellent feedback and important encouragement. A similar group at the University of Notre Dame, composed of Michael

Coppedge, Fran Hagopian, Mala Htun, Wendy Hunter, and Scott Mainwaring, helped me greatly to improve the first two chapters. And I am very grateful to John Higley for his continued support and faith in me.

In addition, I gratefully acknowledge the excellent comments on draft chapters that I received over the years from Daniel Béland, Jeffrey Berejikian, Catherine Boone, Sarah Brooks, Alberto Díaz Cayeros, Jorge Domínguez, Robert Fishman, Carol Graham, Merilee Grindle, Stephan Haggard, Darren Hawkins, Evelyne Huber, Andrew Karch, Peter Katzenstein, Stephen Kay, Robert Kaufman, Marcus Kurtz, Isabela Mares, Covadonga Meseguer, Gabriela Nava-Campos, Juan Carlos Navarro, Joan Nelson, Irfan Nooruddin, Guillermo O'Donnell, Mitchell Orenstein, Nita Rudra, Ben Schneider, Kathryn Sikkink, Richard Snyder, Barbara Stallings, J. Samuel Valenzuela, Edurne Zoco, Jonas Zoninsein, and seminar participants at Arizona State University, Brown University, the Federal Reserve Bank of Atlanta, Harvard University, Ohio State University, Stanford University, Syracuse University, University of Notre Dame, University of Texas at Austin, and Universidad de la República in Montevideo, Uruguay. I am especially indebted to Raúl Madrid, Mitchell Orenstein, and Jeremy Shiffman for their excellent, detailed comments on large parts of the book manuscript.

I thank the Kellogg Institute at the University of Notre Dame for generously funding my fellowship in 2004–05 and for offering a highly congenial research environment. Ample support for my field research was provided by the Teresa Lozano Long Institute of Latin American Studies at the University of Texas at Austin from funds granted by the Andrew W. Mellon Foundation. I am grateful to *World Politics* and Johns Hopkins University Press for granting me permission to draw very heavily on Weyland (2005b) in the first half of chapter 2 and a small section of chapter 1. I also thank Chuck Myers for shepherding this book through the review process so smoothly, and Deborah Tegarden and Anita O'Brien for their excellent help with the production and copy editing of the book.

As always, it is a special pleasure to thank my wonderful wife, Wendy Hunter, skillful multitasker, doting mother, ferocious minivan driver, incisive critic of highfalutin political science theorizing, and outstanding *brasilianista*: ¡Gracias por acompañarme en toda esta aventura! The book is dedicated to my sons, Andi and Niko, the joys of my life. They adjusted admirably well to unexpected circumstances—such as attending Spanish- and Portuguese-speaking daycares—during our trips to Bolivia, Brazil, and Peru. These experiences gave them the important insight that most of humankind does not enjoy the luxuries of middle-class life that we take for granted in beautiful Austin, Texas.

Abbreviations

ACS	Agente Comunitário de Saúde (Brazil)
AFP	Administradora de Fondos de Pensiones (Chile, Bolivia, El Salvador)
ANFIP	Associação Nacional dos Auditores Fiscais de Contribuições Previdenciárias (Brazil)
ANSAL	Análisis del Sector Salud de El Salvador
ARENA	Alianza Republicana Nacionalista (El Salvador)
BONOSOL	Bono Solidario (Bolivia)
CCSS	Caja Costarricense de Seguro Social
CEPB	Confederación de Empresarios Privados de Bolivia
CLAS	Comité Local de Administración en Salud (Peru)
EBAIS	Equipo Básico de Atención Integral de Salud (Costa Rica)
EPS	Empresa/Entidad Prestadora de Salud (Peru)
EPS	Entidad Promotora de Salud (Colombia)
ESS	Empresa Solidaria de Salud (Colombia)
FMLN	Frente Farabundo Martí para la Liberación Nacional (El Salvador)
FUSADES	Fundación Salvadoreña para el Desarrollo Económico y Social
GDP	Gross domestic product
HMO	Health maintenance organization (United States)
IDB	Inter-American Development Bank
IFI	International financial institution
IL	Instituto Liberal (Brazil)
ILO	International Labour Organisation
IMF	International Monetary Fund
IO	International organization
IPEA	Instituto de Pesquisa Econômica Aplicada (Brazil)
IPS	Institución Prestadora de Servicios de Salud (Colombia)
IPSS	Instituto Peruano de Seguridad Social
ISAPRE	Institución de Salud Previsional (Chile)
MPAS	Ministério da Previdência e Assistência Social (Brazil)
NDC	Notional defined-contribution [pension system]
NGO	Nongovernmental organization
PAHO	Pan-American Health Organization
PAYG	Pay-as-you-go [pension system]
PCB	Partido Comunista Brasileiro
PCI	Partito Comunista Italiano

PFSS	Programa de Fortalecimiento de Servicios de Salud (Peru)
PSBPT	Programa de Salud Básica para Todos (Peru)
PSF	Programa Saúde da Família (Brazil)
SEG	Seguro Escolar Gratuito (Peru)
SIBASI	Sistema Básico de Salud Integral (El Salvador)
SMI	Seguro Materno Infantil (Peru)
SNMN	Seguro Nacional de Maternidad y Niñez (Bolivia)
SUS	Sistema Único de Saúde (Brazil)
UDAPSO	Unidad de Análisis de Políticas Sociales (Bolivia)
UNICEF	United Nations Children's Fund
USAID	United States Agency for International Development
WB	World Bank
WBIEG	World Bank Independent Evaluation Group
WHO	World Health Organization

Bounded Rationality and Policy Diffusion

CHAPTER 1

The Puzzle of Policy Diffusion

WHY DO DISSIMILAR countries adopt similar policy innovations? Why do some new policy models therefore diffuse across regions of the world, spreading like wildfire from the originating nation to countries with different economic, social, or political characteristics? Examples of such striking waves of diffusion abound. The social security system enacted by Otto von Bismarck in Imperial Germany quickly found emulators, first inside Europe, but soon on other continents as well. In this way, a policy scheme designed to pacify a powerful, well-organized, and increasingly militant working class spread to countries where workers constituted a small minority—sometimes noisy, but certainly without much clout. In subsequent decades, the Bismarckian model was imitated by nations at ever lower levels of socioeconomic development, which clearly lacked the domestic needs accounting for its initial adoption in Germany. Why would such different countries enact the same basic model?

Similarly, Ronald Reagan's income tax simplification of 1986 found imitators in countries with very different socioeconomic structures. For instance, Brazil adopted a similar reform in 1988 despite its exceptionally high degree of income inequality, which the reduction of marginal tax rates threatened to exacerbate. Also, since only a small number of middle- and upper-class Brazilians earn enough income to be liable for tax payments, lowering their tax rates jeopardized state revenues. Yet despite the divergent socioeconomic context, Brazil imitated a reform designed for the more developed United States.

Last but not least, the pension privatization enacted by Chile in the early 1980s has spread in Latin America and beyond. Strikingly, even poor countries such as Bolivia and El Salvador have privatized their social security systems although they seem to lack important preconditions for making private pension funds operate successfully. For instance, the formal labor market comprises only a small part of the workforce, severely restricting the coverage of the new social security system. Capital markets may be too underdeveloped to invest affiliates' individual pension funds profitably. And the state's institutional capacities for regulating private pension funds are limited as well. Yet despite the absence of presumed prerequisites for drastic pension reform (WB 1994a: 231, 245,

280; WB IEG 2006: x, xv, xvii, 18–29), these underdeveloped nations followed the lead of the more advanced frontrunner.

The spread of similarity amid diversity that policy diffusion entails raises a puzzle. Why do countries eagerly emulate foreign models that do not seem to fit their own domestic characteristics? Why do they adopt innovations despite lacking crucial prerequisites for making the new policy scheme work (cf. Collier and Messick 1975)? As functional needs cannot account for this rush to imitation, what drives waves of diffusion? Why do so many countries follow the leader, although this herd-like behavior may not be best suited for their specific needs? In short, what causal mechanisms underlie the diffusion of policy innovations across countries?

The present study addresses these important questions by analyzing the spread of pension privatization and health reform in Latin America. The difference between these two issue areas and the variation across the five countries under investigation—Bolivia, Brazil, Costa Rica, El Salvador, and Peru—provide analytical leverage for unearthing the causal mechanisms that drive innovations' spread. Diffusion plays out differently in an area such as social security in which a singular policy model exists, compared to a highly complex field such as health care, where various sources of inspiration exist.

The topic of policy diffusion is of great importance in this era of globalization. Because continuing improvements in communication and transportation intensify the cross-national exchange of information, inspiration from foreign models and principles affects more and more issue areas in more and more countries. As the world grows smaller, policymaking is no longer a domestic affair, but increasingly shaped by external inputs. Nowadays, many decision-makers participate in transnational networks that strongly influence choices at the national level, and they engage in ever denser cooperation and rule making at the international level (Haas 1992; Risse-Kappen 1994; Slaughter 2004). Moreover, a multitude of international organizations seeks to persuade, coax, push, or force governments to adopt policy blueprints or ideas they advocate (Barnett and Finnemore 2004; Pincus and Winters 2002; Vreeland 2003).

Above and beyond this welter of specific exchanges and influences, which often pull in divergent directions (Rosenau 2003), there has been a worldwide advance of liberal economic and political arrangements during the last three decades. The international diffusion of democracy and markets has forged increasing homogeneity as alternative systems such as communism have collapsed and lost adherents (Simmons, Dobbin, and Garrett 2006; Meseguer 2002; Levi-Faur 2005; Domínguez 1998). The range of political choice has shrunk, although scholars continue to debate how narrow it has become; for instance, can Europe's generous welfare states withstand the onslaught of market forces (Pierson 1994; Garrett 1998; Huber and Stephens 2001; Swank 2002; Hall and Soskice 2001; Campbell and Pedersen 2001)?

The present study helps assess how far market mechanisms are likely to advance. Neoliberal principles spread first in the economy yet soon expanded to the social sectors as well, prompting efforts to improve efficiency through increased competition or outright privatization. But in the social sphere, opposition to neoliberalism is particularly strong; many people do not want the profit motive to determine the fulfillment of basic human needs such as health. By analyzing the diffusion of reforms in social security and health care, the current frontiers of the market project, this book examines the strength of the neoliberal wave. Has it already crested and stalled, or is it continuing its advance, extending the logic of competitiveness to ever wider spheres of life? Will society soon be governed by uniform market principles, or do alternative goals and mechanisms, such as social equity and public provision, retain support, puncturing the trend toward global homogeneity and preserving sectoral and national diversity?

Beyond addressing this crucial substantive theme, my study elucidates what is perhaps *the* major theoretical issue in the social sciences, namely, the question of rationality. Do decisions emerge from the best possible pursuit of clear and firm self-interests, as the rational choice framework postulates, which according to some authors has sought to gain a hegemonic position in political science (Lichbach 2003)? Or does this interest-maximizing scheme offer an unsatisfactory account of political action because actors do not have an effective margin of choice; are not guided by clear, firm interests; or do not pursue such interests in optimal ways? That is, do structural pressures determine decisions and suppress choice? If there is latitude, are actors driven more by other-regarding motives such as appropriateness and legitimacy than by self-interests? Or if interests indeed prevail, do actors lack the cognitive capacity and computational resources to pursue them in a systematic, unbiased, comprehensively rational way and rely instead on the cognitive shortcuts of bounded rationality? By using the study of policy diffusion to analyze these three aspects of the rationality issue, my book sheds light on a controversial question that has attracted enormous scholarly attention (Cook and Levi 1990; McFadden 1999; Gigerenzer and Selten 2001; Lupia, McCubbins, and Popkin 2001; Gilovich, Griffin, and Kahneman 2002).

First, do international forces overwhelm domestic actors in the era of globalization, or do countries retain a significant degree of autonomy? Authors such as Armada, Muntaner, and Navarro (2001) argue that waves of diffusion result from the pressures of powerful international actors, which push new policy models on weak developing countries. International financial institutions (IFIs) like the World Bank (WB) and International Monetary Fund (IMF) use their tremendous leverage—especially loan conditionality—to impose reforms on dependent nations. Thus, diffusion emerges from central coordination. As external pressures have great force, globalization undermines national sovereignty. In this view, domestic actors do not have an effective choice; the question of their rationality is moot.

The alternative position argues that external pressures matter but are far from decisive (e.g., Nelson 1996). Even in the era of globalization, national sovereignty persists and gives countries—including weak underdeveloped countries—significant room for maneuver. Due to this autonomy, nations retain a considerable margin of choice in deciding whether to adopt a foreign model or not. In this view, IFI demands backed up by loan conditionality constrain governmental decision making but by no means determine its outputs. Given that domestic actors do have effective choices, analyzing the rationality of their decisions is meaningful.

To the extent that Third World governments enjoy policy latitude, scholars need to examine the motives guiding their decisions. Is the emulation of innovations driven mostly by self-interests, as the rational actor framework assumes, or do other-regarding considerations play a significant role as well? Embracing the latter view, sociologists and constructivists argue that normative appeal and the quest for international legitimacy prompt the emulation of foreign innovations. To look good in the eyes of global public opinion, decision-makers want to be modern and up-to-date and therefore imitate new policy models. They are determined to avoid the stigma of being backward and therefore try hard to keep up with the latest trend. On a deeper level, they are influenced by new international norms that redefine proper state action. An innovation raises the standards of appropriate behavior, and decision-makers urgently try to catch up to this new benchmark. Accordingly, political action—including the adoption of foreign models—cannot be reduced to rational interest calculation.

Many political scientists claim, by contrast, that appropriateness and legitimacy are pushed into the background by considerations of self-interest. These interests are essentially given, reflecting decision-makers' institutional position and the incentives and constraints facing them; for instance, all policy-makers need to be concerned about maintaining their power, a universally shared instrumental goal. Decision-makers therefore imitate foreign models not if they look modern and normatively appropriate, but if cost/benefit calculations suggest that they help to reach clear, preexisting interests. Utilitarian notions of goal attainment—not symbolic and normative concerns for legitimacy—drive policy diffusion. Which view is closer to the truth? By analyzing actor motivations, my study of policy diffusion sheds new light on this important aspect of the rationality issue.

To the extent that interests do matter—and who would deny them any role in human motivation?—the question shifts to the procedures with which actors pursue their goals. Do they make decisions in a comprehensively rational way, processing the relevant information with systematic and unbiased procedures? To learn from foreign experiences, do they proactively scan the environment for promising models, tally their advantages and disadvantages, and maximize their expected utility by adopting the option that scores highest in their cost/benefit assessment, as theorists of comprehensive rationality assume (e.g., Meseguer 2002)? Alternatively, actors may be overwhelmed by abundant information and save computational costs by resorting to cognitive shortcuts that turn decision making more efficient, but at the risk of distorting inferences substantially. In this view, rationality is distinctly bounded as hard-pressed decision-makers regularly and automatically rely on heuristics that facilitate the complicated process of making choices, but that can also cause significant biases.[1]

These three specific issues—external imposition vs. latitude for choice; legitimacy vs. self-interest; and comprehensive cost/benefit calculation vs. reliance on cognitive shortcuts—lie at the heart of the debate about rationality in politics, which has agitated political science during the last two decades. To make a contribution, my study examines the three aspects through an in-depth analysis of the policymaking process. This approach is particularly well-suited for assessing how "realistic" the contending frameworks are (cf. Tsebelis 1990: chap. 2). Thus, while focused on a specific topic—the diffusion of social policy innovations in Latin America—the present book hopes to elucidate a much broader question.

THE MAIN ARGUMENT

My research finds that a distinctly bounded form of rationality prevails in the cross-national diffusion of policy innovations. While decision-makers do have an effective choice, and while they largely pursue fixed and clear interests, they do so in ways that differ greatly from the as-

---

[1] Bendor (2003), Jones (1999), Kahneman (2003), and Simon (1985) provide excellent background on theories of bounded rationality.

sumptions underlying conventional rational-choice approaches. Even the impressive specialists involved in Latin American pension and health care reform, whose professional training should make them "most likely cases" (cf. Eckstein 1975) for conducting ample, systematic cost/benefit analyses, lack the time and the informational, computational, and financial resources to follow the ideal-typical norms of comprehensive rationality.[2] As numerous interviews with leading policy-makers and their rich paper trail demonstrate, they do not proactively scan the international environment and engage in a wide-ranging search for promising external models. Instead, they are attracted to certain foreign experiences for more "accidental," logically arbitrary reasons, including geographic and temporary proximity. And rather than evaluating the models that grab their attention through systematic, balanced cost/benefit analyses, they tend to assess the promise of foreign innovations more haphazardly.

Especially where a bold, integrated, coherent, and simple reform model such as Chilean-style pension privatization has emerged, policy-makers commonly rely on the main inferential shortcuts that cognitive psychologists have documented, namely, the heuristics of availability, representativeness, and anchoring (Kahneman, Slovic, and Tversky 1982; Gilovich, Griffin, and Kahneman 2002). These automatically used shortcuts facilitate the processing of overabundant information by focusing—and thus limiting—people's attention and by supplying simple inferential rules that lower computational costs and allow actors to navigate uncertainty. In this way, they enable people to cope with the flood of information that besieges them and that leaves little time for proactive efforts to search for even more information, as the postulates of comprehensive rationality would demand. By filtering information and channeling inferences, however, these heuristics can also introduce biases and distort the conclusions that people draw from the evidence. Therefore, despite people's best efforts, the outputs of humanly feasible decision making often diverge from the results that the ideal-type of comprehensive information processing and systematic cost/benefit analysis would yield. In sum, cognitive heuristics are crucial for allowing people to arrive at decisions, but they can significantly impair the quality of those decisions.

As this book documents, the heuristics of availability, representativeness, and anchoring shape the diffusion of social policy models. The availability heuristic induces people to assign disproportionate weight to particularly striking, vivid, memorable information and to overestimate the significance or relative frequency of such cognitively available infor-

---

[2] For a well-documented similar finding, see Tetlock (2005: chap. 4).

mation (Kahneman, Slovic, and Tversky 1982: chaps. 1, 11–14, 33; Gilovich, Griffin, and Kahneman 2002: chaps. 3–5). In the paradigmatic case of this heuristic, most drivers slow down after witnessing a car crash—although in strictly logical terms, seeing one accident should not affect their assessment of the risks of driving. But the drastic experience of seeing an accident has an immediate impact on most drivers' behavior—until the memory fades away and people speed up again.

In a similar vein, having close knowledge of Chile's dramatic, bold introduction of a novel pension system grabbed the attention of Latin American decision-makers and turned social security privatization into an obligatory point of reference for all experts in the region. Its special availability in Latin America put this innovative model on the policy agenda in the region, much more so than in other areas of the world. Thus, the availability heuristic helps explain why pension privatization spread first and foremost inside Latin America; it helps account for the geographical clustering of policy diffusion, a typical characteristic of this process. While no similarly clear, neat, and integrated policy model emerged in the complex area of health care, decision-makers also followed the availability heuristic and paid disproportionate attention to recent changes in neighboring countries. Rather than concentrating on one singular model, however, they often learned from the experiences of several countries in the region. Thus, in both policy arenas, the availability heuristic focused policy-makers' attention in geographic and temporal terms and thus skewed the process of policy diffusion.

Once a new model has appeared on policy-makers' radar screen, the representativeness heuristic shapes assessments of its quality and promise. This inferential shortcut induces people to overestimate the extent to which a small sample represents true population values; for instance, they tend to draw excessively firm conclusions from a limited set of data, such as a short time series (Kahneman, Slovic, and Tversky 1982: chaps. 1–6; Gilovich, Griffin, and Kahneman 2002: chaps. 1–2). In this vein, many social security experts inferred from the initial success of Chile's privatized social security system—such as the high rates of return achieved by private pension funds—and from its coincidence with the country's striking growth spurt that this new model was of inherently superior quality. Therefore, a number of countries soon rushed to emulate this seemingly successful model. In health care, the absence of a single comprehensive model made assessments of success more diffuse, but an innovative change like Colombia's health reform of 1993 also attained an aura of success—before its serious implementation problems, which reflected its complicated design, became obvious. The Colombian reform therefore triggered emulation efforts, but they were not as widespread and strong as in the case of Chilean-style pension privatization. Thus, to the extent that early success gives rise to impressions of high promise, the representativeness heuristic induces policy-makers to jump on the bandwagon of a diffusion process. It thus helps account for the upsurge in policy emulation that underlies the wavelike nature of innovations' spread.

Finally, the heuristic of anchoring limits the adjustment that policy-makers introduce to adapt a foreign import to the specific characteristics of their own country. According to this inferential shortcut, initially provided information—even of an arbitrary nature—significantly ties down later judgments; while not precluding modifications, it keeps them limited and confines them to peripheral aspects (Kahneman, Slovic, and Tversky 1982: chaps. 1, 33; Gilovich, Griffin, and Kahneman 2002: chaps. 6–8). In this vein, all Latin American countries that enacted structural pension reform during the 1990s instituted the central innovation encapsulated in the Chilean model, namely, pension privatization and the creation of individual retirement accounts in the mandatory social security system. While the absence of a single outstanding model left more room for adjustments in health care, anchoring led to some copying even in this policy arena, including sometimes the very names of new institutions. Thus, by keeping adjustments limited, the heuristic of anchoring helps to account for the spread of similarity amid diversity, a defining characteristic of policy diffusion.

In sum, cognitive shortcuts significantly shape the spread of innovations in Latin American social sector reform. The heuristics of availability, representativeness, and anchoring help account for the geographical clustering, wavelike progression, and basic nature of diffusion. As interviews and documents show, policy-makers did not follow the ideal-typical postulates of comprehensive rationality but applied the inferential strategies of bounded rationality. These shortcuts were required for processing the flood of information facing them but created the risk of significant distortions and biases.

As regards the second aspect of the rationality issue—the main motivation driving policy reform—my research suggests that utilitarian goals have been significantly more important than symbolic and normative considerations, especially in the area of social security reform. Depending on the maturity of a country's pension system, policy-makers confronted long-standing financial problems and a virtual collapse of the social security system (as in Argentina); growing pension deficits that required increasing budget subsidies (as in Bolivia); or actuarial projections that foresaw such difficulties in the future (as in Costa Rica). By enacting pension reform, all of these nations addressed clear, "given" problems that were obvious to experts; they did not search for a problem in order to rationalize the enactment of a new model to which they had become attracted for symbolic or normative reasons, as sociological institutionalists surmise (March and Olsen 1976; cf. Kingdon 1984).

The need to find a definite solution for a pressing preexisting problem was the main argument used by reform-minded experts to justify the adoption of pension privatization. This utilitarian argument was most important for garnering broad political support for reform. Given the high stakes that major societal groups had in social security reform, a typical "redistributive" issue area (cf. Lowi 1964), normative and symbolic considerations did not play a major role. Instead, interests prevailed, and instrumental arguments about problem solving therefore carried the day. The same is true for efficiency-oriented reform efforts in health care, which were designed to cope with the financial constraints tightened by the debt crisis of the 1980s and the adjustment measures of the 1990s. Proposals to introduce competition and performance incentives or to privatize parts of the health system responded to clear problems, such as waste, low productivity, inefficiency, and corruption; and since they affected crucial interests of powerful societal groups and bureaucratic agencies, they elicited strong, often fierce conflict. These redistributive struggles were driven by clashing interests, leaving little room for symbolic and normative concerns.

Equity-enhancing reforms in health care, especially efforts to extend effective coverage to long-neglected poor sectors of the population, could often be pursued through add-on programs that instituted new benefits without imposing visible costs. In political terms, these pro-poor initiatives therefore had a distributive character (cf. Lowi 1964; Corrales 1999: 5–6). Since these measures did not face much political opposition, normative developments could exert significant influence on their adoption. Specifically, financially weak but highly legitimate international organizations like the World Health Organization (WHO) and the United Nations Children's Fund (UNICEF) had since the late 1970s promoted the goal of "health for all by the year 2000." This new normative message helped to trigger the reform wave that sought to expand ("universalize") health care coverage in Latin America during the 1990s. Economic conjunctures, namely the attainment of economic stability and return to growth, provided a permissive condition for this reform wave. The region's recovery made new financial resources available, allowed for "distributive" add-on programs that extended benefits to the poor without taxing the better-off, and thus paved the way for new norms to drive policy change.

Thus, under specific conditions, the normative appeals stressed by sociological institutionalists and constructivists did make a difference. Usually, however, utilitarian efforts to resolve pressing "given" problems and advance clear, preexisting interests played a much more important role. Overall, interest-based, pragmatic problem orientation pre-dominated. Thus, although decision-makers apply a distinctly bounded form of rationality, they are guided primarily by self-regarding goals.

Turning to the third aspect of the rationality issue, political actors also seem to have a significant margin of choice. My research shows that policy diffusion did not result from external imposition. Certainly, external pressures, especially the general policy guidelines and specific reform recommendations advanced by international financial institutions (IFIs), played a significant role in the spread of social policy innovations in contemporary Latin America. By the mid-1990s, pension privatization and efficiency-enhancing health reforms were part of the neoliberal policy package promoted by the World Bank and IMF. To support such reforms, the IFIs offered substantial financial aid, generous technical assistance, and frequent normative exhortations.

But while contributing to innovations' spread, these forms of influence by no means determined the outputs of national decision making or eliminated the latitude for choice. The very variety of policy changes enacted in Latin America, especially in health care, shows that the IFIs did not impose a uniform blueprint on the region; domestic factors clearly mattered. In fact, the IFIs' most powerful instrument of coercion, loan conditionality, has proven to be a blunt weapon in the enactment of complex institutional reforms. Reforms of social security and health systems involve a wide range of actors. This multiplicity of "veto players" and the resulting need for political negotiations make it difficult for external actors that lack democratic legitimation to exert much influence. Thus, the IFIs cannot impose such institutional reforms but seek to influence them through financial incentives, technical assistance, and persuasion—often with limited success (Nelson 1996; Brooks 2004).

Furthermore, IFI influence was most important when a wave of diffusion was already under way. Pension privatization started to spread from Chile to other Latin American countries before the World Bank placed major emphasis on this reform in the mid-1990s (cf. WB 1994a). And as the case studies below show, external conditions were often requested by domestic experts, who sought to enhance their leverage with domestic political actors. Thus, the very distinction of external vs. internal agency is much less clear-cut than external pressure arguments assume (see in general Vreeland 2003). For all these reasons, the IFIs have had only limited influence on the spread of innovations in Latin American social sector reform. In particular, they have certainly not managed to impose concrete policy models, such as Chilean-style pension privatization. And while they have succeeded in pushing countries to advance toward general policy goals, especially efficiency in health care, governments have differed greatly in how far they have moved and in what specific way they have implemented these broad guidelines; in fact, efficiency-oriented reforms have encountered much greater resistance than equity-enhancing efforts. Thus, domestic decision-makers have enjoyed considerable latitude for making real choices; they have often resisted IFI exhortations or failed to implement them.

Therefore, national sovereignty seems to be alive and well in the age of globalization, at least in the area of social policy reform. While external pressures undoubtedly influence domestic decision making, they are usually not the driving force behind social policy reforms and therefore cannot account for the wavelike spread of innovations. As the IFIs' promotion of pension privatization and efficiency goals in health care attained only limited success, diffusion resulted more from horizontal contagion—mediated by cognitive heuristics—or new normative appeals than from central coordination and imposition.

In sum, this study arrives at a clear conclusion on the rationality question. Political actors do have choices, and they make those choices guided more by interests than by legitimacy considerations. But they commonly rely on cognitive shortcuts that deviate from comprehensive rationality. Thus, conventional rational-actor approaches inspired by "economic" versions of rationality need to be modified in light of the consistent findings of cognitive psychology, which the present analysis corroborates.

A FOCUS ON PUBLIC POLICY

In analyzing the diffusion of innovations in public policy, this study pays sustained attention to a subject area that has long been neglected in political science, namely, the output side of politics. The more scientific the discipline has tried to become, the more it has looked down upon public policy as an allegedly atheoretical, largely descriptive field. The present book trespasses on this division between political science and policy studies. In my view, public policy is a proper topic for political science inquiry. It can and should be analyzed from a broader theoretical perspective that goes beyond the specificities of the issue area. As just explained, this study brings three major theoretical questions, which are all aspects of the fundamental rationality issue, to bear on the analysis of social policy: the relative weight of international vs. domestic forces; the role of symbolic vs. utilitarian motives; and the prevalence of comprehensive vs. bounded rationality. I hope to show that the in-depth investigation of social policy in faraway countries can suggest important insights on these crucial questions. The output side of politics definitely lends itself to theoretically driven inquiry.

Furthermore, public policy can and should be the subject of explanatory analysis, not mere description. The present study seeks to unearth the causal mechanisms that drive the cross-country diffusion of innovations and therefore applies process tracing based on intensive field research (Hall 2003; Brady and Collier 2004; see Bates, Greif, et al. 1998). Utilizing a different strategy of inference than statistics (George and Bennett 2005; Abell 2001; Collier, Brady, and Seawright 2004), this case-study method systematically examines a wealth of information that escapes quantification. It thus yields a particularly rich, comprehensive understanding of the factors that shape political decision making.

Political science indeed may be well advised to pay more attention to public policy. The long-standing and increasing overemphasis on the input side of politics that prevails in the discipline threatens to diminish the relevance of its findings. Political parties and elections are certainly crucial aspects of politics, but so are policy programs that affect the lives of millions of citizens. In fact, parties and elections are important in part because of their potential impact on policy outputs. As political scientists of various stripes stress (e.g., Ames 1987: chap. 3), many politicians pursue not only instrumental interests of power preservation and reelection, but also substantive goals that require the creation or transformation of public policy programs. Partisan actors thus want to shape political outputs. And in evaluating parties, governments, and even political regimes, citizens strongly consider policy performance. For these reasons, the output side of politics deserves more scholarly attention than it has received in recent decades.

A reorientation toward public policy is especially important for the field of comparative politics. By contrast to the "limited government" prevailing in American politics, the state is much more active in most countries investigated by comparativists, even after the wave of neoliberal reforms. In those nations, governmental decision making—i.e., public policy—deeply affects vast areas of economic, social, and political development. This obvious fact receded into the background during the "third wave of democratization," when the regime issue attracted most scholarly attention. As elections turned into the decisive mechanism of political choice and as the redefinition of institutional rules seemed pivotal for the new democracies' future, large numbers of scholars were understandably drawn to the input side of politics, away from public policy.

But by now, the third wave of democratization has come to an end. Many new democracies are either consolidating (especially in Latin America and Eastern Europe) or decaying into old or new forms of authoritarian rule (especially in the former Soviet Union, Africa, and the Middle East). As the special politics of regime transition has passed and political life has returned to more normal, regular patterns, scholars should moderate the excessive focus on institutional issues and pay more attention to substantive questions, namely, decision making on the important subjects that are in the purview of states—that is, public policy.

A direct focus on public policy and the decision-making process is especially important because despite some promising contributions (e.g., Tsebelis 1995; Haggard and McCubbins 2001), the institutionalist analyses stimulated by the third wave of democratization cannot account well for policy outputs. For instance, both "potentially dominant" and "potentially marginal" presidents (cf. Shugart and Mainwaring 1997: 49) have managed to pass pension privatization in Congress, and chief executives with an equally wide range of legislative powers have failed to achieve this reform. Moreover, political parties and congressional politicians, the actors highlighted by institutionalist approaches, have played a strikingly limited role in health and social security policy, as the secondary literature and my extensive field research show (Piola, Vianna, and Consuelo 2001: 56; Kaufman and Nelson 2004a: 489–504; Nelson 2004: 31–32; Grindle 2004: 55–57; Ewig 2000: 490–96; Weyland 1996a: chaps. 6–7). While parliamentarians retain "the last word" over crucial institutional changes, such as pension privatization, many important policy decisions are made directly through presidential decree or ministerial regulation and thus bypass congressional deliberation.

Where parliamentary approval is required, the initiation, elaboration, and negotiation of crucial bills lie largely in the hands of technical experts and political appointees inside the executive branch. Congressional politicians may serve as "veto actors," but they rarely play any role as "proposal actors" (Orenstein 2000). They usually do not set the political agenda, choose among available policy options, and design the content of bills. Certainly, parliamentarians can reshape bills in committee, but most amendments focus on specific aspects (often particular benefits or exemptions for certain groups of constituents) and leave the framework of the law for an up-or-down vote. For these reasons, policy analysts stress "the modest role of legislatures" in Latin America (Kaufman and Nelson 2004a: 504). Because assemblies are mostly reactive, the process through which the region's proactive presidents (cf. Cox and Morgenstern 2001) initiate and elaborate bills and other norms deserves particular scholarly attention. The case studies below therefore analyze the policymaking process, which unfolds largely inside the bureaucratic agencies of the state and is not driven in any direct way by electoral incentives and calculations (see, e.g., Sugiyama 2008).

Even partisan politics matter surprisingly little in social policymaking. Many Latin American parties lack well-defined programmatic positions on issues such as health care. They often care more about patronage than policy; as a result, their support is effectively "for sale." And where parties do engage in policy debates, as in Costa Rica, they normally leave it to party-linked experts inside the state to define their issue positions (interviews with Céspedes 2004 and Durán 2004). For these reasons, the opposition's ascent to power rarely brought great change in the content and direction of social policymaking. As the case studies show, there was strong continuity in pension and health reform projects between governments headed by rival parties in Bolivia, Brazil, Costa Rica, and Peru.[3] Experts inside the state bureaucracy promoted similar proposals regardless of partisan politics and often managed to attain their goals sooner or later (e.g., Martínez Franzoni 1999; cf. Heclo 1974).

By focusing on public policymaking, especially proposal design and negotiations inside the state, this book thus analyzes a neglected topic that merits much greater scholarly attention. It helps to fill a gap that contemporary political science with its predominant input focus and its embrace of institutionalist approaches has left wide open. Furthermore, the study concentrates on major theoretical issues and thus hopes to contribute insights that are of central interest to political scientists.

RESEARCH DESIGN

To examine the causal mechanisms that drive policy diffusion, this study draws on in-depth field research, especially personal interviews with leading decision-makers and a close reading of the numerous documents that they processed and produced. I apply a qualitative approach because a number of the theoretical factors investigated in this book, such as the above-mentioned cognitive heuristics, would be difficult to quantify properly. In fact, the burgeoning statistical analyses of policy diffusion, which have undoubtedly made important contributions, often suffer from indicators of questionable validity. For instance, authors commonly operationalize external pressures via the presence of a loan agreement with an IFI. But as mentioned above, such an agreement is by no means proof of external imposition; instead, domestic experts often request IFI conditionality to boost their own bargaining power in internal policy disputes. Only in-depth field research can uncover whether an IMF agreement resulted from such deliberate domestic self-restriction or from external imposition. Thus, case studies are crucial for the present effort to uncover the causal mechanisms that propel the spread of innovations.

---

[3] In El Salvador, the same party led the government during the period under investigation.

In methodological terms, a focus on causal mechanisms means that "positive cases" in which innovations have actually spread are of particular interest. These cases allow for examining in depth the operation of diffusion's engines. But this special attention to positive cases does not imply a no-variance design, which has drawn ferocious criticism (King, Keohane, and Verba 1994; Geddes 1990). Instead, any analysis of diffusion seeks to account for intertemporal variation: Why do many countries enact dramatic *change* by emulating the same reform model or advancing toward the same principle? Furthermore, this study examines geographic variation: Why do countries emulate primarily models that emerge in their own region while often ignoring interesting innovations developed in faraway places? In sum, the book seeks to account for significant variation by investigating the causal mechanisms that drive diffusion and thus create commonality amid diversity.

Moreover, the present study deliberately analyzes two issue areas that differ in important ways. In social security, a bold, neat, well-integrated model has arisen and triggered a wave of reforms, namely, Chilean-style privatization. By contrast, the highly complex, multifaceted health arena has not allowed for a single, coherent, encompassing model to emerge; instead, the diffusion of reforms has been stimulated by various factors, including IFI exhortations, new international norms, and recent experiments in neighboring countries. This difference across issue areas offers analytical leverage on the operation of crucial causal mechanisms, especially external pressures, normative appeal, and cognitive heuristics.

These methodological considerations inform my case selection. Logistics requires confining field research to one region. Since pension privatization spread first in Latin America, this region deserves special attention. It also experienced a series of health reforms that offer sufficient material for examining diffusion in that issue area. While the study's regional scope holds constant various context factors, it also encapsulates substantial differences among the countries under investigation.

Bolivia, Brazil, Costa Rica, El Salvador, and Peru diverged in the institutional features of their prereform welfare states, such as the extension of social security coverage and the relationship of the public and private health sector; in the financial and administrative problems plaguing the established schemes and in the preconditions for reform, such as the extent of capital market development; in their reservoir of technical expertise; and in the relative strength of various social and political forces with a crucial stake in pension and health reform. If, despite these differences, the study uncovers important similarities—such as limited IFI influence and a common focus on the highly available Chilean model of pension privatization coupled with a neglect of alternative reform models—these findings are likely to have broader applicability. Thus, in trying to unearth the causal mechanisms underlying diffusion, this book gains analytical leverage from the points of agreement among diverse countries inside the Latin American context.

But the same causal mechanism can produce different end results when operating in different contexts (McAdam, Tarrow, and Tilly 2001). A tornado devastates a trailer park while leaving a fortress unharmed, and a virus may kill a poor, malnourished child but not a well-fed, strapping youngster. Similarly, diffusion processes in Latin American social policy produced different end states. Many countries emulated Chilean-style pension privatization, but several did not. Health reform advanced even more unevenly. In fact, while diffusion entails the spread of similarity amid diversity, emulating countries often introduced limited modifications to the model they imported. Despite crucial similarities, postreform systems therefore differed in some characteristics.

The selection of Bolivia, Brazil, Costa Rica, El Salvador, and Peru captures these two levels of variation, namely, diffusion vs. nondiffusion and second-order differences among cases of diffusion. The five countries represent the whole gamut of outcomes in the pension arena (Mesa-Lago 1997), namely, a substitutive private system (Bolivia, El Salvador); parallel public and private systems (Peru); a mixed public-private system (Costa Rica); and a reformed public system (Brazil). In the complex health arena, the five countries also adopted different reforms, ranging from more social-democratic measures (Brazil, Costa Rica) to a more neoliberal policy course (Bolivia, El Salvador, Peru). The case studies below seek to uncover the different initial conditions and intervening factors that made the causal mechanisms driving diffusion produce these specific outcomes.

Thus, in explaining why many different countries adopted similar reforms, this analysis of policy diffusion focuses on commonalities. But it also encapsulates several types of variation. In particular, the effort to unearth the causal mechanisms that propel innovations' spread seeks to account for change over time and regional differences while stressing points of agreement among diverse countries inside one region. And the variegated end results of these diffusion processes suggest that divergences among Bolivia, Brazil, Costa Rica, El Salvador, and Peru also mattered.

The Concept, Types, and Characteristics of Diffusion

Definition

This study applies a broad concept of diffusion that includes various horizontal and vertical patterns of propagation. Accordingly, diffusion takes place if the likelihood that a reasonably autonomous decision-making unit (A) will adopt an institutional or policy innovation is significantly increased by influences that emanate from outside this decision-making unit, especially by the adoption decision of another such unit (B); the influence of a promoting actor that contributed to B's adoption decision; or the proselytizing efforts of the unit (C) that first created and enacted the innovation (see also Levi-Faur 2005: 23; Elkins and Simmons 2005).

To allow for an assessment of the above-mentioned theoretical frameworks, this definition deliberately casts a wide net. In particular, it includes not only horizontal influences among units that adopt an innovation, which rational-learning and cognitive-heuristics arguments emphasize, but also vertical influences, such as pressure or "teaching" by international organizations, which normative-imitation and especially external-pressure theories stress. In fact, elements of vertical pressure often interact with horizontal linkages; for instance, from the mid-1990s onward, the World Bank strongly encouraged and supported the emulation of Chilean pension privatization by other Latin American countries, which had started first in a horizontal fashion. Given this synergy of various causal mechanisms, a narrow definition of diffusion may hide more than it reveals. The present study therefore uses a broad conceptualization.

Model Diffusion vs. Principle Diffusion

The prototypical instances of diffusion involve the wavelike spread of a compact policy model, such as the Bismarckian social security scheme, Chilean-style pension privatization, the Bangladeshi microlending institution Grameen Bank, the Bolivian Emergency Social Fund, or the Brazilian cash stipends conditioned upon school attendance (Goodman 2004). In these cases, a growing number of emulators import a neat, concrete, well-defined blueprint, largely replicating the original model. The innovation thus spreads in a rapidly expanding wave that sweeps across whole regions of the world.

But diffusion can also take a looser form, in which decision-making units enact a principle adopted by a frontrunner, such as capital account liberalization, central bank autonomy, or universal access to primary health care. They emulate a new guideline but enact it in various concrete incarnations. The basic thrust of these adoption decisions is the same, leading to a recognizable wave of reforms, but specific design features and institutional characteristics differ.[4] While principles can thus

---

[4] Certainly, however, model diffusion can be nested inside principle diffusion. Countries may imitate the specific institutional way in which a frontrunner enacted a new principle.

spread to large numbers of countries, the resulting pattern of change is not as profound and uniform as the contagion effect unleashed by a neat, clear policy model.

While model diffusion constitutes the most striking form of innovations' spread, has a particularly strong impact on the emulating countries, and therefore attracts disproportionate attention from scholars (Strang and Soule 1998: 285; Meseguer and Gilardi 2005: 4, 17, 22–23), principle diffusion is probably more common because the complexity of many issue areas prevents a singular, neat, well-integrated policy model from emerging. Besides the pension arena, where such a bold, compact model did arise, the present book therefore analyzes the vast and disparate field of health care, where principle diffusion predominated. Thus, my study deliberately analyzes different forms of diffusion. The contrast between model and principle diffusion provides additional analytical leverage on the causal mechanisms driving innovations' spread.

To clarify the distinction between model and principle diffusion, it is necessary to define both terms. A principle is a general guideline for designing programs or institutions. Such a maxim provides a broad orientation for policy-makers that encompasses several specific design options. It charts an overall direction but not a specific course of action. By contrast, a model is one specific option from the menu offered by a policy principle; a model embodies a general guideline and turns it into a concrete, specific blueprint. It prescribes a coherent, integrated way of organizing a policy program or designing an institution. Such a neat, unified blueprint condenses a broad policy orientation or paradigm into a specific incarnation. It crystallizes a policy maxim into a neat, simple package. Thus, whereas a principle is general and vague on details, a model is specific and concrete.

Characteristics of Diffusion

The ample empirical literature on diffusion across countries and across the U.S. states has consistently documented three main features that characterize the spread of innovations. They are especially pronounced in model diffusion but are common in principle diffusion as well.

First, diffusion tends to occur in waves. It usually starts slowly as a few countries or states try out a new model; then it picks up steam as large numbers of nations or states jump on the bandwagon; and finally it levels off as most countries or states have already adopted the change or as the reform wave hits an insurmountable barrier. As a result of this wavelike pattern, the cumulative frequency of reform adoption over time follows an S-shaped curve (Rogers 1995: 11, 22–23; Li and Thompson 1975: 65; Berry 1994: 443; Strang and Soule 1998: 283; Lazer 1999:

466–67, 473; Kogut and Macpherson 2003: 19, 32; Levi-Faur 2005: 18; Orenstein 2003: 179–80; Brooks 2005: 275).

Second, diffusion often displays strong geographical clustering. Neighborhood and regional effects are usually pronounced.[5] New institutions or policies enacted in one country are much more likely to stimulate emulation in a close-by nation than halfway around the globe (Collier and Messick 1975: 1311–13; Starr 1991; Berry 1994: 442; Mintrom and Vergari 1998: 129, 139–44; Strang and Soule 1998: 275; Kopstein and Reilly 2000; Walt 2000: 41; Guisinger 2003: 4, 9, 31–34; Simmons and Elkins 2004: 172; Way 2005: 132, 137–40; see also Mooney 2001). It is noteworthy that this geographical clustering prevails even in the age of globalization, when advanced information technologies facilitate access to innovations on a worldwide basis. In fact, the most powerful international financial institutions, the World Bank and International Monetary Fund, have a global mandate and deliberately advertise interesting innovations worldwide. Nevertheless, even recent instances of policy diffusion, such as the spread of Chilean-style pension privatization, have continued to display clear geographical clustering (Orenstein 2003: 174, 178, 185–86).

Finally, diffusion produces the spread of similarity amid diversity. A number of countries with variegated socioeconomic, political, and cultural characteristics adopt the same basic institutional feature or policy framework. While they may well introduce some modifications to adapt the external import to their specific needs, they replicate the fundamental design of the foreign innovation. Diffusion thus causes convergence.

These three patterns are clearly observable in the spread of social security reform because privatization decisions constitute focal events whose temporal unfolding and geographical clustering are easy to document. Thus, pension reform in Latin America (and Eastern Europe) has followed the typical S-shaped curve of diffusion (fig. 1.1). It actually spread faster than the Bismarckian social security system (Orenstein 2003: 181, 185–86), despite a somewhat delayed start: Only when Chile returned to democracy yet maintained the private pension system did its association with the brutal Pinochet regime ease, allowing the new democracies in the region to import this innovation. The privatization wave then surged quickly, as soon as the regime divergence was overcome.

Pension privatization has also displayed strong geographical clustering. Almost all of the first emulators were located inside Chile's subregion, South America; in fact, three of the first six importing countries

---

[5] Bonds of cultural, political or historical similarity—for instance, among the Anglo-Saxon countries or among Communist countries—can overpower the effects of geographical proximity.

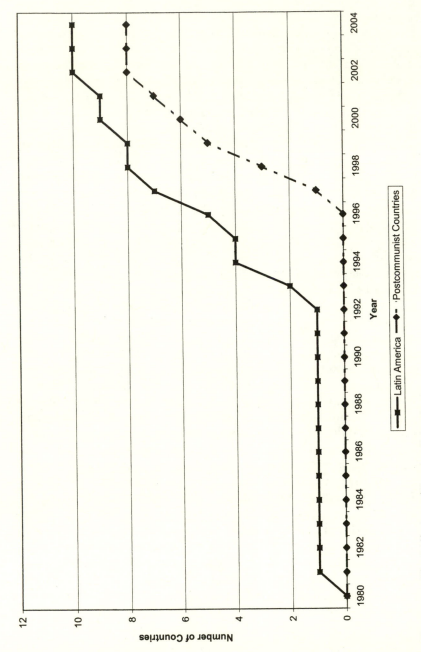

Figure 1.1. The Diffusion of Pension Privatization

(Argentina, Peru, and Bolivia) were Chile's next-door neighbors, and two more (Colombia and Uruguay) shared borders with initial adopters. After Mexico privatized its social security system in 1995, the wave of diffusion reached the Caribbean Basin, affecting El Salvador, Costa Rica, Nicaragua,[6] and the Dominican Republic. Thus neighborhood effects have been pronounced. Finally, while introducing significant modifications, all of these countries instituted the core of the Chilean model of pension privatization by creating individual retirement accounts in the obligatory social security system and by making social security benefits dependent on accumulated contributions and investment returns. As these countries differed considerably in socioeconomic development level, the wave of pension privatization thus entailed the spread of similarity amid diversity.

In the complex area of health care, no singular neat, integrated proposal of a comprehensive revamping has emerged.[7] Reforms have therefore advanced in a more disparate and piecemeal fashion. Yet the three features of diffusion are nevertheless visible. As regards temporal patterns, there has been a clear upsurge in efforts to privatize parts of the health system or introduce competitive principles during the 1990s, inspired in part by Chile's introduction of private health insurance in the early 1980s. Similarly, after a slow start in the 1980s, programs to extend primary health care to the poor have proliferated in the 1990s. Thus, the initially gradual, but then rapid spread of reforms that is captured in the S-shaped curve of cumulative frequencies is observable in health care.

Neighborhood effects have also been significant. For instance, Chile's partial health privatization had an impact primarily on other Latin American countries, such as Argentina, Colombia, and Peru. Similarly, Colombia's health reform affected its neighbor Peru, which also learned from Bolivian innovations. Thus, geographical proximity stimulates emulation efforts in health care. Finally, while the absence of a singular outstanding model allows for less spread of similarity amid diversity in the health arena, basic policy principles, such as the introduction of private competition or the extension of primary care to the poor, did affect many dissimilar countries in similar ways. In sum, while less clear-cut than in social security, health reform has also displayed the three features of diffusion, namely, its S-shaped temporal unfolding, its geographical clustering, and the spread of similarity amid diversity.

---

[6] Nicaragua adopted a privatization law in 2000 but has postponed implementation and may well backtrack (Enríquez and Bow 2004; interview with Bonilla 2005).

[7] As chapter 6 discusses, Colombia's ambitious reform of 1993 was widely seen as overly complex, contrasting with the simple Chilean model of pension privatization.

DIFFUSION IN LATIN AMERICAN SOCIAL POLICY

Model Diffusion in Pension Reform

What are the main innovations in pension and health policy that have spread across Latin American countries during the last two decades? In both issue areas, the most important reform impulse arose from the new paradigm of neoliberalism, that is, the effort to introduce or strengthen market mechanisms in economy and society. After combating economic crises through orthodox stabilization and structural adjustment, many governments, often under IFI prodding, sought to extend market reform to the social sectors (see recently Corrales 2003; Wise 2003a). These attempts to enhance efficiency through competition or privatization thus formed part of the broad wave of liberal change that has swept across many world regions in the last thirty years.

In social security, Chile's radical privatization of 1981 constituted a neat, compact model that attracted widespread attention inside Latin America and beyond. This bold change comprehensively restructured a national pension system along the lines proposed by neoliberalism. Chile's reform diverged strikingly from the principles and models that had guided international pension policy since the inception of national social protection in Bismarck's Germany and that had shaped Latin American social security systems.

While differing significantly in coverage, generosity of benefits, and specific institutional features, the region's prereform pension systems shared many fundamental characteristics. In particular, they were obligatory, publicly administered defined-benefit schemes, financed largely by payroll contributions. As current workers and their employers funded a large proportion of benefit payments, these schemes rested on intergenerational redistribution and approximated "pay-as-you-go" (PAYG) systems. In financing the pensions of retirees, the present generation trusted that their offspring would pay for their own future benefits. To guarantee a reasonable standard of living in old age and forestall a stark income drop upon retirement, these benefits were calculated as a fixed percentage of a worker's last few salaries. This predictability of benefits, combined with the PAYG financing scheme, meant that any resource shortfalls had to be covered by increased contributions from current workers. To enforce this intergenerational contract, the state mandated affiliation and monopolistically administered the pension system, mostly via more or less autonomous social security institutes. Effective coverage was limited, however, to the formal sector of the economy, where official labor registration and regular, predictable wages made the withholding of social security contributions feasible. Since the system was financed mostly out of payroll contributions (not general taxes), urban informal workers and the rural poor, who received irregular incomes "off the books," in most cases remained excluded (see especially Mesa-Lago 1978; also Malloy 1979).

These PAYG systems easily guaranteed social protection for old workers and employees when Latin America's populations grew rapidly and the dependency ratio was therefore favorable. As long as there were substantial numbers of current workers paying social security taxes per retiree receiving benefits, reasonably generous pensions could be funded out of social security taxes that were not too onerous. But in the course of Latin America's demographic transition, falling birth rates led to fewer people joining the workforce, while population aging increased the proportion of retirees. This secular shift, which sooner or later affected all countries in the region, threatened the actuarial balance of the PAYG system. With falling dependency ratios, governments undertook parametric reforms: They began to raise contributions and tighten entitlement conditions; outright benefit cuts usually proved too costly in political terms. Thus, financial problems in and political conflicts over the social security system were on the rise across the region (Mesa-Lago 1989).

In this context, Chile's pension privatization created a radical alternative to the PAYG system, namely, a defined-contribution system run by competitive private pension fund administrators (*administradoras de fondos de pensiones*—AFPs). Affiliated workers and employees had their social security contributions deposited in individual accounts, which the AFPs invested in the capital market. Upon the account owner's retirement, the amount of the accumulated funds and investment returns determined the value of each individual's pension benefit. Thus, contrary to the intergenerational solidarity underlying the prereform systems, the Chilean model embodied purely individualistic principles: Every person would receive in old age what they had saved in the course of their own work life and what they had gained in the form of investment returns. While this new system made the value of the future benefit uncertain, it provided a clear incentive for people to contribute to their own pension funds. Since the Chilean model rested purely on self-interest, the state could take a residual role and transfer the administration of pension funds to private firms, which freely competed for affiliates. This market system was designed to improve efficiency, boost investment returns, and lower administrative costs, partly by precluding any political manipulation of the social security system. Privatization also gave individuals freedom of choice, which allowed them to sign up with the pension fund administrator that best served their interests. And by giving up most responsibility for social security, the state unloaded a thorny task and depoliticized an issue area that had given rise to innumerable demands from special interests.

In sum, the Chilean model instituted a radical alternative to established pension systems. Embodying the main maxims of neoliberalism, it differed in its basic philosophy and in several important design principles. Yet while the pension reform debate in Latin America has focused almost exclusively on the two polar opposites of PAYG vs. privatized systems, European countries have developed notional defined-contribution (NDC) schemes that ingeniously combined features of both extremes. Like the Chilean model, NDC systems make pension benefits dependent on individuals' accumulated contributions. But rather than investing those funds in the capital market and crediting individuals' accounts with actual investment returns, NDC systems create virtual accounts that are remunerated with an interest rate defined by the government. Instead of accumulating in their own capital accounts, workers' contributions are used to fund current retirement benefits—just as in a PAYG system.

Thus, the NDC scheme is similar in its individualistic system of benefit calculation to the Chilean model while emulating the PAYG system in its mechanics of benefit payment, which retains an intergenerational contract. Since it does not invest individuals' contributions in the capital market and since affiliates would therefore benefit little from competition, it is administered by the state. And since it does not channel individuals' contributions into private pension funds, it does not create the fiscal transition cost that plagues full-scale privatization. But due to the lack of capitalization, the NDC scheme does not hold the promise of boosting national savings and productive investment that economists attributed to the Chilean model: Individual contributions are not capitalized in forced savings accounts, but credited to notional accounts and used to fund current retirement pensions. In sum, NDC schemes are novel hybrids that open up a "third way" between the PAYG system and the Chilean model; but the latter blueprint has inspired most pension reformers in Latin America since the late 1980s.

Principle Diffusion in Health Care

By contrast to the clear focus on the Chilean privatization model in social security, the field of health care is highly complex, and reform efforts have therefore varied. But two basic maxims have stood out as guidelines of Latin American health policy during the last twenty years, giving rise to considerable principle diffusion. One group of reform efforts has sought to guarantee universal health coverage by extending effective medical attention to the urban and rural poor. Since in Latin

America, publicly provided health care emerged as a complement of so-cial security coverage, it traditionally included workers in the formal sector, who paid social security contributions and were therefore entitled to the services provided by the relatively well-endowed social security institutes. To the present day, these sectors have much better access to medical facilities than the poor because the countryside and urban squatter settlements are covered precariously by the ministry of health out of general budget funds, which are notoriously scarce. The poor therefore have difficult access to health care, which tends to be substan-dard. Thus, Latin American health systems have been deeply segmented and structurally unjust.

In response, one group of reforms has sought to establish universal coverage by extending decent health care to the poor. These efforts have tried to turn good services from a privilege acquired through social secu-rity contributions into a general right guaranteed to all people as citi-zens. To advance toward this equity goal, states have tried to "raise the bottom" by expanding coverage through add-on programs targeted at the rural poor and marginal urban sectors. Yet financial constraints have often prompted efforts to draw on resources controlled by the well-en-dowed social security institutes; therefore, efficiency-oriented reforms (see below) have been seen—and depicted—as preconditions for helping the poor by universalizing health coverage.

Usually, equity-enhancing reforms have also included efforts to change the allocation of resources among different levels of the health system. Reformers have deemphasized complicated, expensive curative treat-ments, which are accessible disproportionately to the better-off, and have assigned priority to improving primary care, which addresses the simple but pressing health needs of poorer people. In many Latin Ameri-can countries, for instance, a shocking number of children in rural and marginal urban areas still die of easily preventable or treatable diseases, such as gastrointestinal or respiratory infections, against which the mid-dle and upper class can protect themselves. In the eyes of reformers, the state should therefore concentrate on extinguishing these simple but deadly scourges for the sake of social equity.

This primary care strategy also enhances the cost-effectiveness of the health system: Each dollar spent on simple preventive and basic curative measures yields a much greater benefit for human well-being than in-creased investment in expensive hospital treatments, which help rela-tively few people, disproportionately from better-off sectors. Thus, improving primary care promises to enhance social equity as well as economic efficiency.

The efficiency goal inspires a second strand of reform efforts, which seeks to contain the constant increase in medical spending and to produce more and better services with the available resources. The underlying push factor for rising health expenditures arises from continued technological progress, which makes ever more sophisticated yet costly treatments feasible. Desperate patients demand as much medical help as possible, putting political or legal pressure on governments by invoking generous declarations of principles enshrined in constitutions. Thus, technical possibility and human need create pressure to disregard fiscal limitations.

Governments' economic agencies and international financial institutions therefore see efforts to enhance efficiency and productivity as imperative. This economic concern, which is often inspired or reinforced by neoliberal thinking, is fairly new in the health arena, which has traditionally concentrated on need satisfaction—that is efficacy, not efficiency. Accordingly, medical doctors, who used to fill all administrative positions in the health field, resent the attempts of economic experts from the finance or planning ministry to establish financial control over this area and to reshape service provision in accordance with efficiency criteria. Despite this tenacious active and passive resistance, clear fiscal constraints have prompted numerous efficiency-enhancing reform efforts. In a variety of ways, governments have sought to control costs, limit waste and corruption, monitor performance, offer incentives for higher productivity, and outsource some services. These changes have remained disparate and piecemeal as governments have used "salami tactics" to limit opposition and as only some proposals have passed.

The efficiency agenda is particularly controversial because it raises the specter of privatization. Neoliberal economists and health specialists argue that the public sector is inherently inefficient due to weak economic incentives and excessive politicization; only a transfer of part of the health system—especially service provision, but also insurance and financing—to the private sector can bring significant improvements. These experts take inspiration from the Chilean experiment with health privatization and advocate its emulation by other countries. By contrast, a majority of social sector specialists claim that the introduction or extension of the profit motive would further increase costs; it would also threaten social equity because the vast number of less well-off people could not afford to buy quality medical insurance in the market. And the "exit" of the middle and upper class from the public health system would hurt poorer sectors by depleting the state's revenues for health care. Given these polarized viewpoints, steps toward privatization, which a number of Latin American countries have attempted to take, have mostly remained circumscribed to specific aspects of the health system.

A diverse group of health specialists has tried to find a compromise in the acrimonious privatization debate. They have sought to strengthen the public sector by instituting efficiency-oriented incentives and competitive mechanisms inside it. They have called for introducing quasi-markets, especially negotiated, contractual relationships between public and private service providers and the governmental institutions that administer health care finances and insurance. They have also pushed for decentralization as a means to make medical personnel more attuned to the specific needs of their patients and give them more flexibility in service provision. In their view, greater autonomy and stronger incentives should replace the rigid bureaucratic commands and controls that had turned established health systems into slow-moving dinosaurs. Many Latin American countries have indeed introduced quasi-contractual mechanisms and have decentralized their medical systems.

In sum, the health arena has seen a large number of variegated reform initiatives. Change has mostly been gradual, limited, and fragmented, affecting only specific aspects of this complicated issue area; a comprehensive restructuring like Colombia's ambitious reform of 1993 has remained the exception (Nelson 1999). Contrary to the pension arena, no single, neat, compact model has emerged that has stimulated widespread emulation. Nevertheless, these disparate, not always cumulative reform efforts have followed two main tracks, which lead toward social equity and economic efficiency. As these goals have given rise to a range of efforts to extend health care to the poor, emphasize preventive and primary care, strengthen incentives for service providers, introduce competition inside the public sector, etc., health policy has been characterized primarily by principle diffusion, not model diffusion.

Organization of the Volume

Chapter 2 discusses the theoretical ideas guiding this study. To establish a clear focus, it first examines the causal mechanisms driving the diffusion of Chile's compact model of pension privatization. External pressures and normative concerns were not decisive in propelling this innovation's spread. Furthermore, decision-makers diverged significantly from comprehensive rationality and followed the shortcuts documented by cognitive psychologists. By contrast, principle diffusion in health care is influenced by various factors. External pressures are more effective in promoting general guidelines than concrete models; they helped induce governments to adopt efficiency-enhancing reforms. And international norms motivated governments to improve equity by giving the poor access to health services. Last not least, cognitive heuristics shaped the frequent yet disparate diffusion of specific health reform experiences.

Finally, the chapter analyzes the context factors that condition the outcomes produced by these causal mechanisms in specific settings. It thus explains why the moving causes of diffusion can yield different end results—for instance, why some countries do not adopt a foreign model or principle emulated by their neighbors.

Given the differences between model diffusion in social security and principle diffusion in health reform, the study then analyzes the two issue areas separately, yet in a comparative perspective. Chapters 3 and 4 examine the spread of Chilean-style pension privatization, while chapters 5 and 6 analyze the dissemination of equity and efficiency principles in health care. Chapter 3 investigates the impact of external pressures and international norms on the diffusion of pension privatization. It shows that the IFIs did not set off this reform wave in the late 1980s. Moreover, they exerted limited pressure on countries that emulated the Chilean model, namely, Bolivia, El Salvador, and Peru, and had little success in pushing reluctant nations, namely, Costa Rica and Brazil. Normative and symbolic concerns also had modest effect. Advocates of social security privatization like the World Bank did not reshape policymakers' interests by emphasizing new goals but merely highlighted new means for pursuing old goals.

Chapter 4 probes the crucial issue of comprehensive vs. bounded rationality. Extensive field research shows that decision-makers in Bolivia, El Salvador, and Peru did not actively search for the relevant information and process it in a systematic, balanced fashion. Instead, they relied on cognitive shortcuts. Following the availability heuristic, they paid disproportionate attention to the Chilean model and neglected other valuable sources of information. In line with the representativeness heuristic, they drew excessively sanguine conclusions from Chile's initial success and rushed to emulation. And anchoring led them to imitate the Chilean model closely and limit adaptations. In Costa Rica and Brazil, the Chilean model also was uniquely available, and powerful actors followed the representativeness heuristic in extolling its success. But higher levels of technical capacity widened the bounds of rationality and allowed forces concerned with social equity to stress the downsides of the Chilean model. In Costa Rica, the absence of an acute pension crisis and the strength of social-democratic commitments limited the reform impulse and gave rise to a mixed model. Similar aversion to neoliberalism, combined with multiple institutional obstacles to radical change, caused a lengthy stalemate on pension privatization in Brazil. An escape from this impasse opened up only when the European NDC scheme suddenly became cognitively available. In sum, cognitive heuristics deeply shaped the reform process in all five nations, although they produced different outcomes in these specific settings.

Chapter 5 investigates the impact of IFI exhortations and new normative trends on health reform. By contrast to model diffusion in social security, external pressures played a greater—but far from overwhelming—role in driving principle diffusion in health care, especially in advancing efficiency-seeking changes. The IFIs also supported equity-oriented efforts to improve basic services for the poor. But the driving force was a global norm shift, namely, the codification of the maxim "health for all" in the late 1970s. Since governments could pursue this new goal through distributive add-on programs, legitimacy considerations carried the day.

Chapter 6 demonstrates that rather than approximating the postulates of comprehensive rationality, health policy-makers relied strongly on cognitive shortcuts. Due to the absence of a singular, neat, and compact model, however, the heuristics of availability, representativeness, and especially anchoring did not exert as strong an effect as in the pension arena. Certainly, the Chilean and Colombian experiences with health privatization attracted significant attention in Latin America, but their moderate success and complicated nature limited emulation. Various other reform experiences also attracted and influenced policy-making. Due to the availability heuristic, these effects were confined mostly to neighboring countries. Bounded rationality thus led to a more dispersed, "decentered" process of learning in health policy, which contrasted with the wavelike spread of a singular model in social security.

Chapter 7 draws theoretical conclusions and places the empirical findings in a broader comparative perspective. The first section highlights the main results emerging from the case studies. The second section addresses the debate about the nature of rationality in politics and develops the theoretical and methodological implications of my bounded rationality approach. The last section discusses the implications of my study for theories of globalization and the worldwide advance of economic liberalism. The present analysis of policy diffusion suggests that despite homogenizing pressures toward global convergence, significant regional and national diversity in institutional arrangements and policy programs will persist. The resulting complexity reinforces the need for policy-makers to rely on cognitive heuristics in order to process the growing flood of decision inputs. Thus, while information flows are becoming ever more unbounded, rationality remains bounded.

CHAPTER 2

Toward a New Theory of Policy Diffusion

As CHAPTER 1 shows, the cross-national spread of innovations raises three major issues that speak to the basic question of rationality in politics, namely, external imposition vs. domestic autonomy; normative and symbolic vs. utilitarian motivations; and comprehensive vs. bounded rationality. These three issues give rise to a nested set of four theoretical approaches to the study of policy diffusion. First, an argument that emphasizes external pressures stands in contrast to three theories that claim a significant degree of domestic latitude and depict symbolic and normative appeal, comprehensive rationality, and bounded rationality, respectively, as the main mechanism propelling diffusion. Among the latter approaches, the normative appeal framework, which sees decision-makers as driven by the quest for legitimacy and recognition from others, diverges from the emphasis on utilitarian goal orientation that characterizes the comprehensive and bounded rationality frameworks. Finally, among those interest-based frameworks, rational-learning theories claim that decision-makers approximate the ideal-typical postulates of comprehensive rationality. According to the bounded-rationality approach, by contrast, policy-makers commonly rely on cognitive shortcuts that are crucial for processing overabundant, uncertain information but can cause significant deviations from full rationality (see fig. 2.1).

Which one of these approaches offers the most persuasive account of the causal mechanisms propelling policy diffusion? Given the variety of institutional patterns and policy programs that have spread across countries, it is unlikely that one theory alone can offer a full explanation. Causal complexity and heterogeneity are likely to prevail (cf. Ragin 2000; Meseguer and Gilardi 2005: 17–20). Various mechanisms may contribute to innovations' spread, and these causal combinations may differ across issue areas and countries. A grand unified theory of diffusion is therefore unlikely to emerge. A middle-range approach appears more fruitful. Drawing on extensive field research, this chapter therefore assesses which framework provides the best explanation of the causal forces that help to spread social sector innovations in contemporary Latin America.

The analysis first turns to model diffusion, namely, the wave of Chilean-style pension privatization. Cognitive heuristics have made an espe-

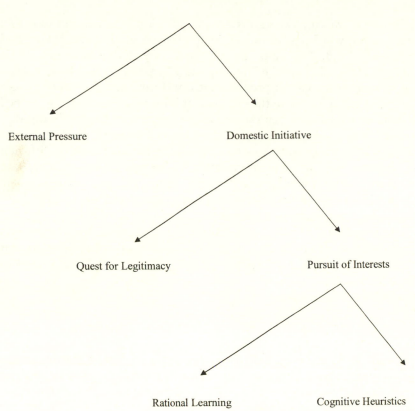

External Pressure   Domestic Initiative

Quest for Legitimacy   Pursuit of Interests

Rational Learning   Cognitive Heuristics

Figure 2.1. Causal Mechanisms Driving Diffusion

cially important contribution to the spread of this clear, outstanding blueprint. This bold model has attracted special attention from boundedly rational decision-makers, and as inferential shortcuts made it look highly successful and promising, they rushed to adopt it. Thus, policymaking in social security has clearly diverged from comprehensive rationality. External pressures and new normative appeals have also had little influence on model diffusion. By contrast, a greater variety of factors has fueled principle diffusion in health care. Cognitive heuristics have played a significant role in the spread of health reform but have not predominated. External pressures have also shaped the adoption of reform principles, and new international standards have inspired changes in some areas of health policy. Thus, principle diffusion is causally more heterogeneous than model diffusion.

In assessing the four theoretical frameworks, this chapter seeks to identify the causal mechanisms driving diffusion. The concept of causal mechanism, which has attracted great scholarly interest (Hedström and Swedberg 1998; McAdam, Tarrow, and Tilly 2001; Mahoney 2003; Mayntz 2004), denotes the "moving cause" (Aristotle) that brings about an outcome—the causal process that transforms initial conditions into an end result. To explain the outcome, it is therefore necessary to embed causal mechanisms in their context and specify the initial conditions that trigger their operation and affect their force. Therefore, the last section discusses the main context factors that shape the operation of diffusion mechanisms and account for variation in outcomes; in particular, why do some countries emulate a foreign model or principle, whereas others do not? Whereas political economy and institutional approaches have highlighted a variety of sociopolitical forces in state and society and the configuration of political institutions, I argue that deliberation and bargaining inside and among state agencies have an especially important effect on the causal mechanisms that propel the differential spread of innovations.

Four Theoretical Accounts of Diffusion Mechanisms

How do the four theoretical approaches to the study of diffusion, which emphasize external pressure, normative and symbolic appeal, rational learning, and cognitive heuristics as the principal causal mechanism, account for the spread of policy innovations?

The external pressure framework attributes the rapid adoption of similar reforms in dissimilar settings to central coordination and vertical imposition emanating from the core of the international system. This argument, often inspired by assumptions underlying dependency and world systems theory (Stallings 1992: 48), depicts the international system as a hierarchy. Innovations are developed in the center and pushed on the weak periphery. Powerful core actors promote an institutional or policy change and use "carrot and stick" to induce less developed countries to adopt this reform. While great powers impose changes directly in their sphere of influence, international organizations (IOs) are nowadays particularly well positioned to exercise forceful pressure on a worldwide scale. In fact, a few core countries, especially the United States, dominate the international financial institutions and use them to advance their agenda. The IFIs command important means of influence, especially strong economic incentives and painful sanctions. Globalization has increased their clout because they decide on much-needed financial aid and certify whether a country is in good standing with the international investment community. Therefore, many scholars of various persuasions depict the IFIs as prime movers in the diffusion of innovations (Stallings 1992; Ikenberry 1990: 99–101; Jacoby 2000: 28–30; Appel 2004: 4–7; Simmons 2001); some even apply terms like "coercion" (Guisinger 2003; Henisz, Zelner, and Guillén 2003; Simmons, Dobbin, and Garrett 2006: 790–91; Armada, Muntaner, and Navarro 2001).

While acknowledging that external promoters such as the IFIs contribute to the spread of reforms, the other three frameworks argue that domestic decision-makers retain considerable latitude. In this view, external pressure matters but in no way amounts to imposition. Above all, it does not determine the extent of policy change in the target countries. The IFIs indeed try hard to promote a range of reforms, but countries do not necessarily follow their instructions. They often resist IFI recommendations or simply fail to implement them. They enjoy significant autonomy, even in the era of globalization. National sovereignty continues to shield them from external pressures. Why then do so many nations enact similar reforms at roughly the same time? If vertical imposition is not decisive, what accounts for this striking horizontal contagion?

The remaining three frameworks stress different forms of learning, which quickly make a foreign model attractive to large numbers of countries. Yet they differ on the main motive driving this learning. Whereas comprehensive and bounded rationality arguments depict decision-makers as driven by clear, "given" interests, scholars who stress normative or symbolic appeal see commitment to appropriateness as the engine of innovations' spread. In the original version of this approach espoused by sociological institutionalists, policy-makers seek to enhance their international status and prestige by importing advanced innovations that demonstrate their modernity. Shunning the stigma of backwardness, they are eager to adopt new policy models, regardless of functional need. An innovation quickly spreads because it raises the standard of modernity. In this view, the effort to look good before global public opinion, not any kind of interest calculation, drives diffusion (Meyer and Rowan 1977; DiMaggio and Powell 1983).

In a variant that contrasts interests and legitimacy concerns less starkly, constructivists in the field of international relations argue that new international norms of appropriate behavior trigger waves of diffusion by reshaping state interests themselves. To comply with higher standards of proper behavior, decision-makers redefine their own goals and modify policy programs accordingly. In this view, interests are constructed and cannot simply be taken as given; their definition is profoundly influenced by normative concerns. When international society raises its standards, governments feel compelled by moral suasion to adopt these new norms. For instance, the global community has enjoined states to guarantee ever more social rights for their citizens, thus redefining what development means. As states adopt this new goal definition to conform to international expectations, they upgrade their own preferences and change their behavior accordingly. In this way, the spread of new international norms soon brings forth a wave of policy innovations.

Where international society has a clear "opinion leader" that sets the norms for advanced, modern behavior and appropriate state action, this constructivist argument paints a picture of central promotion that has some similarities to the external pressure framework: A prominent actor induces the spread of innovations to a wide range of backward countries. In fact, normative appeal arguments often emphasize the role of international organizations, which are well-positioned to promote new norms (Barnett and Finnemore 2004). But these authors depict the emulating nations as eager, willing followers of international trends, not as hapless victims of external imposition (Finnemore 1996a). In this view, state leaders genuinely commit to new standards and norms, rather than complying with outside demands begrudgingly. They change their goals, not only their behavior. According to constructivists, concern for international legitimacy thus leads to a much more profound absorption of outside influences than external pressure arguments imply.

By contrast, the two utilitarian frameworks assume that legitimacy considerations play only a minor role in public policymaking, which is driven primarily by clear, firm, and largely immutable interests. In this view, basic concerns for external and internal safety, economic well-being, and social order guide state action; societal groups also pursue well-identified interests. Problems that threaten these interests produce receptivity to new solutions, which are adopted if they seem to produce a net benefit over the status quo. Thus, while goals are largely given, the means with which they are pursued can change depending on circumstances, including the emergence of challenges to old solutions and the appearance of new decision options.

According to these utilitarian arguments, states enact reforms not because of novel international standards or norms, but because new problems jeopardize old interests or because new opportunities for improvement arise. For instance, governments began to combat environmental degradation not because international society designated this task as a modern, appropriate course of action, but because environmental destruction produced economic damage and health problems, threatening real interests. Decision-makers thus follow a problem-solving logic. Displaying conventional goal orientation, they identify difficulties in light of preexisting interests and seek solutions that seem to promise the greatest possible improvement.

Yet while agreeing on decision-makers' main motivation, these interest-based frameworks differ significantly on the procedures used by policy-makers to identify and evaluate solutions to problems. The rational learning framework assumes that people approximate the postulates of comprehensive rationality. To prepare decisions, they collect the relevant information and process it thoroughly and systematically. In this vein, they scan the environment and conduct a wide-ranging search for promising solutions to problems. Then they ascertain these options' payoffs and assess the likelihood of successful implementation. When such a cost-benefit analysis demonstrates the superiority of a new model over established policy approaches and other alternatives, they enact it. Since these procedures follow the general maxims of inferential logic, for instance through Bayesian updating (Meseguer 2002; Chamley 2004: chap. 2), decision-makers in various countries often reach similar conclusions. As they maximize their utility by adopting a beneficial innovation, a wave of diffusion gets under way. Policy convergence thus results from rational learning (Meseguer 2002; Jacoby 2000: 9, 24).

Whereas this framework invokes the postulates of comprehensive, economic rationality, the cognitive-psychological argument rests on solid empirical findings about bounded rationality. This approach argues that people face overabundant uncertain information with limited computational capacity. Therefore, it is infeasible to process all the relevant information in a systematic, balanced way. Being finite, attention has to be selective. People commonly and automatically resort to inferential shortcuts, which highlight some information and apply simple rules to process it. These heuristics make it much easier to cope with information overload and arrive at decisions. But by limiting and skewing information processing, these shortcuts risk creating systematic distortions and biases. While they are essential for coping with excess information, they can significantly impair decision quality (Kahneman, Slovic, and Tversky 1982; Gilovich, Griffin, and Tversky 2002; Gowda and Fox 2002; McDermott 2004: 58–69).

According to this explanation, a bold, striking innovation attracts the attention of decision-makers in neighboring countries, who by contrast neglect less immediately available, but equally relevant, experiences from faraway places. Thus, attention is skewed, privileging vivid information over less striking information, regardless of its substantive importance. A particularly available model grabs the attention of policy-makers, who are more reactive than proactive. Once a new model has entered their radar screen, they tend to "jump to conclusions" regarding its likely performance. Drawing excessively firm inferences from short stretches of apparent success, they adopt the new model more on the basis of its promise than of a demonstrated track record. An aura of success inspires policy-makers in a number of countries to emulate the innovation, thus triggering a wave of diffusion. Moreover, they often import this policy framework without thoroughly assessing its fit with their specific requirements and needs. Preferring imitation over redesign, they tend to replicate the foreign model and limit modifications and adjustments. In all of these ways, they diverge from the postulates of comprehensive rationality and conform to the patterns of bounded rationality.

Like rational learning, this cognitive-psychological explanation depicts as the driving force of diffusion the interest-based, goal-oriented effort to solve problems. But it points to inherent limitations of human information processing that make problem solving difficult and lead policy-makers to rely on inferential shortcuts. Those heuristics are useful for coping with the flood of information storming in on people, but they can seriously distort judgments.

This new version of bounded rationality differs significantly from the variant developed by behavioral organization theorists in the 1950s (Simon 1957, 1985; March and Simon 1958; Cyert and March 1963; Wildavsky 1964; Allison 1971: chap. 3; Bendor 2003). Derived from the cautious behavior of U.S. business firms, the older variant postulated that decision-makers satisfice rather than maximize. They choose the first option that reaches a preset aspiration level and do not hold out for the best of all options, given their limited computational capacities and the resulting costs of continuing search. Change is therefore gradual and incremental. When the status quo becomes untenable, decision-makers adopt the smallest necessary adjustments that are required for restoring satisfactory performance. Drastic transformations are rare, and they are dangerous because grand novel schemes have unforeseeable effects (Lindblom 1965).

Since this older version of bounded rationality was based on the study of complex organizations in an unusually stable setting and lacked the robust microfoundations provided by cognitive psychology, its findings may lack generalizability. Specifically, its predictions of local search and minimal change cannot account for waves of diffusion, in which external sources inspire decision-makers to adopt ambitious innovations. These bold contagious transformations clearly deviate from incrementalism (see also Jones and Baumgartner 2005: 3–5, 44–45, 50–53, 92, 111, 280–81). Behavioral organization theory expects path dependency: Each decision-making unit's past ties down its future. But in diffusion processes, outside influences interrupt this line of continuity and prompt strikingly new departures. Cross-sectional momentum prevails over longitudinal inertia. The present study therefore assesses the bounded rationality arguments derived from modern cognitive psychology, not the older approach advanced by behavioral organization theorists.

CAUSAL MECHANISMS IN MODEL DIFFUSION

Which one of the causal mechanisms highlighted by the four basic frameworks best explains the waves of diffusion in Latin American social sector reform? In particular, which theory convincingly accounts for the three characteristics of diffusion discussed in the introduction, namely, its S-shaped temporal unfolding, its geographical clustering, and its outcome of spreading similarity amid diversity? And which framework sheds most light on the decision-making processes that underlie the spread of innovations? The assessment first focuses on model diffusion, the type of diffusion with the greatest, most profound, and most uniform impact on a wide range of emulating countries, as is obvious in the spread of Chilean-style pension privatization. The presence of a bold, neat blueprint turned decision making in social security more focused and clear-cut than in the complicated health arena. Theoretical patterns are therefore clearly visible. Thereafter, attention turns to the more variegated mechanisms that drive the spread of innovations in health care.

External Pressure

The external pressure approach seems to account well for the adoption of similar reforms in a wide range of countries and for the speed with which pension privatization diffused; but given the global reach of the most powerful international organizations, it has difficulty explaining the geographical clustering of this innovation's spread. Forceful promotion by a central actor offers the most straightforward explanation for the enactment of the same policy model in a variety of settings; such commonality in diversity seems to result from vertical imposition. As their critics claim, the IFIs have pushed a uniform neoliberal blueprint on the Third World. Furthermore, the powerful means of influence that international organizations such as the IMF and World Bank command seem to account for the rapid spread of innovations; in this view, when the IFIs push for a reform, many weak developing countries soon enact it.

But the external pressure argument cannot easily account for the geographic clustering of diffusion, especially its pronounced neighborhood effects. The most important IFIs, the IMF and World Bank,[1] have a global perspective and promote models from all around the planet. For instance, the 1993 *World Development Report* highlighted health re-

---

[1] Headed by officials from the target region, the Inter-American Development Bank (IDB) is less powerful and insistent on conditionality than the IMF and WB.

forms in a wide range of nations, such as Chile, Korea, Russia, Tunisia, and Zimbabwe (WB 1993b: 161–71); and the World Bank manual on pension privatization (1994a) targeted a global audience. While IFI influence helps explain why policy diffusion eventually "jumps" over to other regions—as pension privatization did in the mid-1990s (Orenstein 2003: 185–86)—it cannot explain why an innovation spreads first and foremost inside one region. This geographic clustering is especially puzzling because the predominantly socioeconomic (rather than cultural) perspective of the IFIs highlights the considerable diversity inside many regions; in terms of socioeconomic development, countries may have more in common with nations on other continents than with their neighbors. For instance, Bolivia may do better by adopting innovations designed in Asia or Africa than by following its much more advanced neighbor Chile, as it did by privatizing its pension system.

As chapter 3 documents, my field research casts further doubt on the explanatory power of external pressures. Despite their seemingly impressive arsenal, the IFIs often do not exert effective influence. Problems of compliance are particularly pronounced when broad institutional issues are at stake; when reforms require parliamentary deliberation and approval; and when numerous sociopolitical forces can therefore gain access to decision making (Naím 1995; Nelson 1997; Pastor and Wise 1999). Under those circumstances, all of which apply to pension reform, IFI conditionality often carries little weight. The concession or disbursement of loans is difficult to tie to the lengthy process of deliberating on complex laws. Also, influential actors fail to be impressed by IFI conditions that do not directly affect their interests. Above all, patronage-obsessed politicians worry about "pork" for their bailiwick, not fiscal equilibrium.

Even presidents can put political calculations ahead of compliance with IFI recommendations. For instance, Bolivia's Gonzalo Sánchez de Lozada (1993–97) wanted to gain electoral benefits by applying the proceeds of public enterprise privatization toward a new social program. He therefore refused to give in to very strong World Bank and IMF pressure to use these resources for covering the transitional costs of pension privatization. In the end, he simply invoked Bolivia's national sovereignty and insisted on making decisions as he pleased (interview with Peña Rueda 2002). This decision exacerbated the country's fiscal deficit and forced Sánchez de Lozada during his second term (2002–03) to enact stringent adjustment measures, which unleashed a severe political crisis culminating in his violent ouster. Yet even on such a consequential issue, this poor, highly indebted, aid-dependent country managed to resist strong IFI pressure.

For these reasons, loan conditionality—the main instrument of international pressure—has little effectiveness for pushing major institutional innovations (Nelson 1996; Hunter and Brown 2000; Brooks 2004; Appel 2004: 4–9). In fact, IFI conditionality need not even constitute an *external* effort at exerting influence; to enhance their own bargaining leverage with domestic opponents or hesitant chief executives, reform-minded experts often ask IFIs to "impose" conditions on their country (interviews with Gottret 2002, Meloni 2002, and Peñaranda 2002; Meseguer 2002: 13–14; Vreeland 2003: 13–16, 46–48, 51–54, 62–64, 103). The clear distinction of external vs. internal factors that the external pressure approach draws is questionable.

Thus, closer inspection of the policy process shows that diffusion does not result primarily from external imposition. IFI admonitions and pressures certainly constrain the options available to national policy-makers and influence their choices among those options; but they by no means determine those decisions. Attention therefore turns to frameworks that acknowledge the autonomy of domestic decision-makers.

Normative Appeal

Among these theories, the normative appeal framework has affinities with the external pressure approach. IFI promotion may turn an innovation into a normatively appropriate model or an attractive symbol of modernity. Moral suasion or the quest for international legitimacy may induce many countries to import the new policy scheme. Thus, the IFIs may exert influence less by pressuring governments to adopt unpalatable changes than by convincing them that those changes are actually palatable. While IFIs cannot impose innovations on domestic decision-makers against their will, they may make them willing to adopt new models by reshaping their preferences. The normative appeal approach thus claims that the IFIs profoundly influence policy-makers—not from the outside, via carrots and sticks, but from the inside, by persuading them what they themselves should want.

This constructivist view differs starkly from an important premise of the rational learning framework, which takes actor interests as given and, in its methodological individualism, brackets the possibility that they may be socially constituted. Whereas rational choice depicts decision-makers as atomistically autonomous, the normative appeal approach conceptualizes them as members of an international society, which also exerts coordination, though in a looser, less heavy-handed way than the IFIs do according to the external pressure approach (Meyer and Rowan 1977; Finnemore 1996a, 1996b; Finnemore and Sikkink 1998; Lutz and Sikkink 2000; Barnett and Finnemore 2004).

By stressing moral suasion and legitimacy, the normative appeal framework diverges from the interest-based foundation of the two learning theories, especially rational choice. Contrary to those approaches, it depicts a model's adoption not as the result of a goal-oriented choice, but of magnetic attraction. Rather than seeking a promising solution to a previously identified problem, decision-makers in this view are drawn to an innovation that looks modern and appropriate, therefore attracts followers, and precisely for that reason turns even more attractive. Indeed, the solution may well appear before the problem and, in some sense, search for a problem that can justify—i.e., rationalize—its adoption (cf. March and Olsen 1976; Kingdon 1984).

This approach seems well suited for explaining the adoption of the same model by variegated countries as well as the rapid spread of innovations. Indeed, the normative appeal approach emphasizes the puzzle of commonality amid diversity, which it invokes to debunk rational learning arguments: Why would countries that display starkly different characteristics and therefore have divergent functional needs embrace the same model? As such striking commonality seems to lack a rational justification, advocates of this framework infer the predominance of normative and symbolic appeal (e.g., Finnemore 1996a: 42–47). In this view, concern for appropriateness and legitimacy also provides the driving force for the remarkable speed of diffusion. As new fashions spread like wildfire (Lieberson 2000), innovative, modern, and normatively appropriate models may quickly find supporters, much faster than a careful cost-benefit analysis would suggest. The desire to appear modern and comply with new norms induces governments to emulate innovations even if a track record for assessing their advantages and problems is missing. Countries rush to keep up with new trends before they have the relevant information to ascertain the reform's likely effects.

But the geographical clustering of diffusion is more difficult for the normative appeal approach to explain. International prestige should have induced Latin American countries to import the notional defined-contribution scheme of pension reform developed in Europe (Cichon 1999) rather than emulating the privatization plan designed by their underdeveloped neighbor Chile. Also, as mentioned above, the leading IFIs, especially the World Bank, promote worldwide learning about policy models. Thus, legitimacy is increasingly defined at a global level. Why should decision-makers continue to adopt a regional focus and pay attention primarily to innovations developed by their neighbors? In the era of globalization, the normative appeal framework cannot easily account for this limited perspective.

Moreover, given modern means of instant communication, the normative appeal framework would expect an even faster diffusion of innovations than is captured in the slow initial upswing of the S-shaped pattern. If the quest for legitimacy drives policy choice, the appearance of a novelty should immediately trigger emulation. Since it takes little time to recognize a new model as cutting-edge, diffusion should get under way in more explosive fashion. And since there is an urge to appear more advanced than one's neighbors, countries should enact the legitimacy-enhancing reform very quickly. Moreover, the rapid spread of reforms would put increasing pressure on laggards to jump on the bandwagon in order to avoid the stigma of embarrassing backwardness. For these reasons, the normative appeal framework would predict a dramatic upsurge of diffusion along an exponential trajectory.[2]

But rather than sweeping across the world like a sudden tsunami, diffusion follows a well-behaved wave pattern. It takes most countries some time before they adopt a foreign model. Novelty as such is not sufficient for triggering imitation. Decision-makers wait for an innovation to attain a minimal track record before they consider emulating it. The desire quickly to enhance one's legitimacy does not carry the day; some assessment of experience is required before policy-makers are willing to incur the political costs and risks involved in enacting significant change.[3]

This insistence on some track record is especially pronounced where an innovation's adoption would affect powerful sociopolitical forces. Such an impact is much more likely in "redistributive" policy areas such as pension reform, where decisions have broad categories of winners and losers, compared to "distributive" decisions that have concentrated winners, yet diffuse losers (cf. Lowi 1964). Distributive decisions are politically attractive because they make some constituents happy without making anybody unhappy (except for the finance minister). Thus, distributive decisions are easily triggered by normative or symbolic concerns. For instance, governments eagerly prove their modernity by creating a science institution, even if there is no domestic scientific community (Finnemore 1996a); this decision imposes no visible cost on powerful constituencies but allows political leaders to make patronage appointments in the new agency.[4]

Decision making tends to be very different in redistributive policy areas because the losers are clearly defined, large groups that resist having

---

[2] In fact, constructivists depict the spread of norms and models as a "cascade" that quickly gathers momentum (Finnemore and Sikkink 1998: 902–4; Lutz and Sikkink 2000: 638, 655–59; see also Kuran and Sunstein 1999: 687, 714, 728–31).

[3] Even sociological institutionalists now stress this (Strang and Macy 2001: 147–56).

[4] Its official purpose to plan and coordinate scientific activities would make such an institution fall under Lowi's (1964) regulatory category, but in underdeveloped countries without a significant science community it simply allowed politicians to make additional patronage appointments, which turned this innovation into a distributive decision.

their interests sacrificed on the altar of international legitimacy. Trying to overcome this opposition, reformers need to invoke an innovation's track record to prove its beneficial net result. Thus, the absence of an easy political consensus makes redistributive policy areas inhospitable territory for the purely legitimacy-enhancing emulation of innovations. The clash of interests subjects external models to close scrutiny, making decisions dependent on the evaluation of some amount of experience with the new policy approach. As a result, redistributive policymaking is a goal-oriented activity in which interests and power acquire great importance. While concern for legitimacy may well restrain the pursuit of interests and influence the outcome of power struggles (cf. Kahneman, Knetsch, and Thaler 1986), the desire to appear modern or comply with new international norms does not seem to be the main motivating force in such conflict-ridden issue areas.

The examination of the policy process in chapter 3 indeed shows that in the redistributive field of pension reform, diffusion proceeded differently than theorists of normative and symbolic appeal claim. Rather than a new policy approach looking for problems that could rationalize its adoption, the Chilean model attracted attention and support by promising to resolve serious difficulties that had been identified long before. In particular, pension privatization claimed to overcome the worsening actuarial disequilibria plaguing social security systems in many Latin American countries (Mesa-Lago 1989). Chile's innovation thus seemed to address preexisting problems (e.g., interviews with De los Heros 2002, Salinas 2002, and Tamayo 2004). The Chilean model appeared as a new instrument to pursue given interests, especially long-term fiscal equilibrium, a core goal of the state.

Other instrumental considerations linked pension privatization to economic development, a long-standing aspiration of Latin American countries. In particular, the temporal coincidence of Chile's social security reform with the start of a sustained increase in domestic savings, investment, and eventually growth induced many experts and policy-makers—in a logically problematic inference (see below)—to postulate a causal connection. The resulting claim that pension privatization makes a decisive contribution to economic prosperity was crucial for winning support from chief executives and legislative politicians for this change. For instance, Peru's president Alberto Fujimori (1990–2000), who was reluctant to introduce market principles in the social sectors, accepted pension privatization only because his key economic advisers stressed its presumed macroeconomic benefits (interviews with De los Heros 2002, Du Bois 2002, and Peñaranda 2002). This pragmatic, instrumental argument was crucial for setting in motion the wave of Chilean-style reform (Madrid 2003b: 31–40).

In sum, normative appeal cannot account for model diffusion in redistributive policy areas such as social security. While the concern for legitimacy may shape distributive decisions, which look politically cost-free, contending interests override this motivation in decisions on pension privatization. Where major benefits and losses for powerful sectors are at stake, the desire to look advanced and comply with new international norms cannot carry the day.

Rational Learning

Given the insufficiency of the approaches discussed so far, can the rational learning framework explain waves of diffusion? Derived from rational-choice assumptions, this approach emphasizes the autonomy of decision-makers, thus diverging from the external pressure framework. And by contrast to the normative appeal framework, rational learning sees political action as a goal-oriented choice driven by interests. Thus, these approaches' deficiencies make rational learning look like a promising alternative.

Upon closer inspection, however, this framework confronts great difficulties in accounting for the three characteristics of diffusion. Above all, commonality in diversity poses a serious puzzle for rational choice. Why would countries of such different characteristics adopt the same policy paradigm? As the emulators of Chilean pension privatization differed in the severity of financial stress and other characteristics of their old social security systems, functional need does not seem to account for the spread of innovations. While diffusion is triggered by preexisting problems, it seems questionable that the same reform approach would offer the best possible solution to these problems in a great variety of countries, as rational choice's utility maximization postulate claims.

In fact, a number of emulating countries seemed to lack prerequisites for the proper functioning of a private pension system. Such a scheme, which includes primarily formal-sector workers, does not fit well in Bolivia and El Salvador, where formal labor constitutes a narrow minority.[5] Those poor nations also did not have well-developed capital markets, which the World Bank depicts as a precondition for successful pension privatization (WB 1994a: 231, 245, 258–60, 280; cf. WB IEG 2006: xv–xvii, 18–29). Thus, the diffusion of the Chilean model to much less developed nations does not look like a rational choice.

---

[5] A new WB study (Gill, Packard, and Yermo 2004: xvii) indeed finds that Latin American pension privatization has yielded "significant disappointments, chief among them the failure to extend access to social security to a broader segment of society." This failure reflects the narrowness of formal labor markets in the region (93–104).

Rational learning also has difficulty explaining the geographical clustering of diffusion. To maximize utility, decision-makers should be equally receptive to innovations from anywhere in the world, rather than paying attention mostly to models from their own region. Striking improvements in communication facilitate information exchange on a global scale. And due to the internal diversity of many regions—for instance, the stark differences between Chile and Bolivia—countries may well have greater similarities in functional needs with nations on other continents than with their neighbors. As a result, experts and policy-makers have the opportunity and incentive to search for innovations worldwide. There is no rational justification for the limited, regional perspective that they do in fact apply.

Diffusion's S-shaped temporal pattern also diverges from rational-choice predictions. Certainly, this approach *would* expect the slow start of diffusion, that is, the absence of the explosive pattern implied by the race for modernity. But the subsequent upsurge, during which many countries adopt a model fairly soon after its first appearance, deviates from rational learning, which requires a careful cost-benefit analysis that considers a longer track record. Given significant cross-country differences in functional needs, the quick adoption of the same policy framework by a variety of countries does not seem to result from rational learning.

The eventual slowdown of diffusion also contradicts some rational learning theories, especially arguments emphasizing economic competition (cf. Ikenberry 1990: 101–2). If diffusion were driven by decision-makers' belief that a new model was important for enhancing competitiveness or for attracting foreign capital, then competitive pressures should cause it to keep accelerating rather than to peter out. The more countries adopt a promising innovation, the greater the competitive pressure on laggards to follow suit (Simmons, Dobbin, and Garrett 2006: 292–95). Accordingly, diffusion should follow an exponential curve. The actual S-shaped pattern, especially the eventual deceleration of diffusion, contradicts this prediction and casts doubt on economic competition arguments, a subset of the rational learning approach. In sum, this framework has difficulty accounting for all three characteristics of diffusion.

The analysis of policymaking in chapter 4 also fails to find much evidence of rational learning. As leading participants stress (see also interview with Naím 2000; Morales 2004; Weyland 2004b), decision making "in the real world" diverges clearly from rational information processing. Rather than systematically assessing the relevant information and performing careful, well-balanced cost-benefit analyses, policy-makers often act under considerable time pressures and confront great uncer-

tainty. Scrambling to address several urgent problems, they find it difficult to devote sustained attention to any issue. Thus, actual decision
making deviates significantly from the normative postulates of comprehensive rationality, approximating instead the empirical patterns of
bounded rationality. This finding points the analyst of diffusion to theories that invoke cognitive-psychological insights on decisional inferences
and heuristics.

Cognitive Heuristics

Like rational learning, the cognitive heuristics framework sees diffusion
result from goal-oriented activities driven by actor interests. In this view,
external models are attractive because they promise to resolve real, previously identified problems. Yet despite agreement on the motives that
propel the spread of innovations, cognitive psychology disagrees with
rational choice on the ways and means by which actors pursue their
goals. Rational choice starts from simplifying ideal-typical premises, especially utility maximization and the comprehensive, systematic processing of the relevant information. While there may be idiosyncratic deviations from complete rationality, they cancel out in the aggregate and
diminish over time due to individual learning and "natural" selection
(Tsebelis 1990: 32–38). Decision making therefore should not be affected by systematic, lasting divergences from cost-benefit calculations.

By contrast, cognitive psychology has established the robust empirical
finding that human rationality is inherently bounded by innate, insuper-
able limitations on information processing. Since attention is finite and
scanning the environment for the relevant information is costly, people
cannot comply with the ideal-typical standards of rational choice. To
proceed efficiently despite the inherent limits on information processing,
they commonly resort to inferential shortcuts. These heuristics make it
much easier to arrive at decisions, especially on novel, unprecedented
reforms with highly uncertain costs and benefits such as pension privatization. Only the efficiency gain provided by cognitive shortcuts allows
people to cope with all the demands and challenges they face. But these
heuristics also risk causing significant, systematic, and lasting biases in
human inference. Therefore, decision making in the real world diverges
significantly from ideal-typical rational choice postulates (Simon 1985;
Jones 1999, 2001; Bendor 2003).

While acknowledging that people do not follow the principles of inferential logic in their actual decision making, advocates of rational choice
have claimed that the results of bounded rationality closely approximate
the conclusions that comprehensive rationality would yield. According
to this argument, which has been applied to the mass public, decision

heuristics, such as the simple cues of partisanship, allow "rationally ignorant" voters to arrive at choices that are in line with their preferred
outcomes. These information misers apply easy guidelines that relieve
them of the need to make up their mind on multiple issue positions,
but that lead them in the same direction as the complicated cost-benefit
calculations prescribed by comprehensive rationality would do.[6] Relying
on decision heuristics is individually rational because the infinitesimal
impact that any single voter can exert on an election outcome makes it
irrational to invest much time in defining vote choices; in this low-
salience situation, "ignorance" is rational (Downs 1957). Common citizens' usage of simple cues is also collectively rational because individual
mistakes cancel out and thus do not affect aggregate outcomes, which
reflect popular preferences quite faithfully (Page and Shapiro 1992; see
in general Tsebelis 1990: chap. 2).

These arguments, which question the empirical significance of cognitive-psychological findings for political analysis, do not apply to important policy decisions made by a few experts and politicians, however.
Social security and health reforms are high-salience choices that have
significant economic, social, and political repercussions and often unleash serious conflicts. It is not rational for the few designers of these
momentous changes to be "ignorant" and follow simple cues. Whereas
political leaders have limited knowledge of these complicated issues,
many specialists who shape the decision options command thorough,
often impressive, expertise. These experts participating in high-stakes
decisions constitute "most likely cases" for the prevalence of fully rational procedures (Fiorina 1996: 88; cf. Eckstein 1975). Their regular reliance on cognitive heuristics is therefore especially noteworthy, offering
strong evidence against conventional rational choice approaches. This
application of inferential shortcuts is certainly not fully rational at the
individual level. But it is unavoidable in the real world of information
overload, great uncertainty, and high time pressures (cf. Morales 2004).

In fact, the institutional conditions under which Latin American decision-makers elaborate crucial reforms often exacerbate these problems,
intensify the need to resort to cognitive shortcuts, and thus heighten the
risk of distortions and biases. Since many bureaucracies in the region
diverge starkly from Weberian principles, political appointees and even
technical experts often face uncertain tenure. In many social agencies,
turnover in the upper, decision-making echelons is exceedingly high; in
Peru, for instance, health ministers have lasted for little more than one

[6] See especially Popkin (1991) and Lupia and McCubbins (1998). In a general cognitive-
psychological treatment of these issues, Gigerenzer and Selten (2001) stress the adaptive,
functional features of heuristics but reject rational choice's maximization postulate.

year on average since 1990 (cf. Corrales 2002; see also WB 2000a: 13, 17; Santiso 2006: 56–59). Appointees and their aides therefore know from the outset that their days are numbered. Unless they rush to enact changes, they cannot make any mark and thus miss the opportunity to boost their careers. They therefore design reform projects under tremendous time pressure and cannot afford a comprehensive, proactive search for relevant information. Instead, they rely on inferential shortcuts to learn about models they can emulate, gain a sense of their performance, and quickly translate them into domestic reform proposals. For these reasons, even well-trained, highly competent specialists are compelled to apply cognitive heuristics—and to incur the corresponding risks of distortions and biases (cf. in general Bendor 2003: 449, 457, 460, 463).

Furthermore, the reliance on inferential shortcuts is not collectively rational because decision-makers tend to apply the same heuristics; therefore, problematic inferences may well not cancel out in the aggregate. The resulting distortions can prevail especially in public policymaking, where—contrary to a mass election—effective choices are often made by few people, if not a single individual, the president. The law of large numbers that individual mistakes wash out in aggregate decisions (cf. Tsebelis 1990: 34–36) therefore does not apply to public policymaking, especially to program design inside the executive branch. And since the executive branch can enact many changes on its own and executive bills put congressional deliberations on certain tracks, authoritative decisions and policy outputs are frequently shaped by the problematic inferences that cognitive heuristics suggest.

In sum, cognitive psychology offers a clear alternative to rational choice, especially as applied to public policymaking. The decision heuristics documented in innumerable experiments and field studies produce judgments, choices, and policy outputs that diverge significantly from the postulates of comprehensive rationality.

THE HEURISTICS OF AVAILABILITY, REPRESENTATIVENESS, AND ANCHORING

The three principal shortcuts highlighted by cognitive psychologists are the heuristics of availability, representativeness, and anchoring (Kahneman, Slovic, and Tversky 1982; Gilovich, Griffin, and Kahneman 2002). The availability heuristic refers to people's tendency to place excessive importance on information that—for logically accidental reasons—has special immediacy, strikingness, and impact, that grabs their attention, and that is therefore uniquely "available." People do not pay balanced attention to all the relevant information, as strict rationality requires, but are drawn especially to vivid, drastic events. This skewed attention distorts judgments. After seeing a car crash, for instance, most drivers slow down and proceed more cautiously for a while. In logical terms, witnessing a single accident should not change people's assessment of the likelihood of car crashes and alter their driving behavior. But in fact, such a drastic, vivid experience has precisely that effect (Kahneman, Slovic, and Tversky 1982: chaps. 1, 11–14, 33; Gilovich, Griffin, and Kahneman 2002: chaps. 3–5). In allowing dramatic incidents to shape their judgments and actions, people overrate the importance of directly available information and modify their behavior based on a selective, distorted perception. Cognitive psychologists call this automatically and unthinkingly used, yet logically problematic, strategy of inference the availability heuristic.

Whereas the availability heuristic skews people's attention and memory,[7] the representativeness heuristic shapes their evaluation of experience. This cognitive shortcut induces people to draw excessively clear, confident, and firm inferences from a precarious base of data. They overestimate the extent to which patterns observed in a small sample hold true for—i.e., are representative of—the whole population. People commonly generalize from a narrow set of observations and prematurely infer a broad regularity (Kahneman, Slovic, and Tversky 1982: chaps. 1–6; Gilovich, Griffin, and Kahneman 2002: chaps. 1–2). For instance, they see a powerful long-term trend in a limited stretch of data. The representativeness heuristic makes people eager to extrapolate from conjunctural up- or down-swings and interpret them as clear evidence of structural developments that will persist. As people overestimate the systematic component of observable processes and neglect random factors, such as regression toward the mean, they place undue weight on short-term successes or failures, which they mistake for proof of the inherent quality of the underlying program or model.

While the representativeness heuristic shapes people's evaluations of success and failure and their decisions on whether to adopt a model, the heuristic of anchoring limits the extent to which they adapt this model to their own specific needs. Anchoring induces people to attach undue weight to an initial value, which strongly affects their subsequent judgments. This inferential "stickiness" appears even if the initial value is produced arbitrarily. For instance, after being asked in the early 1970s whether Turkey's population exceeded five million, experimental subjects gave much lower estimates of the country's number of inhabitants than when the initial question asked whether it was lower than sixty-five million (namely, seventeen million vs. thirty-five million: Kahneman and Tversky 1982: 503; see also Gilovich, Griffin, and Kahneman 2002:

[7] While classical experiments documented how the availability heuristic shapes memory recall, cognitive psychologists have also stressed that it guides and focuses attention (Ross and Anderson 1982: 138–39; Taylor 1982: 192).

chaps. 6–8). Thus, while by no means precluding adjustment, initial values have a strong impact in limiting the range of such modifications. They exert a pull of "gravity" that substantially affects subsequent assessments. Decision-makers are reluctant to diverge radically from this starting point. To save computational effort, they orient their judgments by any available piece of information.

COGNITIVE HEURISTICS IN MODEL DIFFUSION

These three heuristics provide a good explanation for the basic features of diffusion, namely, its geographical clustering, its S-shaped temporal unfolding, and its product of creating commonality in diversity. The availability heuristic can account for the regional pattern of innovations' spread. As people are disproportionately influenced by events they witness directly, so drastic policy change enacted "next door" has particular immediacy, salience, and, thus, availability. Like car drivers, who are unavoidably affected by seeing an accident, decision-makers cannot fail to pay attention to a bold reform adopted by a neighboring country. Such an innovation appears to have much greater relevance than a change occurring halfway around the globe. Thus, geographic and cultural proximity make a new foreign model stand out and induce specialists to study it closely. As decision-makers do not scan the environment systematically and comprehensively for all the relevant information, but are disproportionately influenced by experiences that grab their attention, the unique availability of a neighboring country's reform often puts that innovation on the policy agenda in a whole region.[8] Thus, the availability heuristic helps explain why diffusion first gets under way on a regional scale and displays strong neighborhood effects.[9]

Once the availability heuristic has placed a new foreign model on the agenda, the representativeness heuristic influences assessments of the success of this bold innovation, giving rise to diffusion's S-shaped temporal pattern. This inferential shortcut induces decision-makers to jump to conclusions and overestimate the evidential value of a very limited base of experience. This tendency to overemphasize recent trends leads policy-makers to attribute great inherent value to innovations that attain

[8] Similarly, Mintrom (1997: 756–59, 761) found that among the U.S. states, neighborhood effects influence especially agenda setting.

[9] Geographic proximity operates largely through denser information channels. In turn, professional, political, or ideological networks can make more remote information available and extend decision-makers' radar screen beyond their home region. Transnational professional associations (cf. Haas 1992) spread information; so do political or ideological organizations, such as the Socialist International. Conversely, ideological gulfs can block availability. For instance, Fidel Castro was not impressed by Chilean pension privatization but looked to his Communist brethren for inspiration.

initial success, although this short track record may well be distorted by chance factors. The representativeness heuristic thus fuels the rapid emulation of a seemingly successful innovation and produces the dramatic upsurge in the S-shaped pattern. If a bold change—via the availability heuristic—has attracted regional attention and if early signs of success—via the representativeness heuristic—turn it into a "hit," it may spread like wildfire. But the unfounded expectations of long-term success that fuel this upsurge are sooner or later revised in light of actual experience, dampening enthusiasm for the model and slowing down its further spread.[10] This updating thus causes diffusion to level off. In sum, the representativeness heuristic inspires exaggerated hopes, which eventually give way to greater realism.

In this way, the representativeness heuristic can account for all three phases of the S-shaped curve. The relatively slow start of diffusion reflects decision-makers' insistence on some performance evaluation, which requires a minimal track record; therefore, innovations do not spread instantaneously, as the normative appeal framework implies. But these performance assessments are less careful and systematic than strict rationality demands; instead, decision-makers eagerly act upon early signs of success. The representativeness heuristic thus speeds up diffusion soon after it gets under way. Finally, diffusion peters out as more evidence about the reform's costs and benefits becomes available and the initial enthusiasm therefore fades away. Thus, as time wears on, countries that hitherto failed to adopt the new policy approach become ever less likely to do so now. The representativeness heuristic thus drives the wavelike pattern of diffusion—its slow start, sudden upsurge, and eventual decline.

Finally, the heuristic of anchoring helps explain the result of diffusion, namely, the spread of commonality amid diversity. Once a government has decided to adopt a foreign model, anchoring limits the adaptation of the extraneous policy approach to the specific needs of the importing country. While anchoring by no means precludes such modifications, it keeps their range limited and preserves the basic nature of the imported model. Comprehensive rationality would often call for more profound adjustments, including alterations of a model's fundamental design. But anchoring confines changes to more peripheral aspects; in particular, an innovation's domain of application may be delimited differently, and the new model may be combined with other reforms to make it more palatable.

In this vein, pension privatization was not always as radical as in

---

[10] In fact, innovations may be abandoned (Strang and Macy 2001: 150–55), a topic that has received insufficient attention in the diffusion literature.

Chile. Argentina, for instance, applied this model only above a certain income threshold, maintaining a basic public scheme to provide some protection to all contributors. Thus, Argentina faithfully instituted the new design principle developed by its neighbor, but in a narrower domain. Other countries complemented Chilean-style radical reform with new programs tailored to their specific needs. Given large-scale poverty, for instance, Bolivia combined social security privatization with a universal pension benefit designed to guarantee the basic livelihood of all older people, including people not covered by social security.[11] Thus, while anchoring does not predict apish mimicking, it restricts adaptations to nonessential elements, such as the range of an innovation's application, and maintains the foreign model's core. This heuristic thus helps explain the spread of the same policy approach to a wide variety of countries.

In sum, the heuristics of availability, representativeness, and anchoring offer good explanations for the main characteristics of diffusion, namely, its geographical clustering, temporal sequence, and principal outcome. Since none of the other approaches accounts well for all three features, the cognitive heuristics framework appears superior. My ample field research provides further corroboration. As chapter 4 shows, deliberations and decisions on pension reform in contemporary Latin America have been deeply shaped by inferential shortcuts. Chilean-style pension privatization was highly available among neighboring countries and therefore spread first and foremost inside Latin America; its initial success was interpreted as an indication of inherent quality and therefore triggered an upsurge in emulation; and decision-makers remained anchored to the Chilean model, importing an existing design with limited modifications. Thus, policy-making in pension reform clearly deviated from the postulates of comprehensive rationality and displayed instead the empirical patterns of bounded rationality.[12]

In fact, the heuristics of availability, representativeness, and anchoring arguably made Latin American pension privatization rationally suboptimal. As the striking availability of the Chilean model captured the attention of decision-makers in the region, they neglected other promising innovations such as the notional defined-contribution scheme, which may have offered a more beneficial reform option for countries such as Bolivia, as chapter 4 analyzes in depth. Furthermore, the enthusiasm for Chilean-style pension privatization stimulated by the representativeness heuristic has been recognized as excessive, even by officials of the World Bank, which used to advocate this change strongly. Remarkably, the

---

[11] On these variations, see Mesa-Lago (1997) and Kay and Kritzer (2001).

[12] Interestingly, Meseguer (2005: 72–79) arrives at a similar general conclusion.

bank's chief economist in 1999 unveiled most of the promises attached to radical pension reform as "myths that have . . . derailed rational decision-making" (Orszag and Stiglitz 1999: 4).[13] Finally, anchoring induced policy-makers to follow the Chilean model more closely than they find in retrospect advisable; for instance, the Salvadoran reform team leader nowadays wonders whether a less drastic, mixed model would not have been preferable (interview with Brevé 2004). Thus, decision-makers' reliance on cognitive shortcuts produced policy outputs that appear as rationally suboptimal. The distortions caused by the heuristics of availability, representativeness, and anchoring had real costs.

Combining Causal Mechanisms: Availability Enhancement

While cognitive shortcuts prevail among the causal mechanisms that drive model diffusion, some mechanisms stressed by other theoretical approaches can extend the bounds of rationality selectively. In particular, international organizations can make information available that would otherwise not enter decision-makers' radar screen. While the availability heuristic focuses policy-makers' attention on geographically proximate and culturally similar countries, IOs with a global reach can bring to their attention interesting experiences in faraway places. As a result, they take a closer look at foreign models that went hitherto unnoticed. Since IOs act selectively and promote only best-practice models that embody their own preferences, this extension of the bounds of rationality does not cause information overload. It redirects attention but does not swamp it.

This availability enhancement can be especially effective in two types of situations. First, when the emulation of a highly available model has proven economically or politically infeasible, policy-makers are at a loss about how to combat a problem they are facing; therefore, they tend to be especially receptive to new suggestions on how to resolve this difficulty. Second, when decision-makers have decided to enact a new policy principle but no concrete, promising model that embodies it has entered their radar screen, they appreciate specific proposals for putting the new maxim into practice. In sum, where the availability heuristic has not produced an acceptable solution to a problem, policy-makers—unable to conduct the wide-ranging proactive search for alternatives prescribed by comprehensive rationality—are particularly open to IO suggestions that make hitherto unknown options available.

---

[13] The chief economist for Latin America also admits that the bank "oversold" neoliberal reforms, which included pension privatization (Perry 2005: 3). Moreover, see the critical assessment of the bank's role in pension privatization in WB IEG (2006).

IOs, in turn, seek to promote their own policy principles by selectively advertising models that embody these maxims. Thus, where their efforts at availability enhancement capture decision-makers' attention, IOs can exert significant influence. By making decision-makers aware of foreign models that hitherto escaped their attention, they can lead policymaking in new directions and trigger the emulation of foreign models in otherwise inhospitable territory. IO assessments of a new model's success can also affect policy-makers' cost-benefit analyses and reinforce the performance evaluations derived through the representativeness heuristic. In these ways, IOs can significantly shape innovations' spread.

Availability enhancement may offer external actors, including the powerful international financial institutions, the most effective path for shaping domestic policy decisions. Since direct pressure and loan conditionality are of limited use in social sector reform, this more subtle form of influence assumes particular importance. Rather than attempting imposition, the IFIs have increasingly relied on knowledge provision, advice, and insinuation. From their own perspective, this softer strategy has the advantage of avoiding the political and reputational costs of trying to force governments to enact reforms against their will. As the World Bank has noticed (Pincus and Winters 2002: 12–13; Mallaby 2004: 233, 239, 243, 253; Stiglitz 1999), complex institutional changes have lasting success only if a government "owns" the reform and genuinely commits to it.

Thus, availability enhancement may be one of the principal ways for the IFIs to promote innovations' spread. Their influence, which is more limited than their impressive arsenal suggests, may derive mainly from the bounds of rationality. The very limitations in human attention and computational capacity turn IFI efforts to make decision-makers aware of otherwise neglected policy options so significant. In a hypothetical world of comprehensive rationality, in which decision-makers proactively scan the environment for relevant experiences, such provision of information could not make a significant difference. But in the real world of bounded rationality, in which even experts tend to overlook important bodies of information, IFI promotion of novel models can broaden policy-makers' horizon and make them aware of reform options that had hitherto gone unnoticed. Precisely because the availability heuristic narrows decision-makers' attention, IFI efforts at availability enhancement can trigger the spread of innovations.

CAUSAL MECHANISMS IN PRINCIPLE DIFFUSION

As the preceding discussion shows, model diffusion in the social sectors is driven by distinct causal mechanisms. Above all, decision-makers follow cognitive heuristics and clearly diverge from the postulates of comprehensive rationality. They pursue interests in a conventionally goal-oriented fashion; symbolic and normative considerations play only a minor role in redistributive issue areas. External pressures from powerful IFIs exert some effect but are not the main engine of innovations' spread.

The outstanding importance of cognitive shortcuts is typical of model diffusion. When bold reform ideas crystallize in a concrete, integrated package of organizational features, experts and policy-makers pay special attention. A neat new model is much more vivid and memorable than a general principle. As a result, the availability heuristic operates with particular intensity. While a general guideline can also attract disproportionate attention (cf. Zaller 1992), a distinct model captivates people in a more immediate, profound, and exclusive fashion. A new model also gives boundedly rational decision-makers a clear blueprint for enacting a general principle, which relieves them of the complicated task of developing their own institutional design. The paradigmatic example of a frontrunner impresses itself with special force on the minds of decision-makers in nearby nations. The availability heuristic therefore highlights models more than principles.

Furthermore, the concrete precedent of a model enacted by a frontrunner country greatly facilitates the performance assessments shaped by the representativeness heuristic. A general principle constitutes a pure promise, whereas the implementation of a model is an actual realization. The stretch of experience that it yields gives rise to judgments about success and failure that follow the representativeness heuristic. Certainly, the specific realization of a principle also provides clues about the usefulness and results of this general guideline. But those judgments are less conclusive because other ways of putting the principle into practice are easily imaginable. And the generality of a principle means that performance standards are often unclear. Whereas a model seeks to attain specific goals that allow for measuring its performance, it is more difficult to assess whether the abstract concerns embodied in a principle—for instance, strengthening incentives in health service provision—have been fulfilled. When instituting a model, decision-makers must make choices that specify the goals of the policy reform. Advocates of a broad guideline can avoid these choices. For instance, incentives can be understood in various ways; what counts as an advance by one definition—such as increased service production—may not qualify as progress by another definition, which may emphasize service quality. Therefore, the performance of a principle is hard to ascertain, offering less opportunity for the representativeness heuristic to come into play.

Moreover, only a concrete model can exert the "stickiness" that gives rise to anchoring. Due to its lack of specificity, a general principle cannot tie down judgments in this way. Instead, its very generality allows for a variety of concrete realizations. Thus, a principle is more open to variation and cannot tie down judgments and decisions. By contrast, a concrete model induces decision-makers to remain close to the original source of inspiration and to prefer replication over redesign.

For these reasons, the cognitive heuristics that shape model diffusion do not play an equally important role in principle diffusion. They put policymaking less firmly on specific tracks. By not guiding decision-makers' attention and judgments as clearly toward some options, they have less force in filtering out alternatives.

But these shortcuts—especially availability and representativeness—do exert considerable influence on principle diffusion as well. Among the various considerations that are on decision-makers' mind, one principle can become especially available and therefore prevail, pushing other maxims into the background. For instance, a striking event or perceived crisis can give one principle outstanding salience. The terrorist attacks of September 11, 2001, impressed on Americans the importance of public safety precautions while softening the commitment to strict protections of individual liberty. Such surges in the availability of certain principles are evident in public discourse. For instance, the hyperinflationary crises afflicting several Latin American countries in the late 1980s created lasting concern for price stability (but governments retained leeway over what type of stabilization plan to apply). Thus, the availability heuristic operates at the level of principles as well.

Similarly, successful realizations of a principle can trigger the representativeness heuristic and give rise to optimistic judgments about the attainability of this maxim. If, for instance, the extension of basic health care to the poor yields a striking decline in maternal and infant mortality, decision-makers in neighboring countries feel encouraged to pursue this principle with greater determination. They tend to hold the new governmental effort responsible for this success, inappropriately discounting the role of other contributing factors. And they tend to overestimate the sustainability of this initial success, disregarding regression toward the mean. Thus, overenthusiastic judgments shaped by the representativeness heuristic can propel principle diffusion as well.

Furthermore, the enactment of a new policy program that embodies a general principle can attract attention from neighboring countries and spread if it looks successful, thus disseminating the general principle as well. Even if such programs are not as neat, bold, striking, and widely available as a policy model, the heuristics of availability and representativeness can bring about some diffusion. But their effect is less strong than in model diffusion. Thus, where an innovation does not crystallize into a clear, simple, integrated model, it spreads in a more sporadic fashion, not in the broad, wavelike pattern of model diffusion. Some countries try to emulate the new program and a few nations actually enact it, but not many. Rather than unleashing a wave, this innovation creates some trickles.

For instance, managed competition helped to inspire the Colombian reform of 1993, which boldly sought to restructure the whole health system. But this change was too complicated and eclectic to turn into a neat model; it was difficult for boundedly rational decision-makers to grasp. As chapter 6 explains, the Colombian reform therefore did not stimulate a wave of imitation comparable to Chilean pension privatization. But it did inspire some countries, especially neighbors such as Peru. Enacted across the border, the Colombian reform was especially available in Peru, and its initial success in extending health coverage stimulated imitation efforts, which furthered the diffusion of its underlying principles. Thus, by helping to spread new policy programs, especially to neighboring countries, the heuristics of availability and representativeness contribute to the sporadic dissemination of general maxims.

In sum, cognitive shortcuts, especially the availability and representativeness heuristics, do influence principle diffusion. But they have less force in directing decision-makers' attention and shaping their performance assessments than in model diffusion. As a result, principle diffusion produces less profound and wide-ranging change than model diffusion. As cognitive heuristics play less of a role, there is less striking diffusion. The variation in process and outcome between social security and health care thus confirms the importance of cognitive heuristics as the main causal mechanisms propelling the spread of innovations. Where inferential shortcuts can attach themselves to a clear, neat model and therefore operate with considerable force, they produce a wave of change. Yet where such a model does not emerge and cognitive heuristics therefore focus attention less strongly and give rise to less exalted impressions of success, diffusion remains weaker and less uniform.

As cognitive heuristics operate less forcefully, other causal mechanisms assume a greater role in principle diffusion than in model diffusion. External pressures attain some success in inducing governments to advance toward general guidelines. Whereas the IFIs cannot easily force a country to adopt a specific policy model, exhortations to move in a general direction can yield results. Model imposition would require control, a much greater degree of power than mere influence, which is often sufficient for propelling principle diffusion. Drawing on the conceptual literature on power (Dahl 1984; March 1966), I argue that actor A exerts control if it causes actor B to comply fully with A's preferences. By contrast, A has influence if it induces B to change its intended course of action in line with A's preferences. Thus, influence merely yields a change of direction, whereas control guarantees the attainment of an end point. Accordingly, a mother who wants her recalcitrant son to eat five carrots commands influence if she can coax him into eating two of the crunchy roots; but she exerts control only if she makes him chomp down all five pieces of health food.

Accordingly, an IFI would need control to impose an external model, but influence suffices for inducing a government to advance toward a principle. Compared to model diffusion, the IFIs therefore have greater success in promoting general principles. From the perspective of a recalcitrant government, yielding to IFI imposition by importing a full-scale model carries much greater political cost than accommodating IFI pressure by taking some steps toward a general principle, yet retaining a significant margin of choice over how far to go and how to enact this principle.

IFI recommendations indeed contributed significantly to the spread of general guidelines, especially efficiency maxims in health care, as chapter 5 shows. In promoting this principle diffusion, the IFIs successfully used political pressures, economic incentives, technical advice, and the provision of information, i.e. availability enhancement. Thus, causal mechanisms highlighted by the external pressure and cognitive heuristics approaches propelled this spread of efficiency-oriented innovations. Due to these IFI efforts, many Latin American countries have taken some steps to enhance productivity and cost effectiveness in health care.

But governments have considerable latitude in deciding how far to advance in the direction advocated by the IFIs and in what specific way to enact new principles. Often, they are more hesitant than these institutions recommend. Rather than making comprehensive changes, they proceed in a piecemeal fashion. They tend to experiment with a new principle in one segment of the vast health arena. In fact, they may try out this limited innovation in a specific region by instituting a pilot project. Costa Rica, for instance, first introduced performance contracts designed to improve efficiency in seven hospitals and extended this World Bank-sponsored innovation only gradually to the whole health system. This caution is often motivated by (anticipated) resistance from interest groups inside the state and in society that have a strong stake in the established ways of administering ample resources and allocating positions of power. But it also reflects policy-makers' reluctance to give up procedures that are working—however badly—for new rules that may not work at all.

In sum, the IFIs play a significant role in principle diffusion. While they cannot make governments adopt specific policy models, they are more successful in promoting general guidelines. Although governments often advance with hesitation toward those goals, IFI recommendations have clearly made a difference, especially in helping to spread efficiency maxims in health care.

In some areas of social policy, normative and symbolic appeal can also propel principle diffusion. While the interests and power of contending social groups leave little room for concern with international legitimacy to make a difference in redistributive decision making, social policy also comprises choices that approximate distributive decision making. In particular, some programs introduce or expand benefits for certain groups at limited cost, and this cost is often shouldered in an "invisible" fashion by broad, diffuse societal sectors (Corrales 1999: 5– 6). Accordingly, poverty alleviation measures that are cost-effective, claim few financial resources, and are often funded through IFI loans can escape the push and pull of major interest groups and political forces. Such targeted schemes are usually created by addition; since they do not require the restructuring of established systems of service delivery, conflicts with entrenched interests can be avoided. Since antipoverty programs tend to have limited, largely imperceptible political and economic costs, normative and symbolic considerations can influence their adoption. Accordingly, the quest for international legitimacy has contributed significantly to the advance of equity maxims in health care, as the latter part of chapter 5 shows. For instance, new global norms have inspired efforts to combat maternal and infant mortality among the poor (Shiffman 2003).

In sum, several causal mechanisms drive the international spread of principles. Whereas cognitive heuristics stand out as the driving force behind model diffusion, principle diffusion can result from boundedly rational judgments shaped by such shortcuts, from the promotional efforts of IFIs, or from normative and symbolic considerations fueled by concern for international legitimacy. As general maxims are less specific than neat models, their diffusion is a more eclectic process as well.

CAUSAL MECHANISMS IN DIVERSE CONTEXTS

The preceding analysis has unearthed the main engines of diffusion—the contagious agents that drive innovations' spread across countries. It has thus examined causal mechanisms, which are the "moving causes" (Aristotle) propelling change (cf. Hedström and Swedberg 1998; Mahoney 2003; Mayntz 2004; Hall 2003). Causal mechanisms are the transformatory forces that produce outcomes; they affect given starting conditions and bring forth effects. As McAdam, Tarrow, and Tilly (2001) stress, causal mechanisms operate in the same way in variegated contexts.

But causal mechanisms do not necessarily produce the same end result under all circumstances; rather, they tend to bring about different outcomes in diverse settings. Their specific effect depends on the initial conditions under which they spring into action and on intervening factors that condition their operation and force. Therefore, the same causal mechanism can produce different consequences. To invoke a natural-science analogy, fire is a causal mechanism that has the same nature—combustion—in a wide variety of settings. But its specific outcomes differ starkly depending on initial circumstances and intervening factors: for instance, whether a fire breaks out in a rain-soaked cloud forest or a tinder-dry pine grove; and whether a strong wind fans it. Causal mechanisms direct attention to commonality amid diversity, a frequent product of diffusion. This approach to explanation is therefore well suited for investigating the spread of innovations.

But like the destruction caused by fire, diffusion is not uniform, even inside a geographic region. For instance, a number of Latin American countries, including Brazil and Venezuela, have not implemented Chilean-style pension privatization. And the countries that followed the regional leader reformed their social security systems in somewhat different ways. Specialists distinguish three subtypes, namely, substitutive reforms, which completely replace the public social security system with private pension funds; mixed systems, which maintain a public PAYG scheme as a basic pillar and in addition create an obligatory private pillar; and parallel systems, which give individuals a choice between the new private pension funds and the old public system (Mesa-Lago 1997). Principle diffusion in health care has produced even greater variation; as chapters 5 and 6 show, Latin American countries differ significantly in their efforts to enact components of the equity and efficiency agenda (see also Murillo 2002).

To account for this cross-national variation in diffusion outcomes, the initial conditions and intervening factors that affect the causal mechanisms highlighted in this study need to be considered. Due to contextual differences, the same causal mechanisms exerted differential force and yielded variegated results. While they produced a notable degree of commonality amid diversity, the background characteristics and intervening variables with which they interacted also brought about differences in the spread of foreign models and principles.

Some context factors affected the very operation of diffusion's main causal mechanisms, especially the intensity and force with which cognitive heuristics shaped policy-makers' information processing. Other factors conditioned the effect that the judgments and actions derived from these heuristics had in policy deliberations and decision making. Diffusion outcomes varied depending on what other actors the experts and policy-makers most influenced by cognitive heuristics had to confront. What interests resisted the spread of policy models and principles, and what power capabilities and institutional opportunities did these opposing forces have? These two sets of factors explain why the same causal mechanisms, which produced a good deal of policy diffusion, also yielded different outcomes in different contexts. While drawing on the established literature, which has analyzed the role of societal forces and political regime structures, the following discussion emphasizes an underexplored aspect, namely, divergences between different types of state officials and state agencies.

The principal causal mechanisms highlighted in this study, especially for model diffusion, are cognitive heuristics. These individual strategies of inference can have differential results at the aggregate level, turning the bounds of rationality more or less confining. Cognitive psychology focuses on the individual level and tends to emphasize commonalities among people. But political decision making is a collective process. Due to technical and institutional factors, it can be more or less narrowly bounded.

The depth of a country's domestic expertise influences the aggregate operation of cognitive heuristics. In nations with a broad, diverse community of experts, the bounds of rationality are less narrow. Decision-makers have a greater chance to find out about alternatives to a highly available model; they are faster in updating the conclusions suggested by the representativeness heuristic in light of a model's actual performance; and they are more willing and able to loosen anchoring and adjust a foreign import to their country's specific needs. Thus, the more expertise policy-makers command, the less bounded is their collective rationality; cognitive shortcuts—while still operative—are less confining in their effect.

Furthermore, the institutional background and composition of the group that deliberates about the emulation of a foreign model affects the force exerted by cognitive heuristics. Trained issue area specialists command prior knowledge and have access to alternative sources of information that make them less susceptible to the problematic inferences suggested by cognitive shortcuts. Certainly, the appearance of a striking novelty such as Chilean pension privatization creates considerable uncertainty for these specialists, which induces them to rely on inferential shortcuts as well. But they have background knowledge that helps to limit the resulting distortions and biases. Therefore, established experts are not as easily swayed by cognitive heuristics.

By contrast, generalists without much prior knowledge in the issue area have little immunity from cognitive shortcuts.[14] They lack the background to double-check the inferences suggested by the availability and representativeness heuristics. Since they do not have a network of trusted contacts in the issue area, they lack access to multiple sources of information, which may suggest less enthusiastic performance assessments of a striking innovation and make alternative models available. Thus, where generalists—nowadays especially economic technocrats—displace issue area specialists and control decision making, cognitive heuristics have especially free rein. Accordingly, if finance ministry economists elaborate a pension reform (cf. Madrid 2003: 50–52), cognitive heuristics likely hold greater sway than if long-standing social security specialists participate in these deliberations.

Interestingly, cognitive heuristics themselves can shape the range of actors that design emulation decisions. Inferential shortcuts may suggest to generalists that an issue they had hitherto neglected crucially impinges on their institutional interests. These previously uninvolved actors may therefore seek to control policymaking. In making new reform options available and highlighting their success, cognitive heuristics can alter actors' interest calculations and redirect their behavior. Whereas basic goals are largely given (contrary to constructivist arguments), new information filtered and distorted by inferential shortcuts can change instrumental preferences (see in general Blyth 2002; McNamara 1998: 3–8, 56–71; Goldstein and Keohane 1993: 13–17). Due to the availability and representativeness heuristics, actors may end up pursuing old interests in novel ways. They may therefore become interested in topics they had seen as unimportant before, trying to push aside specialists who had so far dominated the issue area. In this way, cognitive heuristics can change the constellation of decision-makers.

Accordingly, the macroeconomic benefits that the representativeness heuristic associated with pension privatization gave economic generalists a strong interest in the Chilean model. The promise of increased domestic savings turned this reform into a priority for economy ministries. This hope induced economic technocrats to seek command over the issue area and displace pension specialists; it also handed these generalists powerful arguments for persuading presidents to give them such control (Madrid 2003b: 31–40, 49–52). Cognitive heuristics thus affected the composition of the change team that elaborated social security reform. As this composition in turn conditioned the aggregate results of cognitive heuristics, the causal mechanisms profiled in this study assumed special importance.

---

[14] Several reform team members, especially in Bolivia and El Salvador, volunteered that they were not social security specialists when they started working on pension reform.

Thus, cognitive heuristics shaped the constellation of decision-makers and the content of their specific preferences. These psychological mechanisms had clear political effects. Rather than being mere instruments in policy debates, cognitive shortcuts affect who engages in such debates and what specific goals they pursue. While the operation of heuristics is influenced by background conditions, they themselves mold this context in an interactive fashion. Thus, they are not merely epiphenomenal but real.

As cognitive heuristics affect the range of decision-makers who are interested in an issue area, the institutional and political strength of various state agencies conditions their effective role and influence. If an existing social security agency is discredited by a deep financial crisis and severe administrative problems, economic generalists can monopolize reform decisions. By contrast, if established agencies function reasonably well, social security experts successfully demand a place at the table and marshal their issue-specific expertise to keep the inferences suggested by cognitive heuristics in check.

Political-institutional factors also condition the impact that causal mechanisms such as cognitive heuristics exert on decision outputs. Since policymaking is not the dispassionate search for truth, the constellation of interests and power play an important role. As bounded rationality rests on an interest-based framework, it stresses that actors use heuristics in pursuit of their interests. They apply inferential shortcuts to address problems and elaborate solutions in line with their preferences. Accordingly, actors with different goals may advance divergent proposals. For instance, finance ministries may advocate Chilean-style pension privatization to overcome actuarial disequilibria, whereas social security agencies defend the established system as an instrument for poverty alleviation. Thus, policy-makers' goals obviously direct their actions.

Decision-makers' proposals are derived both from their goals and their beliefs, which are shaped by cognitive heuristics. Interests guide the overall course of action, while information filtered by cognitive shortcuts shapes instrumental preferences and suggests specific steps to take. For instance, experts who prioritize efficiency in health care advocate different types of reform than promoters of equity. Cognitive heuristics then condition which specific proposal among a range of options each group advocates. Based on their goals and ideological orientation, actors thus have differential receptivity to external models and principles. Interests clearly matter. But cognitive heuristics crucially affect the ways in which actors pursue those interests; as discussed below, they even shape actors' success in attaining their goals.

The political fate of proposals to emulate foreign models or principles thus depends to a good extent on the push and pull of conflicting interests, the power capabilities of the contending forces, and the institutional rules governing their interaction. The rich insights unearthed by political science, especially analyses of social policy reform in Latin America and beyond (Brooks 2002; Corrales 1999; Grindle 2004; Huber and Stephens 2001; Kaufman and Nelson 2004; Kay 1999; Madrid 2003a, 2003b; Murillo 2002; Nelson 1999; Orenstein 2005; Pierson 1994), are crucial for understanding the specific outcomes of diffusion processes.

The literature has demonstrated how "veto players" can block or moderate drastic reform, including the emulation of foreign innovations. First, in social sectors such as health (and education), service delivery depends on cooperation from providers, whose performance is difficult to guarantee and control. This autonomy enables delivery personnel to offer powerful active and passive resistance, which can influence the course of change (Kaufman and Nelson 2004; Clark 2005; Grindle 2004; Corrales 1999). Second, broader societal segments that lack the purchasing power to exit to private insurance have a great stake in public service delivery. Depending on their collective organization, labor movements, in particular, may manage to impede or hinder externally inspired efforts to privatize social security and health care (Pierson 1994; Madrid 2003a; Murillo 2001).

Last but not least, political parties have an interest in the broad outlines of social policies that affect millions of voters. For programmatic and patronage reasons, they are reluctant to accept benefit cuts and consent to privatization, which would remove voluminous resources from political discretion and thus circumscribe party influence. However, serious financial problems, neoliberal ideological commitments, and a share in governmental responsibility can mitigate parties' skepticism toward painful efficiency-seeking reforms. Furthermore, prevailing patterns of party competition affect the balance of support and opposition; centripetal competition among few parties tends to facilitate reform, whereas centrifugal outbidding and polarization in a fragmented party system hinder it (Haggard and Kaufman 1995: chap. 5; Brooks 2002: 503, 515).

While the literature highlights the role of interest groups and parties, I argue that institutional divergences inside the state also have crucial repercussions for emulation decisions. Pension privatization and efficiency-enhancing health reforms are promoted primarily by finance and planning ministries, which hope to attain the macroeconomic spillover effects suggested by the representativeness heuristic (see above). Where social security and health care agencies are technically capable, institutionally consolidated, and politically powerful, as in Brazil and Costa Rica, they exert a strong counterweight to these pressures (see also Coelho 1999). These agencies' influence arises from their expertise, esprit de corps, and control over resource distribution. It also depends on their financial solvency. Acute deficits legitimate the pressures of economy ministries for structural reforms inspired by foreign models or principles; indeed, they may allow economy ministries to marginalize social sector agencies from decision making or colonize them by imposing their own appointees. Conversely, successful efforts to overcome a severe institutional crisis, boost organizational efficiency, and restore financial equilibrium bolster the veto power of social agencies.

By contrast to societal opposition, which operates primarily at later stages of the decision-making process, resistance from social sector agencies can derail efforts to import foreign models or principles at the outset. As mentioned above, the participation of long-standing pension and health experts broadens the composition of change teams and thus keeps in check collective judgments suggested by the heuristics of availability, representativeness, and anchoring.

Debates and struggles inside the state have indeed affected a wide range of emulation proposals. They have held up or filtered out many projects that governments never ended up submitting to congressional deliberation. In fact, divergences among state agencies can fuel resistance from other veto players. Invoking equity goals against the cold logic of economic constraints, social sector agencies that are hard-pressed by finance ministries in intrastate negotiations can mobilize societal or congressional opposition to reform; for this purpose, they can draw on their patronage networks, leak internal proposals, and selectively offer information and data. For instance, officials in Brazil's Social Security Ministry derailed efforts at pension privatization in 1992 by stimulating resistance from members of Congress and a strategically placed interest association. What looks like societal opposition may actually originate inside the state. Intrastate conflicts, often hidden from public view, thus condition the diffusion of innovations in crucial ways. My book highlights these internal divergences, which have received insufficient attention in the literature.

In sum, this study embeds cognitive-psychological mechanisms in their political context by analyzing how the interests and power capabilities of state and societal actors affect the emulation of foreign models and principles. Obviously, policy diffusion is part of a broader political process shaped by power and interests. Heuristics are cognitive strategies that actors use in pursuing their goals. While interests guide actors, cognitive shortcuts shape the translation of these goals into specific proposals and projects. For instance, officials of economy ministries have a professional and institutional interest in raising domestic savings. In the early 1990s, the representativeness heuristic suggested they could accomplish this goal by emulating Chile's social security privatization.

This cognitive shortcut induced them to mobilize their influence and push for pension privatization as a new means for attaining an old goal. By contrast, traditional pension specialists focused more on social equity and were therefore unimpressed by this promise attached to Chilean-style privatization. Thus, interests shape what actors try to do, and cognitive heuristics condition how they try to do it.

Cognitive heuristics cannot be reduced to power and interests. They are not mere instruments in the struggle among sociopolitical actors. For instance, advocates of pension privatization do not manipulate the representativeness heuristic in order to win support for their cause; instead, this inferential shortcut makes them believe in certain promises attributed to a foreign model, and this conviction induces them to push for its emulation. None of the often very candid interviews conducted for this study yielded evidence that pension reformers made claims on behalf of social security privatization that they themselves did not believe in. They themselves fell prey to cognitive heuristics and did not, in a Machiavellian manner, use them to lure others.

Cognitive shortcuts influence what actors find to be in their interest and what specific measures they seek to attain with their power capabilities. The availability heuristic may attract decision-makers' attention to a model that is suboptimal for their own interests while making them neglect alternatives that hold higher utility. And the representativeness heuristic can make them overestimate the utility of this available option. Thus, cognitive shortcuts mold the pursuit of interests; they are not epiphenomena of actors pursuing their interests. They have a causal force of their own, rather than being mere derivatives of other driving forces.

Heuristics also affect the success with which different actors can "activate" their power resources (cf. March 1966). The claim derived from the representativeness heuristic that Chilean-style pension privatization would boost domestic savings and fuel growth gave economic generalists a crucial argument against opposition forces such as trade unions. They could invoke the common good of the whole country and discredit opponents as defenders of special interests (see in general Blyth 2002: 35–40; McNamara 1998: 65–70). Similarly, the expectation of stellar rates of return, which the representativeness heuristic derived from Chile's initial experience with private pension funds, made the public social security system look like a comparative failure and thus helped to delegitimate the state as the mainstay of the established PAYG system. Highly available foreign models can also serve as rallying points for proponents of change and facilitate their concerted action (see in general Goldstein and Keohane 1993: 17–20). By contrast, opposing forces lacked an outstanding, attractive counterproposal because the availability heuristic confined their attention to Latin America. In all of these ways, cognitive shortcuts can affect the "force activation" of contending sociopolitical actors.

In sum, the operation and outcomes of causal mechanisms such as cognitive heuristics are shaped by the political-institutional context and the divergent interests of various sociopolitical forces. But cognitive heuristics in turn affect this constellation of forces, empowering some actors while putting others at a disadvantage. Political and ideational factors interact; neither side can be reduced to the other.

CONCLUSION

This chapter proposes a new theory of social policy diffusion. Above all, it argues that the wavelike spread of bold, neat policy models is shaped primarily by cognitive shortcuts. The striking experience of a nearby country grabs decision-makers' attention and serves as an obligatory reference point for reform discussions. Where such a highly available model attains initial success, the representativeness heuristic makes policy-makers jump to the conclusion that the innovation is of inherently superior quality and deserves emulation. Due to anchoring, these adoption decisions often stay much closer to the original than the needs of the importing country justify. Thus, cognitive heuristics are the principal causal mechanisms that drive model diffusion.

External pressures make a contribution, but even powerful IFIs lack the capacity to force sovereign states to enact their concrete policy recommendations. While they can nudge countries to advance toward general principles, they face great difficulties in imposing specific blueprints. And since clear, "given" interests guide redistributive policymaking on social issues that affect broad societal sectors, new symbolic and normative considerations originating in international society have little room to affect domestic politics. Thus, cognitive shortcuts predominate among the causal mechanisms driving model diffusion.

The spread of general principles, by contrast, is a more heterogeneous process pushed by various causal mechanisms. Cognitive shortcuts are important; the heuristics of availability and representativeness can help general guidelines spread, both directly and by propelling the emulation of experiments that embody those principles. But these shortcuts do not exert the same causal force as in model diffusion. An abstract guideline is not as striking, vivid, and "available" as a neat, bold model; and since it allows for various forms of implementation, it does not as easily trigger exalted judgments of success nor tie down judgments through anchoring.

Conversely, external pressures play a greater role in principle diffusion than in model diffusion. While unable to impose specific reforms, IFIs often can coax governments to follow general guidelines, albeit at their own pace and in their own ways. In addition to leverage, the IFIs' provision of information and technical advice, which extends the bounds of availability, promotes principle diffusion. Furthermore, new international norms and symbols can propel the spread of maxims that call for states to assume additional tasks. Distributive programs that extend benefits without undermining budget equilibrium and upsetting powerful sociopolitical forces do not create visible costs; therefore, the quest for legitimacy can inspire their adoption. By contrast to model diffusion, several causal pathways can thus lead to principle diffusion.

Causal mechanisms operate in different contexts and therefore produce different outcomes. In the redistributive arenas of pension and health policy, the interests and power of major sociopolitical forces condition the fate of emulation initiatives. But cognitive heuristics shape how actors pursue their interests and apply their power capabilities. For instance, the representativeness heuristic suggested that pension privatization would produce macroeconomic benefits for the whole country. This expectation motivated economy ministries to push hard for change, and it allowed them to discredit opposition from societal groups as the pursuit of special interests. Cognitive shortcuts thus altered the constellation of relevant political actors, reshaped their instrumental interests, and conditioned the effectiveness of their power capabilities.

Those interests and power capabilities in turn influence the strength of cognitive heuristics and their impact on decision outputs. In particular, if the change teams that deliberate on model and principle emulation are small, homogeneous, and full of economic generalists who lack strong training in an issue area, cognitive shortcuts hold more unchallenged sway than if established social policy institutions have seats at the table; in the latter scenario, conclusions derived from cognitive heuristics will likely be cross-checked.

The balance of power between social agencies and economy ministries also affects the political fate of the emulation proposals that these change teams elaborate. Both in social security and health care, the economy ministries pushed for adopting foreign models and principles; the social agencies frequently offered active or passive resistance. The outcome of this intrastate conflict depended on the institutional strength and performance of the pension and health systems and the political alliances in Congress and society that these institutions managed to forge.

In sum, the institutional setting and constellation of sociopolitical forces affected the operation of cognitive heuristics and the decision results that these causal mechanisms produced. But as just mentioned, these shortcuts in turn influenced the configuration of power and interests. The availability heuristic limited the range of options that actors considered in pursuing their interests, and the representativeness heuristic conditioned their judgments about the utility offered by an available option. These ideational factors thus shaped "real" politics, that is, the pursuit of interests and mobilization of power. Due to this interaction, cognitive heuristics were in no way epiphenomenal.

The following chapters substantiate these arguments through in-depth analyses of model diffusion in social security and principle diffusion in health care. Attention first turns to the impact of external pressures and new international norms on the spread of Chilean-style pension privatization; chapter 3 examines this topic.

External Pressures and International Norms in Pension Reform

To what extent have external pressures and new international norms shaped pension privatization in contemporary Latin America? The frameworks that highlight these factors see policy diffusion arise from powerful foreign influences on decision-makers' goal pursuit. According to both approaches, external influences induce domestic policy-makers to act in ways that differ from their original goals. These two frameworks thus diverge from the rational learning and cognitive heuristics frameworks, which assume that foreign experiences affect the instrumental calculations, but not the goal pursuit and interest definition of domestic policy-makers.

But despite this basic commonality, the external pressure and normative appeal approaches differ on the origin and nature of this goal shift. The former framework stresses coercion, whereas the latter invokes persuasion and conviction. The external pressure approach claims that international financial institutions use their enormous leverage to impose their own goals on reluctant developing countries. In this view, the IFIs force poor, aid-dependent nations to pursue goals that those countries do not genuinely embrace. By contrast, the normative imitation approach argues that the promoters of new international norms apply persuasive powers. Inducing developing countries to embrace new international ideas, they transform the goal definition of Third World governments and thus manage to implant their own goals in an especially profound fashion. Rather than imposing foreign goals, they convince domestic policy-makers to change their own goals. They thus prompt a genuine redefinition through which international norms are incorporated into domestic preference schedules.

Both of these approaches claim to account for the wave of pension privatization in Latin America. The external pressure approach emphasizes that leading IFIs, especially the World Bank, promoted this reform with its whole arsenal of power. In this view, the spread of radical social security reform resulted from external coercion (Armada, Muntaner, and Navarro 2001). By contrast, the normative appeal framework claims that neoliberal ideas, espoused especially in the World Bank's

pension reform program (WB 1994a), reshaped global thinking on social security. These promotional efforts spread norms of individual responsibility and thus induced governments genuinely to pursue pension
privatization.

Can these arguments explain the diffusion of social security privatization in Latin America? To what extent did external pressures or new
international norms contribute to this striking wave of change?

IFI INFLUENCES ON PENSION REFORM

The IFIs command an impressive arsenal of power. Since underdeveloped countries frequently need financial aid, the World Bank, International Monetary Fund, and Inter-American Development Bank hold
great leverage as providers of development loans or emergency assistance. In addition to controlling voluminous resources, the IFIs serve as
crucial gatekeepers. Many private lenders insist that the IFIs approve a
government's economic policies before they extend loans to that nation.
Thus, the IFIs seem to hold many trump cards. Can their usage account
for the spread of pension privatization in Latin America?

Investigations of this question need to keep in mind an important selection problem that may distort conclusions about IFI influence. The
IFIs—especially the World Bank—put much more pressure on governments that are reluctant to follow their guidelines than on administrations predisposed to enact pension privatization. Accordingly, the World
Bank did not push much for social security reform in Bolivia, El Salvador, and Peru but sought to exert more influence on Costa Rica and
Brazil. For instance, the leader of the WB pension privatization project
during the 1990s, Estelle James, did not visit El Salvador but maintained
intense, forceful discussions with Costa Rica's pension reform team (interviews with Brevé 2004, Cercone 2004, and Durán 2004; James
2006). Indeed, because the Salvadoran government was already committed to social security privatization, the World Bank did not include this
change in its loan conditionality. Thus, the bank did not see the need to
use its most powerful weapon.

In sum, the IFIs applied their means of influence strategically and
saved the heavier artillery for more recalcitrant clients—yet with limited
success. A simple correlational analysis would therefore yield mistaken
conclusions: Radical pension privatization—as in Bolivia, El Salvador,
and Peru—is associated with low IFI pressure. By contrast, countries on
which the IFIs leaned more heavily proceeded slowly and hesitantly,
such as Costa Rica, or rejected privatization, such as Brazil. Thus, in my

sample there is a negative correlation between social security reform and IFI pressure.[1]

The methodological complication caused by this strategic use of influence requires an in-depth qualitative analysis. Two questions are crucial. First, where governments' initial goals diverged from IFI preferences, did the IFIs manage to impose their recommendations? Did the IFIs successfully force governments to adopt reforms, as the external pressure approach predicts? Second, where governments looked favorably upon pension privatization, had the IFIs instilled those preferences through prior imposition? Did governments' convergence with IFI preferences result from a goal shift forcefully promoted by the IFIs? The following two sections investigate these questions in turn.

TOOTHLESS GIANTS? THE LIMITED SUCCESS OF IFI PRESSURES

My field research clearly suggests that the IFIs did not apply their means of influence with great success. IFI support contributed to radical social security reform in Bolivia and El Salvador, and IFI exhortations helped to induce Costa Rica and Brazil to consider pension privatization. But IFI pressures did not impose reform on any one of those countries. Prodding from the World Bank, in particular, contributed to privatization efforts in several cases, but those efforts yielded decisions that diverged greatly from WB goals, and the bank's attempts to push countries closer to its preferred position yielded strikingly little success. Even a weak, aid-dependent country like Bolivia ended up resisting strong WB pressures on crucial reform decisions. Thus, the Latin American wave of social security reform did not stem from IFI coercion.

As regards reform initiation, the privatization projects of Bolivia, El Salvador, and Peru did not originate in WB recommendations, that is, vertical imposition. Instead, as chapter 4 analyzes in depth, horizontal connections to Chilean experts who had spearheaded reform in that country provided the trigger. These intense contacts, stemming from 1989 to 1991, preceded the World Bank's heavy engagement in the pension area, which started in 1992. As local reform team members stress, the World Bank at that time did not even have much in-house expertise on the topic (interview with Salinas 2002). Only when the Bolivian and Salvadoran reform efforts were already under way did the bank provide

---

[1] Obviously, the IFIs did not press countries that a priori rejected pension privatization. Thus, the relationship of IFI pressure and predisposition toward radical reform is curvilinear.

advice and support, especially by bankrolling the heavy usage of Chilean consultants. Thus, horizontal, not vertical, diffusion set in motion the reform process in countries that were sympathetic to the neoliberal agenda.

By contrast, the World Bank did provide an impulse for putting pension privatization on the political agenda in Costa Rica and Brazil, whose governments were less predisposed toward adopting this radical change. As these nations hesitated and did not pursue privatization projects in the early 1990s, the bank forcefully advocated this reform in the mid-1990s, after it had codified its own thinking on the topic in its high-profile study (WB 1994a) and turned social security privatization into a priority goal. Visits by leading WB experts and policy studies (especially Demirgüç-Kunt and Schwarz 1995) provided an important impulse for the reform discussions of the mid-1990s in Costa Rica (interviews with Durán 2004 and Aguilar 2004). Similarly, the special pension reform commission appointed by Brazilian president Fernando Henrique Cardoso in 1997 took its inspiration in part from the WB pension program of 1994 (interview with Moraes 2003).

But the bank's contribution to agenda setting by no means allowed it to shape decision outputs. Despite continuous prodding from the IFIs, both Costa Rica and Brazil chose to proceed in very different ways from those the World Bank recommended. Given the firm commitment to a solidaristic welfare state among Costa Rica's civil society and political class, both the governments of social democrat José María Figueres Olsen (1994–98) and of Christian democrat Miguel Angel Rodríguez (1998–2002) were unwilling or unable to enact radical social security reform. Specifically, they did not want to confine the existing public pay-as-you-go system to a poverty reduction function and create an extensive scheme of private pension funds, as the World Bank continued to advocate (WB 1998b). Costa Rican reform team members strenuously resisted strong WB pressures for slashing replacement rates in the public social security schemes (interviews with Aguilar 2004, Carrillo 2004, Cercone 2004, Céspedes 2004, Durán 2004, Jiménez 2004, and Rodríguez 2004). Space for private pension funds has therefore remained limited. In fact, the reform law eventually passed in 2000 allowed public institutions to run their own pension funds, and a whopping 79.3 percent of affiliates have stayed with public pension fund administrators (Martínez Franzoni and Mesa-Lago 2003: 27; Leal 2004). As a result, Costa Rica's reformed social security system differs greatly from WB blueprints.

Costa Rica's success in resisting IFI pressures is due to four main factors. First, the great technical capacity of the country's social security experts forestalled dependence on WB advice. The principal public pension agency, Caja Costarricense de Seguro Social (CCSS), has a strong cadre of well-trained experts who are recruited in a meritocratic fashion and carefully instructed in the complexities of the social security system. These career specialists claimed to command more expertise than the leader of the WB pension privatization project, who was an economic generalist (interviews with Aguilar 2004 and Durán 2004). Second, Costa Rica had made a concerted effort during the 1990s to pay down its external debt (Hidalgo 2003: 217–18) and therefore did not require IFI approval for renegotiation deals. And the country's last structural adjustment loan was canceled in 1995, before the pension reform came to fruition (WB 2000b: 6–9). Therefore, the IFIs had little financial leverage. Crucial instruments of power—both loan conditionality and technical assistance—gave the IFIs only limited influence on Costa Rica.

Third, the widespread sense among Costa Rican experts and policymakers that, despite looming financial problems, the country's system of social protection was highly successful intensified their reluctance to embark on a drastic transformation (see Comisión Técnica de Pensiones 1990: 13–14; interviews with Aguilar 2004, Carrillo 2004, and Durán 2004). The absence of an acute financial crisis (WB 2003c: 113) strengthened Costa Rica's hand vis-à-vis the IFIs. Last but not least, the deeply rooted commitments to the established welfare state and the consensual nature of politics posed an insurmountable obstacle to external pressures for dramatic policy change. Experts and politicians of various partisan orientations knew that radical neoliberal reform was politically infeasible (interviews with Aguilar 2004, Barahona 2004, Carrillo 2004, Céspedes 2004, Durán 2004, Jiménez 2004, and Rodríguez 2004; on these four factors, see also Martínez Franzoni 1999: 166–67).

For these reasons, this small, not very powerful country managed to resist significant IFI pressures. While WB exhortations contributed to Costa Rica's decision to take a step toward pension privatization, the very cautious mixed system that the country implemented diverged greatly from IFI preferences. Thus, the World Bank did make a difference—but a rather limited one.

By contrast to Costa Rica, Brazil is a giant and aspiring great power that has always been reluctant to give in to IFI pressures. Reflecting this nationalistic position, social security experts commonly expressed aversion to WB exhortations.[2] During most of the past two decades, the country has indeed diverged from IFI recommendations on social security reform (WB 1989, 1995, 2001b), shied away from pension privatization, and sought to correct the established public system mostly with

---

[2] Confidential author interviews with three leading pension specialists, Brasília, June 1995 and June 1999.

parametric reforms. Although Brazil is Latin America's most important holdout against the wave of social security privatization, the IFIs have had only minimal influence on the country's pension policy. External pressures have clearly not borne fruit.

This resistance to IFI demands was due to similar factors as in Costa Rica. Brazil commands a well-trained corps of social security specialists with a long tradition of expertise (Malloy 1979; Hochman 1992; Weyland 1996a: 89–91, 132–33; Kay 1998: 175–76). Newly recruited experts are quickly socialized into this technocratic culture and proudly stress that domestic specialists know much more about the Brazilian social security system than the World Bank (interviews with Carvalho 1992 and Moraes 1995). The social security ministry (Ministério da Previdência e Assistência Social—MPAS) gave these specialists a powerful political base for resisting external pressures.

Furthermore, despite rapidly increasing expenditures, the general social security system for private-sector workers did not suffer from significant deficits until the late 1990s (Ornélas and Vieira 1999: 33; WB 2003b: 599). The 1988 constitution had created ample funding sources for Brazil's social policies, and the MPAS had successfully claimed the most dependable revenue base, namely, the payroll tax. As the established pension system was not confronting severe financial problems, demands for drastic reform found limited resonance. Last but not least, Brazil's political system is highly fragmented, and the resulting dispersal of power impedes profound change. The party system is weak (Ames 2001; Mainwaring 1999), interest groups lack cohesion and encompassingness, and infighting among state agencies is rife (Weyland 1996a: chap. 3). Therefore, it is exceedingly difficult, if not impossible, to marshal majority support for controversial, politically costly projects, such as pension privatization (Weyland 1996b). These factors give Brazil a high level of defensive autonomy from external pressures.

On one occasion, however, WB exhortations did help to set in motion a privatization effort. In 1997, when it had become clear that parametric reform efforts would make only halting progress, President Cardoso appointed a special commission to design a structural transformation of the social security system. Prodded by domestic experts who had for years advocated a mixed system akin to the World Bank's multipillar approach, the leader of this team, André Lara Resende, took his inspiration partly from the bank's 1994 pension program (Pinheiro 2004: 129). In secretive meetings, the commission elaborated a project along these lines.[3] In 1998, this proposal gathered political force; for the first time,

[3] This project was never published but was similar to Giambiagi, Oliveira, and Beltrão (1996), Oliveira, Beltrão, and Marsillac (1996), and Oliveira, Beltrão, and Marsillac Pasinato (1999); see also Resende (1998), Drummond (1998), and Oliveira (2001).

pension privatization seemed to have a real chance to go forward. Certainly, the powerful social security ministry opposed drastic change, but its capacity to stand up to the even more powerful ministries of finance and planning, which had long advocated privatization, was questionable (interview with Moraes 2003).

But a serious goal conflict between the two leading IFIs helped to abort this reform effort. By 1998, Brazil's international financial position had worsened greatly. The IMF therefore worried intensely about the fiscal deficit. While the World Bank kept advocating drastic pension reform from a long-term perspective, the IMF vetoed this change due to its tremendous transition cost in the short and medium term (interview with Moraes 2003; Pinheiro 2004: 129–30).[4] Thus, one IFI blocked the reform project pushed by another IFI. Such goal conflicts can neutralize external pressures and allow governments to play various IFIs off against each other. For instance, the IMF has never shared the World Bank's enthusiasm for pension privatization, which threatened hard-won fiscal equilibrium (cf. Holzmann and Hinz 2005: 61). And the Inter-American Development Bank, led by Latin Americans themselves, has often been less "pushy" and more accommodating to regional governments, limiting the influence of the more orthodox World Bank and IMF. These divergences give countries additional protection against external pressures.

In sum, since Costa Rica and Brazil were not pursuing structural pension reform on their own initiative, the World Bank applied significant pressure to advance the privatization agenda that it had codified in the mid-1990s. Yet while this influence helped to get some reform efforts under way, either these attempts failed to come to fruition, as in Brazil, or the ensuing changes differed greatly from WB preferences, as in Costa Rica. In both countries, pension specialists who had been socialized into the existing pay-as-you-go system commanded a high level of technical expertise, which created significant immunity from foreign influences. These specialists were entrenched in powerful state institutions that commanded substantial political clout and counterbalanced economic agencies like the finance ministry, which were more supportive of the IFI project. Moreover, both countries had an antimajoritarian constellation of political forces and decision-making structures. Both Costa Rica's consensual mode of policymaking, which gave the major parties, business, and labor significant voice, and Brazil's fragmented institutional system, which empowered numerous veto players, made it very difficult to impose controversial change. Thus, a number of domestic factors account for the limited results of external pressures.

Interestingly, however, even poor, aid-dependent countries that lacked

[4] In fact, the IMF was internally divided on this issue (IMF 1998).

many of these sources of strength—such as Bolivia, El Salvador, and Peru—managed to resist IFI pressures on some economically and politically crucial issues. While the overall policy course charted by these countries during the 1990s was in line with the IFIs' market-oriented program, they diverged from WB recommendations on important specific points. Although these countries lacked the technical and political capacity to design an independent reform program, as Costa Rica and Brazil did, they managed to act autonomously when highly salient political issues were at stake. In fact, it did not prove particularly difficult or excessively costly to face down international agencies that are often depicted as supremely powerful. Thus, weak countries also maintained considerable defensive autonomy.

Even governments of a broadly neoliberal orientation, such as the administrations of Gonzalo Sánchez de Lozada in Bolivia (1993–97), Alberto Fujimori in Peru (1990–2000), and Armando Calderón Sol in El Salvador (1994–99), deviated from important IFI recommendations on a number of occasions. While they took technical advice from the World Bank and other IOs seriously, crucial political concerns and calculations could push them in a different direction. Once a government had decided to give political goals priority, technically solid WB objections and strong external pressures could not force compliance. Thus, even when facing weak countries such as Bolivia, El Salvador, and Peru, the IFIs could not simply impose their preferences.

Bolivia, for instance, clearly commanded fewer assets in its negotiations with the IFIs than did Costa Rica and Brazil. The institutions that administered the old social security system lacked the high level of technical expertise and political clout that the CCSS and MPAS enjoy. And the formation of partisan coalitions, which were necessary for electing presidents, allowed for a decision-making style that is more majoritarian than consensual; for instance, the pension reform itself was quickly pushed through Congress at the end of a lengthy decision-making process (interviews with Peña Rueda 2002 and Fernández Fagalde 2002).

Despite these differences from Costa Rica and Brazil, Bolivia successfully resisted external imposition where the government's political goals clearly diverged from IFI preferences. Above all, the administration of Gonzalo Sánchez de Lozada (1993–97), which enacted drastic pension privatization, faced down strong IFI pressures on the essential question of how to cover the reform's fiscal transition cost. The IFIs pushed very hard for applying the proceeds from public enterprise privatization, which the government was promoting at the same time, toward paying off existing pension entitlements (interviews with Gottret 2002, Vargas 2002, Peña Rueda 2002, Guevara 2002, Grandi 2002, Pantoja 2002, and Bonadona 2002). In this way, the Bolivian state would use the sale of its productive patrimony for liquidating its social debt. This solution would avoid any additional drain on public coffers. But the Bolivian government rejected this proposal tenaciously. After repeated "frank discussions," the president finally countered very strong IFI pressures by invoking Bolivia's national sovereignty, that is, the country's right to make decisions as it pleased (interview with Peña Rueda 2002).

For reasons of social equity and political expediency, President Sánchez de Lozada insisted on placing the revenues from public enterprise privatization into a collective capitalization fund, in which all Bolivians would hold property rights; the dividends from this fund would finance annual payments of US$248 to all citizens above the age of sixty-five. This basic scheme of universalistic old-age security benefited more than 300,000 older people in 1997, helping to alleviate widespread poverty (Graham 1998: 151–68; Müller 2004). This "solidarity bond" (BONOSOL) also contributed to the president's reelection victory in 2002. But it forced the Bolivian state to cover the pension reform's transition cost through regular budget revenues or debt. As a result, the public deficit grew significantly, amounting to 4 percent of GDP from 1998 onward (WB 1999b: 10; Escobar and Nina 2004: 17–20; Holzmann and Hinz 2005: 148). Without the burden caused by the social security reform, the Bolivian state would not have been in the red at all.

To combat this fiscal disequilibrium, which caused concern among the IFIs and elicited strong pressure from the IMF, President Sánchez de Lozada in his second term (2002–03) tried to raise taxes. This adjustment plan triggered violent unrest in February 2003 and made the government vulnerable to further protests, which in October of that year forced the president's resignation. Ironically, the politically motivated decision on the pension reform's transition cost, which contributed to Sánchez de Lozada's reelection in 2002, set in motion the chain of events that led to his ignominious ouster in 2003 (Arellano 2004; Laserna 2003).

Yet despite the fiscal imprudence of President Sánchez de Lozada's BONOSOL decision and its dangerous political implications, the IFIs were unable to force the Bolivian government to cover the fiscal burden of social security privatization with the revenues from public enterprise privatization. Strikingly, even a weak, underdeveloped, highly aid-dependent country like Bolivia managed to face down strong IFI pressures on a decisive issue. National sovereignty clearly survives in the age of globalization.

In a similar vein, political considerations made the Peruvian government diverge from IFI recommendations on the process and sequencing of pension privatization. Aware of his precarious position in the government and of President Fujimori's skepticism toward neoliberalism, Economy and Finance Minister Carlos Boloña tried to take advantage of the political opportunity offered by Peru's hyperinflationary crisis and push through a comprehensive package of profound market reforms as quickly as possible. Fearing that his window of opportunity might close soon and that the "period of extraordinary politics" (Balcerowicz 1994: 84–87) might come to an end (Boloña 1993: 170), Boloña pressed for pension privatization when the Peruvian economy still lacked minimal stability.

This tremendous rush disregarded the IFIs' advice on the proper sequencing of economic stabilization and structural reform. Given the enormous transition cost of pension privatization, it seemed especially dangerous to enact this drastic change at a time when the Peruvian economy continued to suffer from severe disequilibria. The WB as well as the IMF, whose main mission it is to guard countries against fiscal imbalance, therefore warned Peru's economic team and urged a slowdown of its ambitious reform program. But Minister Boloña and his close-knit group of aides, firmly committed to neoliberalism, discarded this advice and stormed ahead with full force (interviews with Boloña 1996, Du Bois 2002, and Peñaranda 2002). IFI exhortations could not prevent them from being "more Catholic than the pope." Although the Fujimori administration was trying hard at that time to reestablish good relations with the IFIs, which the predecessor government of Alan García had ruined, it decided not to listen to IFI recommendations—and did not incur any negative consequences.

While the IFIs cautioned against Minister Boloña's neoliberal zeal, they were less happy with the skepticism toward the market agenda that induced President Fujimori to decide at the last minute against full-scale pension privatization. Listening to the head of the established social security agency, the Instituto Peruano de Seguridad Social (IPSS), and to other opponents of radical change, the chief executive kept the existing public pension system open and gave affiliates the option to switch to the new private pension funds or stay with the IPSS. While this decision was true to the neoliberal principle of freedom of choice (cf. Roggero 1993), it limited the expansion of the private scheme and seemed to threaten its very viability. Together with Minister Boloña's aides and other domestic neoliberals, the IFIs therefore pressed the Peruvian government in subsequent years to make the private scheme more attractive to affiliates and eventually close the public system (Kane 1995: 2–4; Arévalo and Cayo 1997: 2–3; Queisser 1998; Graham 1998: 114, 117; Arce 2001; WB 2004e). Yet while the Fujimori government enacted some of the recommended changes, it maintained the parallel structure of the new social security system, which lay at the root of the difficulties emphasized by the World Bank. Thus, once again IFI pressure attained only limited success.

Firmly committed to neoliberalism, El Salvador's Alianza Republicana Nacionalista (ARENA) government also rushed into pension privatization more precipitously than the World Bank found advisable. While agreement on the general direction of change precluded open conflict and kept WB involvement in the reform process limited (interviews with Brevé 2004, Ramírez 2004, and Solórzano 2004; WB 1996b: 20–23), the bank had urged governments to prepare a firm institutional framework for a private pension system, for instance by developing and regulating the capital market (WB 1994a: 231, 245, 255, 258–59, 280; WB 1996b: 22). The administration of Armando Calderón Sol, however, enacted only perfunctory, insufficient measures in 1995 (Mesa-Lago and Durán 1998: 9, 34–44) and quickly advanced toward radical pension privatization in December 1996. As in the Peruvian case, this lack of sequencing diverged from IFI recommendations. The underdevelopment of the capital market threatened the investment returns of the new private pension funds, which indeed have been lower than expected (interviews with Martínez Orellana 2004 and Ramírez 2004; WB 1996b: 22; Acuña 2005: 23–24, 34–38, 45–48).

Thus, even weak countries that depended on financial assistance from the IFIs deviated from WB recommendations on a number of important issues and resisted IFI pressures; Bolivia's decision on the fiscal transition cost of pension privatization is the most striking case of such immunity to external coercion. These instances of open goal divergence show that the IFIs are not particularly successful at imposing their will on recalcitrant governments. Despite their impressive arsenal of influence, they have difficulty forcing governments to deviate from their preferred course of action and comply instead with IFI exhortations.

In conclusion, the IFIs are much weaker than the external pressure approach claims. This finding from my field research corroborates a number of careful empirical studies, which show that the IFIs' seemingly strongest weapon, loan conditionality, is of limited use. The IFIs have only moderate influence on second-stage market reforms like pension privatization, which are highly complex and pass through a lengthy decision-making process. The participation of numerous political actors keeps the IFIs from applying their leverage effectively (Nelson 1996, 1999; Kahler 1992; Hunter and Brown 2000; Brooks 2004, 2005: 286–87; Madrid 2003b; cf. Holzmann and Hinz 2005: 63–70). Therefore, IFI pressures cannot account for the Latin American wave of pension reforms.

THE EXTERNAL IMPOSITION OF REFORM GOALS?

The preceding discussion takes for granted the distinction between external and domestic actors and between external and domestic goals that straightforward versions of the external pressure approach draw.[5] In this line of reasoning, powerful international actors force their own will on weak domestic governments that hold divergent preferences but have to comply with these external dictates. But external pressures could have even more profound effects by forcing national governments to redefine their own goals and adopt the preferences pushed by the IFIs. In this case, even governmental decisions that were not the product of external pressures targeted at that specific choice could in fact result from international coercion, namely, the imposition of a whole preference schedule. If the IFIs can impose their principles on a Third World government in this way and oblige it to shelve its own goals, then this government's compliance with IFI exhortations is not the result of genuine conviction, but of coerced consent.

The countries under investigation yield little evidence of such an external imposition of goals. Costa Rica and Brazil persistently diverged from IFI preferences, especially in the pension arena. While the WB and IMF had some influence on specific decisions, they certainly did not manage to reshape governments' overall policy orientation in significant ways. And in Bolivia and El Salvador, reform-oriented presidents were intrinsically committed to neoliberalism, not as a result of IFI pressures. A longstanding neoliberal, Gonzalo Sánchez de Lozada had been a driving force behind Bolivia's shock program of market reform in 1985 (see especially Goedeking 2003: chap. 5); he was not a recent convert pushed forward by the IFIs. And El Salvador's ARENA governments drew their strong neoliberal orientation from connections with the country's powerful business community and a high-profile neoliberal think tank, the Fundación Salvadoreña para el Desarrollo Económico y Social (FUSADES) (interview with Daboub 2004; Segovia 2002: 27–31), not from IFI pressures. Thus, the WB and IMF did not succeed in imposing their preferences on Costa Rica and Brazil and did not need to impose their will on Bolivia and El Salvador.

But IFI pressures did play an important role in inducing President Alberto Fujimori of Peru to make a radical shift of policy course immediately after his first election victory in 1990. Although he had campaigned on the promise of avoiding a neoliberal shock program, he decreed a brutal adjustment plan upon taking office and embarked on a program of market reforms. While the hyperinflationary crisis that was exacerbated by the election of this dark-horse candidate was the crucial reason for this policy switch (Weyland 2002b: 109, 116–18), the carrots and sticks controlled by the IFIs strongly pushed Fujimori in this direction. In fact, direct contacts during which WB and IMF leaders condi-

[5] This line of reasoning stresses external "leverage" (cf. Stallings 1992: 55–58).

tioned their urgently needed financial support on an orthodox policy approach triggered the president-elect's decision to abandon the heterodox ideas that his economic advisers had elaborated (Stokes 2001: 69–71). Thus, Fujimori embraced neoliberalism under duress; in this case, external pressures clearly contributed to a change of presidential preferences.

Peru in 1990 faced exceptionally dire circumstances, however, which gave the IFIs an unusual degree of influence. Besides hyperinflation, the country suffered from a civil war unleashed by the brutal Shining Path guerrillas (Wise 2003b: 165–73). Thus, the need for external assistance was particularly high. Furthermore, the president-elect seemed to lack clear, fixed preferences on economic issues. He fought the first round of the election campaign with the simplistic slogan of "honesty, technology, and work" and adopted the antishock plank only for the second round, in which he faced neoliberal ideologue Mario Vargas Llosa. While Fujimori initially hired heterodox economic advisers, the market reform program with its emphasis on individual effort and hard work had affinities with his disciplinarian, moralistic streak. In addition to his own openness on economic issues (interview with De Soto 1996), Fujimori lacked any strong party organization or firm links to interest groups that could have impeded his policy switch. Thus, the tremendous depth of Peru's crisis and the president-elect's feeble ideological and organizational commitments gave the IFIs an unusual opportunity to pressure successfully for a shift of course. But this case looks more like the proverbial exception that proves the rule. Under more normal conditions, the World Bank and IMF cannot force governments to change their policy preferences.

In fact, Fujimori never converted to neoliberalism. While he adopted a host of market reforms, he did so under the pressure of the severe crisis, not out of genuine conviction (interviews with Boloña 1996 and Vásquez 2002; see Boloña 1993: iii–ix, 169–73, 202). Committed neoliberals—namely, Economy and Finance Minister Carlos Boloña and his hand-picked group of aides—guided the government's economic policy only for the limited time period during which Fujimori regarded this delegation as indispensable. Fujimori had initially rejected Boloña's conditions for serving as the leader of the government's economic team; in July 1990, precisely when IFI pressure was at its highest level, Fujimori chose a pragmatist over this neoliberal zealot (Boloña 1993: 25–26; interview with De Soto 1996; Weyland 2002b: 117–18). Only when his first economy minister failed to guarantee economic stability did Fujimori appoint Boloña and give him free hand to enact his ambitious program of market reforms, including pension privatization. Yet as soon as Peru achieved the first stages of economic recovery, the president fired his principal economic aide. Thus, the fervent embrace of neoliberalism that inspired the early pursuit of radical social security reform arose more from the severity and persistence of Peru's crisis than from IFI pressures; in fact, as mentioned above, the World Bank and IMF cautioned against the launching of pension privatization at a time of continuing economic instability.

In sum, while the IFIs clearly contributed to President Fujimori's switch to neoliberalism, the particularly zealous promotion of an ambitious market reform program that led to the rushed enactment of pension privatization was a response to the extraordinarily profound crisis afflicting Peru. The available evidence suggests that WB pressures cannot account for this temporary intensification of Peru's march toward neoliberalism. Among the five countries under investigation, the external imposition of goals therefore played only a limited role.

Moreover, what at first sight looks like external imposition is often the product of an interaction—even collusion—between domestic and international actors. Rather than being the passive victims of IFI coercion, national decision-makers, especially reform-minded experts, often ask the WB, IMF, or IDB to impose conditions on their country. These domestic actors are committed to neoliberal goals yet need help from powerful foreign institutions to overcome domestic political opposition. They therefore ask for external conditionality to force the hand of Congress or of the president himself; in addition, they try to create constraints on their own successors and oblige future experts to continue their earlier initiatives. Consequently, a government's enactment of IFI-sponsored reforms often does not result from unilateral imposition, but from a much more complex interaction and bargaining process (see in general Vreeland 2003: 13–16, 46–48, 51–54, 62–64, 103).

Thus, the clear distinction of external vs. internal interests and goals assumed by the external pressure approach does not hold. Often, the IFIs do not force their will on recalcitrant Latin American governments, but domestic experts cooperate with IFI officials in designing loan conditions that are of interest to both sides. Reform-oriented national specialists collude with IFI representatives to gain leverage on the domestic front. Domestic and international actors share interests. The main line of cleavage does not fall between the IFIs and a nation state. Instead, domestic specialists often have more in common with IFI officials than with politicians inside their own country, especially if those politicians are interested primarily in patronage, not in programmatic issues of economic and social reform.

In this vein, Bolivian pension reform experts at several points during the lengthy reform deliberations asked their IFI counterparts, "Póngame esta condición, por favor," that is, "Could you please impose this condition on us?" (interviews with Salinas 2002 and Gottret 2002). In this way, they sought to gain leverage vis-à-vis domestic politicians and ensure the continuation of the privatization project despite the change of government in 1993. More strikingly even, Peru's economy minister Carlos Boloña and his team requested the IFIs to impose conditions on Peru that they then used to coax President Fujimori himself into supporting their neoliberal reform goals. Whereas the chief executive had initially refused to decree certain changes, he gave in to this domestically solicited IFI conditionality (interview with Peñaranda 2002). Thus, "external" pressure can help technocrats to invert the institutional hierarchy by pushing their political superior, the president, into compliance with goals that they share with the IFIs.

In sum, the main division often does not pit external against domestic actors, but international and national experts against domestic politicians. A transnational community of specialists pools its influence to lean on politicians and win approval for its projects (cf. Teichman 2001: chap. 3). On many technical issues that are not highly salient to politicians, this transnational alliance is successful—although politicians retain the last word and impose their will on questions that are crucially important to them, as the above-mentioned case of the transition cost of Bolivia's pension reform shows.[6]

This transnational collusion is facilitated by the fact that a number of IFI officials are citizens of the country on which—and sometimes, in which—they work. For instance, the director of the World Bank's pension reform project for Bolivia, which sought to protect the privatization effort against any political risks emerging from the presidential election of 1993, was a Bolivian national, Pablo Gottret. As a result, IFI officials sometimes have particularly close personal and professional ties to the domestic experts on whom they "impose" conditions. National specialists, in turn, often aspire to a prestigious and lucrative career as an official or consultant for an IFI; therefore, they have a personal interest in nurturing a collaborative relationship with the IFIs. Indeed, a considerable number of domestic specialists who participated in pension privatization projects in their own country later worked as IFI consultants on social security reform in other nations. For instance, the leader of Bolivia's first reform team, Helga Salinas, later advised the Nicaraguan government, and Gustavo Demarco, a crucial participant in Argentina's privatization effort, did consultancies in several Latin American countries (see also interviews with Durán 2004 and Brevé 2004).

Thus, the web of mutual interests and linkages is more complex and

[6] Sánchez de Lozada's political choice also faced strong opposition from domestic experts (interviews with Bonadona 2002 and Peña Rueda 2002).

less hierarchically structured than the external pressure approach assumes. There is little evidence of clear external imposition in Latin American pension privatization. Under most circumstances, the IFIs cannot force their will upon countries, even on weak, aid-dependent nations. And even where imposition seems to occur, as in instances of loan conditionality, the goals "imposed" by the IFIs are often not strictly external. As the IFIs cannot successfully push new models, diffusion does not proceed vertically. While IFI influence and power certainly promote and facilitate the spread of policy innovations, they are not the principal causal mechanism.

The Timing of IFI Involvement in Latin America's Pension Reform Wave

The temporal sequence of events also suggests that the IFIs did not set in motion the wave of pension privatization in Latin America. This diffusion process started before the IFIs, especially the World Bank, geared up promotional efforts. In Argentina, Bolivia, Brazil, Costa Rica, El Salvador, Mexico, Peru, and Venezuela, serious interest in social security privatization emerged between 1989 and 1991, years before the World Bank published its famous pension reform program in 1994, and even before it prepared that massive study by commissioning numerous consultant reports in 1992. From 1989 to 1991, the WB and other IFIs actually paid little attention to social security; and when they did focus on this arena, they did not advocate Chilean-style privatization (see, e.g., WB 1989; Mesa-Lago 1991).

In the late 1980s and early 1990s, most Latin American countries were confronting acute economic crises and therefore concentrated on immediate tasks of economic stabilization. These countries, and the IFIs as important promoters of adjustment, focused on pressing first-stage reforms, rather than on complicated institutional changes such as social security privatization, which had less urgency and required more time. As mentioned above, the IFIs deliberately advocated a sequential approach to market reform. Governments should guarantee economic equilibrium before moving on to technically complicated, politically controversial, and economically costly changes such as drastic social security reform, whose fiscal transition cost threatened to undermine precarious economic stability. Therefore, the IFIs did not push for pension privatization at this early point.

In the social security arena, the IFIs concentrated instead on parametric reforms, which sought to restore financial and actuarial equilibrium in existing public pension systems, especially by limiting the accumulation of costly entitlements. For instance, in 1991 the IDB gave El Salvador a grant designed to improve the performance of the two public pension institutes. At this point, the IDB did not push for structural reform but hoped to ease the administrative and financial problems plaguing the existing social security system. That this grant—through the hiring of Chilean consultants—set in motion the privatization effort (as analyzed below) was an unintended consequence (interviews with Ramírez 2004 and Tamayo 2004). Similarly, the WB in 1989 focused on "fiscal and financial issues" in Brazil's social security system, stressed the fiscal transition problem as an insurmountable obstacle even to partial privatization, and endorsed instead a scheme to guarantee actuarial equilibrium inside the public system (WB 1989: 21). Thus, the IFIs were not pushing for pension privatization at the time when many Latin American governments developed a serious interest in this project.

In the perception of Latin American reform team members, the IFIs actually did not have much in-house expertise on social security reform in the late 1980s and early 1990s. According to the initial leader of Bolivia's privatization effort, Helga Salinas, the World Bank did not know much about this topic and had only a couple of specialists on its payroll at that time; expertise was really concentrated in Chile (interview with Salinas 2002). And the IDB commissioned the special section on social security in its annual report of 1991 from an independent academic specialist, Carmelo Mesa-Lago, who was not a neoliberal advocate of drastic privatization (Mesa-Lago 1991). In sum, the IFIs did not trigger the pension reform wave of the 1990s in Latin America.

But the IFIs, especially the World Bank, significantly reinforced this wave once it was already swelling. They provided technical, financial, and political support to countries that had initiated structural reform projects on their own and tried to coax more reluctant governments to follow their lead. As regards autonomous emulators, the WB and IDB underwrote numerous consultant missions to Bolivia and El Salvador, for instance. Furthermore, they offered technical advice and financial assistance on specific problems, such as calculations of the fiscal transition cost of privatization (interviews with Gottret 2002, Salinas 2002, Solórzano 2004, and Vargas 2002). And they protected structural reform projects against political uncertainty arising from presidential elections, for instance in Bolivia in 1993. As regards laggards such as Brazil and Costa Rica, the WB eventually tried to press their governments to jump on the privatization bandwagon—though with limited success, as discussed above. Thus, the IFIs contributed to the spread of pension privatization once this process was already under way. They supported ongoing diffusion rather than initiating it. They were followers, not leaders.

In the late 1980s and early 1990s, the primary promoters of pension privatization were Chilean experts who had participated in that country's pension reform, especially José Piñera and his former aides. This group provided the initial impulse for the spread of structural social security reform in Latin America. As Chile's return to democracy in 1989–90 eased the stigma stemming from pension privatization's first enactment by the Pinochet dictatorship,[7] Piñera himself, the minister presiding over that reform, turned into a missionary who advertised the Chilean model worldwide, especially in Latin America. A number of Chilean specialists who had helped to design the reform or to administer the new pension system also became international consultants and eagerly spread the Chilean blueprint (Madrid's interviews with Iglesias 1996 and Larraín 1997).

Thus, when the diffusion of pension privatization in Latin America started to gather steam in the late 1980s, Chilean experts—not the IFIs—were the primary promoters of this innovation. Their missionary zeal, which often made them push beyond the specific consulting tasks for which they had been hired, provided the spark for this reform project to catch on in several countries. It led domestic specialists to see a new, definitive solution for problems that they had faced for years and unsuccessfully sought to overcome (interviews with Ramírez 2004, Salinas 2002, and Tamayo 2004; WB 1996b: 20; see the in-depth discussion in chap. 4 below). The persuasive power of Chilean experts, led by the charismatic Piñera, managed to lift social security reform to a qualitatively new level. It induced specialists in several countries to leave behind parametric adjustments and elaborate radical privatization projects.

This success is noteworthy because Chilean consultants did not command any real means of influence. Since their advice went beyond the tasks for which they had been hired (for instance, in the Salvadoran case), they could not invoke the authority of the IFIs that underwrote their technical assistance. And as foreigners, they lacked political clout. Thus, their impact did not arise from any form of pressure but had a purely ideational character. As chapter 4 analyzes in depth, the new solution they proposed convinced domestic experts in policymaking positions as well as their political superiors.

In conclusion, powerless Chilean experts, not the powerful IFIs, were the prime movers in the diffusion of pension privatization in Latin

---

[7] See Kay (1998: 6, 58, 137). This stigma never disappeared completely, however. For instance, in 1996 El Salvador's reform team flew twelve influential legislators to Chile to impress on them the advantages of pension privatization. But one FMLN deputy commented that despite the apparent benefits, she could never approve Chilean-style reform because pension privatization had been constructed with the blood of so many human rights victims (interviews with Solórzano 2004 and Ramírez 2004).

America. This wave arose at a time when the IFIs focused primarily on economic stabilization, not structural and institutional reform. The WB, in particular, soon supported the further spread of the privatization wave, however. Thus, the IFIs reinforced diffusion; but they did not set it in motion (similar for education reform, Grindle 2004: 47, 198).

THE PROMOTION OF NEW NORMS?

As the IFIs' heavy weaponry—especially loan conditionality—did not prove decisive for the spread of pension privatization in Latin America, and as Chilean consultants with minimal power capabilities triggered this wave, has "soft power," especially the power of persuasion, been the crucial causal mechanism? Did the IFIs or Chilean experts manage to convince Latin American governments to embrace neoliberal goals and maxims, reshape their definition of interests, and instill a genuine commitment to social security privatization? Did the wave of radical social security reform in Latin America thus result from the spread of new norms and ideas, as sociological institutionalists and constructivists would claim?

A private pension system rests on maxims that differ starkly from the ideational foundations of the old PAYG system. Whereas the established scheme was built on social and intergenerational solidarity, a private scheme is inspired by individualism and freedom of choice. The PAYG system promised social equity and protection guaranteed by the state; by contrast, the new system rewards individual effort and harnesses the efficiency of market competition for maximizing people's benefits. Pension privatization thus brings fundamental change; to what extent was it driven by the normative principles inspiring this change? Did new ideas and values promoted by international organizations provide the crucial impulse for the wave of radical pension reform in Latin America?

Among the international organizations that could promote neoliberal ideas and values, the IFIs once again stand out. The organization that had helped to build the old PAYG systems, the International Labour Organisation (ILO), certainly did not advocate pension privatization; instead, it criticized and resisted this neoliberal recipe (Beattie and McGillivray 1995). The main proponents of the new credo were the IFIs, especially the WB. In the 1980s and 1990s, the IFIs indeed undertook a host of efforts to spread their market-oriented message and convince governments of the specific benefits and general validity of neoliberalism. They produced a wealth of publications, which they distributed widely. They held a large number of international conferences and seminars to proselytize for their creed and to advertise "best practices" that embodied neoliberal maxims in various policy arenas. These promotional efforts were especially intense in the area of social security reform. After a huge research effort, the WB produced a widely read pension privatization program that explained its main goals and gave countries a menu of reform options from which to choose (WB 1994a).

The normative appeal argument claims that the IFIs are quite successful in their promotional efforts, which are said to go beyond mere technical assistance and to shape governmental goals. New norms embody higher standards of modernity and legitimacy and therefore win over the hearts and minds of policy-makers and the broader public. To what extent can this line of reasoning account for radical social security reform?

The neoliberal wave that included pension privatization was certainly driven in part by the spread of new economic ideas (Edwards 1995; Leiteritz 2003), and these ideas contained a normative component. The attraction of neoliberalism arose not only from new or revived technical arguments, but also from the ethics of individual responsibility, hard work, and independence from governmental handouts. Neoliberalism had a heroic ring: Self-reliant individuals were supposed to take life into their own hands and assume responsibility for their choices; and reform-minded experts were supposed to take on rent-seeking interest groups and populist politicians to create a free society in which well-being would depend on hard work, not lobbying and "connections."

Thus, while presented first and foremost as a scientific edifice, neoliberalism also embodied a moral—even emotional—message. This normative, ideological component helps account for the fervor with which some leading experts and policy-makers, such as Peru's economy minister Carlos Boloña and his aides, held market-oriented views. In fact, reform team members sometimes characterized their embrace of pension privatization in emotional or religious terms: "We fell in love with the project" and had "faith" in it (see in general Boloña 1993).

Yet while the IFIs' normative message imbued some committed advocates of neoliberalism with special missionary zeal, it did not hold the broad public appeal in the pension arena that new norms enjoy according to sociological institutionalists and constructivists. Whereas novel maxims of human rights, for instance, sooner or later marginalize the power interests that initially resisted their advance (see, e.g., Hawkins 2002), neoliberal norms never won such hegemony in the social security sphere and always remained heavily contested. In fact, the ethic of individual responsibility faced an uphill battle against prevailing views on the importance of social solidarity, which prereform pension systems claimed to embody. Advocates of those systems, such as trade unions and leftist or populist parties, strongly criticized the neoliberal message and defended established norms that seemed gentler and kinder and therefore retained considerable public support. In countries where those traditional values had particularly deep roots, such as Costa Rica, reformers deliberately avoided the neoliberal message. Instead of preaching individualism, they stressed the congruence of their proposals with the solidaristic principles underlying the old system (Rodríguez and Durán 1998: 228–35; MIDEPLAN 1998a: 29).

In fact, the World Bank itself downplayed the normative change it was promoting in the pension area by endorsing a complex, multipillar system that included important solidaristic components (WB 1994a; see also James 1998). The bank did not advocate abandoning the traditional maxims inspiring social security and adopting completely new goals. Instead, it promoted the differentiation of the old goals that in its view had been mixed up in existing social security systems. According to this line of reasoning, all pension systems need to fulfill three functions, namely, redistribution, insurance, and saving. Whereas pay-as-you-go systems used one institutional scheme to attain all three goals, the World Bank recommended assigning them to separate institutions (WB 1994a: 10–16, 73, 76, 99, 162–63). A basic redistributive pillar should guarantee social solidarity and poverty alleviation; individual pension accounts in the second and third pillars should ensure sufficient savings; and all three pillars together would provide insurance (WB 1994a: 233–54). Thus, the WB message did not propound conversion to a new goal, but a more effective and efficient pursuit of already established goals. Deemphasizing social solidarity was merely an implicit subtext (e.g., WB 1994a: 82).

In sum, the central thrust of the IFI message was pragmatic. It presented pension privatization as a new solution to long-standing problems that were inherent in PAYG systems. The very title of the WB program, *Averting the Old Age Crisis*, highlights this instrumental effort to combat threats to existing goals. In the World Bank's technical analysis, PAYG systems were financial and actuarial time bombs. They granted generous entitlements that future generations eventually could not pay, due to the inherent maturation of the pension system and to increasing life expectancy and falling birth rates. This demographic transition increased the proportion of pensioners and diminished the percentage of active workers in the population. Sooner or later, there would not be enough current workers to fund the increasing number of pensioners. Therefore, PAYG systems would inevitably become unsustainable (WB 1994a: chap. 4).

By the 1980s, experience seemed to provide some corroboration of this gloomy analysis. A number of Latin American social security systems, especially in the Southern Cone, where the demographic transition had advanced the farthest, were already suffering from severe financial problems. Other countries with a younger population were facing less dire straits, but in the World Bank's eyes, they were well-advised to transform their pension system soon in order to limit the accumulation of pension entitlements, which would make the unavoidable reform more costly later on.

In sum, the World Bank's advocacy of structural pension reform rested first and foremost on pragmatic considerations. The bank stressed threats that existing social security systems posed to long-established goals derived from the inherent core interests of the state, especially fiscal equilibrium. It was this instrumental, technical argument—not normative subtexts about individual responsibility—that had the greatest impact on pension specialists, policy-makers, and the broader public, as chapter 4 shows.

The World Bank's second main selling point of structural pension reform had a more novel character. Based on Chile's experience in the 1980s, when social security privatization was followed by a significant increase in national savings and investment, reform advocates postulated a causal connection between these phenomena. This argument, advanced quite cautiously by the World Bank (WB 1994a: 92–93, 126, 202, 209, 307–10), but embraced with much greater confidence by Latin American reformers (see chapter 4), was important in giving pension privatization a broader economic rationale as a crucial stimulus to national development and in thus widening the circle of governmental decision-makers that had a direct interest in this change. Consequently, ministries of economy and finance, the most powerful governmental institutions, often led the charge for pension privatization. The hope that social security reform would boost savings, investment, and growth indeed contributed significantly to the adoption of this change by many Latin American governments (Madrid 2003b: 31–36; Brooks 2002).

But this argument embodied a new technical claim, not a novel norm. It did not frame radical social security reform in terms of legitimacy or modernity, but in terms of economic benefit. The savings and investment argument linked social security reform to an existing goal that had long commanded broad public support, namely, socioeconomic development. It did not introduce a new goal but depicted pension privatization as a new instrument for accomplishing this old goal.

In sum, the World Bank's promotion of structural pension reform did contain a normative subtext, the ethic of individual responsibility, which inspired the narrow circle of ideologically committed privatization advocates. But the bank's official core message, which had much broader appeal and greater political weight, linked a Chilean-style reform to previously identified goals that governments had pursued for decades. These pragmatic arguments about economic benefits were decisive for allowing the true neoliberals to win the necessary political backing for designing and approving social security privatization. Thus, pension reform arose primarily from conventional ends-means considerations, not from a normative shift: It promised new solutions for old goals. Contrary to sociological-institutionalist and constructivist hypotheses, the IFIs' main arguments had an instrumental, not normative character.

Interestingly, considerations of international prestige did not shape the diffusion of structural pension reform either. Sociological institutionalists claim that developing countries look up to the First World and for symbolic and legitimacy reasons take their inspiration primarily from advanced, modern nations (see, e.g., Bergesen 1980). But instead of learning from North America or Europe, for instance by importing the novel NDC scheme, Latin American governments eagerly emulated the private pension system enacted by another underdeveloped country; even Argentina, which traditionally saw itself as superior to its Andean neighbor, took this step. This diffusion among equals diverges clearly from sociological-institutionalist predictions that innovations spread downward in the hierarchy of global prestige (as the Bismarckian social security system indeed did; see Orenstein 2003: 183–85). As the current U.S. government tried to enact changes inspired partly by Chilean pension privatization, it became obvious that international status does not shape the diffusion of innovations.

CONCRETE PROBLEMS AS TRIGGERS OF PENSION REFORM

Latin American policy-makers also diverged from sociological-institutionalist arguments by applying conventional goal orientation in deciding on pension privatization. They saw the Chilean model as a promising means to resolve clearly visible, previously identified problems. They adopted this new solution to pursue long-standing, firm interests. This instrumental posture diverges from theoretical arguments that stress the role of new norms in reshaping actor interests. In this view, the appearance of a new solution that embodies or symbolizes a novel, modern principle or value raises standards of legitimacy and attracts support; once embraced, this novel solution then triggers the search for a problem that could justify its adoption (Meyer and Rowan 1977; March and Olsen 1976; Kingdon 1984). Sociological-institutionalist theories thus invert the conventional order of goal orientation. Applied to social security, they argue that the desire to prove a country's modernity and legitimacy prompted the emulation of the novel Chilean model, which was rationalized through the identification of deficiencies in preexisting

PAYG schemes. After decision-makers became committed to privatization, they searched for problems to legitimate the adoption of this reform and therefore came to diagnose difficulties in the long-established system of social protection.

My field research shows, however, that most policy-makers proceeded in the sequence corresponding to conventional goal orientation. Public officials who turned into leaders of pension reform teams had for years sought to resolve worsening financial and actuarial difficulties that were plaguing established public pension systems. These problems had been diagnosed by a wide range of observers, even by scholars who were distant from neoliberalism. For instance, the foremost academic expert on Latin American pension systems, Carmelo Mesa-Lago, gave his 1989 book, which analyzed six country cases in the region, the dramatic title *Ascent to Bankruptcy*. Some countries, especially in the Southern Cone, where the demographic transition had advanced the farthest and where pension entitlements had therefore risen substantially, faced acute fiscal crises. Argentina, for instance, had to declare pension emergencies in the 1980s because the state lacked the cash to pay social security benefits, which claimed 30.5 percent of current government spending in 1989 (MTSS. SSS 1991–92; Alonso 2000: 93–98). And in Uruguay, state pension spending claimed a clearly unsustainable 14.34 percent of GDP in 1994 (Filgueira and Moraes 1999: 14).

At the opposite extreme, fiscal problems were much less severe in countries with a younger population and a less mature social security system. El Salvador, for instance, had created a consolidated public pension system only in 1969, and the demographic transition had not advanced far in the country. As a result, the country was not facing acute financial stress in the early 1990s. But trends were worrisome, as experts of various ideological persuasion agreed (Mesa-Lago, Córdova, and López 1994: 34, 59–62; Ramírez 1994b: 95–99; Synthesis 2000: 1–3). The economic crisis of the 1980s, which twelve years of civil war had exacerbated in El Salvador, shrank the formal sector of the economy and pushed many workers into the informal sector, where payment of social security contributions is low. This change in occupational structure limited the number of active contributors per retiree. Actuarial simulations showed that the financial situation of the pay-as-you-go system would deteriorate greatly in future decades. Thus, disequilibria were fast approaching.

Many other Latin American countries that lay in between these extremes, such as Bolivia, Brazil, Costa Rica, and Peru, were already suffering from significant though not overwhelming financial problems. Social security systems were older and had accumulated a large stock of pension entitlements. The demographic transition had advanced further, especially in Costa Rica, or was proceeding at an accelerated pace, as in Brazil. The "lost decade" of the 1980s had changed the occupational structure and limited or reduced affiliation with the social security system; as a result, the ratio of active contributors per retiree had deteriorated significantly. Therefore, Bolivia's pension system by the late 1980s needed special subsidies from the government budget to remain liquid, and Peru's social security institute was close to financial and administrative collapse at that time.

Despite looming problems, Brazil and Costa Rica faced less dire straits, though for opposite reasons. In Brazil, accelerating price increases allowed the government to limit the real value of pension benefits surreptitiously by adjusting nominal benefits below the rate of inflation. This corrosion of governmental outlays maintained precarious financial equilibrium in the general social security system until the mid-1990s, when—ironically—the government's success in ending hyperinflation eliminated this subterfuge and caused a growing imbalance in the pension system (Bacha 1998: 13–14, 53, 56; MPAS 1995b: 31). In Costa Rica, by contrast, early, gradual, and externally cushioned adjustment to the crisis of the 1980s had limited the deterioration of the occupational structure (Mesa-Lago et al. 2000: 493–99; Clark 2001: chap. 3), and the country's very good health care system gave people a strong incentive to maintain their affiliation with the social security system. Thus, although actuarial projections forecast financial disequilibria for the future, Costa Rica's general social security system was not suffering from acute problems in the early 1990s.

In all of those countries, however, occupational categories with particularly high bargaining power, especially civil servants, had successfully pushed for special pension regimes that offered very generous benefits financed by subsidies from the public treasury and that therefore put a significant, increasing drain on state budgets (Mesa-Lago 1978). Bolivia, for instance, had twenty-two such "complementary funds"; many were actuarially unsound, and some suffered from large deficits (Mercado 1991: 16–21, 27). In Costa Rica, the special schemes for school teachers and for civil servants experienced severe disequilibria by the late 1980s (Programa Reforma Integral de Pensiones 1998b: 3–22). In Peru, the rule that civil servants' pensions were increased with every readjustment of public sector salaries imposed enormous costs on the treasury (IPE 1997: 78–98; Roggero 1993: 27–29). In El Salvador, the social security institute for civil servants was in much more dire financial straights than the scheme for private-sector workers (Mesa-Lago, Córdova, and López 1994: 59–61). And in Brazil, the special regimes for civil servants at the federal, state, and municipal levels, which conceded unprecedented privileges such as an additional salary and pension increase at the time of retirement, spent on their three million retirees almost as much as the general social security regime paid its eighteen million beneficiaries (Oliveira, Beltrão, and Ferreira 1998: 363–64). Since civil servants paid only low contributions, this regime confronted severe actuarial and financial disequilibria (Schwarzer 2003b: 178; WB 2003b: 599).

In sum, special pension regimes for strategically placed occupational groups caused significant, sometimes enormous, deficits and thus greatly exacerbated the financial problems in the social security system. To attain or preserve economic stability, governments therefore faced an urgent need to restore actuarial equilibrium. In addition to being financial time bombs, these special regimes also brought substantial regressive redistribution. Through tax payments, broad segments of the population, including poorer sectors, helped to fund the disproportionately generous retirement benefits of middle-class groupings. For fiscal and equity reasons, the need to reform these privileged schemes therefore seemed especially urgent.

In conclusion, Latin American social security systems were suffering from real problems that had been diagnosed for years. Specialists of various stripes agreed on the need for change and were interested in finding solutions. As chapter 4 examines in depth, these problems made economic specialists in governmental positions, especially in finance and economy ministries, receptive to the Chilean model of pension privatization. Thus, Latin American governments initiated structural social security reform in a conventionally goal-oriented fashion: After identifying a clear, important problem, they pursued what appeared to be a promising solution. They did not invert this order, as sociological institutionalists claim: They did not embrace an attractive, novel, modern scheme and then search for a difficulty that could rationalize its adoption. Instead, the broad outlines of means-ends rationality prevailed.

But the problems afflicting Latin American pension systems did not determine the solution that policy-makers adopted. Financial and actuarial disequilibria did not require and necessitate social security privatization. In fact, Chilean-style reform was bound to aggravate the medium-term drain on public budgets through its huge fiscal transition cost, which had to be paid for decades. For many years to come, parametric reforms and the elimination of privileges would bring much greater financial relief than pension privatization. Thus, the emulation of the Chilean model was not the logical solution to the difficulties that triggered reform efforts. These problems did not in any direct, functionalist way bring forth this recipe for change.

The wave of radical reforms was not purely demand-driven. While real problems triggered this change, they cannot fully account for its shape and nature. Instead, a supply-side factor, namely, the availability of the Chilean privatization model, played a decisive role as well. Information about this innovation made a crucial independent contribution to the decision of so many Latin American governments to adopt structural social security reform. If this blueprint had not appeared on decision-makers' radar screen, they would most likely have continued to tinker with the existing pension system. It was the availability of the Chilean model that made policy-makers go beyond incremental, piecemeal reforms and embark instead on a systemic transformation.

Thus, the wave of pension reforms in Latin America was decisively inspired by learning from the Chilean model, as chapter 4 demonstrates. Reforms are not the direct product of domestic problems and the sociopolitical interests that respond to these difficulties, as conventional political economy frameworks assume. Instead, external ideas, models, and experiences often make a crucial contribution as well, as diffusion approaches claim (see Orenstein 2003: 173).

Conclusion

This chapter has shown that two approaches that are often invoked to explain the diffusion of innovations across countries and that emphasize external pressures and normative appeals, respectively, cannot account for the wavelike spread of pension privatization in Latin America. The impressive power resources of the IFIs did not serve as the main causal mechanism that made governments emulate the Chilean model. The IFIs did not initiate this wave of change but only supported it once it was already under way. They helped governments who embraced privatization to carry through this project, as in Bolivia and El Salvador, but did not manage to impose their will on administrations that were reluctant to take this step, as in Costa Rica and Brazil. In sum, these seemingly powerful institutions made some contribution to the spread of pension privatization, but this process was clearly not the result of vertical imposition.

The diffusion of the Chilean model did not result from the normative appeal of novel ideas either. While the ethic of individual responsibility inspired some strongly committed neoliberals among pension reformers, it never achieved public hegemony and did not guarantee the privatization project the necessary broader support. Instead, traditional norms of social solidarity and state protection continued to hold considerable sway in the social security arena and blocked the advance of individualistic norms. These old ideas were so firmly entrenched that leading privatization advocates, including the WB, depicted their novel ideas as a mere effort to pursue established goals more transparently and efficiently. Instead of preaching new norms, they advanced mostly instrumental, pragmatic arguments and claimed that pension privatization would augment individual and collective economic benefits.

In sum, the wave of drastic social security reform did not result from vertical imposition. Domestic decision-makers retained considerable autonomy; they chose to enact pension privatization, inspired by horizontal learning from the Chilean model. Moreover, their main motivation was not concern for legitimacy and modernity, but the pursuit of clear, long-established interests that seemed to face new challenges from acute financial problems or looming actuarial deficits in existing social security systems. Decision-makers thus acted primarily in a goal-oriented, instrumentally rational fashion.

Yet how did they pursue those goals? Did the process of deliberation and policymaking approximate the postulates of comprehensive rationality as specialists and politicians actively searched for solutions to the problems they were facing and derived their reform decisions from systematic, balanced cost-benefit analyses? Or did experts and policymakers, besieged by uncertainty and time pressures, resort to cognitive shortcuts that made the processing of overabundant, ambiguous information easier, yet at the risk of yielding distorted, rationally suboptimal inferences and conclusions? Thus, was decision making shaped by the patterns of bounded rationality? Chapter 4 analyzes these crucial questions.

CHAPTER 4

Cognitive Heuristics in the Diffusion of Pension Reform

EXTERNAL IMPOSITION and new norms were not decisive for propelling pension privatization, as chapter 3 shows. Instead, this reform wave resulted primarily from instrumentally driven domestic efforts to resolve pressing problems that threatened long-established interests. The present chapter investigates the crucial question of whether national decision-makers pursued these goals by approximating the ideal-typical postulates of comprehensive rationality or by applying bounded rationality. Did they proactively search for the relevant information and process it in a systematic and balanced fashion, or did they rely on cognitive shortcuts that selectively guided their attention and skewed their judgments?

My field research shows that policy-makers deviated significantly from the maxims of full rationality. They displayed the limitations of information processing highlighted by theories of bounded rationality. Logically arbitrary factors attracted their attention to one outstanding model, namely, Chile's bold pension privatization, while making them neglect other foreign experiences that also deserved consideration. Cognitive shortcuts also skewed their evaluation of the main model that they did consider: They overestimated the significance of the limited stretch of success that Chile's private pension system had attained by the late 1980s and attributed a good part of Chile's impressive growth after 1985 to social security privatization, which they associated with increased national savings and investment. And where policy-makers decided to follow in Chile's footsteps, they were so captivated by this model that they adopted it with limited modifications; as is typical of boundedly rational decision-makers, they preferred imitation over redesign.

The heuristics of availability, representativeness, and anchoring—rather than the standards of comprehensive rationality—thus shaped the spread of pension privatization in Latin America. These inferential shortcuts had particular force in Bolivia, El Salvador, and Peru, where limitations in domestic technical capacity, the small size and fairly homogeneous composition of pension reform teams, and the dearth of broader political debate kept the bounds of rationality particularly narrow. As a result, pension reformers focused almost exclusively on the Chilean model, accepted its aura of success, and inferred that it held high promise for their own countries. In fact, the Bolivian, Salvadoran, and—to a lesser extent—Peruvian change teams drew heavily on advice from Chilean experts who actively promoted their model.

By promising significant macroeconomic spillover effects, the representativeness heuristic induced economic generalists in governments' economic agencies to push hard for pension privatization. In Bolivia, El Salvador, and Peru, social security institutes with a stake in defending the established systems were weakened by administrative troubles and actuarial or financial problems. Trade unions and left-wing parties were debilitated by the legacies of hyperinflation and orthodox adjustment in Bolivia and Peru and of a lengthy civil war in El Salvador. As a result, small technocratic change teams dominated by economic generalists gained free rein to follow cognitive shortcuts and advance drastic pension reforms. The heuristics of availability, representativeness, and anchoring molded decision outputs and produced rather faithful replications of the Chilean model.

In Brazil, the cognitive availability of the Chilean model also captivated decision-makers' attention and confined reform discussions to the privatization question for most of the 1990s. The representativeness heuristic induced especially officials and advisors of the powerful economic ministries to expound the promises attached to Chilean-style privatization and press for its emulation in Brazil. Under three consecutive governments, change teams therefore elaborated drastic reform proposals. But specialists from the Social Security Ministry, which has considerable technical capacity and institutional clout in Brazil, focused on social equity and stressed the downsides of Chilean privatization. Since clientelist politicians who wanted to maintain politically distributable patronage had great influence in Brazil's fragmented party system, and since trade unions and leftist parties opposed to privatization commanded political weight, social security officials found allies in Congress and society in their struggles with the economy ministries. The pressure for pension privatization inspired by the Chilean model therefore encountered insurmountable resistance, and the debate remained stalemated for many years.

By limiting the reform discussion to the question of full privatization vs. parametric reforms, the availability heuristic perpetuated the impasse for almost a decade. Only when the World Bank made the notional defined-contribution scheme, which was designed in Europe, available to Brazilian experts did an escape from this stalemate finally open up. Availability enhancement by an IFI offered a third reform option and laid to rest the polarized debate between privatization advocates, who propounded sanguine assessments of Chile's success in line with the representativeness heuristic, and the opponents, who highlighted the negative repercussions of the Chilean model for social equity. And as more information on the actual performance of private pension systems has become available, the high hopes that some sectors had attached to pension privatization have gradually faded, making the resumption of drastic reform efforts in Brazil unlikely.

The availability heuristic also made Costa Rican policy-makers initially focus on the Chilean model, and the representativeness heuristic led economic generalists to extol the macroeconomic benefits of privatization. But the high technical capacity and institutional strength of the existing social security agency guaranteed pension experts ample participation in the reform debate, which allowed for broadening the bounds of rationality. Firm, broad commitment to social-democratic values, which had allowed Costa Rica to attain great social progress, made sector specialists skeptical about the promises that the representativeness heuristic attached to the Chilean model. They stressed the downsides of full privatization, such as limited coverage and high transition costs. Therefore, they sought inspiration in a moderate reform model, namely, Uruguay's mixed system. After concertation with societal interests and lengthy deliberations in Congress, which are typical of the country's consensual policy process, the government found approval for this project, which instituted obligatory individual pension accounts, but privatized only a limited segment of the extensive social security system.

In sum, experts and policy-makers in all five countries deviated greatly from the principles of comprehensive rationality and applied cognitive heuristics in deliberating on pension reform. These causal mechanisms encountered few obstacles and profoundly shaped decision outputs in Bolivia, El Salvador, and Peru, These countries therefore emulated the Chilean model with surprising faithfulness, despite its questionable fit with their underdeveloped economies and societies. In Brazil, the availability heuristic also held sway for years, concentrating the political debate on the pros and cons of the Chilean model. But political-institutional divergences blocked radical privatization, until availability enhancement by the World Bank finally allowed for an escape from this impasse. In Costa Rica, cognitive heuristics also put pension privatization on the policy agenda, but a diverse group of experts widened the bounds of rationality and sought a reform option that was politically feasible in this consensual, social-democratic country.

RADICAL PENSION PRIVATIZATION IN BOLIVIA, EL SALVADOR, AND PERU

The Availability Heuristic: Fixation on the Chilean Model

The Bolivian, Peruvian, and Salvadoran pension systems suffered from significant administrative, actuarial, and financial difficulties, as chapter 3 shows. These problems were most acute in Peru, where the Alan

García administration (1985–90) irresponsibly doubled the staff of the social security agency (Instituto Peruano de Seguridad Social) and where hyperinflation devastated finances. But all these problems did not "require" full-scale privatization. Other decision options, such as determined parametric reform or the introduction of notional accounts, were feasible and promising. In fact, these alternatives could yield short-term relief—much desired by political leaders—whereas social security privatization created huge transition costs. The striking availability of the Chilean model was decisive for the emergence of privatization proposals in Bolivia, El Salvador, and Peru. Only this cognitive "supply" factor explains why important yet not catastrophic problems gave rise to bold projects for completely revamping social security systems; the problems alone cannot account for this surprising departure from long-standing trajectories of pension policy. By focusing attention on the Chilean model, the availability heuristic provided an essential impulse to social security privatization.

As the paradigmatic case of drivers seeing a car crash suggests, the special availability of Chile's privatization model resulted from two factors, namely, its bold, drastic nature and the direct, personal knowledge that Latin American decision-makers gained. First, privatization constituted an audacious departure from decades of social security policy. Whereas decision making usually proceeds incrementally, Chile's reform radically departed from tradition and broke new ground. Privatization did not just tinker with a specific aspect of social security but put the whole system on a new foundation. Whereas a limited modification may have gone unnoticed, this bold, comprehensive revamping attracted widespread attention. Moreover, the Chilean reform was "out of one piece." Systematically derived from clear theoretical and ideological principles, its logic was easy to grasp. Its essential simplicity made it much more appealing to boundedly rational decision-makers than a complicated eclectic scheme. In fact, the Chilean model promised a definitive solution by taking most decisions on social security out of the realm of public policymaking. Whereas a parametric strategy required frequent adjustments of contributions, entitlements, and benefit values, privatization would resolve these issues once and for all by stipulating basic rules and turning many specific decisions into matters of individual choice (interviews with Brevé 2004, Solórzano 2004, and Daboub 2004). The promise to unload a complicated, conflict-ridden issue area appealed to boundedly rational policy-makers and attracted their attention to the Chilean model. Thus, inherent characteristics of this bold innovation boosted its cognitive availability.

Second, personal contacts were crucial for focusing decision-makers' attention on the Chilean model. In fact, the realization that full-scale privatization could resolve the difficulties afflicting the Bolivian, Peruvian, and Salvadoran pension systems arose in surprisingly accidental ways. Economic experts did not become aware of the Chilean model's potential during a proactive search for a solution to administrative, actuarial, or financial problems. While they had undoubtedly heard of Chile's privatization, they apparently did not see it as relevant for their own countries. Only when they entered into face-to-face contact with Chilean experts who promoted this model did they suddenly come to perceive privatization as a possible solution to the problems facing them.

In Bolivia, this connection "clicked" when the Finance Ministry's budget director, Helga Salinas, attended the annual conference of the business peak association, Confederación de Empresarios Privados de Bolivia (CEPB). The keynote speaker was the architect of Chile's reform, José Piñera (interview with Cuevas 2002). Widely credited with great persuasive powers, Piñera advertised his innovation with missionary zeal. Salinas was so captivated that she took Piñera aside and kept talking to him over lunch. She depicts this encounter as an eye-opening experience, a crucial turning point in her ongoing efforts to combat pension problems, and the starting point of the privatization project, which drew on very extensive advice and consultations with Chilean experts during the following years (interviews with Salinas 2002 and Bonadona 2002).[1]

In El Salvador, the privatization plan emerged in a similarly unplanned fashion as the Chilean model suddenly became cognitively available. An IDB-funded domestic team charged with the limited task of improving the administration and finances of the existing social security agencies was making minimal progress when one of the consultants it had contracted, a Chilean involved in pension privatization, promoted this model as a radical alternative.[2] To assess the relevance of this innovation, which immediately attracted attention from Salvadoran generalists, one of them traveled to Chile and collected information (interview with Ramírez 2004). This first-hand experience put Salvadoran pension policy on a completely new track by giving rise to the privatization project, which was elaborated in intensive cooperation with Chilean consultants (Socimer International Bank 1993; Proceso de Implementación n.d.; WB 1996b: 20). Thus, Salvadoran officials unexpectedly came to see the

[1] Bolivia's business peak association submitted a very brief, general plea for drastic pension reform in June 1991 (CEPB 1991b)—months after Piñera's speech.

[2] Interviews with Ramírez (2004) and Solórzano (2004); Proceso de Implementación (n.d.: 1). On the beginning of the Salvadoran reform discussion, see Córdova (1993: 1–4) and Synthesis (2000: 1–2, 23). At that time, the IDB was not advocating pension privatization à la Chile (see Mesa-Lago 1991).

Chilean model as a potential solution to the problems they were trying to address.

In Peru, the privatization project emerged out of contacts between Chilean experts and advisors of neoliberal presidential candidate Mario Vargas Llosa, who elaborated a comprehensive program of market reforms in the run-up to the 1990 contest (Movimiento Libertad 1988). Piñera himself advertised his innovation at a well-publicized conference in Lima in March 1990. After Alberto Fujimori defeated Vargas Llosa yet initiated neoliberal adjustment, Mario Roggero, a congressional deputy from Vargas Llosa's Movimiento Libertad with close connections to Piñera, kept the project alive and sought parliamentary approval for Chilean-style privatization (Roggero 1993; interview with Roggero 2002). Roggero's unsuccessful efforts attracted the attention of neoliberal Economy Minister Carlos Boloña, who in late 1991 took charge of the project. Thus, Peru's privatization proposal also arose haphazardly out of discussions with Chilean specialists.

Therefore, the special availability of the bold Chilean model, which was advertised by its originator José Piñera and his aides, set in motion the privatization projects in all three countries. Face-to-face encounters played a crucial role in alerting domestic decision-makers to the significance of the Chilean model. While Bolivian, Peruvian, and Salvadoran economists had certainly known about this reform before, they only came to see its potential as a solution to the problems facing their countries when they entered into personal contact with Chilean experts who had first-hand knowledge of this profound change (interviews with Salinas 2002, Bonadona 2002, Ramírez 2004, and Tamayo 2004). Direct, vivid experiences, such as Piñera's rousing speech at the CEPB meeting, created a much stronger impression than a dry technical report. These personal contacts suddenly made the Chilean model look like a plausible response to domestic difficulties. They drew Bolivian, Peruvian, and Salvadoran experts' attention to this striking innovation, which captivated their minds. Thus, as personally witnessing a car crash has a much greater impact than reading about an accident in the newspaper, so personal contact with Chilean experts was decisive for establishing the relevance of pension privatization.

In Bolivia and Peru, geographic proximity facilitated these contacts and enhanced the impact of the Chilean model. Innovations enacted across the border are more directly available than changes carried out in a distant corner of the region—not to speak of other continents. Therefore Chile's three neighbors, Argentina, Bolivia, and Peru, were among the first countries to initiate reform projects inspired by the Chilean model. Contiguity favors cognitive availability and prompts emulation. Argentine, Bolivian, and Peruvian specialists were especially receptive to messages about this next-door innovation.

El Salvador, by contrast, lies far away from Chile. Nevertheless, the Salvadoran team learned primarily from Chile, not from more proximate Mexico, which was designing privatization at the same time. The special availability of the Chilean model resulted from the broader affinity between the two nations that Salvadoran decision-makers perceived. Praising El Salvador as the most dynamic and world-open country in Central America, they were particularly receptive to foreign ideas and focused their attention on Chile, which they saw as the lead innovator in the hemisphere. In fact, they wanted to turn El Salvador into "the Chile of Central America."[3] This quest for emulation arose in part from perceived similarities in historical experiences: Both nations had faced powerful challenges from the revolutionary left—Chile under the government of Salvador Allende (1970–73), El Salvador during the civil war of the 1980s; they had both sought to defuse these threats by enacting comprehensive packages of market-oriented reforms (Daboub 2004b; see Segovia 2002: 27–51). This interpretation of recent history helps account for the cognitive impact of the Chilean model so far away from home.

The special availability of the Chilean model in turn helps explain why El Salvador was the first nation in its subregion to start a privatization project and why—with the exception of Costa Rica—it has remained the only Central American country to implement this change. In Guatemala, Honduras, and Nicaragua, pension reform did not attract the same degree of attention. Proposals to emulate the Chilean model were pursued with less determination and more easily derailed in the decision making or implementation process (e.g., interview with Durán 2004). Although the four countries faced similar problems in their social security systems, the availability heuristic launched El Salvador on a bolder reform course than its neighbors.

As in El Salvador, general ideological affinities enhanced the availability of Chilean-style privatization in Bolivia and Peru as well. The willingness of the Bolivian, Peruvian, and Salvadoran governments to enact market reforms helped the Chilean model gain resonance. This blueprint was in line with the overall orientation of these countries' development policy (interviews with Du Bois 2002 and Peñaranda 2002).

But ideological affinities were neither necessary nor sufficient for the

---

[3] The former finance minister proudly stressed that El Salvador was competing with Chile for highest Latin American ranking in the global competitiveness index (interview with Daboub 2004). On this general point, also see interview with Ramírez (2004).

launching of privatization projects. First, not all government leaders and reform team members were convinced neoliberals. For instance, presidents Fujimori of Peru and Jaime Paz Zamora of Bolivia (1989–93) were pragmatists, not ideologues.[4] Yet despite Fujimori's skepticism towards extending neoliberalism to social sectors (interviews with Peñaranda 2002, Romero 2002, De los Heros 2002, and Du Bois 2002; Graham 1998: 113–15), pension privatization in Peru advanced very quickly. Second, if ideological affinity had been decisive, Bolivian, Peruvian, and Salvadoran specialists would have taken the initiative to gather information about Chile's innovation. But diffusion did not start with such proactive efforts. Instead, the Chilean model only became cognitively available when vivid, face-to-face experiences—such as José Piñera's charismatic discourse at the CEPB convention or the acquaintance of Salvadoran experts with a Chilean consultant—drew their attention to this innovation. Direct contacts were crucial to alert decision-makers to the promise of Chile's reform for resolving the difficulties confronting them. The availability heuristic clearly was at work.

In line with this cognitive shortcut, Bolivian, Peruvian, and Salvadoran pension reformers focused almost exclusively on Chile. The first contacts to Chilean experts quickly gave rise to dense networks of exchange. Bolivian, Peruvian, and Salvadoran experts undertook many study trips to Chile to gain first-hand knowledge (Proceso de Implementación n.d.; interviews with Salinas 2002, Gottret 2002, Vargas 2002, Mercado 2002, Ramírez 2004, and Tamayo 2004). Furthermore, they contracted a number of Chilean consultants to provide detailed information on the new system and advice on their own reform plans (Socimer International Bank 1993; WB 1996b: 20; Madrid's interviews with Iglesias 1996 and Larraín 1997). José Piñera, for instance, co-authored eight reports for Bolivian specialists in 1990/91, and his collaborators contributed numerous additional studies.[5]

In fact, Chilean specialists designed the basic outlines of the Bolivian and Salvadoran reforms, and Peruvian experts for their first privatization effort copied Chilean documents and Movimiento Libertad proposals based on them (Boloña 1995: 78). Even studies authored by domestic experts sometimes appeared under the auspices of Chilean institutions that promoted pension privatization (Banco Mundial. Proyecto de Reforma 1993a, 1993b). And reports by Chilean consultants were occasionally republished as if they had been written by domestic institutions

[4] Peru's former economy minister Carlos Boloña indicates (1993: iii, 169–70, 202) that Fujimori never converted to neoliberalism.

[5] In its two-page bibliography, Price Waterhouse (1993) lists eight consultant reports co-authored by Piñera and Claro y Asociados and four reports submitted by Claro y Asociados alone. See also Bustamante and Tarziján (1993).

(Mesa-Lago and Durán 1998: 75). Thus, the initial encounters of Bolivian, Peruvian, and Salvadoran specialists with Chilean privatization advocates opened the floodgates for a stream of additional information; accidental contacts triggered avalanches (interviews with Peñaranda 2002, Romero 2002, Salinas 2002, Vargas 2002, Pantoja 2002, and Solórzano 2004).

In sum, Chile clearly was the principal point of reference for Bolivian, Peruvian, and Salvadoran pension reformers. By contrast, these experts paid surprisingly little attention to reforms elaborated in other Latin American countries. In the early 1990s, Argentina and Colombia were designing profound changes, which—while emulating Chilean privatization—diverged from the original in some ways. Argentina was creating a mixed system that maintained the public pay-as-you-go scheme and added private pension funds; Colombia was elaborating parallel private and public schemes among which affiliates could choose. Comprehensive rationality called for systematic analysis of these modulations on the Chilean theme. But bounded rationality discouraged wide-ranging, proactive information gathering. Specialists shied away from high computational effort. The availability heuristic focused their attention on the Chilean model. As the striking original captivated their minds, modified versions of it were neglected.

Numerous interviews with reform team members and ample documents show that contacts with Argentine and Colombian specialists remained sporadic.[6] They were mostly confined to occasional conversations at international conferences. Only one Bolivian expert mentioned a study mission to Argentina (interview with Bonadona 2002). Salvadoran specialists reported a visit to Argentina and Colombia (besides Chile), but the paper trail of documents suggests that these contacts remained superficial and had no significance or impact—whereas there is overwhelming evidence of a strong orientation toward Chile. In fact, the Salvadoran team asked Chilean consultants to evaluate a Chilean-style radical reform compared to a mixed system à la Argentina; not surprisingly, the Chileans proved the superiority of the drastic privatization that they had helped to institute in their own country (interviews with Ramírez 2004 and Solórzano 2004; Socimer International Bank 1993). Thus, to the limited extent that Salvadoran experts considered other reform options, they did not assess them in a neutral, unbiased way. Instead, it seems that they became "hooked on" Chile's drastic privatization early on (interview with Brevé 2004). The later trips to Argentina

---

[6] Interviews with Gottret (2002), Grandi (2002), Guevara (2002), Pantoja (2002), and Vargas (2002). Peru privatized its pension system before Argentina and Colombia, using Chile as the crucial reference point (interviews with Du Bois 2002 and Romero 2002).

and Colombia may simply have been efforts to signal more openness and rationality than actually prevailed.[7]

The single-minded focus on Chile and inattention to the Argentine and Colombian reform efforts were rationally suboptimal. To improve decision quality, comprehensive rationality calls for serious, unbiased consideration of all feasible options. But the availability heuristic skewed decision-makers' attention; the Chilean model overshadowed other alternatives. The neglect of the Argentine and Colombian reforms was especially problematic because they could have suggested interesting lessons on the politics of pension privatization. Whereas in Chile this drastic change had been imposed by a dictatorship, Bolivia, El Salvador, and Peru—like Argentina and Colombia—were elaborating reforms in fairly democratic settings. Governments in all these countries faced electoral constraints that Chile's authoritarian regime had simply suspended.

Thus, contacts among emulating countries could have been useful for learning about decision-making strategies and for discussing potential adaptations of Chile's drastic blueprint to democratic contexts. It was no accident that both Argentina and Colombia were charting a more moderate course than Chile (cf. Mesa-Lago and Müller 2002). In fact, some domestic experts also invoked the democratic nature of their polities, which made them foresee societal resistance, to advocate less radical reforms (IBSS 1992: 27–41; Mesa-Lago, Córdova, and López 1994: 86–87). But notwithstanding these rational reasons, contacts among emulating countries remained very limited because Bolivian, Peruvian, and Salvadoran specialists were captivated by the Chilean model. They clearly preferred inspiration from the original and looked down upon the modified privatization schemes designed in Argentina and Colombia.

This neglect is especially surprising in the Bolivian case because there had been earlier contact with Argentine pension reformers. The later leader of Argentina's privatization effort, Walter Schulthess, had elaborated an extensive report on Bolivia's social security system in 1988, which recommended modest changes (Schulthess 1988). But the Bolivian team did not seek out Schulthess again when the domestic agenda shifted to profound reform. As this new departure was stimulated by contacts with Chilean experts, the radical original model now became the main reference point; the more eclectic Argentine reform did not appeal to

[7] The Salvadoran team organized a seemingly balanced briefing of President-elect Armando Calderón Sol in May 1994, pairing a Chilean proponent of full privatization, Augusto Iglesias, with Carmelo Mesa-Lago, a well-known advocate of a mixed system. But a team member admitted that they had already decided on the Chilean model beforehand and did not seriously consider the mixed option (interview July 2004; see also Socimer International Bank 1993). On later occasions, the team outright refused to listen to experts who diverged from its line (Mesa-Lago and Durán 1998: 74–78).

Bolivian experts. Thus, the availability heuristic kept Bolivian specialists' attention fixated on the Chilean blueprint.

Bolivian, Peruvian, and Salvadoran reform team members indeed justified this unbalanced focus with the purity of Chile's privatization. By contrast to Argentina's mixed scheme and Colombia's parallel system, the Chilean model was "out of one piece." Derived from simple, clear principles, it was neater and more coherent than those complicated schemes. Therefore, it was more attractive to boundedly rational decision-makers. By phasing out the pay-as-you-go system, Chile's reform brought definitive change, whereas Argentina and Colombia maintained this system as a basic social protection or a full option. The promise to resolve pension problems once and for all and thus remove a problematic, conflictual issue from the political agenda appealed to overburdened decision-makers and technocrats (interviews with Brevé 2004, Solórzano 2004, and Daboub 2004). Thus, considerations of bounded rationality underlay the fixation on the Chilean model and neglect of other relevant options.

Furthermore, Bolivian, Peruvian, and Salvadoran pension reformers took into account only Latin American experiences. The extensive European discussion on social security reform went virtually unnoticed. In particular, the notional defined-contribution scheme, an interesting combination of PAYG and privatization, remained off their radar screen. This neglect of European experiences is noteworthy; the availability heuristic drowned out normative or symbolic considerations. Given Europe's developmental status, international prestige, and sterling democratic credentials, constructivists would expect the novel NDC system to find more receptivity in Latin America than an innovation designed by a dictatorship in an underdeveloped country. But direct, first-hand knowledge of the bold Chilean model proved far more influential than the normative and symbolic appeal of the European option. Due to the availability heuristic, diffusion proceeded through horizontal South-South channels rather than the vertical North-South channels highlighted by constructivists.

The cognitive unavailability of the NDC scheme diminished decision quality, especially in Bolivia. As discussed in chapter 3, Bolivia's privatized pension system has effectively approximated the core principle of an NDC system: The government has obliged private pension fund administrators to use workers' social security contributions to buy well-remunerated government bonds, which finance current pension benefits. Thus, Bolivia effectively continues to use PAYG funding (interviews with Bonadona 2002 and Pantoja 2002; Evia and Fernández 2004: 17)—yet at a much higher fiscal cost than in an NDC scheme. As the former director of the World Bank pension privatization project for Bolivia,

Pablo Gottret (1999: 16), remarked bitterly, "the only difference between the new and the old system, as far as payments to current retirees
is concerned, is that the new system lends the funding formally through
long term treasury bonds issued at 8% in dollars. . . . In the old system
there was no formal recognition of such borrowing." Thus, the state
now pays high real interest for borrowing workers' contributions, which
it could capture at much lower cost in an NDC scheme.

The resulting fiscal drain has raised Bolivia's public deficit, effectively
burdening the whole population—including the poor majority—with a
cost incurred on behalf of the limited number of social security affiliates,
who tend to be better-off. In fact, the fiscal deficit boosted by the excess
cost of privatization, which reached 4 percent of GDP (WB 1999b: 10;
Escobar and Nina 2004: 17–20; Holzmann and Hinz 2005: 148), soon
required painful adjustment. These stabilization efforts in turn triggered
the severe political crisis that entailed the violent ouster of President
Gonzalo Sánchez de Lozada—the political architect of pension reform—
in October 2003 and that threatened democratic stability and economic
prosperity thereafter (Laserna 2003: 13; Arellano 2004). Thus, the unavailability of the NDC option, a product of bounded rationality, turned
Bolivia's social security reform suboptimal. Cognitive shortcuts can produce deleterious consequences that full rationality would avoid.

In sum, the availability heuristic concentrated decision-makers' attention on the Chilean model, which overshadowed other relevant experiences. It privileged one reform proposal and helped to preclude other
options. By putting policymaking on a narrow track, it diminished decision quality and contributed to problematic policy outputs.

The Representativeness Heuristic: Enthusiasm for the Chilean Model

Contrary to constructivist arguments, a novel model that looks modern
and embodies new norms does not automatically prompt imitation. Instead of being swayed by legitimacy considerations, policy-makers primarily pursue interests, especially in redistributive policy arenas. Therefore, they assess a model's promise—its likely costs and benefits—when
deciding whether to adopt it. They do not jump on the bandwagon immediately after a new model becomes cognitively available but wait for
a stretch of performance to accumulate before they judge the novel blueprint's success. Therefore, the spread of innovations is not instantaneous
but starts after an initial delay, as captured in the S-shaped curve of
diffusion.

The cognitive-psychological approach agrees with rational choice that
interests drive the spread of redistributive policy models and that decision-makers insist on evaluating the success of innovations. But these

frameworks diverge on how decision-makers judge the costs and benefits of novel blueprints. Whereas rational learning postulates a systematic, balanced assessment of the relevant information, cognitive psychology highlights shortcuts that distort inferences. After the availability heuristic has narrowed policy-makers' attention to one outstanding model, the representativeness heuristic skews their conclusions about its success or failure. They tend to overextrapolate from the initial stretch of performance that a model attains. Drawing excessively firm inferences from small samples, they see a successful start as an indication of inherent quality, disregarding the likelihood of accidental fluctuations and regression toward the mean. Applying a similar shortcut, they also draw improperly strong inferences from part to whole and vice versa (Tversky and Kahneman 1982: 84; Jennings, Amabile, and Ross 1982: 215–16). Accordingly, they associate good performance of a system with the success of its constituent units.

The representativeness heuristic clearly shaped evaluations of the Chilean model. The Bolivian, Peruvian, and Salvadoran reform teams were impressed with the initial success of Chile's private pension funds and associated them with the country's stellar growth from 1985 onward. The Chilean model therefore gained an aura of inherent success. In fact, this enthusiasm arose largely from information provided by Chilean consultants who had participated in the new pension system. Yet although these promoters of privatization were not neutral sources, the Bolivian, Peruvian, and Salvadoran teams relied primarily on their reports. In both process and outcome, decision-makers' judgments of success thus deviated from comprehensive rationality.

Specifically, the economists dominating the Bolivian, Peruvian, and Salvadoran reform teams were struck by the accomplishments of Chile's private pension system during its first decade. Following the representativeness heuristic, they overestimated the significance of this initial performance. For instance, Bolivia's national pension secretary justified the decision to emulate the Chilean model in part with the 14 percent average return that Chile's pension funds had achieved until the mid-1990s (interview with Peña Rueda 2002; see also Exposición de Motivos 1993: 1); but he quickly added that this rate had fallen significantly thereafter.[8] Similarly, members of the Salvadoran team claimed that drastic reform was meant primarily to increase pension benefits (interview with Tamayo 2004); this hope rested on projections inspired by Chile's high initial investment returns. But this expectation was soon disappointed; results in El Salvador have been surprisingly meager (interviews with

---

[8] In fact, "the returns on the individual accounts are modest" in Bolivia (Escobar and Nina 2004: 23).

Martínez Orellana 2004, Ramírez 2004, and Tamayo 2004; Acuña 2005: 23–24, 34–35). In Peru, pension reformers also pointed to the initially high rates of return of the Chilean pension funds (interview with Du Bois 2002) and extolled the overall success of the new system (interview with De los Heros 2002).

Furthermore, Bolivian, Peruvian, and Salvadoran reformers commonly associated social security privatization with Chile's growth boom after 1985. Despite the absence of firm empirical evidence—acknowledged even by the World Bank (1994: 92, 209, 307–10)—they held private pension funds responsible for the dramatic increase in domestic savings and investment in Chile during the 1980s, which fueled superb growth. In a typical but logically problematic inference from whole to part, they regarded social security reform as representative of Chile's stellar economic performance (interviews with Bonadona 2002, Du Bois 2002, De los Heros 2002, Peñaranda 2002, Vargas 2002, Daboub 2004, and Solórzano 2004). This jump to conclusions broadened the significance of pension reform and made it appear as decisive for economic development. This new connection to long-standing goals greatly reinforced economy ministries' interest in pension privatization and altered the constellation of political forces in this policy arena. Economists sought to take charge and displace social security experts (Madrid 2003: 31–36, 49–52; Müller 2003: 13–16). Cognitive heuristics thus shaped political struggles.

Chilean consultants and, later, IFI officials widely expounded this associative line of reasoning (e.g., Claro y Asociados 1991; WB 1994: 92–93, 126, 202, 209, 307–10). Dominated by economic officials, the Bolivian, Peruvian, and Salvadoran teams accepted these claims and justified pension privatization with the expectation that it would boost domestic savings, investment, and growth (interviews with Bonadona 2002, Peñaranda 2002, Solórzano 2004, and Vargas 2002; Bonadona 1998: 69–70, 91; Mercado 1994: 10, 15–16; Ramírez 1994b: 102–3; Comisión para la Reforma 1996: 22).

Interestingly, these enthusiastic evaluations of Chilean pension privatization rested largely on information provided by Chilean experts who had participated in the new system and thus had a personal stake in its success. As Bolivian, Peruvian, and Salvadoran reform team members acknowledged, their embrace of this model resulted from the promotional efforts of Chilean consultants, who "'sold' us the Chilean model very well" (interview with Ramírez 2004; similar interview with León 2002). These sources can scarcely count as unbiased.

Indeed, Chilean specialists depicted the private pension system in a disproportionately favorable light, highlighting its positive aspects. For instance, a report coauthored by a leading Chilean consultant for the

World Bank (Vittas and Iglesias 1992: 1, 21–22, 33) extolled the stellar investment performance of Chile's pension funds but failed to consider the substantial costs arising from high administrative fees. If these charges are included, gains drop significantly: "In Chile the return on capital between July 1981 and April 2000 was 11.1 percent, but once commissions are factored in, lower-income earners received a 7.34 percent return, and higher-income earners received a 7.69 percent real average return" (Kay and Kritzer 2001: 48). Thus, the informants on whom Bolivian, Peruvian, and Salvadoran specialists relied painted a rosy picture of the private pension system (see also Apoyo 1992: 9). Yet while some experts pressed Chilean advisers on the downsides of the Chilean model (interviews with Grandi 2002, Peñaranda 2002, and Romero 2002),[9] they did not search for more neutral sources of information, as the principles of comprehensive rationality would have demanded. Bounded rationality made them content with the information that was easily available.

The Bolivian and Salvadoran teams also depended largely on Chilean consultants for assessing the transition cost of privatization.[10] By channeling workers' social security contributions into private pension funds, structural reform forces the state to finance current pension benefits and accumulated pension rights. This need to pay off established entitlements creates a fiscal drain for decades, which can seriously hinder privatization. Governments that are still in the midst of economic adjustment may not want to endanger precarious fiscal stability for the promise of long-term benefits. Therefore, the estimated magnitude of this transition cost crucially affects governments' willingness to privatize.

The Bolivian and Salvadoran teams hired Chilean consultants to estimate the transition cost. Strong circumstantial evidence suggests that these simulations significantly underestimated the actual fiscal drain. Indeed, some reform team members admitted that they started from, "let us say, very optimistic assumptions" (interview with a leading Salvadoran expert, July 2004). Bolivian specialists actually discarded the first simulation elaborated by the Chilean firm Claro y Asociados as absurdly low (interview with Galindo 2002). Nevertheless, they kept working with these consultants and building on their simulation model. Similarly, internationally renowned social security expert Carmelo Mesa-Lago strongly criticized the assumptions underlying the transition cost esti-

---

[9] Tamayo (interview 2004) asked Chilean consultants whether their being Chilean made them find the Chilean system so successful—but they claimed to have technical reasons.

[10] Interviews with Galindo (2002) and Vargas (2002); Proceso de Implementación (n.d.: 2). In Peru, this topic was treated with extreme reservation; even reform participants (e.g., Roggero 1993; Muñoz 2000; Morón and Carranza 2003) do not address it.

mates that Chilean consultants calculated for El Salvador. But the Salvadoran team and its Chilean advisers refused to expose their calculations to scrutiny; to the present day, all this information is secret (author interview with a reform team member, July 2004; see Mesa-Lago and Córdova 1998: 125–26). As the simulation model seemed to have serious problems (Mesa-Lago and Durán 1998: 75–78), it indeed underestimated the actual transition cost by a large margin. Thus, the heavy reliance on Chilean consultants and the enthusiastic assessments of this model's success—a product of the representativeness heuristic that made temporary transition costs look unessential—distorted assessments of the downsides of pension privatization.

These unbalanced evaluations, which systematically overrated its benefits and underestimated its costs, imbued the Chilean model with an aura of success. Bolivian, Peruvian, and Salvadoran specialists were effusive in their praise for this innovation, stressing its numerous advantages (interviews with Du Bois 2002, De los Heros 2002, Peñaranda 2002, Salinas 2002, Vargas 2002, Daboub 2004, and Solórzano 2004). Some team members displayed particularly intense commitment to Chilean-style reform. For instance, a leader of the Salvadoran team stated, "We fell in love with the Chilean model" (author interview, July 2004).

But actual experience failed to confirm many of the high hopes attached to privatization. What reformers had expected, "perhaps with more illusion than rationality" (interview with Martínez Orellana 2004), namely, a replication of Chile's record in pension fund performance and economic growth, did not come true. Rates of return remained lower than expected. Due in part to high marketing costs, the Peruvian and Salvadoran AFPs have charged exorbitant administrative fees, eating into workers' retirement funds (Díaz Ortega 1996: 23; Muñoz 2000: 468–69; Cruz Saco 2001a: 9; Paz Panizo and Ugaz 2003: 18, 21, 27; Mesa-Lago and Durán 1998: 64). Many affiliates will therefore have to rely on state-guaranteed minimum pensions or welfare benefits.

Furthermore, the claim that social security privatization boosts domestic savings has not withstood rigorous empirical examination; statistical investigations yield at best inconclusive results (Samwick 2000; White 2000; Escobar and Nina 2004: ii, 17; interview with Martínez Orellana 2004). The prediction that clear individual incentives would make more people join the social security system has not come true either; instead, privatization has been accompanied by a stagnation or further shrinking of effective coverage.[11] Even supporters of the new

---

[11] See for El Salvador Synthesis (2000: 9) and Acuña (2005: 8–10). An important reason for limited affiliation to private pension funds in Peru's parallel scheme was lack of trust in the new system (IPE 1997: 72–74; Ortiz de Zevallos et al. 1999: 47).

scheme stress this limitation as a serious problem (Morón and Carranza 2003: 18, 47–48, 82–84; Gill, Packard, and Yermo 2004: xvii, 3–8, 89–104; WB IEG 2006: x, xvi, 38, 56). Thus, important promises attached to pension privatization have not been fulfilled. And fiscal transition costs ended up being significantly higher than predicted, due to problems with the initial simulations and to political concessions during reform implementation (interviews with Grandi 2002 and Morales 2006).

In fact, the World Bank, the most forceful advocate of pension privatization from the mid-1990s onward, began to change its tune at decade's end. Chief economist Joseph Stiglitz in 1999 disqualified many promises invoked by the bank as "myths" that could not withstand rational scrutiny in light of experience (Orszag and Stiglitz 1999). Prominently among these myths figured the claims that "individual accounts raise national saving" and that "rates of return are higher under individual accounts" (Orszag and Stiglitz 1999: 8). Thus, two of the main justifications used by the Bolivian, Peruvian, and Salvadoran reform teams seemed unfounded. The IMF, which had always been less enthusiastic about pension privatization due to its huge transition cost, soon published a similarly critical assessment (Barr 2000). Later WB analyses of private pension systems also yield sobering findings (Gill, Packard, and Yermo 2004; Holzmann and Hinz 2005; WB IEG 2006). Thus, the initial enthusiasm was eventually unveiled as a product of problematic inferences, such as the representativeness heuristic.

Yet although the high promises attached to social security privatization lacked rational justification and eventually drew growing criticism, they had a tremendous impact on policymaking in Bolivia, El Salvador, and Peru. Economic agencies, which were especially interested in the economic benefits attributed to the Chilean model, dominated the change teams (e.g., WB 1996b: 20). As a result, the reform proposals inspired by the representativeness heuristic had largely free rein. Holding out prospects of great gains for the country, advocates of full-scale privatization quickly gained the upper hand inside the reform commissions. In fact, commitment to drastic reform hardened over time. Some of the teams initially had internal divergences, especially in El Salvador and in Bolivia at the beginning of the Sánchez de Lozada government (interviews with Tamayo 2004, Ramírez 2004, and Guevara 2002; Gray-Molina, Pérez de Rada, and Yañez 1999: 39). But the enthusiastic assessments of the Chilean model derived via the representativeness heuristic stimulated growing support for its full emulation and led to the skeptics' resignation or dismissal. Uniform agreement with the privatization plan soon prevailed.

The reform teams also advanced their radical proposals with great success in interagency conflicts. The established social security institutes were confronting serious financial, actuarial, and administrative problems (Ausejo 1995; DIES-CENITEC 1993; Gray-Molina, Pérez de Rada, and Yañez 1999: 35–36) and thus lacked the institutional strength, credibility, and clout to guarantee the maintenance of the existing pension system.[12] In Bolivia and El Salvador, their own reform proposals, which advocated moderate changes (IBSS 1992; Mesa-Lago, Córdova, and López 1994: 72–74; interviews with Galindo 2002, Tamayo 2004, Ramírez 2004, and Solórzano 2004; see also Synthesis 2000: 22), fell on deaf ears. Instead, substitutive reforms closely modeled on the Chilean original carried the day.

In Peru, determined and successful efforts to overcome an administrative and financial crisis gave the IPSS somewhat greater veto power (Ausejo 1995; interview with Peñaranda 2002; Graham 1998: 115; Arce 2001: 93–94). IPSS president Luis Castañeda Lossio indeed opposed social security privatization. But powerful Economy Minister Carlos Boloña pushed hard for a complete replacement of the PAYG system (see Boloña 1993: 122). The claim based on the representativeness heuristic that this change would boost economic development strengthened his case. Castañeda therefore cut a deal in mid-1992 that allowed for profound social security reform but shelved the planned privatization of the health system (interviews with De los Heros 2002, Du Bois 2002, and Peñaranda 2002; Roggero 1993: 186–87; Ortiz de Zevallos et al. 1999: 38–39). Thus, even in Peru, the small reform team dominated by economists won out inside the executive branch. By making its project appear as a decisive step toward economic recovery, the representativeness heuristic shaped the instrumental interests of leading decision-makers and swung the political struggle over the emulation of the Chilean model.

These ever more homogeneous change teams also won presidential backing. In El Salvador, presidents Alfredo Cristiani (1989–94) and Armando Calderón Sol (1994–99) were committed to comprehensive neoliberal programs (Segovia 2002: 29–51) and were therefore receptive to the attractions of the Chilean model. In addition to general advice from Chilean experts (CINDE 1994), a presentation by Chilean pension consultant Augusto Iglesias before Calderón in May 1994 further cemented this commitment.[13] In Bolivia, President Jaime Paz Zamora (1989–93) hailed from the left and was more skeptical. He refused to enact radical pension reform at the end of his term to avoid the political costs of a

[12] By contrast, the market reforms of the 1990s often included a strengthening of economic agencies. For Peru, see Wise (2003b: 199–205).
[13] In November 1993, a leading reformer advocated a mixed system, but by May 1994, he embraced a substitutive reform à la Chile (Ramírez 1994a: 16–17; 1994b: 100–102).

controversial change whose benefits only his successor would reap (interviews with Bonadona 2002, Salinas 2002, and Vargas 2002; Mercado 1998: 143; Pérez 2000: 5–6). But his successor Gonzalo Sánchez de Lozada (1993–97) had been the architect of orthodox adjustment in the mid-1980s and was now determined to complete the neoliberal reform program. He supported pension privatization, as foreshadowed in his electoral program (*Plan de Todos* 1993: 80–81). Thus, the Bolivian and Salvadoran reform teams won chief executive backing.

President Fujimori, by contrast, never really converted to neoliberalism. He viewed the extension of market principles into the social sectors with particular skepticism (interviews with Du Bois 2002, De los Heros 2002, and Peñaranda 2002; Roggero 1993: 69, 96, 101; Cruz Saco 1998: 169). Only the promise of pragmatic benefits derived from the representativeness heuristic, especially the postulated spillover effects on savings, investment, and growth, managed to sway this lukewarm chief executive (interviews with Du Bois 2002, De los Heros 2002, and Peñaranda 2002; Ortiz de Zevallos et al. 1999: 36, 42–45, 48–49). Moreover, reform proponents flew in José Piñera, the father of the Chilean model, who in a long conversation used his famous powers of persuasion to convince Fujimori (interview with De los Heros 2002; Roggero 1993: 88–92, 101–3). "The reform might not have been signed into law without José's assistance" (Boloña 1997: 1). In this case of ideological concerns, the positive balance sheet derived through the representativeness heuristic, presented in a personal encounter with a skillful promoter of the Chilean model, garnered presidential support.

The bureaucratic and political insulation of the fairly homogeneous change teams; support from government leaders, especially finance ministers and presidents; and the government's majority support in Congress (in Bolivia and El Salvador) or usage of executive decree powers (in Peru) prevented critics from successfully challenging these drastic reform projects. Societal interest groups and left-wing or populist parties were much less concerned with the financial and actuarial problems that prompted the pursuit of pension privatization. Instead, they emphasized distributional issues and defended acquired rights; in particular, sectors that received privileged treatment in established social security systems, such as small groupings of formal-sector workers, professionals, and civil servants, dug in their heels. They supported their opposition to radical pension reform by emphasizing the downsides of the Chilean model. To legitimate their views, they invited experts linked to the Chilean labor movement, who offered first-hand information on the problems of the private pension system (see, e.g., ILDIS 1996). They pointed especially to its limited population coverage and heavy transition cost. In this way, they sought to counterbalance the overoptimistic assessments that the Chilean consultants hired by the Bolivian, Peruvian, and Salvadoran governments provided (interview with Fernández Fagalde 2002).

The most radical and mobilized opposition to pension privatization arose from the bureaucrats and employees of established pension institutes. While the presidents of these institutions—with limited success—sought to resist the strong pressure from economy ministries in intrastate bargaining, many employees took a societal route and used their unions to protest against privatization. Social service providers are nowadays among the best organized and most militant segments of Latin American labor movements (Nelson 2004: 33–36; Grindle 2004: chap. 5). But in Bolivia, El Salvador, and Peru, these combative groups did not win much support from broader union confederations or other sectors of civil society. The economic crisis of the 1980s, the rigors of neoliberal adjustment, and the disruption of societal bonds caused by armed insurgency and state repression in El Salvador and Peru greatly weakened once-powerful labor movements. For instance, the Bolivian and Peruvian union confederations, which used to succeed in paralyzing the whole country, were mere shadows of their former selves (Balbi 1997; Eróstegui 1996; interviews with Camargo 2002 and Quiroga 2002; Mercado 1998: 176–77). Isolated, service provider unions were unable to stall pension privatization.

The reform teams also tried to shape public debate to their advantage. In El Salvador, political consultant Mark Klugmann, who had worked for years with Piñera, recommended to direct all attention to the problems of the old social security system, not the details of the reform plan. In this way, public opinion would see the urgent need for reform and accept privatization as a necessary solution, rather than dissecting the government's proposal (interviews with Brevé 2004, Ramírez 2004, and Tamayo 2004). In Peru, the Fujimori administration proceeded with greater transparency and published its reform plan in the official gazette. A contentious discussion ensued in the second half of 1992. But legislative decree powers, which the government had grabbed with its self-coup of April 1992, allowed the reform team to push its project ahead. The Bolivian and Salvadoran governments commanded majorities in Congress and therefore could defeat opposition to structural pension reform.

Thus, the lopsided distribution of power made it easy for the privatization projects inspired by the representativeness heuristic to go forward. After the Bolivian, Peruvian, and Salvadoran teams had embraced the Chilean model and obtained support from their political superiors, their governments' positions of strength allowed them to disregard fundamental opposition. Defenders of the status quo found little resonance for their arguments. The sanguine assessments suggested by cognitive shortcuts carried the day.

The Heuristic of Anchoring: Limited Modifications of the Chilean Model

While unable to block privatization, opponents had some success in getting the Bolivian, Peruvian, and Salvadoran governments to introduce limited modifications that made the reform laws diverge in some points from the Chilean original. Besides political pressures, technical considerations can prompt such adaptations. All three countries differed significantly from Chile in socioeconomic characteristics. Their formal labor markets were much smaller, their capital markets highly underdeveloped. Comprehensive rationality would have called for profound adaptations of the Chilean model to the specific needs of these backward nations. Emulators were also well-advised to avoid problems that had become apparent during the implementation of Chile's private pension system. Learning from the frontrunner's mistakes would improve decision quality.

Given these rational reasons for redesigning the Chilean model, it is noteworthy that the privatization decisions in Bolivia, El Salvador, and Peru stayed very close to the original. Indeed, Bolivia and El Salvador followed Chile in enacting substitutive reforms. They phased out the PAYG system and forced (new) workers to affiliate with private pension funds (Mesa-Lago 1997; Mesa-Lago and Müller 2002; Queisser 1998: 133). And President Fujimori decided only at the very last minute to keep the old system open and allow workers a choice (interview with Romero 2002). Yet while he ended up not heeding the pleas of his economic aides and their Chilean advisers to close the old system, the Peruvian reform replicated the Chilean model in many other respects. In fact, change team members in all three countries stressed that their projects largely followed the rules and regulations approved in Chile. "We took 90 percent [of the new system] directly from Chile," including the acronym AFP (interview with Du Bois 2002; similar interviews with Bonadona 2002, Galindo 2002, Gottret 2002, León 2002, Pantoja 2002, Ramírez 2004, Romero 2002, Salinas 2002, Solórzano 2004, Tamayo 2004, and Vargas 2002; FMI 1992: 2; Kotlikoff 1994: 1; Muñoz 2000: 452; Mesa-Lago and Durán 1998: 7).

Staying so close to the Chilean model was a product of the heuristic of anchoring. As experimental subjects use any cue—even an arbitrarily given hint—to guide their judgments (Epley and Gilovich 2002), so boundedly rational decision-makers stuck to the original blueprint and were reluctant to introduce changes. Social security reform is complicated; modifications require considerable computational effort. Decision-makers would need to investigate the adaptation's compatibility with other components of the project; revise the detailed rules for implementing the new system; and perhaps rerun the simulations of fiscal transition costs. It was much easier to replicate the Chilean model and introduce changes only when unavoidable, especially due to political pressures.

Anchoring explains why the first privatization projects in all three countries largely imitated Chile's blueprint. Domestic reformers followed the advice of Chilean consultants and hesitated to introduce significant alterations out of their own initiative. In fact, many team members hailed from economic agencies and lacked training in social security. Thus, the demands of comprehensive rationality could not overcome the inertial force of bounded rationality. For instance, the draft bill that Bolivia's first reform team in 1993 left behind for the incoming government was exceedingly similar to the Chilean system. It provided for full-scale privatization, closed the established system to new entrants, opened the pension market to private fund administrators, created a regulatory agency modeled on Chile's Superintendency of AFP, and instituted a governmental minimum pension guarantee to protect poorer affiliates (Exposición de Motivos 1993; see also Ayuda Memoria 1993). The Salvadoran proposal constituted a similarly faithful copy of the Chilean model (Mesa-Lago and Durán 1998: 6–7; Comisión para la Reforma 1996). And the first privatization decree that the Fujimori government passed in November 1991 mostly replicated the Chilean original yet kept the established PAYG system open and thus created a parallel scheme (Créase Sistema Privado de Pensiones 1991). Specifically, this decree copied a project elaborated for Fujimori's main opponent in the 1990 presidential contest, neoliberal Mario Vargas Llosa, which in turn was strongly inspired by the Chilean model (Roggero 1993: 20, 36, 84; Boloña 1995: 78; interviews with Roggero 2002, Cortez 2002, and Peñaranda 2002; Ortiz de Zevallos et al. 1999: 38). Thus, these initial projects stood out for imitation rather than innovation.

Certainly, Bolivian, Peruvian, and Salvadoran team members asked Chilean consultants what changes they themselves would recommend, based on years of experience with a private pension system (interviews with Mercado 2002 and Pantoja 2002). Predictably, however, experts who had staked their professional reputation on the Chilean model were unwilling to admit many "mistakes" and therefore had few modifications to propose (interview with Peñaranda 2002). Instead, Chilean consultants mostly advised against changes proposed by other actors.

For instance, José Piñera urged Peru's pension reformers to close the established system and not give affiliates a choice between a public and a private scheme (interviews with Peñaranda 2002 and Romero 2002).

This advice was directed against the first privatization advocate under the Fujimori government, Congressman Mario Roggero, who in line with the very name of his political grouping, Vargas Llosa's "Liberty Movement" (Movimiento Libertad), wanted to allow affiliates such a free choice (Roggero 1993; interview with Roggero 2002). IPSS President Castañeda Lossio, who had rescued his agency from a severe financial and administrative crisis (Ausejo 1995), also lobbied President Fujimori to preserve the PAYG system. By contrast, Piñera recommended closing the public scheme and forcing new affiliates to join private pension funds. In this way, he ironically departed from the liberal maxim of freedom of choice, as the Chilean model had done. Typically, the economists dominating Peru's reform team followed Piñera's advice and proposed to bar new entrants from the public system. Thus, even on design questions debated during the elaboration phase, change teams remained largely anchored to the Chilean blueprint.

On some specific issues, however, even Chilean consultants recommended modifications. For instance, they advised Bolivian, Peruvian, and Salvadoran pension reformers to grant the regulatory agency that would supervise the private pension funds greater institutional independence and strength than Chile had originally done (interview with Romero 2002). Furthermore, they admitted that the Chilean system had drawn incessant criticism over the high administrative fees charged by private pension funds. This issue was of special concern in Bolivia, South America's poorest nation. Exorbitant charges would deter affiliation and thus further restrict the private pension market, which was already limited severely by the small size of the formal labor sector. The reform team of the Sánchez de Lozada administration therefore sought to force AFP commissions down (interviews with Gottret 2002, Grandi 2002, Mercado 2002, and Pantoja 2002; Mercado 1998: 152, 168). Since Chilean consultants confirmed that AFPs needed high charges to fund the extensive marketing efforts with which they sought to attract affiliates away from competing AFPs (Claro y Asociados 1994: 6–8; see also Vittas and Iglesias 1992: 5, 9, 22–24, 35), the Bolivian government decided to restrict competition. In fact, technical studies showed that the tight regulation of pension fund investments kept AFPs from competing on issues of risk and return (Kotlikoff 1994: 1). Competition instead focused on "frivolous" aspects such as expensive promotional campaigns, including gifts for people who switched AFPs (cf. Berstein and Ruiz 2005). Since competition did not fulfill its purpose of giving consumers an effective choice on the main dimensions of the product, Bolivia licensed only two AFPs, assigning half the population to each (Mercado 1998: 152, 168; Guérard and Kelly 1997: 103–23; Von Gersdorff 1997: 14–18).

This temporary suspension of competition, necessary for making a private pension system viable in an unusually limited market, was one of the few significant deviations from the Chilean model that Bolivian, Peruvian, and Salvadoran reformers introduced as a result of technical considerations, not political pressures. Chilean consultants themselves offered supportive information that helped to prompt this modification. Thus, the guardians of the Chilean model "authorized" this change. In all other major respects, the initial privatization projects in Bolivia, El Salvador, and Peru closely followed the original. Thus, bounded rationality induced the reform teams to keep revisions at a minimum; the heuristic of anchoring tied them to the Chilean model.

In later stages of the decision-making process, however, political pressures forced some further modifications. In Peru, mobilized unions and—more importantly—IPSS President Castañeda Lossio opposed pension privatization. Since Castañeda impressively improved the IPSS's performance (Ausejo 1995), he had considerable clout inside the government. In fact, President Fujimori had ideological reservations about handing over social services to private companies (interviews with De los Heros 2002, Peñaranda 2002, and Du Bois 2002; Graham 1998: 113–15). Facing strong pressure for full-scale privatization from Economy Minister Carlos Boloña, he devised a last-minute compromise. He authorized private pension funds by decree-law but maintained the IPSS scheme, giving affiliates a free choice (interviews with Peñaranda 2002 and Romero 2002). In this way, Fujimori sought to please both sides. While this parallel public and private scheme significantly modified the Chilean model (and was opposed by Chilean consultants and the WB: interviews with Peñaranda 2002, Romero 2002, and Roggero 2002; Kane 1995: 2, 9), it required only a few changes in the draft bill. Thus, it was easy for boundedly rational decision-makers to enact.

In Bolivia, political calculations and pressures also produced some further deviations from the Chilean original. Above all, President Sánchez de Lozada ("Goni") combined pension privatization with a universalistic scheme of old-age protection, which paid every citizen above sixty-five years of age US$248 per year, corresponding to 42 percent of the minimum wage (Mercado 1998: 155–56, 159–60; Müller 2004: 10; Graham 1998: 34, 151–60, 167). Since social security coverage in Bolivia is exceedingly limited, this "solidarity bond" (BONOSOL) sought to alleviate widespread poverty for equity reasons. Extending social benefits to long-neglected sectors also promised great electoral payoffs; this "generosity" indeed helped Goni win reelection in 2002 (Müller 2004).

Last but not least, the BONOSOL allowed Goni to counter noisy criticism from unions and leftist sectors, which claimed that individual retirement accounts would destroy bonds of solidarity and leave many Bolivians unprotected from the rigors of the labor market (see Fundación Milenio 1994: 4; Manz 1996: 79–82; in general Kohl 2004). By "taking the wind out of the sail" of these accusations, this equity-enhancing scheme made pension privatization politically viable in a nation whose social structure differed markedly from Chile's (interviews with Peña Rueda 2002, Mercado 2002, and Salinas 2002; Graham 1998: 151–68). Thus, political and tactical calculations led pension reformers in this unusually poor country to go beyond the Chilean model. Yet they did so simply by addition, not modification. The BONOSOL did not affect the private pension system as such but merely sought to make it politically acceptable.

El Salvador followed the Chilean original even more closely and kept alterations particularly limited. Because the Calderón government held a majority in parliament, it did not feel compelled to make concessions to the opposition, which rejected privatization (interview with Solórzano 2004). The administration also refused to consider the proposal of a center-left think tank and international pension specialist Carmelo Mesa-Lago to institute a mixed system combining an extensive public pillar with a new private pillar. Since the change team was determined to resolve the social security issue once and for all and thus unburden the political agenda—a goal that is attractive to boundedly rational decision-makers—it was unwilling to retain the public scheme (interviews with Brevé 2004, Daboub 2004, and Solórzano 2004). In fact, it closed the old system more quickly than Chile had done. It also adopted a number of other rules that were stricter than the original (Mesa-Lago and Durán 1998: 7). In this way, it sought to limit fiscal transition costs. Thus, its political strength allowed the Salvadoran government to be more tight-fisted than the dictatorial Pinochet regime.

Even the Salvadoran government, however, had to give in to some blatantly self-interested pressures from strategically placed groupings inside the state. For instance, on the day of the scheduled vote in Congress, Supreme Court judges faxed a message that they would look kindly upon privatization if pensioners who continued to work—as many Supreme Court justices did—were guaranteed a benefit provided in the old system. Concerned that the judiciary could strike down the whole law as unconstitutional, the government felt obliged to give in to this blackmail (interview with Ramírez 2004; for a similar concession, see interview with Solórzano 2004). For similar reasons, reformers in most countries—including Chile itself—exempted the armed forces from the rigors of privatization and maintained their exceedingly generous, privileged pension schemes.

In conclusion, political considerations prompted Bolivian, Peruvian, and Salvadoran pension reformers to modify the Chilean model in some significant ways. But these changes left the core of the private system intact; all three countries closely followed Chile in instituting individual pension funds administered by private operators and in making benefits strictly dependent on accumulated contributions and investment returns. Instead of reshaping the structure of the Chilean model, adaptations merely affected the extension or administration of the private system. For instance, Peru's parallel scheme exposed AFPs to competition from the public system, and Bolivia's admission of only two AFPs made privatization workable in a particularly small market.

In emulating the Chilean original faithfully, Bolivian, Peruvian, and Salvadoran reformers applied the heuristic of anchoring. This model offered a convenient, coherent blueprint that they were reluctant to redesign. They avoided profound changes, which would require great computational effort (cf. Epley and Gilovich 2002). Applying bounded rationality, they preferred imitation over innovation. Since a neat model was cognitively available and certified as successful by the representativeness heuristic, they enacted it to the greatest extent that was technically and politically feasible, making significant alterations only under duress. Anchoring clearly tied them to the Chilean model.

Implementing Chilean-style privatization with few adaptations in settings that differed greatly from Chile was arguably suboptimal. Comprehensive rationality called for much more profound adaptations or a fundamental rethinking of the privatization proposal. Many of the hopes attached to this reform have indeed remained unfulfilled. The new pension systems have achieved only narrow coverage; large segments of the population, working in the countryside or the urban informal sector, have remained excluded (Morón and Carranza 2003: 47–48, 82–84; Escobar and Nina 2004: ii, 12–13; Mesa-Lago 2003: 4–7; Gill, Packard, and Yermo 2004: xvii, 3–8, 89–104; WB IEG 2006: x, xvi, 38, 56). The small number of active contributors has limited economies of scale, raised the operational costs of the private system, as reflected in high administrative fees (Morón and Carranza 2003: 49, 93–107; Mesa-Lago 2003: 14–17), and fueled the concentration of the AFP market (interview with Ramírez 2004).

Also, the underdevelopment of the Bolivian, Peruvian, and Salvadoran capital markets has restricted investment opportunities for AFPs. The reluctance of private businesses to negotiate shares in the stock exchange has kept AFPs from injecting capital into productive ventures; therefore, pension funds have given little impulse to economic development (Morón and Carranza 2003: 72–74; Mesa-Lago 2003: 19–21). In fact, unexpectedly large transition costs induced governments to force AFPs to buy treasury bonds that financed existing pension obligations. Workers' forced savings were thus channeled into the public, not the private, sector (Mesa-Lago 2003: 8–13; Gottret 1999). In sum, the simple transplantation of the Chilean model and failure to adapt it thoroughly to unpropitious settings foiled many promises attached to this foreign import.

Conclusion

Cognitive shortcuts profoundly shaped social security reform in Bolivia, El Salvador, and Peru. The availability heuristic focused decision-makers' attention on the Chilean model of radical privatization. The representativeness heuristic induced them to overextrapolate the initial benefits achieved by Chile's new system and to hold privatization responsible for the overall success of the Chilean economy. And anchoring led them to follow the Chilean model closely and limit adaptations to the specific needs of their own countries.

Cognitive heuristics held particular sway because these reforms were elaborated by small, fairly homogeneous change teams, composed mostly of economic agency officials. Given the financial problems and institutional weakness plaguing existing social security agencies, the powerful economy ministries managed to control reform design and marginalize established social security experts. Thus, economic and financial concerns prevailed, making the Chilean model look especially good. Equity dimensions, on which radical privatization performed less well, played little role. In fact, many reform team members had minimal background in the pension area. These novices were especially susceptible to using cognitive shortcuts to process the ample information they received about a striking innovation. The unprecedented nature of Chilean-style privatization and lack of an extensive track record exacerbated uncertainty and thus reinforced the tendency to rely on heuristics. And the limited diversity of the change teams allowed the individual inferences suggested by cognitive shortcuts to stand uncorrected. Thus, structural and institutional factors provided the setting for the heuristics of availability, representativeness, and anchoring to shape reform elaboration.

Moreover, the Bolivian, Peruvian, and Salvadoran governments had the political clout to guarantee approval for privatization bills. Sánchez de Lozada and Calderón Sol commanded majority support in Congress, and Fujimori used a decree-law right before a newly elected Constituent Assembly started its sessions. Thus, the distribution of political power allowed the reform proposals inspired by cognitive heuristics to turn into law.

The Long Stalemate over Pension Privatization in Brazil

Causal Mechanisms in a Different Context

As in Bolivia, El Salvador, and Peru, cognitive heuristics shaped social security policy in Brazil. But a different constellation of political forces precluded a replication of the Chilean model. Thus, the same causal mechanisms operated, but they produced a divergent outcome in this different setting.

Chile's bold reform, enacted in the same subregion, was uniquely available in Brazil. From the late 1980s onward, it occupied the center of the pension reform debate. Friend and foe alike treated it as an obligatory point of reference. Thus, the availability heuristic clearly held sway in Brazil. And as in Bolivia, El Salvador, and Peru, experts concerned primarily with the financial and economic aspects of social security, especially technocrats from the powerful finance and planning ministries, followed the representativeness heuristic in extolling the benefits and promise of Chile's innovation. They claimed that social security privatization would boost domestic savings and investment and thus lift Brazil out of the economic stagnation of the early 1990s (Collor 1991: 91; MTPS 1991: 26; Reforma da Previdência 1992: 5–6; FIPE 1994: 15–16; Martone et al. 1994: 107; Oliveira, Beltrão, and Marsillac 1996: 1, 7; interview with Bornhausen 2003). As in Bolivia, El Salvador, and Peru, this embrace of the Chilean model was based not on systematic, balanced analyses, but on information provided by Chilean privatization advocates (IL 1991; interview with Zylberstajn 2003).

But contrary to Bolivia, El Salvador, and Peru, the pension privatization proposals inspired by the representativeness heuristic did not carry the day, even inside the Brazilian state. The powerful Social Security Ministry (Ministério da Previdência e Assistência Social, MPAS)[14] tenaciously resisted Chilean-style reform and mobilized allies in Congress and society to block it (Weyland 1996b: 70–75; Coelho 1999). Contrary to the Bolivian, Peruvian, and Salvadoran social security institutes, the MPAS had considerable political clout and could not be marginalized by the economy ministries. The segment of the pension system for which it held primary responsibility, the "general regime" for private-sector workers and employees, did not suffer from acute financial problems for many years (Ornélas and Vieira 1999: 33). In fact, until the successful stabilization plan of 1994 (Plano Real), accelerating inflation allowed the MPAS to compress effective benefit values and thus control expenditures.

---

[14] The ministry's name changed frequently. To avoid confusion, I use MPAS throughout.

The absence of a financial crisis limited economic ministries' leverage. And since Brazil's clientelistic politicians used the pension system for patronage purposes, the MPAS commanded substantial support. In particular, many politicians wanted to keep social security in public hands and rejected privatization. MPAS officials also collaborated with the National Association of Auditors of Social Security Contributions (ANFIP), a very active and surprisingly influential defender of the established system, which managed to mobilize further opposition in society as well (ANFIP 1993, 1995, 2003). For all these reasons, the MPAS could not be excluded from reform deliberations, and its efforts to maintain the state role in social security found considerable backing.

Moreover, the MPAS had a cadre of well-trained specialists with impressive expertise and a strong esprit de corps. A close-knit group of technocrats had directed Brazilian social security policy for decades (Malloy 1979: 74–79, 84–87, 126–30; Hochman 1992). Starting with the democratic transition of the 1980s, a new generation of experts had taken over the baton and become socialized into the MPAS's mission of guaranteeing social protection for the population. Although these specialists were attentive to financial and economic concerns (interview with Moraes 1995), they were determined to defend the basic outline of Brazil's welfare state, and they commanded the necessary expertise to negotiate with the economy ministries on a fairly equal footing.

MPAS experts pointed to the downsides of the Chilean model and thus countered the enthusiasm for pension privatization prevailing among the economy ministries. They argued that a private system would leave large numbers of poor people unprotected. They also stressed the huge transition cost of radical reform, which precarious economic stability throughout the 1990s turned into a prohibitive obstacle (Carvalho 1993: 120–36; Moraes 1995: 240–41; interview with Moraes 1995).

Thus, the sanguine assessment of the Chilean model that the representativeness heuristic suggested to economic generalists confronted negative evaluations advanced by social security experts, whose institutional mission highlighted the social dimensions of Chile's experience. For almost ten years, Brazil's pension reform debate was caught in this divide. The cleavage inside the government gave rise to a prolonged stalemate. While the economy ministries often proved stronger in intrabureaucratic struggles, the MPAS countered this advantage by mobilizing support in Congress and society. All efforts to emulate the Chilean model therefore failed.

Brazil emerged from this lengthy impasse only when another reform model suddenly became available, namely, the notional defined-contribution scheme developed in Sweden. Even faster than Bolivia, El Salvador, and Peru embraced Chilean-style privatization, Brazil adopted this hybrid option.

The Emergence of Privatization Projects and Their Blockage

Radical social security reform was first proposed under the government of Fernando Collor de Mello (1990–92), who initiated market-oriented adjustment to put Brazil back on a dynamic path toward economic growth. In his turn to neoliberalism, Collor wanted to revamp the 1988 constitution, which enshrined many nationalist, protectionist, and so-cial-democratic rules in regulating vast areas of economy and society. In social security, he intended to roll back the concession of improved ben-efits, which he saw as a threat to financial equilibrium.

These fiscal concerns and economic goals made many Brazilians re-ceptive to the Chilean model of pension privatization. Given geographic proximity and long-standing contacts between the two nations, this bold scheme was uniquely available in Brazil. In the early 1990s, a number of Chilean specialists, including José Piñera, promoted their innovation in Brazil, and many Brazilian experts visited Chile to study the new pension system first-hand (interviews with Bornhausen 2003, Mendonça 2003, Solimeo 2003, and Zockun 2003). As a result, Brazilian econo-mists and social security specialists clearly came to see the Chilean model as an obligatory point of reference. Indeed, a Brazilian business organi-zation commissioned a study from a Chilean consultant, Augusto Igle-sias. But given ample technical expertise inside Brazil, other proposals to emulate the Chilean blueprint were elaborated by domestic specialists (in-terviews with Bornhausen 2003, Mendonça 2003, and Zylberstajn 2003).

The inspiration in the Chilean model was particularly obvious in the proposal of the Instituto Liberal (IL), a neoliberal think tank sustained by big business groups, which advocated total privatization—essentially, the simple imitation of the Chilean original (IL 1991: 15–19, 38–43; see also Faro 1993). But the IL proposal was unusually radical for Bra-zil,[15] where pronounced social inequality and widespread poverty made it impossible for large sectors of the population to finance a minimally decent pension out of their own pocket (interviews with Mattos 2003 and Zylberstajn 2003). In fact, Brazil was unusual in Latin America in extending social security coverage to poor rural sectors. Since small farmers could not pay regular insurance contributions, privatization would have threatened their social protection. Moreover, private pen-sion funds had little interest in administering millions of low-value ac-

---

[15] IL leader Roberto Bornhausen claimed that the IL made a deliberately radical proposal to provoke some change but never thought it would be fully enacted (interview 2003).

counts (Giambiagi, Oliveira, and Beltrão 1996: 67). Last but not least, maintaining a basic PAYG system would limit transition costs; given Brazil's precarious fiscal situation, only partial privatization was financially viable.

Therefore, most Brazilian advocates of privatization proposed mixed systems. A public PAYG scheme would cover low-income groups, though with stricter rules than in the 1988 constitution. Above a threshold of three to five times the minimum wage (approximately US$210–350), private pension funds would operate, perhaps in competition with pension funds run by the state and societal associations (Castro and Brito 1992: 46–48, 115–20; FIESP/CIESP 1993: 11–12; Oliveira, Beltrão, and Medici 1992). Thus, Brazilian reform projects diverged from the Chilean original by assigning the state a much greater role in basic social protection.

The Collor government took the lead in designing a privatization plan along these lines. It sought to confine the existing public scheme to guaranteeing redistributive social protection for poorer groups and thus induce better-off sectors to open individual pension accounts (Collor 1991: 93–94; interview with Collor 1995). The new head of the social security agency, José Arnaldo Rossi, who had close links to the private insurance sector, turned these ideas into a package of draft bills (Reforma da Previdência 1992; MTPS 1991: 23–29; interview with Rossi 1992; Oliveira 1991).

But Collor's ambitious market reform program, which pursued a fundamental change of Brazil's development model through one "big project" (*projetão*), elicited vocal opposition from a host of interest groups. Since the president needed to enact his proposal by constitutional amendment, which required super-majorities, he faced high legal hurdles. Brazil's fragmented party system and Collor's lack of a firm congressional coalition made it impossible to win the necessary backing. The market reform plan therefore died in committees (interview with Moreira 1995). And as MPAS officials opposed to social security privatization mobilized their supporters in parliament, Collor never submitted Rossi's draft bills to Congress (interviews with Carvalho 1992, Gabriel 1992, Britto 1992, Kandir 1992, and Stephanes 1992). A later effort to resume pension reform (MEFP 1992: 22–32; interview with Mattos 1992) was stillborn due to the political weakness of President Collor, who faced a serious corruption scandal and was forced from office in late 1992.

Continued Impasse over Pension Reform

Collor's ignominious failure did not halt the push for pension privatization. Instead, the worrisome spending increases mandated by the 1988 constitution and the special availability of the Chilean model induced academic research institutes, business associations, and think tanks to redouble their efforts (e.g., FIPE 1994; Martone et al. 1994: chap. 6; Medici, Oliveira, and Beltrão 1993a). Former members of the Collor government also worked through societal organizations, such as a moderate union confederation (Força Sindical 1993: 183–202). All these privatization projects were clearly inspired by the Chilean precedent. Their proliferation, which reflected the density of civil society and depth of technical expertise in Brazil, was a response to the blockage of the governmental proposal; this stalemate prompted additional actors to jump into the fray.

Privatization advocates in state and society wanted to advance their projects in the constitutional revision of 1993–94, which allowed for amending the 1988 charter without super-majorities (cf. Jobim 1994: 19–21, 33). But aware of the controversial nature of radical reform, the economy ministries pursued a two-step strategy. They tried to use the constitutional revision for removing from the charter many specific pension rules that hindered privatization, but not for stipulating that change itself (cf. Blay 1993). Later, less visible infraconstitutional legislation could lower the income threshold for public benefit provision and thus open space for private pension funds. This goal to "deconstitutionalize" social security found support from some congressional leaders aligned with the government (Jobim 1994: 36, 38–39).

But opponents of privatization, including MPAS officials (Carvalho 1993: 120–36), sought to forestall threats to the public pension system. They prepared alternative reform proposals designed to fix problems in the existing system and thus protect it from attacks. The MPAS undertook a huge research effort, inviting numerous domestic experts and a few foreign specialists for presentations, debates, and conferences (MPS 1993–94). But only one European participated; attention remained focused on the Chilean model and, to a much lesser extent, the Chilean-inspired Argentine experience (see especially Azeredo 1994). Thus, the special availability of Chile's privatization continued to overshadow other potential sources of inspiration and to captivate—and polarize—the pension reform debate in Brazil.

As opponents of privatization mobilized, leftist parties strenuously obstructed the whole constitutional revision. Many legislators from the governmental coalition were reluctant to touch politically sensitive areas such as social security, especially in light of upcoming elections. The weak government of Itamar Franco (1992–94) was therefore unable to advance toward social security reform.

When Fernando Henrique Cardoso won the presidency in a landslide and assembled a large majority coalition in Congress, the opportunity for moving toward pension privatization finally seemed to have arrived. The new administration resumed the two-step plan and submitted to Congress an amendment to deconstitutionalize social security and make major parametric changes, especially in the overly generous, deficit-ridden regime for civil servants (MPAS 1995a, 1995b; Moraes 1995). This tightening of entitlements would bring immediate fiscal savings and lower the transition costs of the privatization efforts planned as a second step. But the MPAS continued to oppose radical change (interview with Moraes 1995), and special interests well-represented in Congress resisted the governmental project to protect their privileges (Weyland 1996b: 75–78).

The reform effort therefore turned into a drawn-out battle over parametric adjustments. In years of negotiation, the Cardoso administration made little headway, due to weak party discipline among its supporters and the obstructionism of the leftist opposition (Coelho 1999; Kingstone 2003; Kay 2001: 6–10). The watered-down bill that finally passed was widely seen as insufficient for resolving the looming problems of Brazil's social security system. It did, however, rein in the most excessive privileges in the special regime for civil servants and delete from the constitution the rules for computing pension benefits for private-sector workers.

This frustrating experience, which demonstrated the great difficulty of enacting parametric reforms, prompted the resumption of the privatization project (Giambiagi, Oliveira, and Beltrão 1996: 65, 68). Thus, due to the cognitive unavailability of alternative options, such as the NDC scheme designed in Europe, Brazil's pension reform debate continued to be caught in the dilemma of adjusting the existing system vs. adopting Chilean-style privatization. As the parametric approach proved unpromising, the pendulum swung back toward privatization efforts. Cardoso therefore convened a commission of economic experts that met in great secrecy to elaborate a drastic reform (Pinheiro 2004: 128–29; Drummond 1998). The group's leader, André Lara Resende, took his main inspiration from the World Bank's (1994a) pension program and outlined a multipillar system (Resende 1998; Pinheiro 2004: 129).

The commission's deliberations were dominated by a team from the government's policy think tank (Instituto de Pesquisa Econômica Aplicada—IPEA) and its statistical institute, who had for years proposed to confine public pension provision to a low income threshold and thus enable private pension funds to emerge (Oliveira, Beltrão, and Medici 1992; Medici, Oliveira, and Beltrão 1993a). These proposals, which took inspiration from the Chilean model yet adapted it to Brazil's particularly unequal society, finally found receptivity and turned into the cornerstone of the commission's plans (Oliveira, Beltrão, and Marsillac 1996; Oliveira, Beltrão, and Pasinato 1999; Giambiagi, Oliveira, and Beltrão 1996; Drummond 1998).

But the traditional opponents of social security privatization again offered resistance. While the commission's low profile prevented large-scale mobilization in society or Congress, the MPAS, which had initially been excluded from participation (interview with Moraes 2003), stressed the downsides of privatization. It questioned the political feasibility of Chilean-style reform and emphasized the huge transition cost, which experts put at 188–250 percent of GDP (MPAS SPS 1998; interviews with Carvalho 1999, Pinheiro 1999, and Moraes 2003). When this intrabureaucratic debate heated up, worsening financial problems exacerbated by the Asian and Russian crises of 1997–98 greatly increased the salience of this fiscal concern. Whereas the World Bank advocated pension privatization as crucial for Brazil's economic health in the long run, the IMF now opposed it out of fear for the short run (interviews with Pinheiro 1999 and Moraes 2003; Schwarzer 2003: 278–79; Pinheiro 2004: 130). Thus, one IFI blocked the proposal of another IFI. Due to these fiscal concerns, Brazil's economic agencies, which had initially supported the project, now vetoed it (interview with Moraes 2003).

Once again, Brazil was stuck on the thorny privatization issue. Social security seemed to require significant change, but the model of change that was cognitively available—a softer version of Chilean-style privatization—was financially and politically infeasible. This dilemma plagued Brazil's pension reform debate for almost a decade.

Availability Enhancement: The Sudden Appearance of the European NDC Scheme

At that point, however, an alternative reform model became available, extending the bounds of rationality and paving a way out of the logjam. In July 1998, two Brazilian pension specialists attended a seminar held by the World Bank and Harvard University and learned about the NDC system enacted in Sweden and Poland (Pinheiro 2004: 130–31; interviews with Pinheiro 1999 and Moraes 2003). This European innovation, which until then had remained off the radar screen of Brazilian policymakers, suddenly seemed to allow them to square the circle. By making pension benefits dependent on an individual's accumulated social security contributions (which are placed in a notional account), the NDC scheme can guarantee actuarial and financial equilibrium in a public pension system. Yet by using workers' contributions for paying current retirement benefits—that is, by applying pay-as-you-go financing—the NDC scheme avoids the huge transition cost of Chilean-style privatization. Thus, it promised to restore actuarial balance without creating prohibitive fiscal problems (interview with Pinheiro 1999; Najberg and Ikeda 1999: 279–86; Pinheiro 2004: 129–31).

This new model immediately stimulated great enthusiasm (MPAS SPS 1999), which—typically—was not based on systematic, thorough performance evaluations, but on the hope that an NDC scheme would turn decisions on entitlements into individual choices and thus remove tricky, controversial issues from the political agenda (Najberg and Ikeda 1999: 286; Pinheiro and Vieira 2000a: 31; 2000b: 11; interview with Pinheiro 1999); this expectation is particularly attractive to boundedly rational decision-makers. Thus, availability enhancement by an IFI, which introduced Brazilian experts to an innovative option that had hitherto escaped their attention, finally opened up a way out of the long-lasting pension reform dilemma. Only the sudden appearance of this new model, not domestic political constellations alone, can account for this new departure. Cognitive factors—first the long-standing focus on Chilean-style privatization, then availability enhancement by an IFI—crucially shaped Brazil's pension reform course.

MPAS experts quickly adapted the NDC scheme to Brazil's peculiarities, such as the precarious, legally questionable information on people's social security contributions before the mid-1990s. Furthermore, they designed an original solution for the problem of determining the "interest rate" for remunerating the contributions credited to notional pension accounts (interview with Moraes 1999). The novel formula discourages the premature retirements that were widespread in Brazil, especially among better-off affiliates, and that created severe financial strain. To guarantee actuarial equilibrium, it produces a low pension value for people who retire early, but guarantees much higher benefits for individuals who work into their sixties and contribute for many years (Pinheiro and Vieira 2000b). This ingenious mechanism, which was clearly a product of innovation, not imitation, leaves people a free choice about when to retire but forces each affiliate—and no longer society—to pay the price for this choice (Pinheiro 2004: 130–33). The NDC system thus promised to reduce a major resource drain (Amadeo 2000: 27–28; Schwarzer 2003b: 289; see even WB 2001b: 14, 19, 32–33, 61–67, 71–74; more skeptical Giambiagi and Castro 2003: 280–81, 290).

The Cardoso government managed to obtain congressional approval for enacting the NDC scheme in the general regime for private-sector workers. Although it preserved some privileges for special interests (Ornélas and Vieira 1999: 42; Pinheiro and Vieira 2000b: 17), this reform entailed a crucial step toward financial equilibrium in this social security program, which serves the largest number of Brazilians. The special regime for civil servants, by contrast, remains actuarially unbalanced, even after the courageous parametric reform that the new government of Luiz Inácio Lula da Silva (2003–present) quickly pushed through Congress at great political cost (see debate in Morhy 2003).

Yet despite this persistent problem and some renewed calls for drastic reform (Ribas 2003: 9–11; WB 2001b: 16–18), a return to the privatization agenda is unlikely. The availability of the NDC scheme has suddenly opened up an innovative, fiscally cost-free solution to the disequilibria afflicting social security. As even the president of Brazil's industrial confederation recognizes (Monteiro 2003: 222–23), the high transition costs will impede pension privatization à la Chile. Moreover, the privatization wave has already crested in Latin America. As ever more solid evidence casts doubt on important promises attached to Chilean-style reform (Nitsch and Schwarzer 1998),[16] the attraction of this model has diminished significantly (Schwarzer 2003: 237–43, 313–19; interviews with Schwarzer 2003 and Carvalho 2003). Brazil is unlikely to jump on the privatization bandwagon precisely as it slows down (cf. Giambiagi and Castro 2003: 266, 284, 290).

In conclusion, the special availability of the Chilean model and the unavailability of other options left Brazil's pension reform debate stalemated on the privatization issue for most of the 1990s. Concerned about actuarial and financial problems in the existing system, the economy ministries extolled the great promise of Chilean-style privatization suggested by the representativeness heuristic. But the MPAS, congressional politicians, and interest groups, who commanded considerable institutional strength and political weight, put priority on social goals, on which the Chilean model performed much less well. Several reform efforts therefore ran afoul of strenuous opposition. A way out of the impasse only opened up when World Bank "teaching" made another reform model cognitively available, namely, the European NDC scheme. Thus, while due to political context factors, decision outputs in Brazil differed clearly from the march toward pension privatization in Bolivia, El Salvador, and Peru, cognitive heuristics also played a crucial role in shaping the policy process.

Costa Rica's Penchant for Deliberation and Compromise

Whereas the bounds of rationality kept Brazil's pension reform debate for many years confined to the pros and cons of the Chilean model,

---

[16] The MPAS (2001: 9–47, 93–159) republished Barr's (2000) critical assessment, counterbalancing a more enthusiastic paper by the World Bank's pension reform team leader, Estelle James.

Costa Rican experts and policy-makers took a more proactive approach and designed a compromise acceptable to the diverse sociopolitical forces with a stake in this controversial issue. Inspired by Uruguay, they elaborated a mixed system that maintained the public pay-as-you-go scheme yet added a small scheme of obligatory individual retirement accounts. After internal negotiations that involved both the economy ministries and the powerful social security agency, the government submitted this proposal to consultation with interest groups and congressional politicians. Due to this careful preparation, parliament approved the reform by consensus. In line with the diversity of participants, the bounds of rationality were thus wider in Costa Rica than in Bolivia, El Salvador, Peru, and even Brazil.

Cognitive heuristics played an important role in starting the Costa Rican reform process. Even in this social-democratic polity, the Chilean model was highly available. The bold, striking nature of this regional innovation attracted specialists' attention. As a result, in 1989—right when Chilean-style privatization began to diffuse in Latin America— Costa Rica sent a group of specialists to study the new model first-hand. Given the institutional strength of the social security agency (Caja Costarricense de Seguro Social—CCSS), which commanded sufficient technical expertise to speak on equal terms with the economy ministries,[17] this group had a diverse composition: Three CCSS experts accompanied a Finance Ministry and a Planning Ministry official. The trip report reflected their different institutional interests. It highlighted the increase in savings widely attributed to the Chilean model, a benefit of special interest to the economy ministries; but it also advised against full-scale privatization because guaranteeing basic social protection for workers was an essential state task, indeed, the CCSS's institutional mission (Comisión Técnica de Pensiones 1990: 14–16; interviews with Aguilar 2004 and Valverde 2004). Thus, despite divergences in interest and focus, Costa Rican specialists paid great attention to the Chilean reform because the availability heuristic turned it into an obligatory point of reference in the region.

The report's emphasis on the increased savings credited to the Chilean model also shows that the representativeness heuristic was at work. Given their institutional mission, the economy ministries were especially receptive to a key promise associated with this innovation. But the social orientation of the CCSS counterbalanced these economic judgments. In fact, the report was remarkably silent on the other success of the Chilean

---

[17] Durán (interview 2004) stressed the lengthy training that CCSS experts undergo. Cercone (interview 2004) highlighted the institutional strength of this career bureaucracy; Martínez Franzoni (interview 2004), its political clout.

model, namely, pension funds' initially stellar rates of return. Furthermore, it attributed Chile's radical privatization decision to a particularly severe pension crisis and concluded that Costa Rica's less acute problems did not require such a drastic solution (Comisión Técnica de Pensiones 1990: 13–14; interviews with Aguilar 2004 and Jiménez 2004).

Indeed, many CCSS officials staunchly defended the basic outlines of the country's generous, universalistic welfare state.[18] Invoking its social-democratic values, they emphasized equity goals, a weak flank of the Chilean model (CCSS Gerencia de División Pensiones 1996: 1–4, 8–9; interviews with Aguilar 2004 and Carrillo 2004; see also Rodríguez 2001: 79). The CCSS also commissioned an annual opinion survey, which demonstrated widespread popular rejection of social security privatization (Garita Bonilla and González Varela 1992: 3, 21; Poltronieri 2003: 54, 61, 133; see also Lehoucq 1997: 63; Jiménez 2000: 260–62). Congruent with this virtual consensus among citizens, politicians from the two centrist parties wanted to maintain the existing system. While neoliberal ideas, pushed by groups of academics and experts, gradually advanced in economic and social policy, they encountered clear limits in this strong commitment to social equity, widely seen as a foundation of Costa Rica's successful democracy. Its national identity as an island of social peace and political liberty in a subregion suffering from frequent oppression and conflict centered on these social-democratic values (interviews with Aguilar 2004, Carrillo 2004, Céspedes 2004, Durán 2004, Jiménez 2004, and Rodríguez 2004; Aguilar and Durán 1996: 138, 140–41; Rodríguez 1996: 1, 6–9).

Thus, although the Chilean model was highly available in Costa Rica and the economic benefits highlighted by the representativeness heuristic made it attractive to the economy ministries, unshakeable values precluded its full imitation. Therefore, nobody seriously pursued such a complete restructuring. Even financial sectors that pushed hard for structural reform and initially advocated radical privatization quickly backed off when government officials pointed to the fiscal transition cost of such a dramatic change, which could result in increased interest rates or taxes (interviews with Jiménez 2004, Durán 2004, Céspedes 2004, Rodríguez 2004, and Carrillo 2004; Rodríguez 1996: 1–2; 2001: 79; Esquivel 1998).

Yet while total privatization was never on the agenda, obligatory private pension funds did appeal to the economy ministries, which were interested in promoting higher savings and boosting economic growth (Córdoba 1995: 1, 4, 25–27; see even Aguilar 1995: 2). The representativeness heuristic thus continued to create support for structural reform.

---

[18] Historical background in Programa Reforma Integral de Pensiones (1998a).

In particular, it induced the economy ministries to push for greater influence over social security policy, which had hitherto been the CCSS's domain. Thus, this cognitive shortcut reshaped the constellation of political forces in this issue area.

Furthermore, actuarial studies by domestic and international experts demonstrated that population aging would soon create increasing financial pressures on the established social security system (Pérez Montás 1994: 9–18; Durán 1995: 13–23; Aguilar and Durán 1996: 139, 145; Rodríguez 1996: 1; Rodríguez and Durán 1998; MIDEPLAN 1998a: 14–17). In fact, the special regimes for civil servants and school teachers were already suffering from acute financial problems (Pérez Montás 1994: 19–23; Tamburi 1994: 3–4; interviews with Aguilar 2004 and Rodríguez 2004; Rodríguez and Durán 1998).

These difficulties, promotional efforts by Chilean designers of social security privatization (interviews with Durán 2004, Rodríguez 2004, and Aguilar 2004), and pressure from the World Bank (Demirgüç-Kunt and Schwarz 1995) induced the government of José Figueres Olsen (1994–98) to create a pension reform commission. While an economic generalist without any background in the pension area headed this grouping, CCSS officials were well represented and had crucial input in the deliberations (interviews with Rodríguez 2004 and Durán 2004). They suggested some of the international consultants that the commission hired and pushed their own proposals, which preserved the principles of the existing public scheme. For instance, Róger Aguilar, a leading expert of the CCSS's actuarial division, long resisted the creation of obligatory individual retirement accounts and then advocated that the CCSS itself—not private companies—should run this second pillar (Aguilar 1994: 14–19; 1995: 6, 9; CCSS Gerencia de División Pensiones 1996: 1; CCSS 1998: 3, 10–14).

Another group in the CCSS, led by a young, well-trained actuary, Fabio Durán, was more flexible and proposed a very moderate version of privatization, precisely to forestall more radical reform (interview with Durán 2004). The commission's head, Adolfo Rodríguez Herrera, held similar views and closely cooperated with this current (see Rodríguez and Durán 1998; Rodríguez 2001). Rodríguez himself was highly attentive to equity issues; for instance, he organized an international seminar about social security coverage, a notoriously weak spot of the Chilean model (Rodríguez 1998b; Rodríguez 1998a: 15–16; see also Acuña Ulate and Durán 1994).

Thus, the change team included various state institutions. Contrary to Bolivia, El Salvador, and Peru, social security experts had a strong voice. Because the existing welfare state continued to perform well and the CCSS had tremendous institutional strength, economic experts did not monopolize the reform process. Moreover, the widespread consensus on social-democratic values immunized Costa Rican policy-makers against the radical Chilean model (interviews with Rodríguez 2004, Durán 2004, and Aguilar 2004; Rodríguez 2001: 79). Strong concern for social equity counterbalanced the overoptimistic judgments about the economic benefits of pension privatization that the representativeness heuristic suggested (e.g., Rodríguez and Durán 1998: 216–22).

Nevertheless, the availability heuristic highlighted the significance of the Chilean experience. Therefore, the reform commission entrusted a Chilean expert, Julio Bustamante, with elaborating a proposal for Costa Rica. But because Bustamante's plan looked suspiciously similar to the Chilean original (Bustamante 1995: 20, 23), not like the moderate reform requested, the commission rejected it out of hand (interviews with Durán 2004 and Valverde 2004). Upon the recommendation of the ILO representative in Costa Rica, the commission then contracted Rodolfo Saldain, the main architect of Uruguay's pension reform, the most moderate privatization in Latin America (interviews with Rodríguez 2004, Bonilla 2005, and Saldain 2006). Thus, while initially guided by the availability heuristic, Costa Rican pension reformers soon redirected their attention to the experience that most conformed to their own preferences. Drawing on its depth of expertise and breadth of international connections, the change team took a more proactive stance than its counterparts in Bolivia, El Salvador, Peru, and even Brazil.

Saldain helped the commission draw up a mixed system that maintained the public pension scheme and kept the new obligatory individual retirement accounts narrowly confined (Saldain 1996; interviews with Saldain 2006, Rodríguez 2004, Durán 2004, Bonilla 2005, Aguilar 2004, and Carrillo 2004). This proposal addressed the looming actuarial disequilibria in the existing public scheme. Because the government could not raise contribution rates at will or increase the retirement age significantly,[19] a gradual reduction in benefit values, especially for better-off sectors, appeared as the only viable option. Private pension funds would compensate for this reduction and thus guarantee the organized working and middle class a decent standard of living in old age. Individual retirement accounts would fill in for the slow, partial compression of the existing public scheme. Because private pension funds were also expected to yield economic benefits, the commission agreed on a mixed system with a broad, comprehensive public pillar and a small, yet gradually growing private pillar (interviews with Rodríguez 2004 and Saldain

---

[19] In 1996, a conflict over this issue turned unusually fierce, forcing the government to back down (interviews with Rodríguez 2004, Céspedes 2004, and Barahona 2004).

2006; Rodríguez 1996: 2, 8–10; Rodríguez and Durán 1998: 228–44; Rodríguez 2001: 83–87; MIDEPLAN 1998: 224–28, 232).

Interestingly, this compromise, which differed greatly from the Chilean original, garnered support precisely as an effort to forestall a more faithful emulation of the Chilean model. Its advocates argued that it was better to make a reasonable, moderate reform than be overwhelmed by more radical proposals later on (interview with Durán 2004). The specter of Chile turned Costa Rica's moderate proposal into the lesser evil. Thus, in addition to inspiring hopes in major macroeconomic benefits, Chile's drastic reform and the wave of emulation it triggered provided a crucial indirect impulse for Costa Rica's limited privatization project.

But by the time the reform design had been elaborated, the Figueres government lacked the political clout to push for partial privatization. In 1995, it had spent a great deal of political capital on reforming the special pension regime for school teachers, which was excessively generous and caused worrisome fiscal deficits (Programa Reforma Integral de Pensiones 1998b: 1, 31–37). Protests by striking teachers had created enormous political costs for the president. At the end of his term, he was unwilling to pursue a similarly controversial change in the CCSS (interview with Durán 2004; see also Lehoucq 1997: 63).

But the successor government of Miguel Ángel Rodríguez (1998–2002) quickly resumed the moderate reform project. Personal connections between the two change teams facilitated this continuity. Although two leading reformers under the Rodríguez government, Ronulfo Jiménez and Victor Hugo Céspedes, belonged to the Academia de Centroamérica, the main promoter of neoliberal thinking in Costa Rica (Hidalgo Capitán 2003: 92–94), they never pursued full-scale privatization à la Chile. They recognized that such a radical proposal—"although it may be technically speaking the best system" (interview with Céspedes 2004)—lacked political viability in this social-democratic country. They therefore embraced a mixed system as designed under the Figueres administration (interviews with Jiménez 2004, Céspedes 2004, Barahona 2004, and Carrillo 2004; see Proyecto de Ley 1999: 4–6; Jiménez 2000: 253–54).

But to engineer agreement to this compromise plan, Jiménez deliberately raised the specter of Chilean-style privatization as a "monster" to scare sociopolitical forces with divergent interests and viewpoints into accepting the mixed system as the lesser evil (MIDEPLAN 1998a: 33; interview with Jiménez 2004). This strategy indeed worked. In particular, the ILO representative who had assisted the reform commission of the Figueres administration managed to persuade recalcitrant union leaders that moderate privatization was the best solution they could realistically hope for (interviews with Jiménez 2004, Castro 2004, and Carrillo 2004; Jiménez 2000: 267). Thus, the special availability of the radical Chilean model and its well-known attraction to some Costa Rican sectors, derived from the representativeness heuristic, were important in making limited structural reform politically viable in this social-democratic country.

Specific aspects of the proposed mixed system indeed elicited much controversy. Disagreements centered on the rélative importance of the solidaristic public pillar vs. the individualistic second pillar that would be open to private pension companies (interview with Barahona 2004). Business sectors and the World Bank advocated a limited first pillar and a large, exclusively private second pillar (WB 1998b; see Jiménez 2000: 267). By contrast, CCSS officials, trade unionists, and party politicians resisted shrinking the existing public system. To diminish this conflict, the government shelved its plan to lower public pension values. Thus, the new individual retirement accounts would not be a partial substitution of the existing scheme, but a pure addition financed through existing social taxes (interview with Carrillo 2004; Rodríguez 2001: 85).

Furthermore, conforming to Costa Rica's consensual policymaking style, the Rodríguez government did not try to ram its proposal through Congress, as Bolivia's Sánchez de Lozada and El Salvador's Calderón Sol—not to speak of Peru's Fujimori—had done. Instead, it convened the political parties and a variety of interest groups to a wide-ranging "Concertation" in 1998 (MIDEPLAN 1998d). By allowing for interissue bargains and by getting societal groups with opposed interests to counterbalance each other, these negotiations indeed achieved consensus on a mixed system (MIDEPLAN 1998b: 10–20; interviews with Barahona 2004, Jiménez 2004, Céspedes 2004, and Castro 2004; Jiménez 2000; Castro 2001; see Proyecto de Ley 1999: 5).

The government had to make further concessions, however. Above all, societal associations and public institutions were allowed to create their own pension fund administrators; thus, the second pillar was not reserved for the private sector (Jiménez 2000: 256, 259; Castro 2001: 82–83). Based on these core agreements, the government elaborated a reform bill in consultation with congressional politicians and interest groups.[20] This cumbersome, slow process allowed the Rodríguez administration to pass social security reform, whereas its other important initiatives faltered on insurmountable opposition (interviews with Jiménez 2004, Barahona 2004, and Castro 2004).

---

[20] Castro (2001: 29, 52–53). Interestingly, governmental experts claimed that political parties lacked a clear stance on pension reform and played virtually no role in these deliberations, but they felt represented by politically aligned governmental experts (interviews with Céspedes 2004 and Durán 2004).

The new law fully preserved the PAYG system and strengthened it with measures to attract more affiliates and combat the evasion of contributions (Chaves Marín 1999: 8–9; Carrillo 2000). As a pure addition, it instituted obligatory individual retirement accounts open to private and public pension fund administrators. Interestingly, a large majority of affiliates chose public providers, and the law designated a public bank as the default option for people who indicated no choice. Therefore, more than 80 percent of affiliates are vested in public institutions (Martínez Franzoni and Mesa-Lago 2003: 27). Furthermore, the second pillar was funded through the reallocation of existing social contributions. Thus, the Costa Rican state avoided fiscal transition costs (MIDEPLAN 1998c: 228; Chaves Marín 1999: 11). In sum, while the Chilean model provided important direct and indirect impulses for pension privatization in Costa Rica, the new mixed system diverges greatly from the original. Due to ample technical capacity, the diverse composition of the change teams, and the firm commitment to social-democratic norms, the heuristic of anchoring did not tie down Costa Rican decision-makers.

Due to looming financial constraints (Martínez Franzoni and Mesa-Lago 2003: 69), however, the successor government of Abel Pacheco (2002–2006) resumed the less palatable side of the original reform plan and proposed the gradual reduction of public pension benefits, which turns the new second pillar into a partial replacement of the PAYG scheme. Lengthy, difficult negotiations among interest groups and state institutions, especially the CCSS, eventually hammered out a compromise that enacts this change and raises social security contributions (Grupo Técnico 2005; Martínez Franzoni 2005: 11–26; interviews with Martínez Franzoni 2004 and Carrillo 2004). With this reform, which proved the continued functionality of consensual policymaking in Costa Rica, the financial survival of social security seems ensured for decades to come.

In conclusion, Costa Rica's moderate pension reform was shaped by cognitive heuristics, though not as deeply as full-scale privatization in Bolivia, El Salvador, and Peru and the stalemated discussion in Brazil. The availability heuristic called decision-makers' attention to the Chilean model, and the representativeness heuristic associated it with high macroeconomic benefits—especially increased savings (interview with Carrillo 2004)—and thus created a nucleus of strong support. But the widespread, firm commitment to social-democratic values and the technical capacity and institutional strength of the CCSS, which was not marginalized by neoliberal experts from the economy ministries, ruled out radical reform. The internally diverse change team therefore searched for a politically viable reform plan, finding it in Uruguay's mixed system. After years of consultation and negotiation, this compromise proposal won congressional approval. It maintained the extensive public, solidaristic scheme, whose benefit levels the parametric reform of 2005 will diminish only gradually, and added individual pension accounts, which are run mainly by public institutions and societal associations, not private companies. Thus, while Costa Rica's reform emulated the core innovation of Chilean privatization, it did so in a highly modified form, displaying little anchoring to the original.

CONCLUSION

Cognitive heuristics shaped the spread of Chilean-style pension privatization, especially in Bolivia, El Salvador, and Peru, but also in Brazil and Costa Rica. Due to the availability heuristic, experts and policymakers in all five countries paid disproportionate attention to Chile's bold innovation and neglected other relevant reform experiences; in particular, the European NDC scheme stayed off their radar screen until the World Bank made it available in the late 1990s. And due to the representativeness heuristic, many decision-makers overextrapolated the initially stellar success of Chile's pension funds and attributed its increased savings and superb growth after 1985 to social security privatization. These excessively optimistic judgments induced the powerful economy ministries to push strongly for drastic reform. As the representativeness heuristic led them to claim control of the issue area, it altered the constellation of actors. Far from being epiphenomenal, cognitive shortcuts thus shaped "real" politics.

But the established social security agencies, which prioritized equity goals and sought to preserve the public pension system, were much less impressed with the alleged economic benefits of a private insurance scheme and emphasized instead its social disadvantages. These disagreements inside the state conditioned the advance of pension privatization. Where the social security agencies had limited technical capacity and little institutional weight, the economy ministries dominated reform design and—inspired by the representativeness heuristic—successfully promoted the emulation of the Chilean model. Anchored to the original blueprint, they introduced only limited modifications to adapt this foreign import to their country's needs. What gave the economy ministries this predominance and thus allowed the heuristics of availability, representativeness, and anchoring to shape the decision process and output so profoundly were the imbalance of institutional power between economic and social agencies and the severe financial and administrative problems plaguing the established pension system.

In Bolivia, El Salvador, and Peru, the social security agencies traditionally served for patronage purposes and therefore lacked strong technocratic cadres and a meritocratic bureaucracy. By contrast, the economy ministries long commanded a higher level of expertise, and the crisis and neoliberal adjustment of the 1980s and 1990s stimulated further recruitment of capable technocrats. These challenges also made the economy ministries' concerns for fiscal equilibrium and renewed growth more urgent than the equity goals advanced by social agencies. For these reasons, the economy ministries gained more power to impose their goals, which under the influence of the three cognitive heuristics came to include pension privatization.

In Brazil and Costa Rica, the availability heuristic also drew disproportionate attention to the Chilean model and the representativeness heuristic suggested its great attractiveness to the economy ministries. Cognitive shortcuts thus induced the economy ministries to get involved in social security policy and push for pension privatization. But social agencies had much greater clout than in Bolivia, El Salvador, and Peru. Equipped with considerable technical expertise and a solid institutional apparatus, they managed to counterbalance the privatizing pressure of the economy ministries. Also, the overall success of Costa Rica's welfare state and the special urgency of the equity goal in Brazil provided political protection against efforts to import the Chilean model. Because the social agencies could hold their own in intrastate bargaining and mobilize support in Congress and civil society, Chilean-style reform proved infeasible. In Brazil, an escape from the resulting stalemate over pension privatization opened up only when an IFI made an intermediate option—the European NDC scheme—cognitively available. In Costa Rica, widespread commitment to social-democratic values limited the disagreement and facilitated a compromise on a mixed system that diverged significantly from the Chilean original. Thus, operating in different political-institutional contexts, the same causal mechanisms, namely, cognitive heuristics, produced different emulation decisions.

In sum, inferential shortcuts profoundly shaped the diffusion of pension privatization, interacting with institutional and economic context factors. As the heuristics of availability, representativeness, and anchoring propelled the spread of policy innovations, bounded rationality prevailed. Experts and decision-makers clearly diverged from the ideal-typical postulates of comprehensive rationality. Rather than searching proactively for the relevant information and processing it in a systematic, balanced fashion, they commonly rely on heuristics that allow them to cope with information overload and uncertainty, but at the risk of significant distortions in judgments and decisions. The cognitive-psychological approach therefore can explain the wavelike diffusion of Chilean-style pension privatization better than can rational learning.

CHAPTER 5

External Pressures and International Norms in Health Reform

IN WHAT WAYS is principle diffusion in health care similar to model diffusion in social security, and in what ways does it differ? This chapter examines pressures from international financial institutions and the impact of new development norms; it thus assesses structural and constructivist arguments, as chapter 3 did for pension privatization. Chapter 6 then investigates whether comprehensive or bounded rationality prevails in decision making. In particular, do the heuristics of availability, representativeness, and anchoring shape health reform, as chapter 4 documented for social security reform?

Chapter 3 showed that IFI pressure helped advance pension privatization but was not the moving cause of model diffusion. These seemingly powerful institutions did not manage to force recalcitrant governments to comply with their exhortations. And they did not provide the main impetus pushing governments that agreed with the neoliberal agenda toward profound social security reform; instead, the decisive inspiration emanated from Chilean consultants with first-hand experience in pension privatization. The highly available Chilean model attracted tremendous attention in Latin America and triggered reform diffusion. The IFIs themselves jumped on this bandwagon only after it had already taken off.

Normative appeal did not propel pension privatization either. The ethic of individual responsibility never came close to gaining hegemony in the social security arena. As traditional norms of social solidarity retained a strong hold, reform advocates such as the World Bank avoided normative messages and promoted privatization with the instrumental promise to guarantee long-established functions with greater transparency and efficiency. The pragmatic goals to put social security on a solid financial foundation and attain macroeconomic benefits such as increased savings indeed carried the greatest weight in swaying presidents and parliaments.

How do these factors play out in health care? The absence of a clear, coherent reform model leads to a more diffuse, eclectic decision-making process. Since the availability heuristic does not focus policy-makers' attention on one singular model, they take inspiration from various sources, such as the recommendations of international organizations and new normative trends (both discussed in this chapter) as well as available country experiences (analyzed in chapter 6). Thus, whereas the Chilean model grabs attention in social security and leaves other influences in the background, health experts and decision-makers are exposed to variegated external inputs.

Reform efforts in the complex area of health care tend to be piecemeal. While pension privatization reshapes the social security system in one fell swoop, health reform rarely constitutes a bold, comprehensive transformation. Instead, governments change one component of the multidimensional health system at a time. Health reform is a drawn-out, gradual process, not a drastic break point like social security privatization. In fact, Chile's pension model became attractive because it promised to resolve problems once and for all. By contrast, health reform is a never-ending process. As prior modifications alter the mortality and morbidity profile and as technological progress makes new interventions feasible, the demands on and capabilities of health systems constantly change and require frequent adjustments.

The complexity of health care precludes a singular, highly available model and induces specialists to be receptive to various sources of inspiration. External pressures and international norm shifts therefore carry more weight than in social security. These mechanisms, which are not decisive for model diffusion, significantly affect principle diffusion, as chapter 2 stressed. First, whereas the IFIs cannot impose a clear blueprint on countries, they can nudge governments to advance toward general principles. In health care, the World Bank has managed to promote maxims derived from two basic goals, economic efficiency and social equity (WB 1993b), as discussed in chapter 1. While resisting more radical proposals for privatization, Bolivia, Costa Rica, and Peru, in particular, have enacted important changes that conform to the IFI agenda and that emerged partly out of discussions and negotiations with the WB. Interestingly, however, this principle diffusion has resulted as much from advice and availability enhancement as from forceful pressure.

Normative appeal has also triggered some equity-enhancing reforms, especially the extension of health care coverage to excluded, poor sectors. These efforts, often pursued through add-on programs, have limited and diffuse costs, yet clear, concentrated beneficiaries. Due to their "distributive" nature (cf. Lowi 1964; Corrales 1999: 5–6), they elicit little opposition, especially when economic recovery generates additional financial resources or when IFIs offer generous credits. Since these benefit programs escape from the push and pull of contending interests that affects redistributive reforms, normative and symbolic concerns can carry the day. Therefore, the new norm of "health for all," promoted in

global conferences since the 1970s, found considerable resonance in
Latin America during the 1990s, when the region emerged from the debt
crisis and sought to improve lagging social standards, depressed further
by the rigors of structural adjustment. Many countries therefore instituted new health programs for the poor.

But naturally, principle diffusion produces less homogeneity than
model diffusion; it leaves governments considerable room to decide in
what way and how far to advance toward a general goal. Accordingly,
health reforms in Latin America are quite diverse and much more heterogeneous than the varying degrees of pension privatization. This diversity suggests that external pressures and normative appeal, which are
fairly uniform, by no means determined decision outputs. Instead, these
external influences encountered varying degrees of domestic receptivity,
as the present chapter analyzes. Moreover, reform decisions were also
shaped by lessons derived from other countries' experiences, as chapter
6 shows.

EXTERNAL PRESSURES IN HEALTH REFORM

The World Bank Proposal—Trigger of the 1990s' Reform Wave?

A simple correlational analysis may suggest that the World Bank was
the main protagonist of health reform in Latin America: As soon as it
expounded its ambitious program, which combined equity and efficiency
in an appealing way, government efforts to restructure health systems
picked up steam. Whereas efficiency-oriented measures had remained
haphazard and equity-enhancing efforts had foundered on resource constraints during the "lost decade" of the 1980s, the 1990s saw a proliferation of reform projects, right after the bank published its high-profile
report, *Investing in Health*.[1]

This document, which received enormous attention, started from the
basic maxim of neoliberal social policy. It advocated concentrating public resources on the poorest sectors that cannot finance their own social
protection; by contrast, the better-off should buy insurance in the private market. Targeting state funds on the needy would further both social equity and cost-effectiveness. A dollar spent on basic care for the
poor yields greater utility than additional investment in complicated,
expensive curative treatments, which better-off sectors use disproportionately (WB 1993b: 1–16, 52–71, 156–71; see also Abel and Lloyd-
Sherlock 2000: 12–15).

---

[1] Before the 1990s, the World Bank did not push a clear health reform project. For
instance, Echeverri (1989: 3) stresses the bank's flexibility and adaptability in this area.

The World Bank therefore advocated a profound reorientation of the health system. The state should extend a basic package of services and preventive measures to the poorest groups, which lacked minimally satisfactory coverage (WB 1993b: 108–19). At the same time, it should transfer the provision of sophisticated curative treatments to the private sector, either by outsourcing them to private hospitals or by allowing patients to choose between public and private health insurance (WB 1993b: 123–33). Given this choice, most of the middle class would leave the public system, which in their eyes offered low-quality care. Their exit would allow the state to concentrate on serving the needy. To make public service provision more efficient, the World Bank recommended the introduction of quasi-market mechanisms inside the public sector. Hospitals should gain autonomy from central bureaucratic commands, and clear incentives should boost their performance and productivity (WB 1993b: 126, 130–31, 161). The bank's main goal was not to improve the public sector, however, but to scale it back and expose it to private competition.

In sum, the bank proposed a comprehensive overhaul of the health system. This plan was inspired by neoliberal principles and emphasized the synergy between two crucial values, social equity and economic efficiency. Since the poor had always been neglected, targeting public resources on them would produce more health at lower cost. In turn, improvements in efficiency, productivity, and cost effectiveness would free up resources for extending basic services to the needy. With this ambitious plan, the bank sought to gain leadership in the health field and displace hitherto predominant actors, especially the World Health Organization (WHO), Pan-American Health Organization (PAHO), and traditional Latin American health specialists. Those forces had put undiluted priority on fulfilling social needs, paying little attention to economic constraints.

Indeed, while trying to make its neoliberal program palatable to these actors by emphasizing social concerns, the World Bank advanced a distinctive concept of social equity, defining it in terms of basic needs. Public health care should target the poor and provide only the most essential services. This minimalist goal diverged from the universalistic plan of the WHO and Latin American health specialists to extend generous, comprehensive health coverage to all citizens. Thus, while the bank's two-pronged equity and efficiency strategy sought to appeal to a wide range of actors, it clearly deviated from established health policy approaches.

At the same time, the WB push for introducing efficiency considerations in the health sector, which appealed to governments' economic agencies, did not hold the same attraction as pension privatization, which the representativeness heuristic made appear as a crucial instrument for fueling economic development. Certainly, finance and planning ministries had come to see health care as a bottomless barrel; even constantly rising spending could never fulfill the social needs stressed by health specialists. Therefore, economy ministries eagerly supported the bank's promotion of efficiency to limit the pressure for expenditure increases and ensure the rational usage of scarce budget funds. For the first time, economy ministries, which had hitherto left health policy to sector experts (usually medical doctors), entered this issue area with proposals for efficiency-enhancing reforms and an insistence on cost-effectiveness.

Yet beyond these fiscal benefits, health reform did not promise the broader economic effects attributed to pension privatization. Whereas the representativeness heuristic suggested that the Chilean model boosted domestic savings and investment, changes in the health system would not foster capital accumulation. Even improvements in human capital would take many years to materialize and fuel economic growth. For these reasons, economy ministries never pushed as hard for health reform as for social security privatization. The World Bank therefore found less domestic support for its health program than its pension plan. For finance and planning ministries, health reform always played second fiddle behind pension privatization. Whenever they had to choose, they prioritized social security reform. In Peru, for instance, neoliberal Economy Minister Carlos Boloña cut a deal with his opponents that allowed pension privatization to go forward yet shelved health privatization (interviews with De los Heros 2002, Du Bois 2002, and Peñaranda 2002). In sum, the WB promotion of efficiency in health care found considerable backing from economy ministries but did not stimulate as much enthusiasm as pension privatization.

Just when the bank published its bold agenda, health reforms in Latin America gathered steam. Many countries that had enacted mere emergency measures (mostly expenditure cuts) during the 1980s now designed projects for overhauling their health systems; a number of—usually piecemeal—changes actually came into effect. In fact, while the region had for decades pursued the equity agenda by extending health care gradually to the poor, the 1990s saw an unprecedented wave of efficiency-oriented measures, which the World Bank advocated with particular zeal. This flurry of reform efforts may suggest that IFI pressures constituted the main impetus for principle diffusion in health care.

An inspection of policymaking yields a more nuanced picture, however. While the WB certainly provided a major impulse for efficiency-oriented reform efforts (cf. Cruz and Carrera 2004: 222–23), Latin American governments advanced much less far than the IFIs advocated. In fact, some changes that did take place, such as the partial privatization of health care in Peru, did not result from WB pressures but were inspired by other countries' experiences. And where governments did follow bank exhortations, their compliance was often more the product of persuasion and availability enhancement than of forceful imposition. Moreover, while the World Bank was the principal promoter of efficiency, it was only one among several advocates of greater equity. Other IOs such as the WHO and UNICEF, which lacked the capacity for exerting pressure, played a very important, more broadly effective role. In fact, these IOs had promoted the new norm of "health for all" long before the World Bank jumped on this bandwagon. Thus, besides external pressures and availability enhancement, normative appeal proved effective.

The Effect of IFI Pressures

Assessments of the effective impact of IFI pressures on Latin American health reforms must keep in mind the selection issue discussed in chapter 3. The IFIs did not see the need to push governments that embraced a neoliberal policy orientation. Instead, their pressures targeted more recalcitrant governments that pursued social-democratic goals; yet those administrations were not particularly receptive to IFI exhortations. To avoid problematic inferences, it is necessary to consider these differences in underlying preferences, which conditioned the WB decision to exert pressure in the first place.

The countries under investigation capture considerable variation in IFI—government relations. Whereas in Costa Rica and Brazil, most health policy-makers rejected the market agenda pushed by the World Bank, the Bolivian, Peruvian, and Salvadoran governments of the 1990s embraced broad neoliberal goals. But in El Salvador, the strongest opposition party, the leftist Frente Farabundo Martí para la Liberación Nacional (FMLN), which commands firm support in the health sector, fiercely resisted neoliberal change. In Bolivia and Peru, by contrast, obstacles to the IFI agenda emerged less from civil society than from populist chief executives, clientelist politicians, and an institutionally weak state. To what extent did IFI pressures overcome these variegated impediments? How far did the World Bank manage to push efficiency- and equity-oriented health reforms in these different settings?

COSTA RICA'S CRITICAL ENGAGEMENT WITH THE IFIS

Costa Rican governments had traditionally defined health policy independently from the IFIs. Those institutions had supported specific projects but not influenced broader policy decisions. Since Costa Rica's health system performed much better than most of its regional brethren, policy-makers did not see a need for outside advice (interview with Miranda 2004). The serious economic crisis starting in the late 1970s, however, which threatened the country's social accomplishments (Castro Valverde and Sáenz 1998: 18–19), made governments receptive to deeper cooperation with the IFIs.[2] Since during the 1980s, Costa Rican governments and the IFIs focused on stabilization and adjustment, however, their negotiations did not touch much on health reform, and the WB had virtually no influence in this area. Only as a nod to the IFIs' neoliberal agenda did the government of Oscar Arias (1986–90) in ongoing loan negotiations stress its experiments with private-public cooperation in health service delivery (interviews with Vargas 2004 and Marín 2004; Martínez Franzoni 1999: 165–66); yet these novel efforts had emerged out of domestic initiatives, without any IFI involvement. And after fulfilling the symbolic function of placating the WB, these experiments remained confined to pilot projects and did not stimulate a revamping of the health sector, which their designers advocated (Marín and Vargas 1990).

This stagnation of market-oriented experiments is noteworthy given that the government of Rafael Angel Calderón Fournier (1990–94) pursued a fairly neoliberal course and for the first time in Costa Rican history negotiated loans for health policy reform with the WB and Inter-American Development Bank. Despite increasing IFI involvement, the state did not cede much greater space to the private health sector, as the WB advocated (cf. WB 2003c: 57). The predominance of social-democratic values among users of health services, public health personnel, and bureaucrats of the Caja Costarricense de Seguro Social left little room for market-oriented reforms. Thus, even under propitious circumstances, the IFIs did not manage to reshape Costa Rica's health system.

While the decision to obtain IFI funding for policy changes implied a willingness to listen to WB and IDB advice, significant interest divergences remained. Domestic policy-makers prioritized equity goals, whereas the WB stressed efficiency goals. Costa Ricans mainly wanted to improve the primary care system, which had suffered financial cuts in the 1980s. By contrast, the IFIs pushed for cost-effectiveness, performance, and productivity and focused on organizational changes, including privatization efforts (interviews with Ayala 2004 and Guzmán 2004; Clark 2004: 197–200; Castro Valverde and Sáenz 1998: 4–5; CCSS 1993: 10–11; Presidencia 1993: 16). Interestingly, domestic policy-makers proved quite successful. The loan document with the WB defined the

---

[2] For excellent analyses of the subsequent negotiations examined in this section, see Martínez Franzoni (1999) and Clark (2004).

new primary care system—Costa Rica's priority—in much greater detail than the efficiency-oriented reforms sought by the Bank, which were left surprisingly vague (WB 1993a: vi–vii, 13–14, 91–116; Banco Mundial 1993: 1–4). And while rushing to implement the new primary care system from early 1995 on, the Costa Rican government took its time to design performance-enhancing measures, which were enacted only gradually from late 1997 onward.

The IFIs were even less successful in shaping reform content. As regards primary care, CCSS specialists insisted on following the basic principles guiding Costa Rica's welfare state, especially comprehensive universal coverage. Demonstrating the broad commitment to these principles prevailing in the country, even the conservative Calderón government made only limited concessions to WB exhortations to target public spending on the poorest sectors and cover only a limited number of basic, cheap health services (interviews with Ayala 2004, Guzmán 2004, and Cercone 2004; Banco Mundial 1991: 3–4; Martínez Franzoni 1999: 167; Clark 2004: 198–99). Invoking the social success of their welfare state and their continued capacity to fund it, CCSS officials managed to win WB acquiescence to their plan to guarantee generous primary care for all citizens by creating a network of about eight hundred Basic Health Teams (Equipos Básicos de Atención Integral de Salud—EBAIS), which would offer integrated preventive care and basic curative services on a capitation basis throughout the national territory.[3]

Thus, Costa Rican specialists used their high technical capacity and invoked their country's social accomplishments, the absence of a financial crisis, and the social-democratic values prevailing among the population and the political class to attain great success in their negotiations with the World Bank. On occasion, they also relied on their discretion in the implementation phase, which the bank could not monitor closely. On a particularly hard-fought issue, they promised to accept a WB demand, although they never planned to comply with it: "We lied," confessed a participant in these negotiations. In sum, rather than imposing its will on this minuscule country, the bank ended up subsidizing Costa Rica's priorities.

Initial disagreements were even more pronounced in discussions about the efficiency agenda. Chilean consultants hired upon the World Bank's instigation advocated radical changes along the lines of their own country's health privatization. They recommended dividing up Costa Rica's comprehensive social security institution CCSS, creating separate financing, insurance, and provider agencies, and allowing for private-sector

---

[3] UPC (1993: 165–77); IDB (1992: 1–2, 12–13, 43). The expansion of primary care indeed proved much more costly than the World Bank (2003c: 13, 23, 26) anticipated.

participation and competition. Essentially, they wanted Costa Rica to follow Chile's introduction of private health insurance companies (Instituciones de Salud Previsional—ISAPRE). But because only the middle class can afford private health plans whereas poorer sectors must stay in the underfunded public health system, the Chilean reform created deep social segmentation. Moreover, many ISAPRE affiliates were discontent. Private companies eagerly insured the young and healthy but used all kinds of machinations to exclude "bad risks," especially older, sickly people.

Costa Rican policy-makers adamantly refused to emulate this reform (interviews with Marín 2004, Miranda 2004, and Salas Chaves 2004; Clark 2005: 12–13, 19). Chilean-style privatization violated the traditional, constitutionally enshrined principles underlying the Costa Rican welfare state, especially universalism and social solidarity. As polls commissioned by the CCSS showed, these values retained overwhelming popular support (Garita Bonilla and González Varela 1992: 3, 21; Poltronieri 2003: 54, 61, 133). Privatization also threatened the institutional interests of the CCSS and its corps of experts. Moreover, Costa Rica's private medical sector seemed too underdeveloped to run part of the extensive health system, especially hospitals. In long negotiations, the WB and the consultants it brought backed off from these proposals, which had initially found some support in Costa Rica's Planning Ministry (MIDEPLAN 1992: 2, 12, 23–28, 32–39; Presidencia 1993: 2, 15, 22–28, 36, 43; Calderón 1993: 4–9; CCSS 1993: 28–34; interviews with Ballesteros 2004, Salas Chaves 2004, Cercone 2004, and Guzmán 2004).

But World Bank pressure did significantly reinforce the impulse for Costa Rica to move toward efficiency-enhancing reforms. Certainly, domestic experts had for years proposed measures to enhance health system performance. But these projects and experiments, including nonprofit health cooperatives contracted by the CCSS, had very limited effect due to bureaucratic resistance from CCSS officials. The WB push was crucial for resuming the efficiency agenda, though in ways that differed greatly from the WB's initial goals (interviews with Ayala 2004, Cercone 2004, and Marín 2004; UPC 1993: 63, 121).

Availability enhancement by another IFI paved the way for a compromise that differed both from the WB's privatization plans and from CCSS officials' defense of the established system. In the mid-1990s, the IDB proposed—and the World Bank soon embraced—the introduction of efficiency-enhancing measures inside the public health sector (Martínez Franzoni 1999: 166–75). Greater autonomy and clearer incentives should induce CCSS clinics and hospitals to improve service production and fulfill targets set in contractual negotiations with central health authorities. And functional specialization inside the CCSS headquarter would allow for a more transparent and efficient discharge of insurance, purchasing, and provision of services. This reorganization would transform a bureaucratic hierarchy into a quasi-market (Trejos et al. 1994: 51–52, 58–63, 85–87; IDB 1996: part 3; Iunes 2001: 215–17).

These novel proposals, which differed from the World Bank's privatizing thrust, proved acceptable to both sides (interview with Ayala 2004). From the bank's perspective, they promised to increase efficiency and familiarize public providers with the market logic of incentives and rewards. From the CCSS's perspective, these performance-enhancing measures would strengthen rather than dismantle the public health system (cf. CCSS 1993: 28–34). By boosting productivity, they would take the wind out of the sail of privatization proposals. They would also allow the CCSS to improve service quality despite tightening resource constraints and thus stem the exit of middle-class people to the fledgling private health sector. Thus, the Costa Rican government embraced quasi-market mechanisms to fortify the public sector and keep the private sector narrowly confined. This partial concession to the WB's logic of competitiveness sought to preserve the basic outlines of the publicly dominated health system (interviews with Ayala 2004 and Sáenz 2004).

As part of this compromise plan, the CCSS introduced performance contracts to commit hospitals and health posts to specific service targets. The central authorities monitored attainment of these goals and applied financial rewards or penalties. From 1997 onward, performance contracts were gradually extended from a few hospitals to all public health care providers, and the targets expanded from simple requirements, such as the availability of basic equipment, to include measures of productivity and quality. While the contracts are still criticized for an excessive emphasis on quantifiable indicators, observers claim that they have fostered greater attention to goal attainment and efficiency (interviews with Cercone 2004 and Guzmán 2004; critical assessments in CCSS and Banco Mundial 2002: 7, and Martínez Franzoni and Mesa-Lago 2003: 51–61).

In conclusion, Costa Rica did enact performance-enhancing changes, but they differed from the privatization agenda initially advocated by the World Bank. WB pressure was crucial for reinforcing domestic efforts at efficiency-oriented reform, which had not made much headway by the early 1990s and needed external support to come to fruition. As in the pension arena, however, this small, seemingly weak country managed to maintain its long-standing welfare state, contrary to IFI preferences for a more radical transformation (Martínez Franzoni 1999: 165–68; Clark 2004: 197–204). Successive governments of differing partisan orientation used loans and policy advice from the IFIs to strengthen the established system and made only those concessions that were compatible with its basic outlines. Yet whereas Costa Rica designed its limited pension privatization without direct WB involvement, it elaborated health reforms in lengthy negotiations with the IFIs and followed important external recommendations, especially in reorganizing the CCSS and introducing performance contracts. Without IFI participation in decision making, the country would not have moved as far toward efficiency goals (WB 2003c: 7, 12). Thus, the IFIs propelled principle diffusion in health care more than model diffusion in social security.

BRAZILIAN HEALTH POLICY-MAKERS' AVERSION TO THE IFIS

Compared to Costa Rica, Brazil forged ahead with even greater independence from IFI pressures. Whereas most Latin American countries adopted some kind of neoliberal health reform, Brazil's new democracy moved in the opposite direction, trying to strengthen the public system and reinforce state control over the extensive private health sector. For many years, Brazil placed social equity ahead of economic efficiency. This priority took hold because the main impulse for health reform arose not—as in most of the region—from experts inside the state (Nelson 2004: 31), but from a leftist professional movement that had emerged during Brazil's lengthy democratization.

This Movimento Sanitário (public health movement), led initially by a small communist party (Partido Comunista Brasileiro—PCB), demanded a fundamental restructuring of the country's unique health system, in which the state contracted most services from the private sector. In the eyes of the sanitary movement, this outsourcing created severe distortions by inducing private providers to foist unnecessary treatments on patients to increase their own revenues; by privileging curative treatments over preventive measures; and by benefiting urban middle-class neighborhoods, where private facilities were concentrated, while neglecting rural regions and squatter settlements. The *sanitaristas* therefore demanded strict public guidance and control over the private health sector, if not its nationalization (Conferência Nacional de Saúde 1987; Escorel 1999; Fleury 1997; Arretche 2004).

These goals found substantial support in the Constituent Assembly of 1987–88 (Rodriguez 1988). The new charter guaranteed generous, comprehensive health coverage for all citizens and prescribed efforts to improve service delivery for poorer sectors, especially by decentralizing health care to bring it closer to users. The 1990s indeed saw a gradual, yet thoroughgoing decentralization of Brazil's health system. The new constitution also mandated greater control over private hospitals and doctors through the creation of a state-guided "Unified Health System" (Sistema Único de Saúde—SUS). But these rules proved difficult to implement because private providers tenaciously resisted increased state intervention.

All these changes were enacted in complete independence from the IFIs. Given its leftist origins, the sanitary movement was averse to cooperating with these mainstays of the global capitalist order. Indeed, Brazil's reforms diverged fundamentally from the privatizing thrust of the World Bank. They sought to limit the costs of service provision through greater state control—the exact opposite of the bank's advocacy of market competition. The sanitary movement's push for generous universal coverage also contrasted with the bank's plea for targeting a minimal service package to the poor. In fact, the World Bank incessantly criticized the guarantee of comprehensive health care for all as far beyond Brazil's financial means (WB 1991: 2, 21, 82, 101–2, 109–10; WB 1994b: xi–xii, xvi, 41, 79, 100–101, 149–52, 158, 163; WB 1996a: 4, 11–12; WB 1998a: 7, 18, 20; WB 2003b: 175; interviews with Campos 2003 and Pawlowski 2003; Sugiyama's interview with La Forgia 2004). Thus, the reform course traced by the sanitary movement deviated starkly from IFI proposals.

This gulf diminished somewhat from the mid-1990s onward because Brazil's health system was thrown into severe financial problems as the Social Security Ministry monopolized the most stable revenue source in the country's comprehensive social budget (GTI 1994: 2). The IFIs' emphasis on resource constraints and calls for greater efficiency therefore found resonance, especially in Brazil's economy ministries. Moreover, the WB health program of 1993 stressed the synergy of equity and efficiency goals underlying efforts to improve primary care. As the Finance and Planning ministries embraced this agenda (GTI 1994; interview with Negri 2003), the government of Fernando Henrique Cardoso (1995–2002) for the first time negotiated a policy-based loan with the World Bank and IDB. While the lion's share of the US$650 million offered by the IFIs was allocated to service infrastructure (thus refurbishing the public health sector), a small part of the project focused on elaborating health reforms. In particular, it sought to institute differential reimbursement rates for private service providers to privilege primary care over expensive curative treatments (WB 1996a: 14–18, 22, 30–32, 63–64, 78–79, 91). This measure would give priority to a basic benefit package in public resource allocation, as the World Bank recommended (interviews with Pawlowski 2003 and Machado de Souza 2003). It would thus advance both equity and efficiency without violating the constitutional guarantee of comprehensive health coverage.

A host of administrative and political problems and stubborn resistance from *sanitaristas* entrenched at all levels of the health system largely blocked these reform efforts, however. Reform design started with years of delay, and the Health Ministry disregarded most proposals and studies produced by the project. Crucial measures, such as differential reimbursement rates for primary care, were not implemented (WB 1998a: 19). The bank therefore classified the whole loan operation as "unsatisfactory"—an unusually harsh rating (WB 2004e: 1, 12–14, 17, 36). Thus, voluminous financial resources failed to elicit compliance. Even when facing serious fiscal problems, Brazilian health reformers proved immune to IFI pressures, which they resented (interviews with Negri 2003, Pawlowski 2003, and Guimarães 2003).

Yet whereas loan conditionality proved ineffective, availability enhancement by the IFIs did make a difference. From the mid-1990s onward, Brazil's Health Ministry concentrated on guaranteeing a package of basic services for poorer people and used economic incentives and sanctions to attain this goal (interview with Negri 2003; Serra 2000: 35–38; MS DAB 2002: 19–20, 49–50, 55–68). These efforts were inspired partly by the 1993 *World Development Report* (interviews with Azevedo 2003, Guimarães 2003, and Pawlowski 2003). Brazilian policy-makers absorbed these new proposals, especially the effort to improve both social equity and economic efficiency.

But although the determined implementation of a primary care strategy moved Brazilian health policy closer to WB recommendations, leading decision-makers adamantly deny any bank pressure and influence (interviews with Negri 2003 and Machado de Souza 2003; see also Serra 2000: 43–46, 86–87 and interview with Pawlowski 2003).[4] The continuing strength of the sanitary movement would have turned direct cooperation with the IFIs into "the kiss of death" for this reorientation of Brazil's health strategy. Instead, decision-makers claimed to apply basic principles of health economics, which were widely available in the international discussion. Yet as the WB was the most prominent exponent of these principles, it influenced Brazilian health reform indirectly through availability enhancement.

Thus, Brazil for many years did not listen to IFI recommendations and enacted ambitious equity-oriented change despite persistent criticism from the World Bank (cf. Serra 2000: 43–44, 86–87). Their leftist ideology turned many health reformers deaf to IFI messages. Even when more moderate forces hailing from the economy ministries extended their influence into the health arena and negotiated a sizeable loan with

[4] For instance, the primary care package was derived not from technical analyses of cost effectiveness, as advocated by the WB (and conducted in Bolivia), but from historical spending patterns and political discussions with stakeholders (interviews with Negri 2003, Andrade 2003, Azevedo 2003, Machado de Souza 2003, and Guimarães 2003).

the IFIs, the impact on policy reform was negligible. Therefore, external pressures cannot account for the course of Brazilian health policy. And only from the mid-1990s on did availability enhancement begin to play a role.

In conclusion, where decision-makers diverged from the IFIs' neoliberal orientation, as in Costa Rica and Brazil, WB influence on health reform remained limited. In Costa Rica, the IFIs used their financial leverage to push the government toward efficiency-oriented changes. This pressure did "make a difference"; left to its own devices, Costa Rica would not have advanced as far. But the country's performance-enhancing reforms strengthened the public sector and differed greatly from the privatizing proposals advanced initially by the World Bank. Furthermore, the bank largely acquiesced to Costa Rica's plans to fortify and extend its generous system of integral primary care.

In Brazil, the leftist ideology of many health policy-makers posed an even greater obstacle to IFI influence. The sanitary movement starkly diverged from WB advice by promoting state control and generous expansions of entitlements. The bank itself recognized that "its leverage with respect to policy reform is limited" (WB 1998a: 18, 23, 30). Even when severe financial constraints moved Brazilian health policy closer to IFI goals, external pressure was not the decisive factor; only availability enhancement played a role.

By contrast, the governments of El Salvador (1989–present), Bolivia (1985–2003), and Peru, especially under President Fujimori (1990–2000), embraced the market reform program promoted by the Washington agencies. Did this agreement on basic goals give the IFIs substantial influence on health policy? Did these countries enact efficiency- and equity-oriented reforms in the WB mold, and can IFI pressure account for these changes?

POLITICAL POLARIZATION AS A HINDRANCE TO IFI INFLUENCE IN EL SALVADOR

Led by the right-wing ARENA, the governments of El Salvador adopted a neoliberal policy orientation. After President Alfredo Cristiani (1989–94) managed to stabilize the economy and end the ferocious civil war, attention turned to structural reforms (Segovia 2002), including health care. In preparation of the successor government of Armando Calderón Sol (1994–99), a group of external funding agencies led by the United States Agency for International Development (USAID), which through the early 1990s played a very influential role in shoring up U.S.-allied governments in this war-torn country, elaborated a comprehensive diagnosis and prescription for the Salvadoran health system. Conducted by foreign consultants with close IFI links, this Análisis del Sector Salud de El Salvador (ANSAL) outlined an ambitious reform project inspired by the World Bank plan (WB 1993b; Avilés 1998: chap. 7). The Salvadoran state should target public resources to the poor and give priority to preventive and basic curative care by subsidizing an essential health package for the destitute. Better-off sectors should fund their own health insurance and make copayments for specific treatments. The state should withdraw from service delivery, transfer primary care to municipalities, community groups, NGOs, or private providers, and privatize hospitals. These providers would be paid on a capitation basis to stimulate efficiency and limit costs (ANSAL 1994a: xvi–xvii, 80–85, 95–100, 118–34; Solari 1994).

The ANSAL plan was designed by foreigners and supported by the Salvadoran Planning Ministry (ANSAL 1994b: 1, 11; WB 1994c: 44; WB 2002: 12). Despite reservations (ANSAL 1994a: v, 151–53; MSPAS GRSS 1995: 70–71, 100; Avilés 1998: 74, 152), the domestic health agencies officially embraced it (MSPAS 1994: 39–40, 57; MSPAS GRSS 1995). The WB and IDB offered ample financial incentives and technical assistance to promote comprehensive, profound health reform (WB 1994c: 40–42; Weinberg 1998). These efforts were inspired not only by neoliberal principles, but also by practical considerations. The Salvadoran state lacked the resources for improving the battered health system; cooperation with private providers, including the privatization of existing facilities, seemed advisable. Resource constraints had also led clinics and hospitals to extract informal payments from patients; the proposed cost recovery mechanisms would simply regularize and regulate these emergency fees. Since a good part of ANSAL's privatization agenda was driven by practical necessities, it found broader support among health specialists, ranging beyond the neoliberal experts who were guiding government policy (interviews with Betancourt 2004 and Silva 2004).

But electoral politicians inside ARENA and bureaucrats in the health agencies were reluctant to pursue ANSAL's efficiency agenda and give in to IFI pressures (Avilés 1998: 74, 152). The health minister himself, a leading ARENA politician, resisted profound change, especially privatization, which would create political costs by upsetting established bureaucratic interests and by reducing his own control over patronage. The ministry therefore dragged its feet on health reform and concentrated instead on institutional modernization (interview with Betancourt 2004; Avilés 1998: 160–62; cf. Silva 1998: 57–59). Moreover, it covered the country with integrated regional health systems (Sistemas Básicos de Salud Integral—SIBASI), which sought to coordinate existing service providers and improve primary and secondary care (MSPAS 1999; MSPAS n.d.; Seiber 2002; see also Lewis, Eskeland, and Traa-Valerezo 1999).

As the World Bank and IDB continued to push for a profound transformation, the Health Ministry simply declined their generous loan offers to avoid the efficiency-enhancing conditions attached to them (WB 2001d: 24; Homedes et al. 2000: 74; Selva Sutter 2000: 587). In subsequent years, the ministry scaled back cooperation with the IFIs and focused it on specific areas or pilot projects. The IFIs sought to use these limited initiatives to introduce and test efficiency-enhancing mechanisms such as performance contracts, cost recovery schemes, and out-contracting to private providers (see IDB 1998). But these experiments did not trigger broader reform efforts.

Thus, despite its neoliberal orientation, the Salvadoran government kept shying away from the IFIs' efficiency agenda, especially privatization. Two political-institutional factors account for this resistance. First, the established health agencies, especially the ministry and the social security institute, wanted to retain control over service delivery and the economic resources and political power accompanying it (cf. CONASA 1999: 1). While the social security institute had not managed to forestall pension privatization (see chapter 4), it offered more successful resistance in the health arena, which was of lower interest to the economy ministries. In fact, the government's reform agenda was already filled up with economically more important projects (interview with Daboub 2004). Furthermore, the Health Ministry lacked the technical and institutional capacity to design and implement central elements of health reform, such as a basic service package (WB 2001c: 12; interview with Silva 2004).

Second, El Salvador continued to suffer from intense ideological polarization, which had until recently fueled armed conflict. Many FMLN leaders and supporters fiercely rejected health privatization, and this position found strong majority support in opinion polls (Cruz, Craig, and Ventosa 1999: 31–34, 39). Thus, efforts to advance the IFIs' efficiency agenda were bound to be highly controversial and politically costly for ARENA. In the run-up to the 1997 legislative elections, the government therefore resisted IFI demands and drastically scaled back loan negotiations (MSPAS 1996: 51; Homedes et al. 2000: 74; Selva Sutter 2000: 587). In sum, strident partisan opposition deterred the Calderón Sol administration from enacting the World Bank's efficiency and privatization goals in health care. Despite its neoliberal convictions and aid dependence, it rejected external pressure from the powerful IFIs.

Resource constraints, however, continued to induce the economy ministries and neoliberal presidential advisers to promote the efficiency agenda. To advance health reform despite political concerns and ideological divisions, presidents Calderón Sol and Francisco Flores (1999–2004) undertook efforts at concertation. They convened commissions with wide-ranging representation and charged them with drawing up a consensus project. But deep disagreement prevailed in the health sector

(Asamblea Legislativa 1999: 36–54; Cruz Saco 2001b: 73–100). The two commissions advanced only some general guidelines and left crucial issues unresolved, especially the thorny privatization question (CONASA 1999; CRSS 2000; see also OPS 2001: 17; Olano 2003: 6).

The IFIs now exerted less pressure than in the mid-1990s (interviews with Betancourt 2004 and Silva 2004). They had come to understand the highly controversial nature of anything resembling health privatization in El Salvador (IDB 2000: 1, 4, A18; WB 2001c: i; annex F: 4–6). Also, the World Bank in general was stressing the need to guarantee the "ownership" of reforms by the domestic government and other veto players (Mallaby 2004: 233–53). Therefore, it refrained from pushing for profound change in El Salvador (WB 2001c: ii, 20; WB 2002: 13). Together with the IDB, it undertook only limited efforts to try out efficiency-enhancing measures and demonstrate their usefulness (IDB 2000: 1–5, A4–6; WB 2001d: 8–11, 14–15, 35–36; WB 2004a, 2004b: 6). In this way, the IFIs hoped to stimulate the broader adoption of such reforms (IDB 2000: A18)—yet without much success.

In sum, the neoliberal orientation of the ARENA governments was not sufficient for the IFIs to promote health reform successfully.[5] Although external funding agencies helped design a comprehensive proposal and offered generous financial support, resistance from established health bureaucrats, foot-dragging among ARENA politicians, and especially fierce ideological opposition from the left posed insurmountable obstacles.[6] Only modest efficiency-oriented measures, such as the out-contracting of some auxiliary services, went forward. The Salvadoran government achieved more advances on the equity front, where the SIBASIs brought somewhat greater emphasis on primary care and an extension of basic service provision (Seiber 2002: 51–53). Thus, persistent IFI efforts to influence Salvadoran health policy produced only limited results.

THE HAPHAZARD ADVANCE OF HEALTH REFORM IN PERU

Compared to El Salvador, the IFIs had greater—yet far from overwhelming—success in promoting health reform in Peru. From the mid-1990s onward, this country enacted some efficiency-oriented measures and a range of equity-enhancing programs that embodied WB-sponsored ideas, received financial support from IFIs, and were elaborated in con-

---

[5] The WB found much more receptivity for its proposals in education, where El Salvador pursued ambitious reforms with generous IFI support (WB 2002: 5, 8, 10; Parandekar 2002; Córdova 1999).

[6] The fierce conflict over health privatization in 2002, which chapter 6 discusses, further demonstrates the depth of ideological polarization.

sultation with them. These changes did not add up to the comprehensive health system reform recommended by the bank, however. They remained partial and incoherent and were often designed and implemented haphazardly (for an excellent analysis, see Ewig 2004). These limitations resulted from two political-institutional factors, namely, the predominance of neopopulist leadership and the fragmentation and institutional weakness of the Peruvian state (see in general Morón and Sanborn 2004).

Both presidents Fujimori and Alejandro Toledo (2001–06) were personalistic leaders who sought to sustain their governments through a plebiscitarian, charismatic, uninstitutionalized relationship to unorganized masses of people (Weyland 2002b: chap. 7). Because Fujimori helped to destroy Peru's party system and dismantle institutional constraints on executive rule, he and his successor had ample latitude for discretion. Using this room for maneuver to garner mass support, Fujimori and Toledo often disregarded technical considerations and made ill-conceived decisions. This haphazard approach to policymaking reflected and reinforced the institutional weakness of the Peruvian state, which lacked a cohesive, well-trained corps of experts, especially in the social sectors. In the Health Ministry, turnover among political appointees has been exceedingly high, and the absence of firm ministerial leadership has exacerbated internal fragmentation (WB 2003d: 2–6, 17–20, 23; Arroyo 2000: 126–36; interviews with Benavides 2002, Bendezú 2002, De Habich 2002, Sobrevilla 2002, and Yamamoto 2002; see in general Morón and Sanborn 2004: 18–19, 30, 42–43). This fragmentation, which obstructs systematic health reform, is aggravated by the numerous IOs and NGOs that collaborate with Peru in the health sector. Each donor pursues its own projects and links up with sectors inside the bureaucracy, and the ministry's top leadership is too weak to coordinate donor activities. Therefore, the ministry is pulled in different directions (interviews with Eiseman 2002, Kolodin 2002, and Manrique 2002).

Yet while these political-institutional problems posed obstacles, Peru's profound economic crisis made cooperation with the IFIs attractive. Hyperinflation had pulverized state revenues in the late 1980s and forced a cutback of health expenditures by 75 percent, causing a collapse of service delivery. A cholera epidemic in 1991 demonstrated the dire situation. After President Fujimori managed to stabilize the economy, attention turned to the social sectors, including the urgent reconstruction of the health system. The destruction wrought by the crisis paved the way for reforms along WB lines. Continuing fiscal constraints created concern for cost-effectiveness; high unemployment allowed the government to hire new health personnel on flexible private-sector contracts and avoid the public sector's rigid labor regime; and the utter neglect of the poor, especially in rural regions, meant that equity-enhancing measures could be enacted via add-on programs that would not elicit opposition.

When Peru began to rebuild its health system in 1993, it therefore turned to foreign donors with a proposal to strengthen essential services for the poor (Lineamientos Básicos 1993; see MEF and BCRP 1993: sections 16, 31). The Health Ministry soon turned this targeted Program of Basic Health for All (Programa de Salud Básica para Todos—PSBPT) into one of its flagship initiatives. The PSBPT greatly increased the supply of services in long-neglected rural areas, especially during President Fujimori's reelection drive in 1994–95 (MINSA PSBPT 1997, 1998; WB 1999c: 3, 6, 11, 26, 29, 53; interviews with Benavides 2002, Espinoza 2002, and Meloni 2002). While this program was financed domestically, the WB and other donors supported equity-enhancing efforts by stressing the need for targeting and by subsidizing infant and maternal care in particularly poor regions (WB 1994d; interviews with Manrique 2002, Benavides 2002, and Abugattás 2002; Ewig 2000: 497–98, 506–7).

Yet simultaneously with this centralized, top-down program, the Health Ministry created a bottom-up scheme for community participation in health care, the Comités Locales de Administración en Salud (CLAS). In exchange for allowing community representatives to help administer service delivery, CLAS formalized the cost-recovery mechanisms that health posts had to adopt during the crisis years (interviews with Freundt 2002 and Vera del Carpio 2002; see MINSA PAC 1996; Graham 1998: 109–13). Organized along opposite principles, the two schemes coexisted uneasily (interviews with Benavides 2002, Bendezú 2002, and Vera del Carpio 2002; Espinoza 1998a: 46, 51, 54; Altobelli 1998: 12; Sobrevilla 2000: 40–41, 74). This divergence reflected the haphazard nature of health policy (Ewig 2004). Thus, while Peru expanded primary care for the poor, it did not enact the coherent, comprehensive reform advocated by the WB.

After President Fujimori won reelection by a landslide in 1995, the IDB and other donors, experts in the Economy Ministry, and some health specialists saw an opportunity for promoting a profound systemic change. Since 1993, the IDB had financed a project that included the elaboration of reform ideas. In 1995, this Programa de Fortalecimiento de Servicios de Salud (PFSS) elaborated ambitious guidelines for restructuring the health system in line with the 1993 WB program (interview with Espinoza 2002). Although the WB was not involved in this initiative, its ideas were highly available and served as a crucial source of inspiration. Accordingly, the reformers proposed universal insurance to guarantee all citizens access to a basic healthcare package. Better-off sectors would pay for this coverage, while the state would help the poor with demand subsidies. The insured could choose among service providers; public agencies, including the social security institute, would compete with private companies.[7]

But President Fujimori was reluctant to revamp the health sector profoundly. In fact, the PFSS project was part of a comprehensive IDB-sponsored proposal for state reform, which included massive dismissals of public employees. Fujimori refused to incur the political costs and risks of this bold neoliberal initiative (Espinoza 1998a: 28–29; interviews with Abugattás 1999, Costa Bauer 2002, Torres y Torres Lara 1999, and Espinoza 2002). As regards health reform, exposing public providers to unfettered private competition would have upset powerful bureaucratic and political interests (cf. Rodríguez 1995: 18, 31). A shift from supply to demand subsidies threatened the financial sustenance of hospitals, which traditionally received public funds regardless of performance, production, and efficiency; they strongly opposed having to compete for patients (see Espinoza 1998b: 9; interview with Sobrevilla 2002). And since most leading health officials, including the minister, were hospital doctors or directors, they found receptivity for their complaints. Furthermore, the universalization of health insurance would have required a massive injection of new funds, which the Peruvian state lacked. For all these reasons, comprehensive IFI-sponsored reform proved unviable (Rodríguez 1995: 30–31; Jara and Vergara 1995: 20; Espinoza 1998a: 11–12).

Peruvian health policy therefore continued on its unsteady course. A domestic initiative that was inspired by the Chilean and Colombian experiences and that proceeded without IFI involvement brought limited health privatization in 1997, as chapter 6 will analyze. Equity-enhancing reform advanced further, though in haphazard ways.

In 1997, President Fujimori suddenly announced free health insurance for all public school children (Seguro Escolar Gratuito—SEG; see Ewig 2004: 240–41). Although this measure was ill-prepared and the Health Ministry had to scramble to fulfill the presidential mandate (Jaramillo and Parodi 2004: 11–16), the general idea to introduce free, state-subsidized health insurance for especially vulnerable groups promised to improve poor people's access to health care. Technical studies showed that the informal payments extracted by many public health providers prevented the destitute from seeking medical treatment (Francke 1998: 50–51). Whereas IFI-inspired efforts to target health care at the poor through the PSBPT had improved the supply of services, many poor people could not afford to use them. Free, state-funded health insurance promised to overcome this demand problem. But public school children were not a

[7] MINSA (1998: 27, 32–45—a copy of a 1995 document). See also Jara and Vergara (1995a, 1995b), Mesa-Lago (1996), Rodríguez (1995), and Espinoza (1998a).

priority group for receiving such help. Truly destitute youngsters had to work and could not attend school (MINSA DGSP 2003: 43). The SEG was also mistargeted in medical terms because school-age children suffer from fewer health problems than infants and pregnant women.

Therefore, the IFIs pressed the Fujimori government very hard to modify the SEG by targeting its resources better and by complementing it with a maternal and infant health insurance program (WB 1999c; IDB 1999b; Pichihua 2005; interview with De Habich 2002). A number of domestic health experts supported this equity focus (Espinoza 1998: 33; Meloni 2005). They were eager to use IFI pressure to promote this goal and to protect their initiatives against any risks arising from the presidential election of 2000 (see WB 2001e: 2). Peruvian experts therefore asked the WB to include maternal and infant health insurance in its loan conditions (interviews with Meloni 2002 and Aguinaga 2002; see WB 1999c: 4, 11, 17; MEF and BCRP 1999: 12; Goldenberg and Suárez 2000: 4; Espinoza 1998a: 34).

Because the IFIs offered generous funds and because neopopulist Fujimori tried with all means to win another reelection, he quickly enacted this new benefit scheme (cf. Espinoza 1998: 37). In fact, the Peruvian government pushed for covering a more generous package of treatments than the IFIs regarded as fiscally viable. Moreover, Fujimori's main competitor and eventual successor Alejandro Toledo, himself a neopopulist leader and always eager to make extravagant promises, trumped the president by calling for "integral" health insurance (Toledo 2001: 12; see also Pichihua 2005).

Thus, for electoral reasons, Fujimori and Toledo tried to go far beyond the targeted approach advocated forcefully by the IFIs. Instead of concentrating public resources on the poor, they wanted to extend free coverage to the whole population. And instead of prioritizing basic health problems that could be resolved with limited expense, they announced comprehensive coverage. The IFIs firmly opposed such irresponsible promises. From 1999 onward, they conditioned their generous assistance for maternal and infant insurance on stricter targeting, but with little success (interview with Kolodin 2002; WB 2004g: 39; IDB 2004c: 9, 18, 28; interview with Espinoza 2002). Neopopulist leaders used social benefit programs for strengthening their fluid mass base and disregarded equity-oriented IFI pressures that hindered this overriding political goal.

In sum, IFI exhortations and support helped trigger some significant health measures in Peru. Generous loans and constant prodding contributed to greater attention to the basic needs of the poor. Yet while IFI pressure played a role, advice and availability enhancement seem equally important. Several changes were inspired by the World Bank's 1993 program, but not imposed with "carrots and sticks." In fact, IFI pressures often ran afoul of the neopopulist strategies of chief executives and the institutional weakness of the Peruvian state. Above all, President Fujimori's political calculations precluded any comprehensive health reform and determined move toward privatization. Once again, IFI pressures made some difference but did not determine the course of health policy.

THE UNEVEN ADVANCE OF HEALTH REFORMS IN BOLIVIA

Compared to Peru, the IFIs had more success in promoting equity-enhancing reforms in Bolivia, but efficiency-oriented changes have remained minimal. Given large-scale poverty, domestic and international actors placed high priority on efforts to give the destitute effective access to health care, especially in underserved rural areas. Therefore, the IFIs generously subsidized numerous add-on programs and significantly shaped their design, stressing the need for cost-effectiveness. By contrast, Bolivia's underdevelopment made privatization plans unpromising; the private health sector is in its infancy, and few citizens can afford private insurance (Cárdenas 2000: 73). Efforts to boost efficiency in the social security health system, which spends a disproportionate share of public resources on its limited number of affiliates, ranked low on governments' crowded policy agenda; and whenever IFI prodding led to a reform initiative, the combative union of social security employees protested immediately. Therefore, IFI-supported universalization measures have far outstripped efficiency-oriented changes (Lavadenz 2001: 58–59).

Bolivia's health system traditionally failed to reach many citizens, especially in the desperate rural areas, where poverty afflicts a staggering 82 percent of the population (PNUD 2002: 65). Maternal and infant mortality therefore ran at very high levels. For years, policy-makers had tried to improve basic care for the poor, and numerous IOs and NGOs supported these efforts. From the late 1980s onward, the WB, IDB, USAID, and UNICEF funded various programs to extend health coverage to specific segments of the destitute (Lavadenz 1993; Homedes 2001; Chávez 1993; Muñoz Reyes 1993; interview with Cuentas Yáñez 2002).

Progress remained slow, however. Fiscal constraints on the Bolivian state and the demands of better-off sectors for expensive curative treatments limited the funds available for primary care. Equity-enhancing projects therefore required continued donor support in order not to be abandoned. Additional obstacles arose from the tremendous institutional weakness of the Bolivian state, which was exacerbated by the patronage hunger of electoral politicians, the politicization of bureaucratic appointments, and the resulting misuse of resources, waste, and corruption. The very multiplicity of IOs and NGOs conducting health projects further weakened the Health Ministry and obstructed the pursuit of a coherent reform program. The lack of coordination among donors and the ministry's failure to set clear guidelines hindered systematic progress toward greater social equity (interviews with Flores 2002 and Pooley 2002).

Change therefore arose from outside the health sector. Inspired by the 1993 WB program, the Social Policy Analysis Unit (Unidad de Análisis de Políticas Sociales—UDAPSO) created by Bolivia's Planning Ministry designed a focused approach to health care universalization (interviews with Pooley 2002, Seoane 2002, and Peña Rueda 2002; MDH SNS SEGRSS 1994). To put Bolivia's limited resources to optimal use, UDAPSO specialists and externally financed consultants defined a basic package of preventive and curative treatments that should be guaranteed to every citizen. For this purpose, they applied the cost-effectiveness model elaborated at the Harvard School of Public Health, which compares the health benefits that resources invested in the treatment of different diseases yield. In line with WB guidelines, they analyzed how many disability-adjusted life years are saved by a dollar spent on childhood diarrhea, by contrast to tuberculosis, pneumonia, or malaria (Cárdenas, Madden, and Contreras Gómez 1997; interviews with Cárdenas 2002, Pooley 2002, Seoane 2002, and Galindo 2002; see also DDM 1995; Myers 1997: 183–86, 189–92; Contreras 1997: 203–5, 209–11, 222–24). Based on these calculations, they composed a minimal package of highly cost-effective measures, focused on maternal and infant care. Thus, these domestic experts and international consultants closely followed WB ideas, applying economic rationality to enhance social equity and universal health care.

An important democratizing reform enacted by the government of Gonzalo Sánchez de Lozada provided a stable funding source for this basic health package.[8] Through ambitious decentralization measures, Goni transferred voluminous resources to Bolivia's municipalities (Grindle 2000: chaps. 5–6; Bossert et al. 2000: 14–17). To ensure the productive usage of these funds, the government pushed municipalities to spend a large share on social services, including health care. After guaranteeing the new program's financial sustenance (interviews with Cuentas Yáñez 2002 and Sandoval 2002), the Goni administration created the National Maternal and Infant Insurance (Seguro Nacional de Maternidad y Niñez—SNMN), which entitled these priority groups to the free provision of the health package defined by UDAPSO (MDH SNS 1997b: 29–30, 47–55). Most of Bolivia's 311 municipalities quickly decided to implement this

---

[8] Using fiscal decentralization to fund primary care was a UNICEF proposal (interview with Pooley 2002). On the alternatives considered, see Loaiza (1997: 43–44).

program (Aponte 1997: 33; Torres Goitia Caballero 2000: 329–30). With this innovative approach, which WB, IDB, and other IOs subsidized with 30 percent of total program cost (Cárdenas, Chawla, and Muñoz 1997: 43–44; Aponte 1997: 28), the Goni government tried to lift the economic barriers that prevented many of the destitute from obtaining medical attention. SNMN reimbursements supplied the necessary funds for treating citizens free of charge and thus liberating poor people from payments that providers had traditionally imposed.

The SNMN constituted an innovative effort to expand access to basic health care in a poor country and reach far beyond the structural limits that Bolivia's small formal labor market imposed to health coverage through the social security system (Aponte 1997: 24–25). More clearly than any other health measure in the five countries under investigation, it followed important WB principles and recommendations (see Torres Goitia Caballero 2000: 357–58). Indeed, Bolivian decision-makers heeded WB warnings about the cost of the new scheme and therefore kept the package of covered treatments minimal, disregarding UNICEF and PAHO proposals for more generous service provision (interviews with Pooley 2002 and Seoane 2002; Seoane 1994; Torres Goitia Caballero 2000: 351). The application of economic calculations for improving social equity was novel and controversial (interviews with Cárdenas 2002 and Sandoval 2002); medical doctors condemned this approach, and UDAPSO had to undertake a special effort to win over the country's health authorities (Contreras 1997: 205; interview with Cárdenas 2002). Without the support gained from following WB guidelines, this important program may well have run afoul of domestic opposition.

But the IFIs disliked some aspects of the SNMN, despite its inspiration in the 1993 WB report. The World Bank criticized its universalistic scope and lack of population targeting; it wanted to reserve public resources for the poor. Furthermore, the bank and especially USAID advised against the free provision of basic care; given the fiscal weakness of the Bolivian state, they advocated cost recovery through user charges (interviews with Sandoval 2002, Cuentas Yáñez 2002, Lugo 2002, and Torres Goitia Caballero 2006). For equity reasons, the Bolivian government insisted on free coverage and forwent USAID funding (interview with Sandoval 2002). And it stressed that widespread poverty made population targeting administratively difficult and not cost-effective. After lengthy discussions, the WB gave in (interviews with Seoane 2002, Cárdenas 2002, Cuentas Yáñez 2002, and Pereira 2002). In particular, it was impressed by the strongly positive findings of an evaluation report it had sponsored (Dmytraczenko et al. 1998; interviews with Lugo 2002 and Pooley 2002; see also John Snow Inc./Banco Mundial 2000; MDH SNS 1997a; Torres Goitia Caballero 2000: 333–37; UDAPE and OPS

2004). As evidence accumulated that the SNMN significantly improved Bolivia's lagging health indicators, the IFIs turned into stronger supporters of this innovative universalization effort.

The successor government of Hugo Banzer and Jorge Quiroga (1997– 2002), however, further deviated from the strict targeting advocated by the IFIs. To trump Goni for political reasons, it greatly expanded the treatments covered (Böhrt Arana and Larraín Sánchez 2002: 37–42); technical studies supported by IOs other than the WB also recommended an extension (e.g., Capra et al. 1998). The 2002 election triggered a further escalation of partisan bidding. The party of former president Jaime Paz Zamora (1989–93) promised to guarantee comprehensive health care for all citizens (Proyecto de Ley del Sistema Boliviano 2002). Party-linked experts themselves estimated that this further extension of the insurance scheme would require five to ten times more financial resources (interviews with Pereira 2002 and Barriga 2002). No wonder that the IFIs raised strenuous objections, for both fiscal and equity reasons (interviews with Flores 2002, Cárdenas 2002, and Valenzuela 2002). In their view, expanding the list of treatments would enable better-off people to lay disproportionate claim to scarce resources and thus cement the effective exclusion of the poor.

The new government, led again by Sánchez de Lozada (2002–03), indeed proceeded with caution (Torres Goitia Caballero 2002: 120) and focused the insurance scheme on pregnant women, young mothers, and infants. But reflecting the escalating dynamic of partisan competition, it extended the list of covered treatments to all illnesses afflicting this population group. In this way, it broke the emphasis on basic needs and primary care, although the IFIs conditioned a generous debt relief scheme for Bolivia on advances in basic health indicators (MSPS DGSS 2000: 2–3; Grupo Consultivo 2000: 3–5; see also WB 2001a: 2–4, 10– 13, 32–33; WB 2004c: 27–30). Thus, political concerns again won out over external constraints. Despite Bolivia's aid dependence, electoral interests trumped IFI pressures.

The government of Evo Morales (2006–present) pushed this escalation to the extreme by promising "free health for all" in the campaign for constituent assembly elections. Since this goal is impossible to finance, the government has as a "first phase" proposed a great extension of health insurance. The new scheme shall cover all medical problems affecting young mothers and people up to the age of twenty-one and guarantee a basic health package for all adults. But despite its projected natural gas bonanza, it is unclear whether Bolivia can fill the exorbitant funding needs for this generous plan (MSD 2006: 13–14).

In sum, Bolivia followed WB ideas in creating maternal and infant health insurance. The 1993 *World Development Report* provided a decisive impulse for this important equity-enhancing initiative. The IFIs also offered crucial financial subsidies; their loans and donations equaled 70 percent of public spending on primary health care (Francke 2002: 9, 55–56; see also WB 2004f: 9, 35, 91). World Bank influence arose from pressure, advice, and availability enhancement. But escalating party competition undermined the cost-effectiveness approach advocated by the IFIs and threatened the fiscal sustainability of basic health insurance (interview with Galindo 2002). Moreover, the striking institutional weakness of the Bolivian state (IDB 2004b: 40–42, 48), which the un-coordinated activities of a multitude of external donors exacerbated (UDAPSO 1993: 5; IDB 1999a: 8–9; WB 2004f: 94; interviews with Flores 2002, Monasterios 2002, Pereira 2002, Cárdenas 2002, and Pooley 2002), hindered program implementation, even in urban centers (Home-des 2001), but especially in poor rural areas, where social needs were most acute.

The very resource needs intensified by partisan outbidding on basic health insurance reinforced IFI pressures for efficiency-oriented mea-sures, however. The central target was the health agencies for social security affiliates, which consumed a disproportionate share of public funds (Cárdenas 2000: 41, 47; Francke 2002: 16, 23) but offered low-quality services. This inefficiency was due to rampant politicization; party politicians, dislodged from much of the Bolivian state by privatiza-tion, used the social security health agencies for patronage appoint-ments. Incompetence, waste, and corruption were therefore rife (inter-views with Flores 2002, Calderón 2002, and Torres Goitia Caballero 2006). The IFIs pushed for profound reform, which would expose these institutions to competition and eventually turn them into mere insurance agencies while allowing their affiliates to use private service providers (IDB 2001; IDB 1999a: 5, 11, 16–18; interviews with Flores 2002, Cuentas Yáñez 2002, and Valenzuela 2002; see also WB 1999a). These proposals clearly embodied the IFIs' efficiency agenda.

Bolivian policy-makers were reluctant to pursue these controversial plans. In the early 1990s already, Chilean consultants had elaborated a privatization proposal inspired by their own country's reform, and Bo-livia's peak business association had advocated this plan (CEPB 1991a; interview with Cuevas Argote 2002). Bolivian health specialists, how-ever, uniformly rejected it as too inequitable (interviews with Bonadona 2002, Galindo 2002, Peña Rueda 2002, and Pereira 2002). Even the Goni government, which enacted an impressive range of neoliberal re-forms, lacked the political will to transform the social security health system (Torres Goitia Caballero 2000: 317, 359; interviews with Cárde-nas 2002, Sandoval 2002, and Seoane 2002). Instead, it prioritized pen-sion privatization, which promised to boost economic development and therefore found more support from the economy ministries and the president himself.

Because the Goni administration enacted much of the IFIs' neoliberal agenda, however, attention shifted to the social sectors under the successor government of Hugo Banzer. A reform-oriented health minister was willing to follow IDB recommendations and begin the restructuring of social security health insurance. Consultants therefore drew up proposals to expose the established public agencies to competition and permit private service provision (Valenzuela 2001a, 2001b; interviews with Cuentas Yáñez 2002, Flores 2002, and Valenzuela 2002). But the union of social security health providers immediately protested these "privatization" efforts. More importantly, clientelistic politicians strongly resisted any further loss of bureaucratic positions that they could use for patronage appointments. A powerful party faction that helped to sustain the weak government therefore vetoed the IDB-sponsored reform plan (interview with Flores 2002; Valenzuela 2002). The second Sánchez de Lozada administration, which rested on a precarious party coalition, did not dare to resume this controversial project (interview with Torres Goitia Caballero 2006; Cueto Arteaga 2002). Therefore, IFI efforts to promote efficiency made minimal progress.

In sum, the Washington banks achieved uneven success in promoting health reform in Bolivia. Equity-enhancing programs advanced considerably, but very few efficiency-oriented measures passed; obviously, the extension of benefits was more attractive to politicians than conflictive efforts to revamp entrenched institutions. The most important initiative, maternal and infant insurance, embodied core elements of the IFI agenda; given its limited stock of domestic expertise, Bolivia imported a good deal of know-how made available by external sources (Contreras 1997: 203–5, 209–11, 222–24; Myers 1997: 185, 189–93). But spiraling electoral competition soon loosened the targeting demanded by the IFIs.

Thus, while the IFIs made a significant difference, they did not manage to attain major goals in this aid-dependent country. In fact, Bolivia's poverty and acute social deficits induced so many donors to offer aid that none of them gained decisive leverage. Taking advantage of this oversupply, the government avoided dependence on any specific source of funds. While affecting Bolivia's health policy through pressure and availability enhancement, the IFIs therefore could not push this weak country to adopt politically costly, controversial reforms.

CONCLUSIONS ON IFI INFLUENCE

The case studies show that the IFIs exerted significant but far from decisive influence on health policymaking. They supported equity-enhancing reforms in Costa Rica and contributed to their design and enactment in Bolivia and Peru. And they pushed forward efficiency-oriented measures in Costa Rica and helped to put them on the agenda—though with limited success—in El Salvador, Peru, and Bolivia (cf. Cruz and Carrera 2004: 222–23, 228 on Mexico). Only Brazil remained largely unaffected by IFI influence. Altogether, the IFIs induced countries to advance toward efficiency and equity, although they did not manage to impose specific reform designs. Thus, they played a more important role in health reform than in pension privatization. As a result, principle diffusion in health care had more of a vertical component than model diffusion in social security, where horizontal contagion, especially direct learning from Chile, predominated.

Yet while IFI influence helped to trigger the waves of equity- and efficiency-oriented health reforms, "soft power" proved more effective than "hard power." The IFIs clearly drew leverage from their generous loan offers, which often came attached with conditions (e.g., interview with Pereira 2002). But as in the pension arena, conditionality in no way gave the IFIs control over decision making; several administrations, even in poor countries that desperately needed aid, simply refused to accept conditional loans or failed to comply with their terms. Many efficiency-oriented reforms, in particular, were blocked by opposition from clientelistic government supporters or ideological foes of "privatization." Thus, IFI leverage often proved ineffectual.

Even when the IFIs failed to attain their original goals, however, as in the institutional transformation of Costa Rica's health system, they often managed to coax governments to advance in the direction they advocated; thus, they contributed significantly to principle diffusion. For this purpose, soft power exerted through availability enhancement, technical assistance, or the "recommendation" of foreign consultants often proved more effective than loan conditionality. Health policy-makers commonly acknowledged the important contribution that technical advice from the IFIs made to their reform decisions.

IFI involvement was especially significant in drawing Latin American economy ministries more deeply into health policymaking. In earlier decades, economic officials had cared only about the fiscal bottom line of the health system and had left policy decisions to health specialists, mostly medical doctors. But the economic crisis of the 1980s and the IFIs' emphasis on efficiency induced economic agencies to elaborate and advocate concrete reform proposals that promoted cost-effectiveness and targeting. The WB thus helped to change the constellation of health policy-makers, and the "new" actors took their main inspiration from its efficiency and equity agenda. In this way, the IFIs guaranteed powerful attention to the principles they were expounding. Thus, softer forms of influence—rather than forceful leverage—allowed the IFIs to propel health reform.

These promotional efforts had a differential impact across countries, however. To account for this varied effect, governments' ideological orientation proved most important. Where health policy was controlled by leftist forces averse to neoliberalism, as in Brazil, or where such forces commanded veto power, as in El Salvador, the World Bank could not make a difference. By contrast, where market-oriented forces prevailed, as in Bolivia and Peru, the IFIs attained greater influence. Social-democratic Costa Rica lies in between these extremes. The significance of ideology demonstrates that the IFIs cannot impose reforms on governments against their will. Only where the relevant domestic actors accept the IFIs' policy orientation can the reforms advocated by those agencies go forward. Ideological divergence is a sufficient condition for blocking IFI influence. In the health arena, the World Bank cannot coerce seemingly weak Third World countries.

Inside these ideological parameters, the institutional and financial strength and technical competence of the existing health agencies made a significant difference. Institutional solidity, good performance, and strong technical capacity gave Costa Rica's CCSS great bargaining power. The EBAIS program was therefore much more generous than Bolivia's SNMN, which embodied the WB's minimalistic approach more faithfully. Yet while giving the IFIs greater leverage on specific decisions, institutional weakness hindered the consistent implementation of the bank's health reform agenda, as the politically driven erosion of targeting in Bolivia's SNMN and the haphazard enactment of disparate changes in Peru demonstrate. These differences demonstrate again that the IFIs faced important limits in their capacity to propel principle diffusion in health care.

NORMATIVE APPEAL IN EQUITY-ENHANCING HEALTH REFORM

The Emergence of the Equity and Universalization Norm

While IFI pressure and availability enhancement helped to advance equity-enhancing health measures in Latin America, this vertical influence cannot account for all the progress made on this front. Brazil and Costa Rica pursued more ambitious and costly goals than the WB regarded as financially viable; indeed, Brazil transformed its health system in complete independence from the IFIs. Even aid-dependent Bolivia, which initially followed the IFI line more closely, gradually made its maternal and infant insurance more comprehensive and generous than the WB recommended.

Thus, IFI influence cannot satisfactorily explain the wave of equity-enhancing, universalizing reforms enacted during the last two decades.

This principle diffusion drew a strong additional impulse from normative appeal, especially the worldwide resonance found by the goal of "health for all by the year 2000," which had been propagated and pursued since the late 1970s. The WB contributed to the resumption of this universalization effort after the "lost decade" of the 1980s, when dire resource constraints caused setbacks in many countries; in particular, the WB's stress on the compatibility of universalization and efficiency legitimated the equity goal before governments' economic agencies, which control the purse strings. But as the bank did not invent pension privatization, it was not the actor that first raised the universalization goal to international prominence and thus set in motion a striking "norm cascade" (Finnemore and Sikkink 1998). Instead, as in social security, the WB supported diffusion when it was already under way.

The goal of guaranteeing satisfactory health coverage for all citizens emerged from the basic needs movement of the 1970s. In the health arena, this amorphous movement achieved the international codification of its principles in the famous WHO conference held in 1978 in Alma Ata. This legendary meeting, invoked to the present day by many health experts and government officials (e.g., MSPAS n.d.: 3–4, 20; interviews with Azevedo 2003, Finkelman 2003, and Salas Chaves 2004), condensed its central recommendation in the pithy slogan: "health for all by the year 2000." Governments from all over the world pledged to devote substantial resources to fulfilling this ambitious goal by extending basic medical services and preventive measures to the poor. This new norm gained tremendous international legitimacy (Cueto 2004: 1866–72).

Thus, the equity goal emerged long before the WB took an important role in the health area. Moreover, its universalistic impulse and comprehensive notion of primary care differed substantively from the later WB version, which insisted on targeting (Cueto 2004). It had a purely social impetus without any admixture of economic goals such as cost-effectiveness. The sponsors of the Alma Ata conference and main promoters of this universalistic equity goal were the WHO and UNICEF. These IOs enjoyed great international legitimacy and had a global network because they helped many developing countries with policy advice and technical assistance. But compared to the IFIs, they were weak and commanded minimal pressure. In particular, they lacked ample financial resources and therefore could not impose any conditionality but relied only on the power of moral suasion and international embarrassment.

The global advance of the universalization principle, which inspired reform efforts all over the world, thus constitutes a genuine norm shift as conceptualized by constructivists and sociological institutionalists

(Finnemore and Sikkink 1998; Barnett and Finnemore 2004). The Alma Ata conference boosted the legitimacy of "health for all." After this famous meeting, the universalization goal was on the mind of health officials, that is, cognitively available (cf. Kuran and Sunstein 1999). And given the uniformly positive value attached to this goal, which set a new standard of appropriateness, nobody dared to argue against it. Indications that governments neglected poorer sectors, as evidenced by high maternal and infant mortality, turned into sources of national shame (see Shiffman 2003; Shiffman, Stanton, and Salazar 2004).

This norm shift triggered a multitude of reforms because governments could often pursue it through add-on programs that had a distributive nature (cf. Lowi 1964). In many Latin American countries, the Health Ministry had the institutional mission to serve people who were not covered by the social security system. Thus, the poor were legally entitled to health care, although insufficient political priority, resource constraints, and the institutional weakness plaguing many health ministries often prevented the fulfillment of this promise. In many countries, effective universalization therefore did not require legal changes, which could have aroused redistributive conflicts over how to finance this equity-enhancing change. Instead, it could be pursued through low-profile administrative rules and decisions on the location of new health facilities. Since costs therefore remained politically invisible, many efforts to expand effective health coverage classify as distributive measures. These add-on programs did not face strong interest-based opposition. In fact, politicians had an obvious self-interest in creating new benefit schemes and eagerly sponsored the cause of "health for all."

Some countries such as Brazil, however, pursued universalization through constitutional changes or large-scale benefit programs. These politically visible decisions elicited resistance from better-off sectors, which feared higher taxes or lower benefits for themselves. But counteracting pressures often neutralized this opposition. Democratization strengthened politicians' interest in catering to the large numbers of poorer people, whose votes could decide elections. As a result, health experts found political support for their equity agenda from newly competitive partisan forces. Brazil's return to democracy and Colombia's efforts to reinvigorate its existing democracy therefore reinforced universalization efforts (Nelson 2004: 41–46). Thus, political interests often counterbalanced interest-group resistance to complying with the international norm shift triggered by the Alma Ata meeting. Since opposing interests "canceled out," normative appeal could carry the day. International legitimacy concerns, which were too weak to shape the redistributive politics of pension privatization, therefore managed to set in motion a wave of equity-enhancing health reforms.

Economic Constraints and Opportunities in Universalization Efforts

While the "health for all" norm inspired the universalizing reforms of the last twenty-five years, it cannot account for the bunched nature of these efforts in Latin America, especially the reform wave of the 1990s. The dearth of extension efforts in the 1980s and their proliferation in the 1990s resulted from changing economic opportunities. Although distributive measures do not carry visible political costs, they require fiscal resources; therefore, finance ministers are crucial veto players. Resource availability is a necessary precondition for advancing the universalization agenda.

The profound economic crisis of the 1980s therefore hindered equity-enhancing measures. Many countries had to slash health budgets and could not extend benefits. Even Costa Rica, which had already attained universal coverage in the 1970s, saw this accomplishment threatened by severe resource constraints. But as Latin America overcame the crisis, new funds became available. Tax revenues recovered, and increased IFI involvement in the health arena led to plentiful loan offers. These resources allowed governments to resume the equity agenda and extend primary care to the poor.

Thus, the wavelike character of equity-enhancing health reforms partly reflects Latin America's economic roller-coaster over the last twenty-five years. While this principle diffusion was initiated by a norm cascade set in motion by two weak yet highly legitimate IOs, the ebb and flow of financial resources conditioned efforts to put the new norm into practice. Reinforced by the political incentives unleashed by democratization, this combination of factors gave rise to a broad-based move to guarantee basic health care for the poor. Normative appeal thus propelled principle diffusion, but it unfolded only under propitious economic and political conditions.

The Wave of Equity-Enhancing Reforms

The universalization norm stimulated many equity-enhancing changes in Latin America. Whereas efficiency-oriented measures were pushed primarily by Finance and Planning ministries, Health Ministry officials usually took the initiative in proposing and elaborating these reforms.

COSTA RICA'S GENEROUS PRIMARY CARE MODEL

Costa Rica prided itself on having fulfilled the standards of Alma Ata even before that famous conference took place (interview with Salas Chaves 2004). But these norms clearly helped to motivate the efforts of the 1990s to make up for ground lost during the economic hardship of the 1980s. Several experts and policy-makers invoked those principles as crucial inspiration for the EBAIS strategy (interviews with Salas Chaves 2004 and Marín 2004; Castro Valverde and Sáenz 1998: 10). Commitment to these values induced Costa Rican decision-makers to resist WB pressures for a much more minimalist concept of primary care, as discussed above. The Alma Ata norms also proved stronger than political interests. Party politicians pushed for implementing EBAIS first in large urban centers, where votes were concentrated. But the program designers insisted on privileging outlying rural areas, where poverty was concentrated (interviews with Marín 2004, Sáenz 2004, and Ayala 2004). While external pressure and assistance and domestic political goals certainly contributed to the enactment of the EBAIS strategy,[9] the norms of Alma Ata played a significant independent role in propelling this ambitious program, which has further improved poor people's access to health care and boosted Costa Rica's enviable medical indicators (Rosero-Bixby 2004; Mortalidad infantil 2005; McGuire 2006).

BRAZIL'S PRIMARY HEALTH MOVEMENT

In Brazil, the norms of Alma Ata reinforced the reform proposals of the sanitary movement (interviews with Campos 2003 and Azevedo 2003) but initially played a less important role than in Costa Rica. Since the *sanitaristas* pursued broader ideological and political goals, they designed a comprehensive vision for a profound health reform, which was deliberately not confined to a primary care strategy. But the ideological nature of the sanitary movement; its heavy emphasis on institutional changes such as decentralization; and its relative neglect of concrete efforts to privilege preventive measures and basic care over curative treatments allowed a primary care movement to arise in the early 1990s (interviews with Girade 2003 and Machado de Souza 2003).

This amorphous movement emerged from a multitude of municipal and state-level efforts to improve health care for the poor and thus guarantee the universal coverage promised in the 1988 constitution. Spearheaded by nurses and health promoters (whereas the sanitary movement was dominated by doctors), this new movement managed to win Health Ministry support for building a rapidly expanding network of community health agents (Agentes Comunitários de Saúde—ACS), who promoted healthful behavior and provided basic care in destitute areas. Supported by the sponsors of the Alma Ata conference, especially UNICEF, this primary care scheme spread first and foremost in the impoverished

---

[9] Presidential candidate José Figueres Olsen used the primary care proposal as a major plank in his 1993–94 election campaign.

Northeast (interviews with Girade 2003, Machado de Souza 2003, Sousa 2003, and Azevedo 2003; Sousa 2001: 47–89). While the mainstream of the sanitary movement criticized this primary care strategy as a concession to the World Bank's advocacy of targeting a minimal health package at the destitute and as the provision of "poor medicine for the poor" (interviews with Andrade 2003, Azevedo 2003, Campos 2003, Girade 2003, Machado de Souza 2003), the IFIs actually played no role in these efforts, which were for years sustained by UNICEF and the WHO.

This persistent criticism, however, helped to trigger an upgrading of the ACS approach, which was folded into a family health strategy (interview with Sousa 2003): A team consisting of a doctor, a nurse, and several community health agents would provide a more comprehensive package of basic health treatments and preventive services to four to five thousand people. From 1994 onward, this Programa Saúde da Família (PSF) was gradually extended to a large proportion of Brazil's municipalities, especially in rural areas (MS 2002; Negri and Viana 2002: chaps. 10–12, 18). After 1998, this expansion drew an additional impulse from the appointment of an ambitious politician and presidential hopeful, José Serra, as health minister (interview with Azevedo 2003). An economist by training, Serra for the first time incorporated economic criteria into ministerial decision making. The resulting concern for cost-effectiveness reinforced the embrace of the primary care strategy, which the ministry promoted forcefully with financial incentives conditioned on clear performance targets (MS DAB 2002: 19–20, 49–50, 55–68). While this marriage of the primary care strategy and health economics resembles the WB approach to health, leading policy-makers adamantly deny that the IFIs had any influence (interview with Negri 2003).

Thus, the primary care movement, which emerged at the margins of the sanitary movement, managed to effect considerable change in Brazil's inequitable health system. Arising from local initiatives, it used the political space opened up by the sanitary movement's decentralization efforts to promote the norms codified in Alma Ata. Supported and legitimated by resource-poor UNICEF (Viana and dal Poz 1998: 20, 26), its persistent advocacy of preventive measures and basic care found increasing receptivity from the Health Ministry; eventually, a powerful "econopol" (cf. Domínguez 1997) turned this strategy into his flagship program. By all accounts, the PSF has significantly improved health care for the less well-off. Problems such as infant and maternal mortality, which used to be disproportionately severe for a country of Brazil's economic development level, have eased (Serra and Faria 2004: 177). Thus, in a nation of record social inequality, the principles of Alma Ata have made a difference.

The universalization norm also inspired reform efforts in Bolivia, the second-poorest country of the Americas. As discussed above, the equity-oriented measures of the 1990s, especially the maternal and infant insurance (SNMN), received crucial inputs from the IFIs. But these efforts also resumed an older primary care strategy, which was initiated in the early 1980s, following Bolivia's tortuous return to democracy. The father of a leading health policy-maker under the two Sánchez de Lozada administrations, Javier Torres Goitia Torres, served as health minister in the leftist government of Hernán Siles Suazo (1982–85) and implemented a primary health strategy through popular participation and mobilization. He promoted the creation of popular health committees that carried out immunization campaigns and provided basic services, especially to the poor (Torres Goitia Torres 1987: 12, 60–61, 74–78, 101–9; interviews with Torres Goitia Torres 2006 and Pooley 2002). He also introduced cost-free medical attention at childbirth (Torres Goitia Torres 1987: 103–4, 136–39), the first kernel of the SNMN.

All these efforts took inspiration from the equity norms codified at Alma Ata (Torres Goitia Torres 1987: 11–15, 53–55, 92; Torres Goitia Caballero 2000: 307; Böhrt Arana and Larraín Sánchez 2002: 17). In fact, UNICEF, which had cosponsored the 1978 conference, called attention to Bolivia's deplorable indicators on maternal and infant health and supported Torres Goitia's bottom-up strategy (interview with Torres Goitia Torres 2006). But the social protests, political turbulence, and hyperinflationary crisis that ruined Siles Suazo's presidency also hindered progress on the health front.

After the drastic adjustment of 1985 restored economic and political stability, Bolivia resumed the universalization effort. The WB, IDB, USAID, and UNICEF provided substantial financial and technical support and in the late 1980s started various projects to improve health coverage for the destitute (Lavadenz 1993; Homedes 2001; Chávez 1993; Muñoz Reyes 1993; interview with Cuentas Yáñez 2002). These initiatives benefited some long-neglected groups. But their multitude and the lack of effective coordination by the Health Ministry created inefficiency and mistargeting; the projects were executed with many problems and delays (Homedes 2001; IDB 1999a: 8; MDH SNS 1994: 38; interview with Cuentas Yáñez 2002).

The desire to create a stable base of domestic funding for universalization efforts stimulated proposals at the beginning of the Sánchez de Lozada administration to extend health insurance to the poor for a small per-capita fee, which the state would subsidize for the destitute (MDH SNS SE-GRSS 1994; MDH SNS 1994: 39, 84; interviews with Seoane

2002, Peña Rueda 2002, Galindo 2002, and Pereira 2002). Experts and political leaders worried, however, that these charges would be difficult to collect and would deter the poor from using medical services (interviews with Sandoval 2002 and Pereira 2002). Yet the fiscal decentralization of 1994–95 created resource availability at the municipal level and thus allowed for the extension of a basic health care package free of charge via the innovative maternal and infant insurance (SNMN).

Thus, while the SNMN incorporated crucial WB ideas, it also emerged from a long line of universalizing efforts that far predated the 1993 *World Development Report* and that were inspired by the norms of Alma Ata (interview with Torres Goitia Caballero 2006). Besides IFI influence, normative appeal stimulated Bolivia's equity-enhancing health reforms of the 1990s. The SNMN's creation was driven partly by the "shame" ("vergüenza") that policy-makers felt about their country's lamentable rates of maternal and infant mortality, which ranked among the highest in the world.[10] This embarrassment prompted a determination to push ahead with the SNMN despite various difficulties that hindered the institution of the new program and seemed to make its postponement advisable (Loaiza 1997: 43).

PERU'S PRIMARY HEALTH CARE PROGRAMS

In Peru, efforts to extend basic curative and preventive services to the poor also started right after the Alma Ata meeting—and long before the WB began pushing for this change. Peruvian health expert David Tejada was the WHO's assistant director in 1978 and helped organize the high-profile conference. The ideas of Alma Ata therefore had an immediate impact on his home country. The outgoing military regime initiated a primary care program in 1979 but lacked the political clout to make much headway with its implementation. The new democratic administration of Fernando Belaúnde (1980–85) enacted a more ambitious scheme to extend basic services to the poor. Although the serious economic problems afflicting Peru hindered its execution, this program was important in establishing principles and committing the government to goals—such as improved maternal and infant care—that later administrations could not renege on (Arroyo 2000: 113).

When David Tejada became health minister in 1985, primary care received an additional impulse. But the economic collapse beginning in 1987 undermined all efforts to extend coverage and improve services for the poor. As health expenditures plummeted by a stunning 75 percent from 1988 to 1990 and as the Shining Path guerrillas occupied large

---

[10] Aponte (1997: 4, 9); UDAPSO (1993: 3–4). In fact, Bolivia had incurred many specific commitments before IOs to improve maternal and infant health (MDH 1995: 10–12).

parts of the national territory, the Peruvian state was unable to maintain services for many poor citizens. Only the strategic defeat of the insurgency and the economic recovery of the mid-1990s allowed the Fujimori administration to restore the health system and resume the primary care strategy. While these efforts received an important impulse from IFIs (see above), they also renewed long-standing attempts to advance toward universalization and greater social equity, driven by the norms of Alma Ata.

THE LIMITED ADVANCE OF PRIMARY HEALTH CARE IN LATIN AMERICA

In sum, the norm cascade unleashed in 1978 triggered equity-enhancing reforms throughout Latin America.[11] Governments of different political and ideological colors extended basic curative and preventive care to less well-off sectors. Due to serious financial problems, these efforts made only limited headway in the 1980s. But greater resource availability allowed for significant progress in the 1990s. The WB gave an important additional impulse but did not initiate this change. Instead, a new norm prompted these efforts. And since add-on programs allowed for "cost-free" distributive policymaking, normative concerns stressed by constructivists managed to shape governmental decisions.

But this political condition also limited the extent and impact of equity-enhancing change. Ambitious concepts of primary care called for a profound transformation of the health system. This "revolution" (Cueto 2004: 1867–68, 1871–72) would take away resources from expensive hospital treatments and reallocate them to simple services. It thus required redistributive change that would hurt the middle class—the primary user of hospitals—to benefit the poor. But hospital directors, medical doctors, service personnel, and social security agencies adamantly rejected such a thorough restructuring and stubbornly defended the status quo. Thus, fierce political opposition ruled out determined redistribution and left room only for distributive measures.

Given the absence of a thorough reallocation of funds, resource constraints—eased but not lifted by economic recovery—limited the equity-enhancing initiatives that governments managed to implement. Although spending on primary care has increased significantly in many countries, both in absolute terms and as a proportion of total health expenditures, the lion's share of resources continues to fund complicated, expensive curative treatments, especially in hospitals. In Brazil, for instance, expenditures on primary care rose from 10.5 percent of Health Ministry

[11] In El Salvador, the confounding effect of the fierce civil war makes it difficult to assess the impact of international health norms during the 1980s. On the impact of the Alma Ata conference on Mexican health policy, see Cruz and Carrera (2004: 221–22).

spending in 1995 to 17.3 percent in 2002 (Serra and Faria 2004: 175); and in Costa Rica, the share of primary care in health expenditures increased from 15 percent in 1997 to 20 percent in 2000 (Arce and Sánchez 2001: 16–18; WB 2003c: 117). But these figures show that secondary and tertiary care continues to receive the largest share of funding.

Thus, there clearly has not been a primary care "revolution." Since reformers had to pursue the Alma Ata agenda through add-on programs, they have achieved only limited success. Because new norms cannot dislodge or overwhelm fairly clear and firm interests of major sociopolitical forces, they fail to trigger a thorough revamping of established institutional structures. The causal mechanism emphasized by constructivists can make a difference in some interstices of the health system, but its very condition of operation restricts its impact.

CONCLUSION

External pressures and new normative appeals, which did not drive model diffusion in social security, provided more important impulses for principle diffusion in health care. With plenty of carrots and some sticks, the IFIs pushed Latin American countries to advance toward greater efficiency and equity in their health systems. Drawing on external financial support and technical advice, several governments, especially in Bolivia, Costa Rica, and Peru, extended services to the rural and urban poor. The IFIs made an even more distinctive contribution with their forceful promotion of efficiency-oriented measures (e.g., WB 2004d: 13); without their constant prodding and availability enhancement, strong resistance from established bureaucratic institutions, unionized service providers, and patronage-hungry politicians would have blocked any advance. Thus, while the IFIs cannot impose specific blueprints and models—neither in social security nor in health care—they can induce countries to move toward the principles they advocate. For this purpose, they use both their financial leverage and the provision of plentiful information, that is, availability enhancement.

But IFI influence fell far short of accomplishing its original goals. None of the countries I investigated has come close to undertaking a comprehensive health reform as expounded in the 1993 *World Development Report*. Most often, externally induced change has remained piecemeal, uneven, and disparate. While some initiatives have gone forward, active or passive resistance or simple inertia have often proven stronger. Privatization proposals have drawn particular fire, as the experiences of El Salvador show. Where efficiency-enhancing measures such as performance contracts have been enacted, they have usually brought more formal than real change; while even Bolivia introduced these modern management instruments, they have not altered the actual operation of its underperforming health system. Countries have advanced the farthest in extending primary care to long-neglected sectors. But they have targeted these new programs less narrowly than the World Bank recommended. In sum, external pressures had a significant but limited impact on principle diffusion in health care.

Indeed, equity-enhancing reforms resulted not only from IFI promotion, but also from an international norm shift, which long predated prominent WB engagement in health care. The codification of the "health for all" maxim in 1978 triggered a norm cascade that put increasing moral pressure on governments to combat embarrassingly severe health problems, especially maternal and infant mortality. As economic recovery and generous IFI loans allowed Latin American governments to pursue universalization through distributive, politically cost-free add-on programs, this new norm managed to shape their decision making in the 1990s. The availability of new funds avoided any clash of interests and allowed the quest for international legitimacy to carry the day. In sum, the wave of universalizing programs resulted from the confluence of IFI pressures and new normative appeals. These two causal mechanisms, which were not decisive in the spread of Chilean-style pension privatization, had a greater impact on efficiency- and equity-oriented reforms in health care.

CHAPTER 6

Cognitive Heuristics in the Diffusion of Health Reform

WHILE EXTERNAL pressures and new norms contributed to the spread of health reform (see chapter 5), cognitive heuristics also shaped this process in important ways. Experts and decision-makers did not proactively scan the international environment and evaluate foreign innovations in a thorough, systematic way, as comprehensive rationality would require. Instead, bounded rationality prevailed, as in the diffusion of pension privatization. Above all, the availability and representativeness heuristic provided a major impulse for efficiency- and equity-oriented health measures in the 1990s. New experiments adopted in the region, especially Chile's partial health privatization of 1981 and Colombia's comprehensive restructuring of 1993, were uniquely available and attracted much attention; early accomplishments of the Colombian reform, especially a striking expansion of insurance coverage, also imbued it with an aura of success that stimulated some emulation efforts.

But Chile's health reform was less drastic than social security privatization because it did not condemn the existing public system to extinction by forcing new labor market entrants into private insurance companies; in fact, only a minority of the population switched. And Colombia's revamping did not constitute a neat, simple, well-integrated model that rested on a few coherent design principles, like Chilean pension privatization. Instead, it was inspired by a variety of country experiences and sought to strike a compromise between different goals (Uribe 2004). Therefore, it was highly complicated in design and administration and was harder to grasp and less attractive to boundedly rational decision-makers. By contrast to a neat, unified blueprint, a complex, eclectic change is unlikely to become an outstanding model. As a result, Colombia's reform never turned into the obligatory, singular reference point in the health arena that Chile's privatization was in social security. Failing to monopolize attention, it did not unleash a broad wave of diffusion, but more dispersed emulation efforts. And where it influenced decision making, it was not the only source of inspiration but had to share the limelight with other country experiences. Whereas social security policy in the 1990s often revolved around a clear-cut choice of whether to enact Chilean-style privatization or not, health policy-makers tended to pick and choose from more than one experiment. This broader range of available options limited anchoring: Since decision-makers were not fixated on one outstanding model, they did not import a specific blueprint wholesale; instead, they often combined elements of various experiments or modified their major source of inspiration in light of other available options.

The absence of a clear, unique model in health care thus meant that cognitive heuristics produced less profound and widespread diffusion. The availability heuristic highlighted different experiments to decision-makers in different countries; the representativeness heuristic did not single out any of them as uniquely successful; and limited anchoring led to significant modification, rather than simple imitation. For these reasons, reform diffusion in health care was less uniform and wavelike than in pension privatization.

But while producing less striking contagion effects than in social security, cognitive heuristics caused significant deviations from comprehensive rationality. For logically accidental reasons, especially geographic proximity and direct contacts, the availability heuristic highlighted some experiences while many other interesting innovations failed to enter decision-makers' radar screen. And the representativeness heuristic triggered early enthusiasm for the Colombian reform, whose actual accomplishments soon turned out to be problematic. Thus, the empirical patterns of bounded rationality diverged from the normative postulates of comprehensive rationality.

THE LACK OF A NEAT, SINGULAR MODEL IN HEALTH REFORM

The health system is much more complex than social security. Rather than paying cash benefits, it offers a wide range of preventive and curative services whose provision and quality are difficult to monitor. Pensioners can certify benefit receipt with a signature; but patients rarely know what, if any, treatment they need and how good the medical quality of the service was. The information asymmetry between providers and patients makes the performance of medical personnel hard to measure and control. Furthermore, while pensioners can be counted on to obtain their benefit, demand needs to be stimulated in health care, especially for preventive services and routine examinations.

For all these reasons, health care is complicated and multifaceted. It involves a host of medical, financial, managerial, informational, and promotional aspects and activities, including countrywide vaccination campaigns, the purchase of high-tech equipment for hospitals, the extension of primary care to the rural poor, the institutional relations of the Health Ministry to the social security agencies, and personnel management in health posts.

Due to this tremendous complexity, no neat, simple reform model has emerged (Nelson 1999: 22–24). Chilean-style privatization, which became the mandatory reference point in social security, was much less drastic in health care: It did not force people to join private insurance companies but introduced free choice. Only a limited segment of the population could afford private insurance plans; even after two decades, 70 percent of citizens stayed in the public system. Thus, privatization remained very partial and did not revamp the whole health system. But as better-off sectors transferred their obligatory insurance fees to private companies, they stopped subsidizing public health care for the large majority of the population. Partial privatization therefore tightened financial constraints on the public system and caused lower service quality. Thus, Chile's reform did not improve the whole health system but favored the middle class and hurt poorer sectors. Rather than lifting all boats, it brought regressive redistribution, as even the WB and Chilean experts acknowledged (WB 1993b: 162; Oyarzo 1994: 139–40).

To make things worse, discontent prevailed among people who had chosen private insurance companies. These Instituciones de Salud Previsional used rules of exclusion hidden in the fine print of their contracts to refuse treatment to many patients. Their profit-driven efforts to attract young, healthy people and push chronic patients off the insurance rolls ("cream-skimming") stimulated great resentment (Oyarzo 1994: 124, 140–41; interview with Lagos 1993). Thus, health privatization was much less successful than pension privatization, which initially produced high rates of return and allegedly boosted Chile's growth. While the ISAPRE scheme was cognitively available in Latin America, it failed to stimulate the enthusiasm that the representativeness heuristic inspired for pension reform.

Furthermore, since health privatization remained partial, it could not resolve organizational and financial problems once and for all, as pension privatization claimed to do. This promise of a definitive solution is particularly attractive to boundedly rational decision-makers and provided a special impulse to the spread of Chilean-style social security reform. By contrast, the ISAPRE scheme did not relieve policy-makers of the continued need for adjustments, modifications, and reforms. The new private system required firm regulation; the underfinanced public system needed constant support; and their coexistence raised new issues concerning the treatment of private affiliates in public facilities. As even the WB (1993b: 162) recognized, Chile's health privatization "experience shows that reform is a permanent process, not a one-time effort, and that countries undertaking reform must have both the capacity and the political will to review and revise health policies continuously."

For all these reasons, the ISAPRE scheme did not constitute a clear, neat model, failed to attract as much attention as social security privatization, and lacked the aura of success that impressed especially economic experts. It also violated the social equity concerns of many health specialists. While a number of Latin American countries considered Chilean-style health privatization, the balance of rejection and support was usually stacked against it.[1]

To avoid the problems of the ISAPRE scheme, Colombia's health reform of 1993 combined partial privatization with an ambitious equity-enhancing effort to extend health insurance to the poor through public demand subsidies. The Ley 100 gave people a free choice among health insurance companies, which in turn contracted with service providers. Better-off people paid the full cost of their coverage in the contributive regime. Less well-off individuals joined the subsidized regime, which entitled them to a basic package of preventive and curative treatments. They paid part of the insurance premium, based on their income, and a solidarity fund fed by an extra charge on better-off people and by tax revenues covered the remainder. The initially distinct benefit packages of the contributory and subsidized regimes were supposed to converge gradually. The combination of an individualized, purely contractual and a subsidized, redistributive insurance scheme would thus guarantee universal, basically equal health care.

In these ways, the innovative Colombian reform sought to strike a balance between economic efficiency and social equity (Uribe 2004). Demand subsidies should incorporate less well-off people into the privatized insurance system and thus overcome the exclusion plaguing Chile's purely market-oriented reform. Solidaristic support was designed to turn poorer people into effective consumers who can exercise similar individual choice as the middle class. Whereas ISAPREs affiliated only the minority favored by the primary distribution of income, the Ley 100 instituted modest redistribution to universalize the effective capacity to fulfill basic health needs through the insurance and provider market. At the same time, this market-oriented solution tried to enhance social equity more efficiently than the paternalistic provision of health services by monopolistic public agencies managed to do. For these reasons, even

[1] Interviews with Bonadona (2002), Cercone (2004), Galindo (2002), Marín (2004), Miranda (2004), Peña Rueda (2002), and Pereira (2002); Miranda (2003: 341, 346). This rejection was particularly pronounced among Brazil's leftist sanitary movement (e.g., Labra 1988).

architects of Chile's ISAPRE system came to advocate a Colombian-style plan (Büchi 1994: 143–47; interview with Sánchez 1993).

Since Colombia's ambitious reform stood out against the limited, piecemeal changes adopted in other Latin American countries, it attracted a good deal of interest, especially inside the region. As the next section shows, health specialists from several countries followed the availability heuristic, paid special attention to this experiment, and placed it on the domestic decision-making agenda. But the Ley 100 never monopolized attention as Chilean pension privatization did. Inherent characteristics made it much less appealing to boundedly rational decision-makers.

Above all, Colombia's health reform was much more eclectic and complicated than radical social security privatization. Inspired by pure neoliberal principles, Chile's pension model was simple, coherent, and "out of one piece." Its neat, integral nature made it easy to grasp and propagate. Its elegant simplicity grabbed the attention of boundedly rational decision-makers. This model opened up a clear new path out of the mess of traditional pension policy. By contrast, the Ley 100 combined divergent principles derived from efficiency *and* equity, individual choice *and* collective solidarity (Uribe 2004: 210–11). It was highly complex and difficult to understand. It created two different insurance schemes and divided responsibilities among a variety of institutions, whose very list of acronyms—EPS, IPS, ESS—was confusing. It introduced managed competition, demand subsidies, productivity incentives, basic benefit packages, a solidarity fund, etc. No wonder that health specialists complained about its complicated nature and the great difficulty of implementing it (Isasi 1998: 5–6; Mendes 1999: 47–48; interview with Vargas 2004).

Thus, the Colombian reform did not constitute a neat, clear policy model. While it had some defining characteristics, such as boldness, it lacked others, especially simplicity and tight coherence. Therefore, although the Ley 100 stood out on the radar screen of Latin American health specialists, it did not turn into the singular focal point, like Chilean pension privatization. It overshadowed other experiments, including Chile's ISAPRE system, but did not monopolize attention. Instead, policy-makers considered other country experiences as well.

COGNITIVE HEURISTICS IN THE SPREAD OF HEALTH PRIVATIZATION

Efforts to Emulate Chile's Private Insurance Scheme

In the early 1990s, the Chilean privatization experiment began to attract significant attention in Latin America. Since Chile's new democracy decided to maintain the ISAPRE scheme, its association with the dictatorial Pinochet regime loosened and it became acceptable to democratic polities. Due to geographic proximity and long-standing connections, Latin American health specialists and economic experts came to study the reform, and Chilean health consultants advertised it in neighboring countries and at international conferences (e.g., Sánchez 1997). In fact, Chilean promoters of social security privatization sometimes drew up health privatization plans as well. The firm Claro y Asociados, for instance, which elaborated Bolivia's first pension reform project, also designed an ISAPRE scheme for the country (interview with Cuevas Argote 2002). Thus, model diffusion in social security began to spill over into health care.

Horizontal connections first made the ISAPRE scheme cognitively available. Direct links to Chilean experts led decision-makers in Peru and Bolivia to discuss ISAPRE-style reforms in the early 1990s, before the IFIs came to promote health privatization forcefully. As in the pension arena, deliberations and emulation efforts started among Chile's next-door neighbors (including Argentina: Lloyd-Sherlock 2004: 103). Typically, the availability heuristic produced geographic clustering of steps toward policy diffusion. Colombia, another Andean country that bordered on first emulator Peru, soon took inspiration from Chile as well (Uribe 2004: 211–12).

In more distant countries, external pressure or availability enhancement by the IFIs helped to put the ISAPRE scheme on the policy agenda. For instance, the IFI-sponsored ANSAL study discussed in chapter 5 created interest among Salvadoran health experts in the Chilean experience; even specialists from the center-left, such as Héctor Silva, who later joined the FMLN, were open to this proposal (interview with Silva 2004; cf. Avilés 1998: 73). In a more forceful fashion, WB consultants advocated this neoliberal innovation in social-democratic Costa Rica (interviews with Marín 2004, Sáenz 2004, and Salas Chaves 2004). Furthermore, the IFIs later supported health privatization proposals where the ISAPRE system had become cognitively available before their involvement, as in Bolivia and Peru. Thus, this plan first spread horizontally, but vertical influence then gave it an additional impulse.

But in Chile, this bold, novel scheme had not attained the striking initial success that pension privatization had achieved; in fact, affiliation with ISAPREs expanded only slowly. Furthermore, health privatization did not boost Chile's economic growth, as social security reform was said to do. Therefore, the representativeness heuristic failed to stimulate strong enthusiasm for the ISAPRE scheme. Even economic experts committed to its underlying principles could not support it with powerful pragmatic arguments.

Indeed, the disadvantages of health privatization had become obvious during its first decade of implementation. The social segmentation of Chile's health system undermined equity, solidarity, and universalism, which most health specialists held in high esteem. Therefore, the ISAPRE system was increasingly seen not as a model to imitate, but a deterrent to avoid.[2] While several countries considered emulating this reform in the early 1990s, it lost support thereafter.

For these reasons, an effort to imitate the ISAPRE scheme only got under way in a unique setting, namely, Peru in 1991. Facing persistent hyperinflation, President Fujimori had delegated economic policy to a free-market enthusiast, Carlos Boloña, who assembled a small, cohesive team of like-minded economic experts (Weyland 2002b: 117–18). This tight-knit group sought to enact a comprehensive package of neoliberal reforms as quickly as possible. Whereas the IFIs recommended the sequencing of stabilization and structural change, Boloña and his aides proceeded to revamp Peru's economic and social institutions immediately (interviews with Boloña 1996 and Peñaranda 2002). The political difficulties facing the Fujimori government, which lacked stable support in Congress, and the precarious position of the economic team, whose neoliberal zeal the president viewed with reservations, suggested to Boloña the need to advance fast. Therefore, he took advantage of presidential decree powers delegated by Congress to pass a host of structural reforms in late 1991 (Boloña 1993: 176). This package of decrees included partial health privatization.

The desire to use this window of opportunity exacerbated time pressures for preparing the project. As a careful assessment of costs and benefits—not to speak of a search for alternative policy options—was infeasible, decision-makers relied heavily on cognitive heuristics. The homogeneity of the small change team precluded any correction of the resulting distortions. In fact, the health privatization decree was elaborated by a single individual, an economist working for the Economy Ministry; the Health Ministry had no input at all (interviews with Yamamoto 2002, Meloni 2002, and Espinoza 2002).

This generalist, José Carlos Vera la Torre, followed the availability heuristic and took his inspiration from the ISAPRE system. At that time, connections between Peru's economic team and Chilean experts who had enacted market reforms under the Pinochet regime, such as Hernán Büchi and José Piñera, were extremely close. Boloña's aides largely emulated Chile, including its experiment with health privatization, which Chilean specialists depicted as a big success (interviews with Vera la Torre 2002 and Yong Motta 2002). In fact, Peru's privatization decree

---

[2] See note 1.

was "directly copied from Chile" (interview with Vera la Torre 2002;[3] similar interview with Meloni 2002); a health specialist who worked in this specific area quipped that Vera simply used the neighbor's legislation and substituted "Chile" with "Peru" (interview with Manrique 2002). Under high time pressure, anchoring prevailed, prompting imitation and precluding adaptation. Shaped by cognitive heuristics, this decision-making process deviated starkly from the standards of comprehensive rationality.

The decree allowed social security affiliates to channel their obligatory health insurance contributions to private companies (Crean el Sistema Privado de Salud 1991). This drastic change intended to expose the social security institute IPSS to private competition. It resulted from direct, horizontal learning from an experiment enacted by a neighbor, not from vertical pressures; the WB was not involved at all. But this hasty, ill-prepared measure was never implemented. The IPSS, which tried hard to overcome its financial and administrative problems and improve health service provision (Ausejo 1995), fiercely opposed private competition.[4] It claimed that the exit of better-off contributors would drain its finances and threaten health care for poorer affiliates (Vera la Torre 1994b: 190–93). The new health minister, a close confidant of President Fujimori, also opposed health privatization (Paredes 2002; interview with Peñaranda 2002).

Eventually, the IPSS reached a compromise with the neoliberal economic team. In exchange for letting pension privatization proceed, IPSS President Castañeda Lossio obtained Minister Boloña's commitment to shelve health privatization (Boloña 1994: 159; interviews with De los Heros 2002, Du Bois 2002, and Peñaranda 2002; see chapter 4). Therefore, the 1991 decree was never implemented, though it stayed on the books.

In 1993, a neoliberal congressman, soon appointed as health minister, and his chief adviser, the author of the 1991 decree, tried hard to unblock health privatization (interviews with Freundt 2002, Vera la Torre 2002, and Meloni 2002; Vera la Torre 1994a, 1994b). This initiative drew support from the economic team and former Economy Minister Boloña, the driving force behind market reform in Peru (interview with Du Bois 2002; Vera la Torre, Petrera, Ruiz, et al. 1994). To win broader backing, privatization advocates organized conferences with foreign experts, especially from Chile and the United States (Vera la Torre et al.

---

[3] The U.S. HMO system also provided crucial inspiration (interview with Vera la Torre 2002).

[4] But to improve efficiency and user satisfaction and thus forestall full-scale privatization, the IPSS itself began to outsource some medical services (Fiedler 1996: 411–16).

1994; ESAN/IDE 1994). Thus, they activated their horizontal links, which had made the reform project available in the first place.

But the IPSS continued to resist health privatization (interview with Freundt 2002; Vera la Torre 1994b: 190–93; Arroyo 2000: 165; see also Paredes 2002). President Fujimori himself had reservations about applying market principles to the social sectors. He also feared that popular aversion to health privatization would lower his chances in upcoming vote contests, including his bid for reelection in April 1995. Since the government was already embroiled in a contentious, politically costly debate over privatization in education (Graham 1998: 32, 100–109; Ortiz de Zevallos et al. 1999: 7–22), the president refused to promote health privatization (interviews with Freundt 2002 and Vera la Torre 2002).

In sum, widespread aversion or skepticism about Chilean-style health privatization allowed emulation efforts to advance only under special circumstances (cf. Boloña 1994: 159; see Arroyo 2000: 39–40). The resulting time pressures gave cognitive heuristics, especially availability and anchoring, free rein. Simple imitation and deficient adaptation greatly lowered decision quality.[5] Even the economic expert who elaborated the 1991 decree and pushed for its implementation in 1993 expresses relief that this initiative failed because it would have deepened the segmentation of the Peruvian health system, further undermining social equity (interview with Vera la Torre 2002).

This equity concern was the principal reason why policy-makers in Bolivia decided not to pursue the ISAPRE scheme. This proposal became cognitively available under the Paz Zamora administration (1989–93). But its regressive features, which even Chilean consultants acknowledged, made Bolivian experts reluctant to promote this plan in the early 1990s (interview with Bonadona 2002). Determined to extend market reform to the social sectors, the Sánchez de Lozada government (1993–97) gave more serious consideration to the Chilean experiment in 1993–94. But the specialists and officials debating this issue worried about the exclusion of the urban and rural poor, who could not afford private health insurance. They also heard about discontent among ISAPRE-affiliates (interviews with Galindo 2002 and Peña Rueda 2002). They rejected emulation because Chile's reform had not attained any clear success that the representativeness heuristic amplified. In fact, in subse-

[5] In 1993, Vera la Torre (1994b: 174–81) introduced some modifications of the Chilean system, but they were designed to benefit only social security affiliates, especially those choosing private insurance companies. Thus, these changes did not address most equity problems plaguing Chile's partially privatized health system (cf. Vera la Torre et al. 1994: 125–28).

quent years Bolivian health specialists have widely seen the ISAPRE scheme as a failure (interview with Pereira 2002).

For the same reasons, interest in Chilean-style privatization faded among Salvadoran health experts, particularly specialists not linked to the neoliberal ARENA governments. Continued political polarization turned any proposal resembling the ISAPRE scheme highly controversial and unviable (interview with Silva 2004). And in Brazil, Chile's privatization scheme and the occasional domestic proposal inspired by it (e.g., Médici, Oliveira, and Beltrão 1993b; IL 1994) were rejected out of hand by the leftist sanitary movement (Labra 1988; Mendes 1999: 78–93).

As a result, Chile's experiment did not spread to other Latin American countries. While many specialists followed the availability heuristic and paid great attention to the novel privatization scheme, it did not attain clear initial success; the representativeness heuristic therefore did not imbue it with the aura of inherent quality that made pension privatization so attractive to boundedly rational decision-makers. Economic experts occasionally promoted the ISAPRE scheme for efficiency reasons. But they did not exert much pressure because it lacked the macroeconomic spillover effects that the representativeness heuristic attributed to pension privatization. Therefore, the equity concerns raised by health specialists, the institutional interests of established public agencies, and politicians' goal to avoid polemical, costly reforms managed to preclude the diffusion of Chilean-style health privatization.

Efforts to Emulate Colombia's Complex Health Reform

The Ley 100 promised to remedy the equity deficit of the ISAPRE system by extending subsidized health insurance to poorer sectors. In fact, it attained its most striking success with a drastic increase in coverage from 20.6 percent of the population in 1993 to 57 percent in 1997. Progress was greatest for lower strata: "In the first [income] decile, insurance coverage went from 4 percent in 1993 to 40 percent in 1997" (Ramírez 2004: 142; see also De Groote, De Paepe, and Unger 2005: 127–28). As the availability heuristic drew the attention of Latin American policymakers to Colombia's ambitious reform, its accomplishments on the equity front triggered the representativeness heuristic, which made the Ley 100 appear as a promising innovation.

The high fiscal cost of the coverage extension and the complicated nature of the new health system dampened this enthusiasm, however. Reform implementation boosted health spending by "21.1 percent yearly . . . between 1993 and 1996" (Ramírez 2004: 144; see also De Groote, De Paepe, and Unger 2005: 125–26, 133–34). Moreover, it was not easy for boundedly rational decision-makers to grasp and evaluate this multifaceted reform. Therefore, the representativeness heuristic triggered moderate but not overwhelming contagion. And where emulation efforts took place, anchoring remained limited; the very eclecticism of the Ley 100 opened the door for picking and choosing. As a result, policy-makers in several Latin American countries sought to emulate certain components of the Colombian blueprint but adapted them to their specific circumstances.

Due to geographical proximity and cultural, educational, and historical connections,[6] Colombia's reform quickly became available inside Latin America. Its architect, José Luis Londoño, codified its lessons and promoted them widely, for instance at a high-profile meeting of health ministers in 1995 (Londoño and Frenk 2000: 56). Following the availability heuristic, Latin American health specialists paid special attention to the Ley 100. And the representativeness heuristic stimulated emulation efforts in several nations.

Territorial contiguity again furthered diffusion. The Colombian reform was immediately available in neighboring Peru. In 1993–94, both the main proponent of health privatization and the leading designer and executor of the CLAS scheme of community health management (see chapter 5) studied the Ley 100 (interviews with Vera la Torre 2002 and Vera del Carpio 2002). In fact, the former expert reports extensive interactions, including mutual visits and discussions with Londoño; as a result, he shifted from embracing Chile's ISAPRE scheme to proposing a universal health insurance system very similar to the Colombian blueprint (interview with Vera la Torre 2002; Vera la Torre 2003b: 158–79). These intensive contacts continued for years (interviews with Costa Bauer 2002 and Meloni 2002; MINSA 1997). To avoid the equity problems of the ISAPRE scheme, even Chilean consultants hired by Peru advanced proposals resembling the Ley 100 (Jara and Vergara 1995a, 1995b; Solimano 1997).

As a result, Peruvian health specialists in 1995–96 elaborated a comprehensive reform project that was strongly inspired by the Colombian restructuring (and followed general IFI guidelines; see chapter 5). They proposed a contributive and a subsidized regime, competition between private and public providers, and demand subsidies, thus incorporating all the major features of the Ley 100 (Mesa-Lago 1996: 7–14, 20–24; Espinoza 1998a: 9–10; Arroyo 2000: 42). This wide-ranging, ambitious

[6] For instance, the executive president of Costa Rica's CCSS (1994–98), Alvaro Salas Chaves, was a classmate of the Ley 100's architect, José Luis Londoño, at Harvard's Kennedy School (interview with Salas Chaves 2004).

emulation plan sought to integrate the disparate programs created by the Fujimori government (see chapter 5) and thus bring a qualitative change in Peruvian health policy.

But facing great bureaucratic and political resistance, a freshly appointed neoliberal health minister and a new, reform-oriented IPSS president designed a more moderate proposal in mid-1996. While intense discussions with Colombian and Chilean consultants made them follow the Ley 100 in many important aspects, they pushed less strongly for privatization and assigned the IPSS a predominant role in health insurance and service provision (Mesa-Lago 1996: 11–25; Espinoza 1998a: 10; interview with Costa Bauer 2002).

Even this compromise threatened to upset powerful bureaucratic interests by curtailing the Health Ministry's role in service provision. In fact, it was part of a broader plan to reform the state, which included the dismissal of thousands of public employees. Yet President Fujimori refused to take this unpopular step and blocked the state reform (interviews with Abugattás 1999, Torres y Torres Lara 1999, Espinoza 2002, and Vásquez 2002). Health reform therefore also came to a standstill (Espinoza 1998: 11–12). In fact, the Peruvian state lacked the voluminous financial resources required for including all citizens in the subsidized regime. A new round of fiscal adjustment in 1996 precluded the extension of health insurance to the poor.

As these political and economic obstacles forestalled a sectorwide reform, Peruvian health policy resumed its piecemeal, fragmented trajectory. The removal of IPSS President Castañeda Lossio, whom President Fujimori increasingly feared as a political rival, allowed for partial health privatization. In mid-1996, a small team with participation from the Economy Ministry elaborated a plan that was strongly inspired by the Colombian and Chilean precedents.[7] Based on intensive consultations with experts from both countries (interview with Costa Bauer 2002; MINSA 1997), it permitted social security affiliates to transfer part of their obligatory health insurance contributions to private provider organizations called Entidades Prestadoras de Salud (EPS). This competition would improve the IPSS's efficiency, and the exit of better-off patients, who made most use of IPSS services, would create room for less well-off affiliates to obtain health care (Ewig 2004: 239–40). Following the Colombian reform and diverging from pure Chilean-style privatization, this change was framed as a first step toward a broader restructuring that would eventually include poorer people in subsidized

---

[7] In a revealing formulation, Isasi (1998: 2), a consultant who participated in this decision, insists that it "was not a mere copy of the models of other countries."

health insurance. Thus, Peru would emulate the Ley 100 in a gradual fashion (Ley de Modernización 1996: 144233–34; see also Pichihua 1998: 4).

In sum, Colombia's reform was especially available to Peruvian policy-makers, and its initial success triggered the representativeness heuristic and thus stimulated its diffusion. But its complexity weakened anchoring. Peruvians therefore chose one component and adapted it to their own needs. Typical of boundedly rational decision-makers, they simplified the privatization scheme. Whereas the Ley 100 confined the EPS (called Entidades Promotoras de Salud in Colombia) to the insurance function and created separate service providers called Instituciones Prestadoras de Servicios de Salud (IPS), President Fujimori and other decision-makers criticized this complexity and insisted on combining the two roles. Therefore, the Peruvian EPS were designed as private insurance and health service companies (Isasi 1998: 2–3, 6).

To keep the IPSS financially viable, Fujimori also confined privatization to the primary and secondary level of medical attention; the IPSS continued to provide all complicated, expensive hospital treatments to social security affiliates. The president therefore limited the proportion of insurance contributions that IPSS affiliates could transfer to EPS to 25 percent; they continued to channel 6.75 percent of their salaries to the IPSS. The health minister and the design team pleaded for a higher percentage, but Fujimori was increasingly averse to neoliberalism (interview with Vásquez 2002). By contrast to Colombia and Chile, health privatization in Peru thus remained limited. The EPS proposal nevertheless elicited vociferous opposition from doctors, medical personnel, and their unions (e.g., Velit Granda 1997; Colegio Médico n.d.; Ewig 2004: 239–40). But the government controlled a majority in Congress, and the EPS scheme passed easily in 1997.

In sum, Peru quickly emulated the initially successful innovation of its neighbor, albeit with substantial modifications.[8] While the complicated Colombian reform did not turn into a neat model and anchoring therefore did not yield faithful imitation, Peruvian policy-makers clearly followed the availability heuristic in paying disproportionate attention to the Ley 100, and they applied the representativeness heuristic in interpreting its initial success as proof of inherent quality.

Typically, however, the new system has disappointed initial expectations. By late 2003, fewer than 250,000 Peruvians had joined an EPS,

---

[8] These modifications are highlighted by Isasi (1998) and Payet (interview 2002). The effort to mark distance from Chile and Colombia probably reflects the aversion to health privatization in public opinion.

amounting to less than 4 percent of the dependently employed; further growth seemed unlikely (SEPS 2002: 15, 19; SEPS 2004: 11).[9] Only four EPS formed, and they have languished, leading to further concentration. As the IPSS has faced little competition, the reform has failed to transform Peru's health system. In fact, the financial constraints that economic crisis and adjustment imposed on the middle class have left little room for health privatization. During the 1990s, purchase of private health insurance and services diminished as better-off sectors had to resort to cheaper care from the public sector (MINSA DGSP 2003: 14–16, 24). Thus, Peruvian decision-makers incurred the political cost of enacting a change that few people took advantage of. Emulating the Colombian and Chilean experiments in health privatization proved to be largely a failure.[10] Once again, the heuristics of availability and representativeness produced suboptimal decision outputs.

Immediately after the politically costly EPS decision, President Fujimori took an ill-prepared step toward the equity-enhancing aspects of the Colombian reform, namely, the extension of health care to poorer sectors through insurance mechanisms. In mid-1997, he announced free health coverage for public school students. As analyzed in chapter 5, this populist measure, which was mistargeted in equity terms, drew withering criticism from the IFIs and domestic health experts. Yet since Fujimori's fiat could not be undone, it was complemented with a state-financed insurance scheme focused on maternal and infant health (Seguro Materno Infantil—SMI).

Peruvian health reformers depicted the SMI as the kernel of a "subsidized regime" à la Colombia (e.g., Pichihua 1998: 4; WB 1999d: 44). They gradually planned to extend coverage to the whole population, introduce cost recovery mechanisms, and open up service provision to private competition. Thus, they kept drawing inspiration from the Ley 100 (e.g., Johnson 1998: 46–50). In fact, the Toledo government continued this slow advance toward a comprehensive subsidized regime. It extended coverage to additional sectors (Vera la Torre 2003a: 22–23) and considered introducing user fees for better-off people (Seguro de Salud 2005). The latter proposal responds to urgent resource needs because the fiscal sustenance of these insurance schemes has remained precarious (interview with Kolodin 2002; Ricse Cataño 1999: 17; Francke et al. 2002: 17–19; Vera la Torre 2003a: 8; MINSA DGSP 2003: 54, 59–60; Jaramillo and Parodi 2004: 11, 64). The Peruvian state simply

[9] In 2001, the Economy Ministry spearheaded an effort to universalize the EPS scheme through demand subsidies (MEF DGAES 2001), but without success.
[10] Carbajal and Francke (2000: 2, 23–28). The limited number of EPS users is quite content with private service provision, however (SEPS 2000: 11–12, 16, 21–22).

cannot fund universal health insurance and thus institute the equity component of the Ley 100.

In sum, Colombia's health reform stimulated important emulation efforts in neighboring Peru. Due to geographic proximity and dense professional connections, this bold experiment was highly available to Peruvian health specialists and decision-makers. And given its initial success in coverage extension, the representativeness heuristic made it look attractive. But its complicated nature and the fiscal penury of the Peruvian state precluded any full-scale replication. Instead, diffusion advanced in a piecemeal fashion and faced continued financial constraints as well as pervasive bureaucratic resistance (Espinoza 1998a: 8, 11, 15, 21, 24; interviews with Benavides 2002, De Habich 2002, and Eiseman 2002).

While the availability heuristic has given the Colombian reform a particularly strong impact in adjacent Peru, it has also shaped health policy in more distant countries. In Bolivia, the Colombian system attracted the attention of health specialists in the mid-1990s; it elicited particular enthusiasm from advocates of privatization, who extolled the benefits of the EPS scheme (Antelo 1997: 28, 32, 34, 39). But since the country's private health sector was underdeveloped and since low prosperity and skewed income distribution limited the market for private insurance (interview with Peña Rueda 2002), Bolivia was not a leading candidate for emulating the Ley 100. Its architect Londoño therefore never visited to promote his innovation (interview with Cárdenas 2002). Moreover, health privatization was not a priority for the Sánchez de Lozada government, which pursued a crowded agenda of market reforms and was unwilling to push another controversial project (interviews with Sandoval 2002, Seoane 2002, and Cárdenas 2002). Therefore, Bolivia did not jump on the bandwagon when the Colombian reform had a particular aura of success, derived via the representativeness heuristic from the initial expansion of insurance coverage.

In subsequent years, the actual experience of the Ley 100's implementation, which proved very difficult and ever less successful (Ramírez 2004: 139–51; Uribe 2004: 212–15), gradually deflated these exalted hopes and prompted an updating of the optimistic judgments suggested by the representativeness heuristic. In particular, Colombia did not manage to universalize insurance coverage and equalize the benefit packages of the contributive and subsidized regimes. Since the Colombian health system remained segmented, Bolivian health specialists came to see the Ley 100 as a failure (interview with Pereira 2002).

The persistent inefficiencies in the health care system for social security affiliates stimulated a reform effort inspired by the Colombian experience in 2001, however. As analyzed in chapter 5, a reformist health minister followed IDB recommendations and planned to expose the social security health agencies to private competition. While the impulse for this project came from an IFI, its content drew heavily from the Ley 100 (interviews with Valenzuela 2002 and Flores 2002; Valenzuela 2001a, 2001b). But the political weakness of the Banzer, Quiroga, and second Sánchez de Lozada governments did not allow this project to go forward (interviews with Cuentas Yáñez 2002, Valenzuela 2002, Flores 2002, and Torres Goitia Caballero 2006; see chapter 5).

The Ley 100 also inspired health specialists in El Salvador to elaborate various reform proposals that followed up on the IFI-financed ANSAL project (see chapter 5). But sharp political polarization led the leftist FMLN, which had strong support among doctors and other health personnel, to attack an emulation of the eclectic Colombian reform as a neoliberal privatization effort. Therefore, governmental decision-makers had reason to hide any influence of the Colombian proposal. Also, they hesitated to design a concrete reform bill and submit it to Congress.

Frustrated by years of stagnation and pressured by private business (ANEP 2002: 5), the economy ministries and neoliberal presidential advisers launched a determined privatization project in mid-2002 (Inglés 2002). This move provoked a lengthy, fierce strike among medical personnel. In October 2002, President Francisco Flores sought to take advantage of the shutdown and sent three bold reform bills to Congress (Flores 2002). These projects, elaborated by economic generalists and neoliberal presidential aides without any input from the Health Ministry,[11] were strongly inspired by the Ley 100 and Chile's ISAPRE system. In fact, a Colombian consultant, together with a U.S. expert, played a crucial role in their elaboration (interview with Daboub 2004; see also Panadeiros 2000; Cifuentes 2000; Segura 2002).

This plan sought to expose the social security institute to private competition and give affiliates a free choice in the selection of insurance and service providers; as in Chile and Colombia, separate entities would discharge these two functions (Ley del Sistema de Salud Previsional 2002: 2, 7–10, 21). Over time, affiliation could be extended to the urban informal sector and rural poor to prevent the social segmentation caused by the ISAPRE scheme (Ley del Sistema de Salud Previsional 2002: 5). Experts recommended this reform as part of the first step toward a comprehensive restructuring à la Colombia, which would require demand subsidies so the poor could buy their own health insurance (Cifuentes 2000: 21–26). While financial constraints prevented the immediate implementation of the Ley 100's equity-enhancing component, the government tried to forge ahead with its efficiency-oriented elements.

---

[11] Cercone (2005); telephone interview with a leading Salvadoran health expert, July 2004.

But the exclusive focus on competition and free choice and the neglect of the equity dimension doomed Flores's project. By raising the specter of privatization, it elicited fierce rejection from doctors (Colegio Médico de El Salvador 2002; Olano 2003: 13–14), further inflamed the medical strike, and guaranteed it widespread popular backing. The leftist FMLN fueled the flames to garner support in the upcoming legislative and municipal elections of 2003 (González 2002). After initial intransigence, the government soon conceded defeat and shelved the health reform (interviews with Betancourt 2004 and Silva 2004). But the strike continued for months, and the FMLN indeed won the electoral contest.

The huge fallout of this conflict has prevented the ARENA government of Antonio Saca (2004–present) to revive the project. Instead, it has tried to make progress on the equity flank by using the revenues from new sin taxes and external donations to extend health insurance coverage to poorer groups, especially the urban informal sector (Jiménez 2005; Laínez 2005). In sum, the sharp ideological polarization prevailing in El Salvador has blocked efforts to emulate crucial elements of the Ley 100.

The Colombian reform also was cognitively available in Costa Rica, due in part to personal connections. Two important experts had studied medicine in Bogotá, and the executive president of the public health agency CCSS had been a Harvard classmate of the Ley 100's architect, who indeed visited Costa Rica several times in the mid-1990s (interview with Salas Chaves 2004). But as in the pension arena, firm social-democratic commitments and the CCSS's good service performance created widespread skepticism toward neoliberal reforms. Leading health experts regarded the Ley 100 as a failure (interviews with Salas Chaves 2004, Sáenz 2004, Vargas 2004, and Cercone 2004), and surveys showed that a vast majority of Costa Ricans rejected health privatization (Garita Bonilla and González Varela 1992: 3, 21; Poltronieri 2003: 54, 61, 133). Persistent and gradually tightening fiscal constraints may soon place a Colombian-style reform on the policy agenda again, however (interview with Durán 2004).

In conclusion, the ambitious nature of the Ley 100 and its initial success in expanding coverage attracted widespread attention from Latin American health specialists in line with the availability and representativeness heuristics. But the complexity of this reform limited anchoring where it did inspire emulation, as in Peru. And spreading awareness of its downsides, especially its exorbitant fiscal cost, forced emulation efforts to remain partial. They focused on the efficiency-oriented components more than the equity-enhancing aspects. Yet this imbalance exacerbated opposition, which precluded the enactment of reform in Bolivia, El Salvador, and Costa Rica. Thus, due to the availability and representativeness heuristics, the Ley 100 triggered a number of emulation efforts. But it did not stimulate a wave of actual change comparable to pension privatization. The absence of a neat, integrated, and seemingly successful model kept policy diffusion in health care more limited than in social security.

THE DISPERSED AVAILABILITY OF HEALTH REFORM EXPERIENCES

While Chile and Colombia's striking experiments attracted particular attention among health specialists and economic experts throughout Latin America, their emulation was politically infeasible in many countries. Furthermore, numerous health issues were not amenable to the privatization solution. In general, most governments did not attempt a comprehensive restructuring of the health system but concentrated on limited, piecemeal changes. In elaborating such projects, reformers often examined the experiences of several other countries. They took inspiration from various sources because no singular, outstanding model emerged in health care (Cruz and Carrera 2004; Uribe 2004).

The availability heuristic shaped this information processing. Even in the absence of a neat model that monopolized attention, bounded rationality precluded a systematic, proactive search for the relevant information. Decision-makers did not examine a wide range of reform efforts. Their radar screen remained limited. They considered only experiences that happened to be easily available to them (or that IOs made available).

Patterns and Channels of Availability

Policy-makers' attention was conditioned primarily by geographic and temporal proximity. Neighborhood effects were pronounced. Information about developments in nearby countries proved particularly accessible and vivid. Dense personal and institutional connections contributed to this special availability. Subregional institutions, such as the Andean Health Organization (Organismo Andino de la Salud),[12] strengthened information exchange among neighbors. Furthermore, only contemporary information counted. Decision-makers paid attention to recent reform efforts, not to experiences of the past. High personnel turnover and weak institutional memory reinforced this bias for the present in Bolivia, El Salvador, and Peru. In sum, most health specialists and pol-

---

[12] Founded in 1971, it comprises Bolivia, Chile, Colombia, Ecuador, Peru, and Venezuela, holds frequent technical and ministerial meetings, and conducts joint projects.

icy-makers considered only information that happened to impress itself on them. Experiences that were nearby in space and time registered much more than distant reform efforts.

Thus, the availability heuristic limited, filtered, and distorted decision-makers' attention and information input even in the absence of a clear model. Without a singular focus, however, this cognitive shortcut operated in a context-dependent, dispersed way and yielded heterogeneous results. Rather than many nations taking inspiration from one common source, decision-makers in specific countries focused on different reform efforts, depending on the location, the time, and the main problem facing them. For instance, Andean countries studied primarily experiences in their subregion. This dispersal of attention precluded the wavelike spread of one blueprint throughout Latin America. Instead, diffusion proceeded at a subregional scale or in a country-specific fashion.

While geographic and temporal proximity commonly limited decision-makers' range of attention, two factors could puncture these constraints and extend their view beyond Latin America, namely, developmental prestige and ideological affinity. First, novel experiences in advanced First World countries stimulated interest among Latin American health specialists and policy-makers. In the 1990s, attention focused primarily on U.S. experiments with managed care (through health maintenance organizations—HMOs) and managed competition, especially the ill-fated Clinton health plan; on Britain's introduction of quasi-market mechanisms; and on innovations in hospital management in Spain, particularly Catalonia and the Basque country.[13] Since Latin America sought to reach the prosperity and status of the First World, its policy experiments seemed worth studying.

International prestige—a factor stressed by constructivists—thus influenced the availability of information in health care. This differs from social security, where the special availability of Chile's privatization model drowned out other sources of inspiration and made experts overlook European experiments with notional defined-contribution schemes. Since in health care, attention was not monopolized by a singular model, it extended farther than in social security. As decision-makers' need for inspiration was not satisfied by an outstanding regional model, they were receptive to extraregional innovations from particularly prestigious countries.

Furthermore, ideological affinity occasionally led decision-makers to

[13] Besides longstanding cultural and historical links to Spain, availability enhancement by IFIs—especially the WB and IDB—helped place the Catalan and Basque experiences on Latin American decision-makers' radar screen (interview with Sáenz 2004). For instance, a Basque health specialist elaborated consultant reports for the IDB-financed PFSS in Peru (Bengoa 1996).

200 • Chapter 6

look beyond Latin America and consider an extraregional experience, especially in a First World country. This factor helped to stimulate interest among Latin American neoliberals in the U.S. HMO scheme and the contractual and incentive mechanisms introduced in Britain's National Health Service. At the opposite end of the spectrum, the Brazilian Communist Party long led the country's health reform movement and paid special attention to the changes spearheaded by their Italian comrades. Thus, ideological sympathies shaped the availability of information and—together with developmental prestige—helped to expand health specialists' radar screen beyond the bounds of geographic proximity.

Ideology, however, can also limit availability and block the consideration of intraregional experiences. Accordingly, aversion to communism prevented most Latin American governments from paying attention to Cuba's health system, which by all accounts has performed very well, especially in equity terms. Although Cuba held interesting lessons, the ideological gulf largely precluded their diffusion inside the region. Thus, ideology cut both ways: Affinity drew attention to geographically distant reforms, while divergence precluded the examination of nearby experiences.

Timing also shaped cognitive availability; in fact, it exerted a more consistent effect than geographic proximity. Even the extraregional experiences that decision-makers considered were recent. For instance, Italy's Communist-sponsored health reform of 1978 immediately reverberated in Brazil; Britain's creation of quasi-market mechanisms in the 1980s quickly elicited interest; and the Clinton health plan provided instantaneous inspiration. Thus, temporal proximity clearly shaped the availability of information. Memories proved short. Rather than conducting an active search for relevant data, decision-makers took into account what happened to be on their mind.

The importance of personal contacts in information transmission contributed greatly to this temporal limitation. Decision-makers liked to invite the architects of foreign innovations so they could share their experiences, explain their blueprints, and give practical advice (interview with Espinoza 2002). Personal testimony made a foreign policy scheme particularly vivid and concrete and thus boosted its availability. Firsthand knowledge therefore had a much greater impact than arid documents. By making personal contacts crucial, the availability heuristic focused attention on contemporary policy experiments and filtered out innovations from the past.

In sum, the bounds of rationality clearly shaped attention and information processing in health care. Rather than undertaking a wide-ranging search for relevant experiences, decision-makers considered only information that happened to attract their attention. Availability, not inherent importance, served as the principal selection criterion for information intake. But the absence of a clear model led to a dispersal of attention. Rather than focusing on a single obligatory point of reference, health specialists and policy-makers took their inspiration from a menu of options and varied significantly in the specific experiences they considered. Due to geography, cultural and historical connections, judgments of prestige, and ideological affinities, the availability heuristic created a complex network of information flows, rather than the Chile-centered radial structure prevailing in social security.

Since policy-makers considered a variety of foreign reform experiences, they could pick and choose the option that seemed best for their country. This broader repertoire also facilitated redesign by allowing boundedly rational policy-makers to combine elements from various alternatives and thus draw up a new scheme with greater ease. While anchoring therefore had limited force, these emulation decisions were not based on the systematic cost-benefit analyses demanded by comprehensive rationality. Since the range of choices was constrained by the availability heuristic and its logically arbitrary selection criteria, much relevant information remained neglected. Bounded rationality prevailed.

As in the pension arena, availability enhancement by international organizations sometimes breached these limitations of information processing. IOs called attention to reform experiences that decision-makers would otherwise have failed to consider. By extending the range of options that was cognitively available, IOs softened the bounds of rationality. But as discussed in chapter 2, this provision of additional information was biased by the ideological orientation and policy goals of the specific IO. For instance, the WB advertised primarily neoliberal experiments, whereas UNICEF promoted community participation. Innovations that were not highlighted by these special lenses remained unavailable. Thus, the information that decision-makers processed was confined by logically accidental factors, namely, geographic and temporal proximity, judgments of prestige, ideological affinities, and the policy orientation of IOs.

The Availability of Neighboring Experiences

While a comprehensive analysis of these complex processes is infeasible, a discussion of important reform efforts can document these patterns of availability. For instance, Peru learned important lessons from neighboring Bolivia for its maternal and infant health insurance scheme (Seguro Materno Infantil—SMI). By the late 1990s, it was obvious that the recuperation and expansion of primary care facilities from 1994 onward had not drastically reduced embarrassingly high rates of maternal and infant mortality. The user charges that many health facilities imposed kept poorer people away from medical services (Francke 1998: 50–52). Based on ongoing direct contacts and a WB recommendation, Peruvian experts therefore studied Bolivia's maternal and infant insurance, which lifted economic access barriers and indeed boosted poor people's usage of primary health care (Meloni 2005; Pichihua 2005). The Bolivian innovation was directly available in adjacent Peru, and its initial success gave rise to judgments of inherent quality derived via the representativeness heuristic (cf. WB 1999d: 42; Cotlear 2000: 9). Cognitive shortcuts thus shaped the diffusion of this equity-enhancing scheme among neighboring countries.

In elaborating their program, Peruvian decision-makers drew on an extensive exchange of information with Bolivian specialists (Meloni 2005; interview with Cárdenas 2002). During the design phase, a group of Peruvian experts, including the leader of the SMI team, took a week-long study trip, met with Bolivian health authorities, and visited field sites. They derived a number of insights on the planning and implementation of this insurance scheme, which informed two pilot projects (Pichihua 1998; Espinoza 1998: 3436). Before upgrading these experiments to a nationwide program, they again obtained advice from a Bolivian specialist (WB 1999c: 82; see also Francke 2002). Thus, Peru's SMI received its initial impulse and many specific inputs from Bolivia's innovative program (which also stimulated emulation efforts in two other neighboring countries, Argentina and Paraguay: interview with Torres Goitia Caballero 2006).[14]

Bolivia in turn learned from its neighbors Peru and Argentina to create mobile medical teams and thus give dispersed rural populations who lived far from health posts effective access to care. In emulating this innovation, Bolivian experts drew on advice from Argentine and Peruvian consultants (interview with Pereira 2002). Thus, neighbors frequently exchanged information and assisted each other in their reform efforts.[15]

Peru's CLAS program, which enlisted community participation for running primary health facilities and thus instituted administrative decentralization (see chapter 5), was also informed by experiences in the subregion. This decision received its first impulse from UNICEF's Bamako Initiative—an instance of availability enhancement by an IO (Graham 1998: 110; Ewig 2000: 499, 504). This program strengthened weak public health institutions through community involvement. Users

[14] IFI intermediation helped Argentina overcome its normal disdain for its poor, underdeveloped neighbor and learn from it (WB 2003a; IDB 2004a: 7).

[15] For other instances, see MINSA (1997) and Novak (2004).

(except for the destitute) paid small service charges, and in exchange, community representatives participated in administering health care delivery. UNICEF promoted this "taxation for representation" scheme worldwide (cf. WB 1993b: 159) and first introduced it to Peru for organizing the supply of essential medicines (Phang Romero 2002: 1124–25; interview with Bendezú 2002). Advised by an UNICEF consultant, the CLAS team adopted major elements of this IO proposal (Sobrevilla 2000: 19–20, 26; Altobelli 1998: ii, 30–31; Ewig 2004: 236; interviews with Freundt 2002, Sobrevilla 2002, and Meloni 2002).

Recent experiments with health decentralization in neighboring countries served as important additional inputs. The CLAS team examined Chile's experience with municipalization; Bolivia's Popular Participation Law; and the "privatization with community involvement" enacted in Colombia through the Ley 100 (interview with Vera del Carpio 2002; Sobrevilla 2000: 17–19, 29, 36; Ortiz de Zevallos et al. 1999: 23). In fact, they held direct conversations with Colombia's health minister and took a study trip to Chile (interviews with Freundt 2002 and Yong Motta 2002). Thus, they paid special attention to contemporary reform initiatives in three of the five countries bordering on Peru—and only to such contiguous countries. The availability heuristic clearly limited their information processing.

These nearby experiences validated the plan to decentralize health administration through community participation and revamp the traditional top-down structure, helping to overcome considerable bureaucratic and political resistance to this bold change (cf. Ortiz de Zevallos et al. 1999: 26–27). For instance, the radical nature of Bolivia's decentralization and participation experiment ("una utopía," interview with Vera del Carpio 2002) made the more moderate CLAS look reasonable and feasible. Given the variety of foreign sources of inspiration, however, the CLAS team typically did not import any of these blueprints but modified them. In line with President Fujimori's determination to bypass municipal governments,[16] community representatives were selected by the health post director and the community, not the mayor (interviews with Benavides 2002, Vera la Torre 2002, and Freundt 2002). In sum, the CLAS designers received important impulses from recent innovations in neighboring countries. A core member of the Peruvian team, in turn, helped set up an experiment with community health participation in El Alto, Bolivia (interview with Bendezú 2002).

The neighborly exchange of information and ideas was less intense

---

[16] This presidential order was motivated by numerous opposition victories in the 1993 municipal elections (Ortiz de Zevallos et al. 1999: 26). It also fit Fujimori's neopopulist strategy to bypass intermediary institutions and create direct links to the people.

among the two Central American countries under investigation. Since the good performance of their health system contrasted with the serious problems afflicting El Salvador, Costa Rican experts saw no reason to learn from their backward neighbor. And their commitment to neoliberalism made Salvadoran government officials find Costa Rica's social-democratic system unattractive. Only occasionally did they consult with their neighbors. For instance, during the controversy over President Flores's proposal to introduce private competition in the social security health system, the Salvadoran government invited a Costa Rican specialist who liked aspects of Colombia's Ley 100 and who validated the Salvadoran reform effort inspired by it; but he had not helped to elaborate this project (Cercone 2005). Thus, for particular reasons, these two Central American countries had unusually little impact on each other's health policies.

The Availability of First World Experiments

While focusing especially on their neighbors, Latin American countries also took into account some reforms enacted in developed countries. First World countries' success and prestige attracted attention to their innovations. Moreover, long-standing connections resulting from training in North America or Europe facilitated information flows by inducing Latin American decision-makers to follow developments in their former host nation. Prior emulation experiences also created lasting bonds and gave special availability to information from the country that had been imitated before. These pathways of availability proved especially important in Costa Rica, whose health system performed at First World levels; therefore, the country showed little inclination to learn from its Third World neighbors.

Because Britain's National Health Service had inspired Costa Rica to pursue the universalization of state-financed health care (Miranda 2003: 96–97; cf. CCSS 1985: 1), policy-makers remained especially receptive to British innovations. As the serious financial problems of the 1980s prompted efficiency-oriented reforms, the CCSS president, Guido Miranda, turned again to Britain for inspiration. Typical of the availability heuristic, this renewed connection arose from a fairly accidental personal encounter. At an international conference, Miranda met British expert Brian Abel-Smith, who had experience with novel payment mechanisms (interview with Miranda 2004).

Abel-Smith advocated a capitation scheme that pays doctors a fixed per-capita fee for covering people's health needs. Contrary to reimbursements for services rendered, this system does not reward doctors for providing unnecessary treatments; in fact, it stimulates improvements in preventive care that avoid expensive curative treatments. And because doctors' income increases with the number of patients who choose them, they have an incentive to offer high-quality care. Miranda became capti-vated by this British innovation, and Abel-Smith visited Costa Rica three times (CCSS 1985; interview with Miranda 2004; see also Miranda 2003: 309–10, 315).

The capitation scheme seemed to address problems plaguing Costa Rica's health system. Above all, it promised simultaneously to enhance economic efficiency, improve service quality, and stimulate the integra-tion of preventive and curative care. Miranda and a group of reform-oriented health specialists were therefore eager to test this innovation in Costa Rica, and British experts helped to elaborate a capitation system. But the rigid personnel rules of Costa Rica's public sector created obsta-cles. Also, doctors did not want to have their income depend on perfor-mance. The reform commission therefore compromised and made less than a quarter of doctors' pay depend on capitation payments (Marín 1986: 14–15; see also CCSS 1986: 3, 10; CCSS. Comisión Proyecto de Barva 1986: 11; cf. CCSS 1985: 6–7). This concession limited the eco-nomic incentives offered by the new system.

The CCSS bureaucracy nevertheless offered strenuous passive resis-tance, and unions of medical personnel vociferously opposed a revamp-ing of service delivery (interviews with Marín 2004 and Ballesteros 2004; see also Güendel and Trejos 1992: 31, 35–36). Miranda therefore tested the capitation scheme only in one isolated pilot project. Although this trial run was plagued by many implementation problems, surveys showed high contentment both among patients and service providers (Alfaro Cascante 1987: 20–25, 41, 44). As a result, Miranda planned to extend the capitation scheme nationwide (Cordero Vásquez 1988: 1–2, 12–20). But this initiative was soon shelved because improvements in service delivery and economic efficiency proved to be less pronounced than expected. In fact, the small size of the pilot project limited competi-tion among doctors and thus reduced the beneficial effects of capitation. And Costa Rica's protectionist public personnel regime hindered the provision of individual incentives (Sáenz and Zamora 1988; Güendel and Trejos 1992: 35; Miranda 2003: 316; interviews with Miranda 2004, Marín 2004, Sáenz 2004, and Ballesteros 2004).

Yet while the capitation experiment ended in failure, this British inno-vation had a lasting impact on Costa Rican health policy by helping to inspire the successful EBAIS program. Health reformers who had helped design Miranda's pilot project escaped from the rigid public personnel regime and created non-profit private cooperatives, which provided inte-gral health care to patients and received per-capita reimbursements from the CCSS (interviews with Marín 2004 and Vargas 2004; CCSS DTSS

1990; Fiedler and Rigoli 1991; Gauri, Cercone, and Briceño 2004: 294–95). This innovative project also faced strenuous resistance from many CCSS officials and service personnel unions, which saw it as a step toward privatization (interviews with Ayala 2004 and Guzmán 2004; see also CCSS DAPE 1995). Cooperatives therefore remained few and far between and did not turn into the seeds of a new health system, as their founders had hoped (Marín and Vargas 1990).

But when IFI influence helped to unfreeze reform efforts in the early 1990s (see chapter 5), leading specialists who had helped design the capitation scheme and later founded cooperatives took advantage of this opportunity to put their long-standing ideas into practice. Accordingly, each EBAIS received funding on a per-capita basis from the CCSS to provide integral preventive and basic curative care to four to five thousand people living in a specific area (UPC 1993: 165–77; Clark 2004: 199–202). Thus, the new primary health system embodied crucial components of the capitation scheme. The financing mechanism created incentives for emphasizing prevention and simple curative treatments and thus addressing health problems before they required expensive hospital care. Despite the failure of the specific emulation effort, the British capitation scheme thus helped to inspire an important change in Costa Rica.

The EBAIS program did not institute the competitive component of the capitation scheme. But to boost efficiency and ease persistent resource constraints, Costa Rican health reformers—under prodding from the WB and IDB (see chapter 5)—decided to introduce quasi-market mechanisms. In deliberating which specific measures to take, they again sought inspiration from Europe. In an unusually proactive fashion, they studied the performance contracts adopted in Britain, Sweden, the Netherlands, and especially Spain (CCSS UCPM 1995: 6, 13: Cercone 1996; Martínez Franzoni 1999: 172–73). Thus, they deliberately focused on health systems based on similar social-democratic principles as their own. Following a WB suggestion, they made heavy usage of Spanish consultants, who transplanted their own provisions and rules to Costa Rica. As in Spain, therefore, Costa Rican performance agreements have concentrated primarily on measurable, quantitative indicators of service provision; moving to quality- and results-oriented indicators has proven difficult (interviews with Arce 2004, León Barth 2004, Guzmán 2004, Sáenz 2004, and Salas Chaves 2004; CCSS 1996; CCSS PM 1997; Sojo 1998).

In sum, considerations of developmental prestige and ideological and institutional affinity have combined with IFI recommendations to focus the attention of Costa Rican experts on European innovations and prompt the emulation of British and Spanish innovations. Costa Rica's tendency to pay primary attention to First World countries, not its own region, transcends the usual bounds of availability. It results from the exceptional performance of the country's health system, which makes learning from backward neighbors unattractive. It also reflects the high competence of domestic health experts and their wide-ranging informational and historical connections. In health policy as in social security, the bounds of rationality were less tight in this technically advanced nation than in the other countries under investigation.

Availability via Ideological Affinity

Given the predominance of market-oriented thinking in Latin America during the last two decades, leftist ideological sympathies have less frequently made an extraregional reform experience available. The most noteworthy case is the disproportionate attention that Brazil's sanitary movement paid to the ambitious change spearheaded by the Italian Communist Party (PCI) in 1978. Because many *sanitaristas* were close to the Brazilian Communist Party (PCB; Escorel 1999: 75, 81–82, 183, 191), they followed the initiatives of their Italian comrades. The PCI was the prototype of a reform-communist party that had abandoned Stalinism and fully embraced democracy. This renovation held special appeal to Brazilian leftists, who sought to use their country's slow transition to democracy (1974–89) to achieve a profound transformation of its highly unequal society.

The resulting ideological affinities stimulated an intense exchange of ideas. The architect of Italy's health reform, PCI deputy Giovanni Berlinguer, visited Brazil frequently and had his main writings translated into Portuguese (Escorel 1999: 82–83; Berlinguer 1978; Berlinguer, Fleury Teixeira, and Campos 1988). Italian and Brazilian experts engaged in many visits, joint conferences, and projects (e.g., Teixeira and Melo 1995). Due to all these contacts, the Italian experience deeply influenced Brazilian health reformers (Escorel 1999: 79, 82–85, 190; Cohn 1989: 123, 132).

In Italy, leftist parties and militant unions had been decisive in pushing for health reform (Berlinguer 1989: 44). This example reinforced the tendency of Brazil's sanitary movement to conceive of its efforts in broad political terms, as part of a struggle for comprehensive socioeconomic change. Whereas health reform in other Latin American countries centered on the health arena and had a predominantly technical character, the Brazilian movement stands out for its politicization. It planned to use health reform as a wedge to gain popular support for an overall restructuring of society (Fleury Teixeira and Mendonça 1989: 207, 217, 227–31; Oliveira 1989; interviews with Campos 2003, Cohn 2003, and Felipe 2003). This ambition was reinforced by the success of the Italian

Communists, who used the health reform plank for finally gaining a share in governmental responsibility in the late 1970s.

The Italian example also strengthened the *sanitaristas*' determination to guarantee all citizens comprehensive health care. They rejected targeting, declared health—defined in an integral way—as a basic right of citizenship, and assigned the state the obligation for its provision. This generous universalistic approach sought to institute a European-style welfare state in underdeveloped Brazil (Pêgo and Almeida 2002: 35–36).

The openly political strategy and ambitious goals of the sanitary movement, which were strongly inspired by the Italian precedent, had both strengths and weaknesses. On the one hand, they allowed the *sanitaristas* to promote a certain level of political activism and mass mobilization, in addition to occupying bureaucratic positions inside the state. This broader support, activated in the high-profile Eighth National Health Conference of 1986 (Conferência Nacional de Saúde 1987), enabled the movement to codify in the new constitution of 1988 its major reform principles, especially the universalization of health coverage and the state's responsibility for service provision (interviews with Sousa 1987 and Arouca 1992; Rodriguez 1988). Despite stubborn conservative opposition, the constitutional mandates triggered a substantial institutional transformation of the health system in the 1990s (Arretche 2004; Negri and Viana 2002). In particular, Brazil narrowed the gulf between social security affiliates and the rest of the population, which creates stark inequality in many Latin American health systems. Thus, the sanitary movement's political strategy produced more profound change than in most of the region (Kaufman and Nelson 2004a: 485).

But the *sanitaristas*' political focus and ambitious approach also posed obstacles to equity-enhancing health reform. Concentrating on institutional changes, they neglected concrete improvements in service provision. They assumed that decentralization—their main institutional demand—would automatically lead to better care. Therefore, they had few specific recommendations on how to extend services, especially to poorer sectors (Campos 1997; Cohn 1989: 126, 134; interviews with Girade 2003 and Machado de Souza 2003). Because the sanitary movement rejected targeting, it was reluctant to enact special programs for the destitute. And the constitutional guarantee of comprehensive health care diverted scarce resources to complicated, expensive treatments, which were more accessible to better-off people. For instance, judicial demands forced the public health system to pay large amounts for treating a few patients.

Important problems, such as significant regional and social inequalities in medical indicators, therefore persisted (Almeida et al. 2000: 153–58). Many health needs of poor people in outlying areas, such as the desperate Northeast, remained unmet. These deficits spurred numerous municipal initiatives to address the most basic problems with simple means. Above all, community health agents (Agentes Comunitários de Saúde—ACS) administered vaccinations and taught people how to prevent and combat simple infectious diseases, such as diarrhea. As the ACS proved their effectiveness in containing a cholera epidemic that struck in 1991, Brazil's federal government soon promoted the nationwide extension of this program. Thus, learning from lower levels of the state led to a federal plan that sought to fill gaps left by the political strategy of the sanitary movement (see also MS 1997: 7–8; Viana and dal Poz 1998: 29–30).

To use this primary care approach for transforming larger segments of the health system, the government upgraded the ACS strategy in 1993–94 by stimulating the creation of family health teams (MS FUNASA 1994), as discussed in chapter 5. This Programa Saúde da Família (PSF), promoted vigorously in subsequent years, again took its inspiration from municipal initiatives (interviews with Girade 2003, and Machado de Souza 2003; MS FUNASA 1994: 21; MS 2002). One of the most influential experiments took place in the city of Niterói (close to Rio de Janeiro), which emulated the family doctor scheme developed in Cuba (interview with Azevedo 2003). A foreign experience made available by ideological affinities substantially influenced the PSF.

Many *sanitaristas* admired aspects of Cuban socialism and therefore paid attention to Cuban health policy (e.g., Capote Mir 1982; interview with Campos 2003). They heard about the recently created family doctor program at a health conference in Havana in the late 1980s. Sérgio Arouca, the sanitary movement's main leader, immediately extolled the Cuban scheme (Rosas 1988: 105; see also Ordóñez 1989: 81). But since Brazil's federal government was in conservative hands, the Cuban experience did not trigger national-level emulation. Instead, a municipal experiment that eventually influenced federal policy served as transmission mechanism.

This import of Cuba's family doctor scheme emerged from an accidental encounter—typical of the availability heuristic. In 1989, Niterói suffered dengue and meningitis epidemics and requested assistance from Cuba, which has special expertise in combating these infectious diseases. Cuba's generous help induced a local intellectual and personal friend of Fidel Castro's to organize a trip to the island for Niterói's mayor and health secretary, during which they held long conversations with the *máximo líder* and studied Cuba's health system. Enthused with the family doctor program, they decided to adopt it. Experts from Niterói went to study the program first-hand, and Cuban specialists supervised its emulation in Niterói, which was directed at the poorest neighborhoods

(Da Cunha, Machado, and Brant 1994: 29; Teixeira, Monteiro, and Miranda 1999: 149; Mendes 1999: 147–48; Senna and Cohen 2002: 526–27).

The Niterói experience was an important input for the PSF (interviews with Machado de Souza 2003 and Sousa 2003; MS 1999: 24, 29; Viana and dal Poz 1998: 18–20). It showed that assigning a doctor-led health team to a certain number of people could further the proactive provision of basic promotional and preventive measures. But the federal government did not simply extend Niterói's scheme to the whole country. Instead, Brazilian health specialists and policy-makers regarded the Cuban system, which used medical doctors as principal care providers, as "extremely luxurious" (MS 1999: 39). Brazil simply lacked the trained doctors and public funds for replicating this program, which Niterói had in fact copied. Instead, the PSF employs doctors only to lead teams of professionals with lesser qualifications; thus, its doctor/patient ratio is much lower than in Cuba and Niterói (interviews with Andrade 2003, Girade 2003, and Machado de Souza 2003).

In sum, ideological affinities have made Italian and Cuban experiences cognitively available to Brazil's sanitary movement and have provided important impulses for ambitious health reform efforts. This emulation of foreign schemes has brought significant improvements, but also created some problems and gaps.

Summary of Findings

The preceding case studies show that geographic and temporal proximity, the prestige of developed countries, and ideological affinities shape the availability of information. Latin American health experts and decision-makers pay attention first and foremost to their subregional or regional neighbors; the exchange of information among the Andean countries is especially intense. Less frequently, they broaden their horizon and consider First World experiences. Ideological affinities occasionally guide their attention as well.

While the patterns of availability differ across countries and decision-makers, in all cases the range of attention is limited, and much narrower than comprehensive rationality prescribes. Bounded rationality prevails. Health experts do not scan the international environment proactively but receive information via cognitive shortcuts. Attention is selective— limited by geographic and temporal proximity, prestige considerations, or ideological links. As in the pension sphere, the bounds of rationality are tighter in nations with lower technical capacity, such as Bolivia, El Salvador, and Peru. Countries like Brazil and especially Costa Rica, which have a strong pool of well-trained cadres, are less limited in their information intake; on several occasions, Costa Rican specialists have been unusually proactive in their information gathering (Martínez 1997). But in many countries much of the time, health experts and decision-makers are more reactive than proactive.

Conclusion

Cognitive heuristics have significantly shaped the diffusion of innovations in health policy. Following the availability heuristic, Latin American decision-makers have paid particular attention to bold experiments inside their region, especially Chile's partial health privatization and Colombia's effort to combine privatization with a universalistic, equity-enhancing insurance program. These bold, novel schemes attracted great interest. They were directly available to policy-makers inside their region of origin. In fact, personal contacts facilitated the spread of information. Therefore they entered the policy agenda in several countries; Bolivia, El Salvador, and Peru considered proposals to emulate the Chilean ISAPRE scheme and the Colombian Ley 100.

But Chile's health privatization remained limited and did not attain the striking initial success that prompts judgments of inherent quality in line with the representativeness heuristic. Therefore, this reform triggered an emulation effort only under special circumstances in Peru. The Colombian reform did quickly boost insurance coverage and attain an aura of success. But the fiscal cost of this accomplishment and the complicated, unwieldy nature of the Ley 100 diminished its attractiveness for boundedly rational decision-makers. Whereas a neat, simple model can spread like wildfire, the multifaceted Colombian reform proved less contagious. While it stimulated emulation efforts in Bolivia, El Salvador, and Peru, only the Fujimori government enacted any change; and Peru's EPS system differs significantly from the Colombian original, especially in neglecting the equity dimension. Thus, the absence of a neat, well-integrated, successful model tempered judgments of availability and representativeness, weakened anchoring, and limited the diffusion of policy innovations.

In other areas of the complex health system, processes of learning and emulation differed even more from the wavelike spread of pension privatization. Instead of focusing on a single regional model, policy-makers considered a variety of foreign experiences in a dispersed, context-dependent fashion (cf. Cruz and Carrera 2004; Uribe 2004). The availability heuristic directed their attention especially toward recent reforms in adjacent countries. Information exchange among neighbors was particularly intense inside South America. Policy experiments in prestigious First World nations also served as sources of inspiration, and ideological affinity sometimes placed extraregional innovations on the radar screen. Furthermore, decision-makers considered mostly recent experiences; information processing thus had a strong temporal limitation.

In sum, learning was shaped by logically accidental factors, especially geographic and temporal proximity, but also international prestige and ideological affinity. Experiences that for these reasons made an impression influenced deliberations and policy decisions. Relying on the availability heuristic, health specialists and policy-makers paid selective attention to their international environment. The bounds of rationality limited their information intake. They did not engage in a wide-ranging, proactive search for the relevant information. Applying the representativeness heuristic, they also did not conduct systematic, balanced cost-benefit analyses but overrated early indications of success. For instance, many experts were unduly impressed by the initial accomplishments of Colombia's Ley 100, and Brazil's sanitary movement fell for Italy's health reform. Thus, cognitive shortcuts strongly conditioned policy-makers' learning from foreign experiences and shaped the spread of innovations across countries.

Due to the lack of a singular, outstanding model, however, health policy did not see a broad wave of diffusion, as it swept across social security. External influences simply did not have as much impact on domestic decision making. Certainly, policy deliberations often took foreign inputs into account; on a number of occasions, foreign experiments provided an impulse for change and shaped the content of health reform. But contrary to pension privatization, external stimuli did not trigger full-scale imitation in health care. Policy emulation went significantly less far; nowhere did it resemble the import of the Chilean pension model by Bolivia, El Salvador, and Peru (interview with Cárdenas 2002).

While generally less profound than in social security, the impact of external influences on agenda setting, policy deliberations, and decision outputs in health care varied across countries. Whereas some nations commonly considered foreign experiences in designing new programs, others acted quite independently of external influences. These differences were pronounced in the early stages of the decision-making process, especially agenda setting, the discussion of policy options, and the design of proposals. As they preceded the politics of the actual policy choice, they did not arise from the broader constellation of sociopolitical interests and power capabilities, but from divergences in attention and information processing that reflected differences in the technical capacity and institutional strength of various state agencies.

As in social security, nations with established, institutionalized communities of well-trained, competent, and knowledgeable health specialists were less likely to emulate foreign experiences than countries that commanded limited domestic expertise. The thinner a country's technical capacity and the less meritocratic its health agencies, the deeper was the influence of external stimuli. Where health agencies suffered from technical and institutional weakness, experts from the economy ministries managed to exert more influence. While these ministries had less interest in health care and played a more limited role than in social security, they advocated efficiency-oriented reforms inspired by the Chilean and Colombian experiments on a number of occasions (interviews with Vera la Torre 2002 and Daboub 2004; MEF DGAES 2001). Where these emulation efforts faced less resistance from equity-oriented health specialists, they had a greater chance of going forward. Thus, the same technical and political-institutional factors conditioned the depth of external influences in health care as in social security.

Therefore, as Bolivia, El Salvador, and Peru followed the Chilean model of pension privatization much more closely than did Costa Rica and Brazil, they also proved more receptive to foreign inspiration in health care. Peru emulated a component of the Colombian health reform, and Bolivia and El Salvador elaborated proposals to that effect. By contrast, Costa Rica and Brazil never considered taking this step. In general, those two countries made decisions on many aspects of health policy without much regard for external inputs. While Costa Rica in the 1990s cooperated more closely with the IFIs than before, it insisted on its own priorities, especially in equity-enhancing reform; in this area, it paid little attention to other countries' experiences, both inside Latin America and beyond. Domestic experts designed the EBAIS scheme— their main priority—with great independence from foreign influences (interviews with Ayala 2004, Cercone 2004, Guzmán 2004, León Barth 2004, Marín 2004, Salas Chaves 2004, and Vargas 2004). The CCSS's outstanding technical expertise, admirable performance, and powerful political position gave domestic decision-makers substantial autonomy. They did not need to seek inspiration in foreign experiences; and neither the IFIs nor domestic economic agencies could push them to adopt foreign blueprints, with the exception of performance contracts.

After the important impulse stemming from the Italian health reform, Brazilian health policy also traced an autonomous course (interview with Negri 2003). As in Costa Rica, health decision-makers counted on rich technical expertise and a fairly firm institutional base and thus had the capacity to design their own programs. Moreover, leftist ideology immunized the sanitary movement against the neoliberal experiments that many neighboring countries considered emulating. And for linguistic, historical, and geographic reasons, Brazil's connections with Spanish-speaking nations were not as strong as the links prevailing inside the

Andean subregion, for instance. Last but not least, the lively experimentation among Brazil's 5,500 municipalities offered a wealth of inspiration for federal policy-makers (see MS SAS 2002). Blessed with this domestic creativity, Brazilian health specialists saw less need for examining foreign innovations.

In sum, cognitive heuristics shaped learning from foreign experiences in health policy, though more intensely in Bolivia, El Salvador, and Peru than in Costa Rica and Brazil. To the extent that specialists and decision-makers considered foreign inputs, their attention and information processing was clearly shaped by the heuristics of availability and representativeness. Logically arbitrary factors such as geographic and temporal proximity, developmental prestige, and ideological affinity channeled information intake; and early signs of success, for instance of Colombia's Ley 100 and Bolivia's maternal and infant scheme, were overinterpreted as indications of inherent quality. Thus, the diffusion of innovations in health care—while remaining more limited than in social security—was shaped by cognitive heuristics as well.

CHAPTER 7

Bounded Rationality in the Era of Globalization

THIS STUDY provides the first in-depth analysis of policy diffusion in Latin America. Focusing on social sector reform, it demonstrates how foreign models and principles enter the radar screen of experts and policy-makers; how they are assessed and evaluated; and how decisions on their adoption and adaptation are made. In this way, it elucidates the reception and emulation of foreign innovations. Whereas a number of authors have analyzed the teaching of new norms and models, especially by international organizations (see recently Barnett and Finnemore 2004), learning by recipient countries has so far elicited insufficient attention.[1] My study helps to fill this important gap.

The central finding is that despite differences between countries and issue areas, similar causal mechanisms have driven the spread of social policy innovations in Latin America. External pressures, especially from international financial institutions, have supported policy diffusion but have not been decisive in initiating the process and determining its outcomes. Domestic policy-makers have retained considerable autonomy in their decisions. As regards their motivations, concern for international legitimacy has had only a limited impact in both issue areas. Rather than being swayed by new international norms, policy-makers have mostly responded to widely recognized, preexisting problems and have been guided by fairly clear, firm, "given" interests.

Most importantly, decision-makers have applied bounded, not full, rationality in pursuing these interests. In both issue areas, they have diverged greatly from the postulates of comprehensive information processing and systematic cost/benefit analysis. Cognitive heuristics have shaped their learning from foreign models, experiences, and principles and have guided the spread of innovations; the availability of a singular, neat, coherent model—Chilean-style privatization—has turned these shortcuts into the decisive causal mechanism in social security. Thus, cognitive psychology yields a more convincing account of policy diffusion than rational choice.

The international financial institutions are often depicted as powerful

---

[1] For initial steps, see Brooks (2005), Gilbert (2004), Madrid (2003b: 36–52, 173–84), and Weyland (2004b).

agents of policy diffusion. Authors claim that in the neoliberal era, these enforcers of global market discipline impose their uniform blueprints on weak developing countries. The IFIs can indeed twist governments' arms successfully on specific economic issues that are decided by a few actors in the executive branch, such as currency devaluations. In the economic realm, they obtain additional leverage from certifying a country's good standing with the international investment community (Stone 2002: 11, 17, 27). But the demands and anticipated reactions of investors hold less sway in social policy reform. Moreover, complicated institutional changes such as social security or health privatization require the consent or acquiescence of such a multitude of domestic actors that the IFIs cannot impose reform from the outside. Whereas the president and finance minister are concerned about a country's attractiveness to foreign investors and its relations to the IFIs, many interest groups and congressional politicians care little and push instead for other policy goals or their own patronage interests. The involvement of numerous domestic actors in social sector reform thus limits external influence. The IFIs therefore cannot compel Third World governments to adopt complex institutional changes in the social sectors (see especially Nelson 1996, 1999; Hunter and Brown 2000; Brooks 2004; Gilbert 2004: 210–11; and in general Vreeland 2003).

My field research corroborates these important findings and disconfirms inferential arguments that attribute the wavelike nature of pension privatization and health reform to central coordination and vertical imposition (Armada, Muntaner, and Navarro 2001; see in general Stallings 1992). The IFIs supported the diffusion of innovations but were not the first movers; instead, Chilean experts initiated the spread of pension privatization. And while many countries followed the broad outlines of the neoliberal program promoted by the IFIs, some nations refused to move in this direction, such as Brazil in both its social security and its health policies. Furthermore, governments diverged on crucial specific decisions from IFI recommendations; even weak, aid-dependent Bolivia disregarded strong pressures on how to cover the transition cost of radical pension reform. For these reasons, diffusion proceeded more via horizontal contagion than vertical imposition.

Where the IFIs did make a difference, their success resulted less from power and leverage than from persuasion and information provision—that is, availability enhancement. On a number of occasions, as in Costa Rica's reform of health care management and Brazil's adaptation of a notional defined-contribution pension system, the World Bank put decision making on a new track by giving boundedly rational decision-makers access to information that had escaped their limited attention. Thus, the incapacity of domestic decision-makers to process the relevant information comprehensively allowed the IFIs to attain influence by making hitherto unnoticed reform experiences cognitively available. IFI influence thus flowed often from informational resources—and from the limited information processing of national policy-makers. Accordingly, the World Bank is better advised to strengthen its role as a knowledge bank than to tighten its loan conditionality (cf. Stiglitz 1999: 6–13; Pincus and Winters 2002: 10–15; Mallaby 2004: chap. 9).

The IFIs also try to give some of their recommendations normative appeal. This effort was especially pronounced in health care. The World Bank's prominent 1993 report advocated a focus on basic needs and postulated a synergy between equity-enhancing and efficiency-oriented change. In this view, cheap promotional, preventive, and curative measures could address the health needs of the poor and thus limit the demand for expensive hospital treatments. But while this message legitimated universalistic health reforms in the eyes of economists and thus facilitated their adoption in numerous countries, the World Bank merely reinforced a norm that had emerged fifteen years earlier, spearheaded by international organizations such as the WHO and UNICEF that lacked financial resources and political leverage. Thus, the bank jumped on the bandwagon of a normative appeal that it had not initiated. As in pension privatization, it reinforced an already ongoing trend rather than being the original trendsetter.

More importantly, normative appeal drove the spread of innovations only where change could be adopted through distributive decisions (cf. Lowi 1964). This was the case especially with efforts to extend health care to long-neglected sectors of poor people. Such add-on programs entailed concentrated benefits but diffuse costs. Therefore, they elicited little opposition, especially when the economic recovery of the 1990s augmented fiscal resources and IFIs offered generous loans. In this favorable setting, the equity goal of guaranteeing "health for all" managed to propel the diffusion of reform initiatives, such as targeted basic health programs and maternal and infant insurance.

Most social policy reforms, however, especially pension privatization and efficiency-oriented health measures, are redistributive or regulatory in nature. They affect the clear, fairly well-defined interests of important social sectors by offering benefits to some constituencies while imposing costs on others. Therefore, they elicit strong support and opposition and can unleash fierce conflicts among powerful sociopolitical forces. While normative considerations can affect this clash of interests by strengthening one side and "mobilizing bias" against the other (cf. Schattschneider 1975: 30), they have played a secondary, largely instrumental role in most of the emulation decisions investigated in this book. Actors have primarily advanced their interests rather than promoting normative maxims, and these maxims have not significantly constrained their interest pursuit. For instance, the ethic of individual responsibility has inspired only the die-hard advocates of pension privatization but has not attained legitimacy—not to speak of hegemony—in public and political debate, where norms of social solidarity have continued to prevail; therefore, proponents of drastic reform, including the World Bank in its high-profile 1994 document, have downplayed or hidden the new normative message.

Rather than being guided by new international norms, domestic decision-makers have primarily pursued fairly fixed, "given" interests, especially established state interests such as fiscal balance, economic development, human capital formation, and social stability. As new problems such as economic crises and population aging have posed threats to existing policy programs or as economic recovery has made it feasible to compensate for past austerity measures and attain further improvements, governments have become receptive to new models or principles adopted in foreign countries. In their emulation decisions, they have acted out of conventional goal orientation, pursuing predefined interests by addressing difficulties or taking advantage of opportunities. Contrary to sociological institutionalism and constructivism, policy diffusion has not resulted from solutions chasing problems, but from problems creating receptivity for solutions.

This search for solutions has not been fully rational, however. Bounded, not comprehensive, rationality has governed policy diffusion. In their quest for promising programs, decision-makers have deviated regularly from the postulates of standard rationality and have instead applied the limited toolkit of bounded rationality. Rather than scanning the international environment broadly and proactively, they have focused on information that happened to become available, often for logically accidental reasons. And they have processed this information not through balanced, systematic cost/benefit analyses but with more haphazard yet commonly applied rules of inference. These cognitive shortcuts, especially the heuristics of availability, representativeness, and anchoring, make it easier to digest overabundant information and navigate uncertainty, but at the risk of substantial distortions and biases.

Demonstrating how these mechanisms of bounded rationality operate and how powerfully they shape policy diffusion constitutes the principal contribution of this book. As chapters 4 and 6 show, the availability heuristic conditions which foreign models, principles, and experiences enter decision-makers' radar screen. For not very rational reasons, it attracts attention to some innovations while leading to the neglect of others. In channeling information intake, it puts policymaking on certain tracks. In issue areas in which a neat, simple, and coherent reform model has emerged,[2] this shortcut concentrates the attention of experts and decision-makers in the region of origin on this singular, outstanding reference point and induces them to disregard extraregional innovations.

This radial structure, clearly visible in the overwhelming interest elicited in Latin America by Chilean pension privatization, contrasts with the more decentered, diverse, and localized patterns of attention that prevail in the complex area of health care, where no simple, neat model has arisen. Due to the absence of a single, obligatory reference point, experts and policy-makers pay attention to various experiences. These sources of inspiration differ depending on location and established communication channels, historical connections and prestige considerations, and ideological affinities. Thus, information processing is also guided— and limited—by logically arbitrary factors. As a result, the availability heuristic shapes the spread of innovations in health care. But due to the diversity of foreign experiences that are cognitively available in various countries, health care has seen a less clear-cut wave of diffusion than social security. Dispersed emulation, not widespread imitation, has prevailed in this multifaceted issue area.

Once policy-makers pay attention to an external model, principle, or experience, they evaluate its success and promise. Since emulation decisions are motivated primarily by interests, not normative or symbolic concerns, decision-makers do not immediately fall for a foreign innovation but first assess its payoffs. Therefore, they wait for some track record to accumulate. The case studies show, however, that they do not conduct thorough, systematic cost/benefit analyses. Instead, early indications of success make them jump to conclusions and impute inherent quality to an innovation. Thus, they commonly follow the representativeness heuristic and draw excessively firm conclusions from small samples, such as limited stretches of successful performance. In similar associative reasoning, they hold specific reforms responsible for the overall performance of a successful country.[3]

In these ways, the representativeness heuristic imbued Chilean pension privatization with an aura of success. Private pension funds initially attained stellar rates of return, and by accumulating ample investment resources, they seemed to fuel Chile's growth boom from 1985 onward. In health care, by contrast, no innovation attained such striking initial success, limiting the inferences suggested by the representativeness heuristic. Chile's private insurance companies were slow to find adherents.

---

[2] Gilbert (2004: 208–12) documents a very similar process in the spread of capital housing subsidies.

[3] In a similar vein, Japan's tremendous economic success from the 1950s to the 1980s led many academic, policy, and business analysts to attribute inherent value to specific aspects of the "Japanese model," such as quality circles (Strang and Macy 2001).

Colombia's bold reform did boost coverage, especially among the poor, but at exorbitant fiscal cost; and this complicated change faced many implementation problems. Due to this mixed record, the representativeness heuristic did not stimulate widespread enthusiasm for the Ley 100. In sum, no health reform gained a halo of success. As various foreign experiences looked attractive to some extent, emulation decisions were dispersed and cautious; partial imports, often with modifications, prevailed over full-scale imitation.

In social security, by contrast, the presence of a single, seemingly successful model put a premium on simple imitation over thorough redesign. Thus, the heuristic of anchoring, according to which initial cues strongly affect later judgments and restrict adjustments, operated with considerable force. Countries with especially limited technical capacity, such as Bolivia and El Salvador, therefore imported most of the Chilean privatization scheme. Nations with ample, long-standing expertise, such as Costa Rica, introduced substantial modifications but nevertheless instituted the core innovation of the Chilean model, namely, privately managed individual pension accounts in the obligatory social security system. Thus, while not precluding adaptations, the heuristic of anchoring limited their magnitude and protected the core of the foreign model.

By contrast, the absence of a clear model in health care did not give anchoring much opportunity to operate. While some copying occurred— as in Peru's creation of private insurance companies and in the spread of maternal and infant insurance schemes in the Andes—adaptation and modification usually prevailed over imitation.

In sum, cognitive shortcuts crucially affected the diffusion of policy innovations in social security and health care. In both issue areas, information processing and decision making diverged from the standards of comprehensive rationality. Rather than scanning the environment proactively for the relevant information and conducting systematic, balanced cost/benefit analyses, experts and policy-makers commonly applied the heuristics of availability, representativeness, and anchoring. These shortcuts made it feasible for them to digest ample uncertain information, arrive at decisions, and thus leave a mark despite the time pressures and precarious job tenure that they often faced.

But the frequent reliance on cognitive shortcuts exacted a price, namely, the risk of significant distortions and biases. Experts and policy-makers often failed to consider relevant information that did not happen to become available. And they drew overly enthusiastic conclusions that motivated them to import a foreign model—a choice that some now regret. In particular, more moderate, less "anchored" emulation decisions may have been more beneficial to their country. Thus, by the standards of comprehensive rationality, many choices concerning policy

diffusion, especially the import of the Chilean model of pension privatization, appear as questionable. Contrary to conventional rational choice,
decision-makers often pursued their interests in suboptimal ways.

The differences between the two issue areas corroborate the significance of cognitive heuristics as causal mechanisms that propel policy
diffusion. Where a clear, neat model emerges and captures specialists'
attention; where such a singularly available model attains an initial
stretch of success and the representativeness heuristic therefore gives rise
to highly optimistic performance evaluations; and where anchoring limits modifications of this outstanding, seemingly successful model, an
impressive wave of diffusion gets under way in the region of origin:
Many of the frontrunner's neighbors soon emulate the innovation.
Availability enhancement by IFIs later helps this wave to reach more
distant continents.

In highly complex issue areas, by contrast, such a neat, compact
model cannot arise and establish immediate success. Policy diffusion
therefore remains less uniform and powerful as the availability heuristic
makes decision-makers in various countries focus on different foreign
experiences. While there is a good deal of learning from neighbors, it
follows diverse connections and channels. In sum, if the heuristics of
availability, representativeness, and anchoring can attach themselves to
a clear, neat model, they attain special force and produce a striking pattern of temporally and geographically clustered, concentric diffusion;
where such a model does not emerge, cognitive shortcuts yield less powerful inferences and diffusion remains dispersed.

The differences between the two issue areas also show that ideology
as such does not drive diffusion. Both pension and health privatization
embodied neoliberal principles of individual responsibility and free initiative. But pension privatization advanced much farther because the
availability heuristic concentrated attention on this model and the representativeness heuristic imbued it with an aura of success; as shown in
chapter 4, the hope for macroeconomic spillover effects was crucial for
convincing presidents and congressional politicians to adopt this change.
Cognitive heuristics that shaped information processing, not uncondi-
tional ideological commitment, made the difference.

Yet while cognitive heuristics serve as crucial causal mechanisms for
spreading policy innovations, they do not alone determine outcomes. In
particular, they cannot guarantee that a foreign model or principle
spreads in a uniform wave. Causal mechanisms bring about different
end results depending on the divergent contexts in which they operate
(McAdam, Tarrow, and Tilly 2001). As a flood washes away makeshift
slum dwellings but not brick mansions, so bounded rationality produces
more policy diffusion in some issue areas and in certain countries than

in others. As just discussed, cognitive heuristics focus policy-makers' attention more sharply and provide a stronger impetus to emulation in policy spheres in which an integrated, coherent blueprint with early signs of success exists than where such a model has not emerged.

Political-institutional and economic differences across countries also matter. Given the predominance of interests among actor motivations, bounded rationality expects decision-makers to consider contextual challenges in their judgments and actions. Accordingly, the depth and urgency of the problems facing a government condition its openness to reform and affect the constellation of sociopolitical forces participating in its design. If there are serious, acute difficulties that affect basic state interests such as fiscal stability, economy ministries try and often manage to control the elaboration of reforms. Where a small, fairly cohesive team of economic generalists therefore monopolizes program design, cognitive heuristics tend to reinforce each other and inspire proposals to import foreign innovations. And where the crisis of established policy approaches limits opposition inside the state and in society, and where presidents can enact reforms via decree or via majority support in Congress, these emulation projects turn into authoritative decisions.

By contrast, where existing social programs achieve satisfactory performance, sector specialists demand participation in reform design, especially if they command long-standing expertise. The resulting involvement of a broader range of actors allows for cross-checking the inferences suggested by cognitive heuristics. A more open, pluralistic policy process, which stimulates debate and negotiation, limits the impact of inferential shortcuts and keeps policy diffusion in check. Rather than rushing to emulate a foreign model or principle, decision-makers proceed more cautiously and prefer partial emulation, for instance by instituting a mixed pension system that combines public and private pillars. Thus, the policy performance and political-institutional characteristics of specific countries can moderate or filter out emulation projects designed under the influence of cognitive heuristics.

In sum, cognitive heuristics—like the other causal mechanisms that contribute to policy diffusion, especially in health care—produce different end results depending on the issue area and the country setting. But while inferential shortcuts do not determine diffusion outcomes, they strongly shape the content of emulation decisions. Especially where a neat, simple, and initially successful model exists, the heuristics of availability, representativeness, and anchoring stimulate its imitation and fuel the spread of similarity amid diversity. Thus, they explain what diffuses when it diffuses, and why it diffuses.

Furthermore, the setting in which cognitive heuristics operate is not given but rather is affected by these causal mechanisms. The constellation of actors that participate in emulation decisions results in part from cognitive heuristics. For instance, economic generalists in Latin America used to pay little attention to social security systems, which for decades were the domain of actuaries and lawyers. When demographic shifts and the economic crisis of the 1980s turned pension deficits into important drains on fiscal equilibrium, finance and planning ministries extended their view to social security, but from a narrow financial perspective. Therefore, they mostly advocated parametric reforms to raise revenues and cut expenditures.

Yet when the Chilean model of pension privatization became cognitively available and when its initial success stimulated great enthusiasm in line with the representativeness heuristic, the economy ministries took a much more forceful stance. They sought to gain control over social security policy and pushed for drastic reform. In particular, the promise that pension privatization would boost domestic savings and investment and thus fuel economic development, which the representativeness derived from Chile's growth record, turned this reform into a core goal of several economic agencies (Madrid 2003b: 31–40, 49–52). This new belief reinforced their interest and induced them to wield their power capabilities in social security policy, trying to displace established policy specialists.

Thus, inferences suggested by cognitive shortcuts led finance and planning ministries to take a keen interest in pension privatization. The hopes suggested by the representativeness heuristic turned pension privatization into a crucial means for the ends pursued by these economic agencies. By reshaping their instrumental preferences, these expectations made the emulation of the Chilean model highly salient to economic generalists. As they therefore sought to control decision making in this issue area, the range of relevant actors changed. Thus, the constellation of sociopolitical forces, which in turn conditioned the impact of cognitive heuristics on policy outputs, was itself conditioned by inferences derived via such shortcuts.

Therefore, cognitive heuristics are not the epiphenomena of more "basic" factors such as sociopolitical forces and their interests, and they are not mere instruments in conflicts among such forces. Instead, they can mould the instrumental interests of powerful sociopolitical actors and thus redraw the configuration of forces that shape policy choices and the emulation of foreign models and principles. External models and principles made available and evaluated by cognitive heuristics shape factors that many theoretical approaches simply take as given. Rather than constituting uncaused causes, power and interest constellations are affected by ideational factors, including boundedly rational learning from foreign inputs (see in general Blyth 2002). While actors' core goals are fairly clear and firm, the specific ways in which they try to realize these goals is mediated by knowledge, including the lessons suggested by cognitive shortcuts (cf. Goldstein and Keohane 1993).

THE NATURE OF POLITICAL RATIONALITY

My study's findings have crucial implications for the debate over rational choice, which has roiled political science over the last fifteen years (Green and Shapiro 1994; Friedman 1996; Jones 2001; Lupia, McCubbins, and Popkin 2001; Weyland 2002a; Lichbach 2003; Shapiro, Smith, and Masoud 2004). Do political actors pursue their goals in a systematic, efficient fashion that approximates the postulates of comprehensive rationality, or do they significantly diverge from these standards? Do they rigorously apply logical rules of inference and cost/benefit analysis or do they resort to easy and expedient but potentially flawed shortcuts and heuristics that can impair decision quality?

This investigation has documented widespread deviations from comprehensive rationality. Experts and policy-makers commonly rely on cognitive heuristics that can substantially distort their judgments. While the bounds of rationality are more or less tight in different political settings, nowhere did decision making embody full rationality; even in Costa Rica, which for technical and institutional reasons came much closer to this standard than Bolivia, El Salvador, Peru, and even Brazil, inferential shortcuts shaped policymaking by focusing and limiting attention and by making some reform options—especially pension privatization—disproportionately attractive to important actors.

These consistent findings are noteworthy because of the technical training and intellectual caliber of the experts and policy-makers involved. Common citizens regularly apply cognitive shortcuts to make choices of low salience, such as vote decisions; given the negligible impact of each vote and the low stakes of casting a ballot, time-saving deviations from complicated rational calculations—even "ignorance"—are paradoxically rational. Indeed, advocates of rational choice argue that simple cues, such as partisan identity, allow citizens to make vote choices that approximate their real preferences. Furthermore, the law of large numbers guarantees that individual deviations from full rationality, which are seen as idiosyncratic, cancel out and do not affect overall election results. These arguments imply that divergences from fully rational procedures do not distort aggregate outcomes (Tsebelis 1990: chap. 2). They are therefore irrelevant for the analysis of collective choices. Political scientists can proceed "as if" comprehensive rationality prevailed (Popkin 1991; Lupia and McCubbins 1998).

But these arguments do not hold for the policy choices examined in the present study, which were prepared by small groups and often made by single individuals, especially presidents; the law of large numbers therefore does not apply. Also, cognitive heuristics are not individual idiosyncrasies, but common rules of inference. Because most people use the same shortcuts, the resulting distortions do not cancel out. Instead, they may get reinforced in small groups (Turner and Pratkanis 1998; Esser 1998; McDermott 2004: 126–27, 249–55). Moreover, the decisions analyzed in this book do not have low salience; the stakes are often high. Structural pension and health reform can create major benefits and costs for broad societal categories and deeply affect countries' social, economic, and political development. Deviating from rational procedures in such consequential decisions is therefore not rational (cf. Fiorina 1996: 88).

Moreover, many of the leading decision-makers are well-trained, highly capable, intellectually impressive experts. These talented professionals are most likely cases for applying the procedures of comprehensive rationality. But as this book demonstrates (see also Tetlock 2005: chap. 4), even they commonly use inferential shortcuts. Given their credentials, this reliance on cognitive heuristics does not arise from individual deficiency, but from deep-rooted bounds of rationality.

The innate tendency to apply cognitive heuristics is reinforced in Latin America by the political setting. Many states are weakly institutionalized and lack meritocratic, Weberian bureaucracies (cf. Rauch and Evans 2000).[4] Political appointees and experts therefore experience high tenure and career uncertainty, and even presidents face frequent challenges to their authority or political survival in these "politicized states" (Chalmers 1977). Therefore, they rush into reform decisions to shore up support and have any chance of making a difference. Given this need to advance quickly, experts and political officials cannot follow the careful, systematic procedures prescribed by comprehensive rationality and transmitted in their professional training (interview with Naím 2000) but commonly rely on inferential shortcuts.

My findings thus support the recent calls in political science and economics to move beyond the simplifying assumptions underlying conventional rational choice (e.g., McFadden 1999; Thaler 2000; Jones 1999, 2001; Kahneman 2003). These ideal-typical postulates are far from approximating decision making in the real world. Policy-makers commonly deviate from these standards in their judgments and choices. By investigating the procedures that decision-makers actually apply in di-

---

[4] Even an otherwise developed country such as Argentina has traditionally suffered from this problem (Teichman 2001: chap. 5; Dezalay and Garth 2002: 37–38).

recting their attention, processing information, weighing options, and making choices, cognitive psychology provides a much more realistic microfoundation for political analysis.

Besides its great theoretical significance, the prevalence of bounded rationality has important methodological implications. In particular, it suggests the need for in-depth case studies and the insufficiency of more scientific methods such as formal modeling and statistics. The parsimonious, schematic notion of decision making applied by conventional rational choice paves the way for rigorous, nomothetic analysis. While claiming to derive all explanations from individual choices, this approach effectively makes the process of individual choice a black box. Individuals are conceptualized as executors of the universalistic principles of instrumental rationality. Their individual characteristics therefore do not matter; they are "interchangeable" (Tsebelis 1990: 40, 43–44): Any rational person who faced the same incentives and constraints would respond identically. For this reason, the situational incentives and constraints in effect explain and "determine" (Levi 1988: 10) individual choices. A rational decision-maker *must* react to this context in a certain way—and any other rational individual would react in exactly the same way. Rational actors have no latitude and thus, in some sense, no choice.

This explanatory scheme greatly facilitates scientific analysis. Scholars do not need to reconstruct the complicated process of decision making and consider variations across individuals (Mercer 2005: 77, 81–85). In particular, they need not unravel subjective interpretations of the situation, complex thought processes, and the variegated translation of individual preferences into specific choices and actions (see especially Satz and Ferejohn 1994). Instead, analysts can simply correlate objective situational characteristics with observable behavior, which—according to a "revealed preferences" approach—even yields the information required for ascertaining individual interests. Strict adherents of rational choice therefore rely on deductive modeling and statistics and bypass process tracing based on intensive field research (e.g., Meseguer 2002).

But this simple methodological scheme requires modification. Because decision-makers commonly deviate from full rationality, scholars need to delve into the policymaking process. As actors' choices reflect not only the objective situation, but also subjective factors such as cognitive shortcuts and the resulting judgments and beliefs, researchers need to ascertain these "softer" phenomena, which are often difficult to measure rigorously and to quantify. Qualitative research, including archival work and interviews with decision-makers, is therefore in order.

In fact, a number of rational-choice theorists acknowledge that pure incentives-and-constraints explanations are insufficient and that cognitive factors such as beliefs and ideas need to be considered (North 1990:

chap. 5; Schofield 1996); some even draw on "interpretivist" approaches (Bates, de Figueiredo, and Weingast 1998; Chong 2000). Accordingly, these scholars forgo the objectivist, correlational mode of analysis and embrace case studies. This important step is codified in the "analytic narratives" project (Bates, Greif, et al. 1998), which stresses the need to examine specific historical choices and test deductive models against concrete empirical evidence. Analytic narratives seek to combine rigorous theorizing with careful research in order to attain both generality and accuracy.

But it is doubtful that analytic narratives can reach this ambitious goal. They rely heavily on analytical simplifications and mere inferences and do not thoroughly reconstruct individual thought processes and choices. For instance, they often stipulate actor preferences without much evidence (Elster 2000: 685, 693; Parikh 2000: 681). Moreover, the usage of equilibrium models leads analytic narratives to focus on periods of stability. They thus fail to capture the suspense and contingency of the dramatic choices that give rise to this stability (Carpenter 2000: 655–63). By concentrating on decision outcomes, analytic narratives neglect the decision-making process. They assume and postulate the operation of rationality in history without offering sufficient empirical documentation.

This book takes a crucial further step by abandoning premises of comprehensive rationality and tracing the empirical patterns of bounded rationality. Because decision-makers face overabundant yet uncertain information and use cognitive shortcuts to process it, the in-depth analysis of decision making is indispensable. Rather than deriving choices from objective constraints and incentives, scholars need to investigate how individuals perceive their context; what stimuli they pay attention to; what inferences they derive; and how they design their responses. It is therefore crucial to conduct process tracing, that is, empirically reconstruct the decision-making process to unearth evidence for assessing theoretical arguments (George and Bennett 2005).

Theory-guided process tracing can capture both the general and particularistic elements of decision making that the usage of cognitive heuristics entails. On the one hand, reliance on these shortcuts is widespread, if not universal.[5] The decision-making process therefore has regularities that are generalizable across individuals. For instance, most

---

[5] New experiments suggest, however, that human cognition may be profoundly shaped by cultural patterns (Nisbett 2003); the findings of cognitive psychologists from the West may therefore not hold universal validity. But because Western culture predominates among Latin American elites, and because many experts analyzed in this book acquired part of their professional training in the West, this culturalist objection is unlikely to invalidate my study.

people pay disproportionate attention to information that is especially vivid and memorable and draw excessively firm conclusions from small samples.

On the other hand, there are also specific, even coincidental factors that affect the operation of cognitive heuristics. For instance, membership in a professional or social network or common educational background may draw the attention of some decision-makers—but not others—to a certain foreign model. Even fairly accidental personal meetings can make crucial information available. As shown in chapter 4, for example, the future leader of Bolivia's pension reform team was captivated by a speech by José Piñera, the missionary promoter of Chilean-style privatization. Indeed, many channels of learning—such as the connections of Brazil's public health movement to the Italian Communist Party—were not determined by objective characteristics of the situation; instead, subjective, ideational factors played a crucial role.

This combination of regularities and contingencies is best captured via theory-oriented process tracing. Interviews with decision-makers and a study of the documentary record are crucial for reconstructing actors' goals and preferences; their access to various streams of information; the constraints they faced and took into account; their judgments and calculations; and the choices they ended up making. This methodological approach does justice to the more realistic notion of political decision making that my study suggests. Individuals are not personifications of universal reason but face significant cognitive limitations in their effort to make rational decisions. Rather than being optimal information processors and utility calculators, they struggle with a flood of complex information that has uncertain relevance and validity. Scrambling to make sense of this over-abundance and facing the urgent need to make decisions, they resort to clues and shortcuts, which can suggest reasonable solutions but also lead to mistakes. Theories of bounded rationality thus capture the human mind with all its capacity and fallibility.

Diffusion and Political Change in the Era of Globalization

Global Homogeneity, National Specificity, or Regional Clustering?

This study sheds light on the impact of advancing globalization on political institutions and political change. As mentioned in the introduction, the last three decades have seen the worldwide spread of liberal ideas and practices, especially democracy and markets. Many foreign models and principles discussed in this book, especially Chilean-style pension privatization and efficiency-oriented health reforms, are part of this liberal wave. In fact, by investigating the extension of market mechanisms into the social sectors, I examine the current edge of this wave. The book thus elucidates how far market reform can advance and how profound its effects will be. Does global liberalism produce convergence and increasing homogeneity as more and more countries follow uniform blueprints, or will national differences persist as governments process similar external inputs in different ways?

Most authors highlight vertical pressures toward global conformity or insist on lasting national specificity. My book stresses horizontal contagion among regional neighbors as an important additional pattern. The world of the future is unlikely to become homogeneous or maintain national distinctness; instead, elements of both patterns will coexist with regional effects, especially clusters of country groupings. As complexity therefore increases and information streams multiply, decision-makers will have to rely on cognitive heuristics at least as much as they have so far. As the world becomes unbounded, the bounds of rationality will continue to affect policymaking.

Among theories of globalization, economic structuralism and sociological institutionalism stress the homogenizing pressures emanating from the core of the world system. Economic structuralists claim that multinational corporations and international financial institutions impose their uniform designs on an ever wider range of countries, especially in the economically dependent, politically weak Third World. Companies' worldwide profit logic forces countries to serve as cogs in the wheels of global capitalism or be starved of economic resources, and the IFIs promote and help to manage countries' integration into this asymmetrical network of production and exchange. Third World nations therefore face overwhelming pressures to streamline their institutions and adapt them to the demands and expectations of global capitalists, for instance by reducing levels of regulation, matching their competitors' low tax rates, and establishing firm guarantees of property rights. In this view, the forces of global conformity sooner or later overwhelm national differences (Cox 1986; Strange 1996; Sassen 1996).

Sociological institutionalists see similar homogenizing pressures at work, though in a less coercive fashion and for less materialistic reasons. In their view, the quest for legitimacy—not economic interests—drives the move toward global conformity. Backward countries eagerly emulate international trendsetters. The symbolic desire to look modern and the normative concern to live up to the advanced standards of world society drive this rush to imitation. Therefore, developing countries commonly import institutional forms designed in the First World. As a result, there is increasing convergence despite different functional needs.

The push and pull of global forces thus induces domestic decision-makers to deviate from the equilibrium solutions that national-level incentives and constraints would bring forth.

By contrast, historical and rational-choice institutionalists predict continuing diversity across countries. Although these two approaches diverge in their basic premises, they share this important claim (Campbell 2004: 65–85, 163–67, 185). Historical institutionalists postulate institutional self-perpetuation and rigidity. This path dependence, explained by self-reinforcing mechanisms of "increasing returns" (Pierson 2004), guarantees that divergences in starting conditions and initial institutional arrangements persist (Mahoney 2000). They even withstand the homogenizing pressures of economic globalization, as the burgeoning literature on the European welfare state, in particular, has claimed (Pierson 1994; Garrett 1998; Huber and Stephens 2001; Swank 2002; see also Hall and Soskice 2001). Thus, rapid modernization preserves national differences and does not forge global convergence.

From different premises, rational-choice institutionalism arrives at similar conclusions. Certainly, its equilibrium approach assumes that institutional arrangements flexibly adjust to prevailing incentives and constraints. But these contextual stimuli differ across countries. Also, political change is not easy to effect. Pervasive collective action problems and intense political uncertainty, especially leaders' fear of offending powerful constituents that benefit from collectively suboptimal arrangements, make it difficult to escape from dysfunctional equilibria (cf. Bates 1981; Ames 1987; Geddes 1994; criticism in Grindle 1991). Economic pressures for change therefore tend to falter on political obstacles. As a result, economic globalization does not produce political homogeneity. Because the relevant incentives and constraints vary across countries, rational choice predicts persistent national specificity as well.

The present analysis of policy diffusion differs from both the arguments about national distinctness and global uniformity. It highlights instead an intermediate pattern, namely, horizontal contagion among neighbors and the geographical clustering of policy programs (see Levi-Faur 2005: 25–27). Where a clear, neat model emerges, similarity tends to spread amid diversity, yet first and foremost at a regional level, due to the availability heuristic. Where such a model does not arise, patterns of emulation are more dispersed and neighborhood effects are especially pronounced, as evident in the diffusion of health reform. Although availability enhancement by international organizations helps the concentric circles of model diffusion eventually to expand beyond their area of origin, regional differences tend to persist. For instance, many East European pension reformers were inspired not only by the Chilean model of full-scale privatization, but also by the notional defined-contribution system designed in Sweden.

The heuristics of anchoring and representativeness reinforce this geographic clustering. Anchoring limits modifications of a model that spreads among neighbors. By keeping country-specific adaptations in check, it helps regional similarity prevail over national differences. And the representativeness heuristic inspires excessive enthusiasm for an initially successful model and stimulates its rapid spread, which starts at a regional scale. By the time the innovation becomes cognitively available on other continents, it may have accumulated a longer, more mixed track record that lowers these exaggerated performance expectations and thus slows down its further advance. As a result, emulation may remain concentrated in the region of origin.[6]

For these reasons, islands of similarity form in a sea of difference. Diffusion spreads similarity amid diversity, but not on a global scale. Innovations travel first and foremost inside geographic regions and culturally or historically defined communities of nations. Geographic or cultural neighbors are linked by especially dense networks of experts, government officials, and civil society organizations. Information about promising innovations therefore extends primarily through these channels. And as Slaughter (2004) has argued forcefully, these networks promote the adoption of similar rules, institutions, and policy programs.

Globalization thus does not advance in a uniform wave that sweeps across the whole world, but as a much more differentiated, fragmented process (Campbell and Pedersen 2001; Rosenau 2003). Rather than yielding global uniformity, it produces convergence in some geographic regions and issue areas while maintaining divergence in others. For instance, as many Latin American countries emulated the Chilean model and privatized their pension systems, differences with other regions, such as Africa, Asia, and Western Europe, increased. Furthermore, some Latin American countries diverged from the regional trend and preserved the established pay-as-you-go system. Thus, while producing greater similarity among many countries, policy diffusion does not eliminate national and regional differences.

Policy Diffusion, Institutional Change, and Path Dependency

Globalization exposes national decision making to strong external influences. Nowadays, domestic policymaking is no longer purely domestic. Experts and government officials commonly consider foreign mod-

---

[6] I owe these arguments to interesting suggestions from Raúl Madrid.

els, principles, or experiences in preparing their own decisions. The present study amply documents this intense exchange of information, its frequent impact on policymaking, and the resulting convergences among countries (see also Dezalay and Garth 2002; Slaughter 2004; Orenstein 2005). As innovations spread especially among neighbors, clusters of similarity emerge inside regions.

These external influences significantly affect the stability of national institutions and policy programs. By offering alternatives to the status quo, they can trigger changes that otherwise would not occur. Bold new models can have a particularly pronounced impact. If such a model emerges in a region, the availability heuristic draws disproportionate attention to it; and if it achieves initial success, the representativeness heuristic leads policy-makers to place excessive confidence in it. This exalted promise puts the performance of existing institutions and policy programs into an unfavorable light; they come to look disappointing, if not deficient. While these arrangements may well produce "increasing returns" (Pierson 2004), the representativeness heuristic suggests that the new model yields even greater benefits. Thus, by stimulating enthusiasm for alternative blueprints, cognitive shortcuts can induce decision-makers to escape from path dependency and opt for change over continuity.

By analyzing the rise and spread of new reform options, the present study highlights the comparative nature of institutional choice. The maintenance of established arrangements does not depend on their own performance alone, but also on the perceived promise of cognitively available, feasible alternatives. Decisions on institutional preservation or change hinge on the range of options under consideration. Policy-makers cannot abandon existing institutions and programs unless they have a better alternative (Campbell 2004: 117–18). Accordingly, the appearance of a promising model can induce decision-makers to abandon the old arrangement and embrace the new blueprint instead. While the diminishing performance of existing institutions creates receptivity to other options and may thus constitute a necessary condition for institutional change, it is not a sufficient cause; a promising alternative must also be available.

Although rational-choice institutionalists and even recent historical institutionalists (Pierson 2004; Thelen 1999) start from choice-theoretic premises, they have surprisingly failed to highlight the comparative nature of decisions on institutional preservation vs. transformation. These theories examine the conditions under which existing institutions produce "increasing returns" (Pierson 2004) and prove self-reinforcing or self-undermining (Greif and Laitin 2004). But they are one-sided in focusing mostly on the established arrangements. While problems with the status quo provide an important push for institutional change, the pull of a cognitively available, feasible, and promising alternative is also required (cf. Clemens and Cook 1999: 459–60).

This supply factor is exogenous to established institutions. Certainly, when existing arrangements are unsatisfactory, decision-makers are more likely to search for alternatives and to see a new option—by comparison—as better. But a crisis does not necessarily bring forth a solution. The emergence of a novel option, the dissemination of knowledge about it, and the rise of enthusiasm for this alternative decisively contribute to institutional reform. By analyzing the supply side of policy change, my study complements extant theories, which overemphasize the demand side by focusing on the performance of existing institutional arrangements.

The rise of an alternative option differs in nature from the exogenous shocks discussed in the institutionalist literature, such as a dramatic economic crisis or a foreign invasion. Whereas those irruptions undermine or destroy established institutions and thus narrow the choice set, the appearance of a new model extends it. Exogenous shocks create a need for change but leave open the direction of this change. By contrast, a promising alternative offers a blueprint for propelling change in a specific direction.

For these reasons, the appearance of an attractive new model can break path dependency. Interrupting long-standing trajectories, it can push institutional development in unanticipated directions. Some drastic changes, such as pension privatization and other neoliberal reforms, indeed seek to reverse earlier institutional developments by restoring market regulation in areas that an interventionist state had administered for decades. Neoliberal reformers are eager to dismantle existing institutions and extinguish their legacies. For instance, they try to privatize the whole social security system and close the old PAYG scheme as soon as possible.

These radical efforts took hold especially where the existing pension system covered only a small proportion of the workforce and where current social security spending and obligations to future pensioners were relatively low. These conditions, which restricted the range of beneficiaries, lowered transition costs, and limited political support for the status quo, prevailed in less developed countries such as Bolivia and El Salvador. The tendencies toward path dependency were therefore comparatively weak. The modest legacies of the existing institutional framework allowed for particularly profound change, namely, the faithful import of the Chilean model.

By contrast, in more developed nations with mature social security systems, such as Argentina, Brazil, Costa Rica, and Uruguay, institutional legacies constrained neoliberal reform to a greater extent. Opposition from current and future beneficiaries and the high fiscal transition cost made complete privatization unpalatable. These countries therefore introduced mixed public/private systems or experimented with the novel NDC scheme. While these reforms also constituted a significant, sometimes radical departure from past trends, they were less profound than a full-scale emulation of the Chilean model. Rather than totally breaking with established arrangements, they combined continuity and change.

Theories of path dependency thus require modification by extension (see also Brooks n.d.). These arguments are inspired by the experiences of advanced industrialized countries with dense, firm organizational networks and institutional structures (Pierson 1994). But the analysis of developing countries, which have less extensive and entrenched institutional frameworks, suggests a more differentiated picture. The strength of institutional and policy feedback varies, depending on the resources at stake and the number and clout of the beneficiaries. The broad, generous coverage of welfare states in the First World strongly hinders drastic reform and tends to keep change incremental. By contrast, the meager social protection systems of underdeveloped countries are easier to dismantle or revamp. Thus, institutional legacies do affect the depth of reform, but they do not preclude radical transformations, as theories of path dependency suggest. Instead, the relative strength of these legacies is decisive.

Interestingly, these differences stimulate efforts to take advantage of the greater ease of reform in Third World nations, establish exemplars of drastic change, and in this way stimulate substantial transformations in the First World. With their weaker institutional structures, developing countries offer special opportunities for profound reform. They can turn into laboratories where U.S.-based proponents of neoliberalism try to test new models. If the novel arrangements attain a stretch of success, they are advertised back to the First World with the intention of diminishing opposition to deep restructuring there (Dezalay and Garth 2002: 141–42; interview with Klugman 1993). Neoliberals thus try to crack weak links in the chain of path dependency in order to put pressure on its stronger links.

Such an effort to enlist a Latin American field experiment for reimporting a model to the First World is currently under way in social security. U.S. advocates of pension privatization, including President Bush, stress the accomplishments of the Chilean innovation, which in turn was inspired by theories of U.S. economists. The World Bank is also invoking the reform momentum triggered by Chile's change to urge European "reform laggards" to jump on the privatization bandwagon (Holzmann, MacKellar, and Rutkowski 2003). If these promotional efforts attain success, the Chilean model will help to derail path dependency in advanced industrialized countries. The shining example of Third World nations may thus provide an opening for reducing the conservative effects of institutional and policy legacies in the First World.

The opportunity for overcoming path dependency and enacting drastic change arises only where a bold, neat model emerges, however. As chapters 5 and 6 show, reforms in the complex health arena, where no such model exists, remained limited, piecemeal, and incremental. Most countries did not revamp their entire health systems but enacted only bits and pieces of the efficiency and equity agendas. In the absence of a striking blueprint, they advanced gradually and cautiously. Despite more ambitious goals, even Colombia and Brazil did not break long-standing patterns of economic inefficiency and social segmentation; in Brazil, for instance, the extension of coverage to the poor led middle sectors to exit the public system, a move that the state subsidized through tax breaks. Thus, the most significant changes in the health arena deflected institutional trajectories somewhat but did not redirect them, as pension privatization did. Without a bold, compact reform model, the inertial force of path dependency prevailed.

The scholarly literature on the spread of innovations has paid disproportionate attention to the dramatic instances of model diffusion (Strang and Soule 1998: 285; Meseguer and Gilardi 2005: 4, 17, 22–23); examples include the waves of imitation triggered by Bolivia's Emergency Social Fund, which sought to cushion the social cost of determined market reform; Bangladesh's Grameen Bank, which offers micro credit to the poor; and Brazil's Bolsa Escola, a conditional school grant program (Goodman 2004). Yet while those striking cases of explosive contagion hold special cognitive availability for scholars, they are uncommon. Most innovations that inspire learning and emulation do not qualify as policy models by the definition of chapter 1. They are not ambitious, bold, neat, systematically integrated blueprints that embody a coherent set of novel principles, but more eclectic, piecemeal experiences or pragmatic compromise proposals. But although these modest projects do not inspire the degree of interest and enthusiasm that models elicit, they often inform reforms in neighboring countries, where decision-makers consider foreign inputs, especially from their immediate environment. Because in the era of globalization, the cross-national exchange of information has become commonplace, learning from foreign models is only one form of policy diffusion. It does not take a brilliant, bold innovation to elicit interest from policy-makers across borders; more limited experiments can also stimulate learning and emulation.

Because the dispersed pattern of diffusion found in health reform seems to be more common than the concentric waves of model diffusion in the pension sphere, path dependency remains strong in many areas of social policy. As historical institutionalists have argued, change is often confined to incremental adjustments. Established institutional and program structures are difficult to break. But when a bold model arises, trajectory-changing transformations are possible. While such dramatic reforms are not very frequent, they produce clear departures from long-standing trends and shape whole issue areas for decades to come.

Global Liberalism: Diversity and Bounded Rationality

All these findings suggest that the diffusion of liberal reforms has brought substantial change to a wide range of countries but is far from forging global homogeneity. Instead, national and regional diversity as well as differences across issue areas have persisted, producing complex mixtures of liberal reforms with social-democratic, nationalist, and similar kinds of elements. While there has been a move toward convergence as the range of feasible political choices has narrowed (for Latin America, see Remmer 2003: 35–39, 42; Domínguez 1998), considerable heterogeneity persists inside these loose bounds; countries pursue liberal reforms in quite different versions and meld them with preexisting institutions and policy programs. Therefore, the world of politics is not turning uniform.

In the last two decades, many nations have implemented a host of changes to strengthen market competition and reduce state intervention in the economy. They have also extended liberalism to the social sectors, enacting elements of privatization, contracting, or other efficiency-oriented measures and pursuing targeting or similar neoliberal approaches to equity enhancement. Thus, there has been a broad advance toward liberalism in economic and social policy. Where change has occurred, it has largely gone in one direction. Few countries have moved against the current (as Brazil did in its health reform). While no nation has implemented the neoliberal program in its entirety, many of them adopted significant parts, and few countries rejected it altogether.

This liberal wave will probably have lasting effects. Drastic reversals are unlikely. Indeed, increasing returns and similar inertial forces, especially the interests and power of new stakeholders, now protect liberal programs against challenges. Path dependency favors the new status quo and hinders a switch to alternatives. In economic policy, competitive pressures and monitoring by global capital markets and international financial institutions will deter departures from prudent, fairly orthodox policy approaches. And the economy ministries will continue their efforts to control social policy; given the amount of resources allocated to benefit programs and the potential economic spillover effects, they will pursue efficiency-enhancing, market-oriented reforms. In fact, governments in the Third and First World are unlikely to escape from the resource constraints that have forced them to enact cost-saving and productivity-raising measures during the last three decades. In Latin America, the burden of foreign and domestic debt service, which devours enormous budget funds, will keep this concern pressing for the foreseeable future. For all these reasons, governments around the world are unlikely to abandon liberal reforms; instead, there will be a continued push for further change, especially advances toward greater efficiency.

Yet while the liberal wave has moved change in one predominant direction, it has by no means produced global uniformity. Many countries that have followed broad liberal guidelines have enacted divergent specific reforms. These concrete measures have reflected considerable regional and national specificity. In fact, liberalism has faced differential obstacles. Purer versions carried the day in some countries, but compromises were forged in others. My book demonstrates such divergences, for instance by comparing the substitutive pension privatizations of Bolivia and El Salvador with the mixed system adopted in Costa Rica. As inertial forces such as support for established institutions and the veto power of existing beneficiaries differed in strength, path dependency was easier to break in some nations than in others. The implementation of neoliberalism therefore varies greatly, as the health reforms analyzed in chapters 5 and 6 show. Even in the economic sphere, "varieties of capitalism" have persisted despite the neoliberal wave (Hall and Soskice 2001; Kitschelt et al. 1999; Huber 2002; Huber and Stephens 2001; Garrett 1998; Swank 2002). And despite their relative weakness, Third World countries retain considerable autonomy in responding to external exhortations and pressures for liberal reform (Remmer 2003: 39–41; Wibbels and Arce 2003: 130–32; Dezalay and Garth 2002: 33, 43, 95).

In fact, global liberalism is internally diverse and heterogeneous, giving national governments the opportunity to pick and choose and to play off advocates of one variant against promoters of another. For instance, market principles call for pension privatization, but the insistence on fiscal balance—another neoliberal plank—hinders drastic change due to its transition cost. As discussed in chapter 3, opponents of privatization in Brazil therefore managed to invoke an IMF veto to counter pressure from the World Bank and domestic economy ministries. And in health care, World Bank recommendations for privatization ran afoul of IDB proposals to introduce quasi-market mechanisms inside the public sector, as the Costa Rican case shows (Martínez Franzoni 1999). Even in the economic sphere, neoliberalism is far from monolithic but allows for a variety of policy approaches, such as flexible vs. fixed exchange rates; the sale of public enterprises vs. "popular capitalism" or voucher schemes; and antitrust measures of differential strictness.

This variety enhances the latitude of domestic policy-makers inside the constraints arising from the global advance of liberalism. The ever faster and more widespread dissemination of information about various policy options allows national decision-makers to enact those institutions and programs that combine the best with established policy structures. Rather than facing a uniform blueprint, they can select from a range of options.

But this increasing production of relevant information and the promotion of numerous models and experiments by a multitude of international agencies and nongovernmental organizations further swell the flood of information that decision-makers face. This overabundance, which is impossible to process comprehensively, intensifies the need to resort to cognitive shortcuts. Therefore, the heuristics of availability, representativeness, and anchoring will continue to shape what reform options decision-makers consider and how they evaluate them. The adoption and adaptation of liberal reforms will therefore depend in part on logically accidental factors that can differ across countries and regions. National decision-makers increasingly look beyond their borders but for this purpose need to rely on inferential shortcuts. As policy-makers overcome the bounds of space, they remain entangled in the bounds of rationality.

References and Interviews

Abel, Christopher, and Peter Lloyd-Sherlock. 2000. Health Policy in Latin America. In Peter Lloyd-Sherlock, ed. *Healthcare Reform and Poverty in Latin America*, 1–20. London: University of London. Institute of Latin American Studies.

Abell, Peter. 2001. Causality and Low-Frequency Complex Events. *Sociological Methods & Research* 30:1 (August): 57–80.

Abramson, Wendy. 2001. Monitoring and Evaluation of Contracts for Health Service Delivery in Costa Rica. *Health Policy and Planning* 16:4 (December): 404–11.

Abugattás, Javier. 2002. Author interview with former head of Programa de Focalización del Gasto Público. Lima: 9 July.

———. 1999. Author interview with former head of Programa de Focalización del Gasto Público. Lima: 8 July.

Acuña, Rodrigo. 2005. *Pension Reform in El Salvador*. Washington, DC: World Bank. Social Protection Discussion Paper No. 0507.

Acuña Ulate, Alberto, and Fabio Durán. 1994. *Diagnóstico y Estrategias para la Extensión de la Cobertura del Seguro de Invalidez, Vejez y Muerte*. San José: Caja Costarricense de Seguro Social, Dirección Actuarial.

Aguilar, Róger. 2004. Author interview with Director Actuarial y de Planificación Económica, Caja Costarricense de Seguro Social. San José: 16 June.

———. 1995. Sistema Nacional de Pensiones: Estrategia para el Fortalecimiento y Desarrollo. N.p.

———. 1994. *Proyecto para la Reforma del Sistema Nacional de Pensiones*. San José: Caja Costarricense de Seguro Social, Dirección Actuarial.

Aguilar, Róger, and Fabio Durán. 1996. La Reforma del Sistema Nacional de Pensiones de Costa Rica. *Seguridad Social* 202 (September–October): 135–49.

Aguinaga, Alejandro. 2002. Author interview with former vice-minister (1994–99) and minister of health (1999–2000). Lima: 16 July.

Alfaro Cascante, Amalia. 1987. Estudio sobre Opinión del Nuevo Modelo de Atención Ambulatoria: Barva–Heredia. N.p.: Caja Costarricense de Seguro Social.

Allison, Graham. 1971. *Essence of Decision*. Boston: Little, Brown.

Almeida, Celia, et al. 2000. Health Sector Reform in Brazil. *International Journal of Health Services* 30:1 (January): 129–62.

Alonso, Guillermo. 2000. *Política y Seguridad Social en la Argentina de los '90*. Buenos Aires: Miño y Dávila.

Altobelli, Laura. 1998. Report on Health Reform, Community Participation, and Social Inclusion: The Shared Administration Program. Lima: UNICEF.

Amadeo, Edward. 2000. Comments in "Seminário Internacional: Reforma da Previdência." *Conjuntura Social* 11:1 (January–March): 26–31.

Ames, Barry. 2001. *The Deadlock of Democracy in Brazil.* Ann Arbor: University of Michigan Press.

———. 1987. *Political Survival.* Berkeley: University of California Press.

Andersen Consulting and Consorci Hospitalari de Catalunya. 1996. *Diseño e Implementación de Mecanismos de Asignación de Recursos y para la Modernización de los Procesos Críticos de las Gerencias Financiera y Médica: Cambios Organizacionales.* San José: Caja Costarricense de Seguro Social.

Andrade, Luiz Odorico de. 2003. Author interview with president, Conselho Nacional de Secretários Municipais de Saúde. Brasília: 14 August.

ANEP (Asociación Nacional de la Empresa Privada). 2002. *Resultados de ENADE [Encuentro Nacional de la Empresa Privada] 2002. Segunda Parte.* San Salvador: ANEP. http://www.anep.org.sv/ENADE2002/2requerimiento.html.

ANFIP (Associação Nacional dos Auditores Fiscais de Contribuições Previdenciárias). 2003. *Análise da Seguridade Social em 2002.* Brasília: ANFIP.

———. 1995. *Ciclo de Estudos sobre Seguridade Social: Seminário Internacional sobre Seguridade Social.* Brasília: ANFIP.

———. 1993. *Compromisso com a Sociedade: Números verdadeiros da Previdência Social.* Brasília: ANFIP.

ANSAL (Análisis del Sector Salud de El Salvador). 1994a. *La Reforma de Salud: Hacia su Equidad y Eficiencia.* San Salvador: ANSAL.

———. 1994b. *Resumen Ejecutivo. Informe Técnico. Borrador Avanzado.* San Salvador: ANSAL.

Antelo, Jack, ed. 1997. *Seguros Públicos y Seguros Privados de Salud. Temas sobre Reforma de Salud.* Vol. 4. La Paz: Asociación Boliviana de Investigaciones en Economía de la Salud (ABIES).

Aponte, Guillermo. 1997. Seguro Nacional de Maternidad y Niñez. In Hugo Loaiza, ed. *El Seguro Nacional de Maternidad y Niñez. Temas sobre Reforma de Salud 1,* 3–33. La Paz: Ministerio de Desarrollo Humano, Secretaría Nacional de Salud.

Apoyo S.A. 1992. El Sistema Privado de Pensiones. Informe Analítico. Lima: Apoyo.

Appel, Hilary. 2004. Western Financial Institutions, Local Actors, and the Privatization Paradigm. *Problems of Post-Communism* 51:5 (September–October): 3–10.

Arce, Claudio. 2004. Author interview with official of Proyecto de Modernización, Caja Costarricense de Seguro Social. San José: 1 July.

Arce, Claudio, and Juan Carlos Sánchez. 2001. Avances del Proceso de Reforma de la Caja Costarricense de Seguro Social. *Revista de Ciencias Administrativas y Financieras de la Seguridad Social* 9:2 (November): 13–21.

Arce, Moisés. 2001. The Politics of Pension Reform in Peru. *Studies in Comparative International Development* 36:3 (Fall): 88–113.

Arellano, Manuel. 2004. Natural Gas, Social Unrest, and the Ousting of a President. Talk presented at panel "Are Latin American Presidents Living Dangerously?" University of Texas at Austin, 8 April.

Arévalo, Gregorio, and Javier Cayo. 1997. A Proposal for Modifying Peru's Current Pension System. Washington, DC: Inter-American Development Bank.

Armada, Francisco, Carles Muntaner, and Vicente Navarro. 2001. Health and Social Security Reforms in Latin America. *International Journal of Health Services* 31:4: 729–66.

Arouca, Sérgio. 1992. Author interview with leader of sanitary movement and Deputado Federal (PPS-RJ). Brasília: 23 June.

Arretche, Marta. 2004. Toward a Unified and More Equitable System: Health Reform in Brazil. In Robert Kaufman and Joan Nelson, eds. *Crucial Needs, Weak Incentives,* 155–88. Washington, DC: Woodrow Wilson Center Press.

Arroyo, Juan. 2002. Acuerdos de Gestión y Nuevos Mecanismos de Pago en los Noventa. *Economía y Sociedad* 44 (March): 42–46.

———. 2000. *Salud: La Reforma Silenciosa.* Lima: Universidad Peruana Cayetano Heredia.

Asamblea Legislativa. Comisión de Medio Ambiente y Salud Pública. 1999. *Seminario de Comparación de Propuestas de Reforma del Sector Salud en El Salvador.* San Salvador: Asamblea Legislativa.

Ausejo, Flavio. 1995. La Reforma del Instituto Peruano de Seguridad Social. In Augusto Alvarez Rodrich and Gabriel Ortiz de Zevallos, eds. *Implementación de Políticas Públicas en el Perú,* 133–44. Lima: Editorial Apoyo.

Avilés, Luis. 1998. Modernized Injustice: The Reform and Modernization of the Salvadoran Health Care System. Ph.D. Dissertation, Johns Hopkins University.

Ayala, Norma. 2004. Author interview with leading member of health reform team (1992–98) and official of Caja Costarricense de Seguro Social. San José: 22 June.

Ayuda Memoria. 1993. Aspectos a ser Tomados en Cuenta antes y al Momento de Efectuar la Reforma a la Seguridad Social a Largo Plazo. N.p.

Azeredo, Beatriz. 1994. As Experiências Chilena e Argentina de Reforma da Previdência Social. In Ministério da Previdência Social (MPS). *A Previdência Social e a Revisão Constitucional. Debates.* Vol. 2, 181–99. Brasília: MPS.

Azevedo, Aline. 2003. Author interview with coordinadora, Departamento de Atenção Básica, Ministério da Saúde. Brasília: 5 August.

Bacha, Edmar. 1998. O Plano Real. In Aloizio Mercadante, ed. *O Brasil pós-Real,* 11–69. Campinas: Instituto de Economia. Universidade Estadual de Campinas.

Balbi, Carmen Rosa. 1997. Politics and Trade Unions in Peru. In Maxwell Cameron and Philip Mauceri, eds. *The Peruvian Labyrinth,* 134–51. University Park: Pennsylvania State University Press.

Balcerowicz, Leszek. 1994. Understanding Postcommunist Transitions. *Journal of Democracy* 5:4 (October): 75–89.

Ballesteros, Róger. 2004. Author interview with former member of health reform team, Caja Costarricense de Seguro Social, and liaison with Inter-American Development Bank. San José: 16 June.

Banco Mundial. 1993. Costa Rica: Proyecto de Reforma del Sector Salud. Misión de Preparación del Banco Mundial, Febrero 22–Marzo 5, 1993. N.p.

———. 1991. Ayuda Memoria. Misión de Identificación (15–25 Julio). San José. N.p.

———. Proyecto de Reforma al Sistema de Seguridad Social a Largo Plazo en

Bolivia. 1993a. *Proyecto de Reforma al Sistema de Riesgos Profesionales*. Vol. 1. La Paz: Corporación de Investigación, Estudio y Desarrollo de la Seguridad Social (CIEDESS).

———. 1993b. *Restructuración del Sistema de Seguridad Social de Largo Plazo en Bolivia*. La Paz: CIEDESS.

Barahona, Manuel. 2004. Author interview with former moderator, Comisión de Pensiones, Concertación Nacional (1998). Heredia, Costa Rica: 16 June.

Barnett, Michael, and Martha Finnemore. 2004. *Rules for the World*. Ithaca: Cornell University Press.

Barr, Nicholas. 2000. *Reforming Pensions: Myths, Truths, and Policy Choices*. Washington, DC: International Monetary Fund.

Barriga, Roberto. 2002. Author interview with Jefe Nacional de Seguro Básico de Salud, Ministerio de Salud y Previsión Social. La Paz: 14 August.

Bates, Robert. 1981. *Markets and States in Tropical Africa*. Berkeley: University of California Press.

Bates, Robert, Rui de Figueiredo, and Barry Weingast. 1998. The Politics of Interpretation. *Politics and Society* 26:4 (December 1998): 603–42.

Bates, Robert, et al. 1998. *Analytic Narratives*. Princeton: Princeton University Press.

Beattie, Roger, and Warren McGillivray. 1995. A Risky Strategy: Reflections on the World Bank Report "Averting the Old Age Crisis." *International Social Security Review* 48:3–4 (July–December): 5–22.

Benavides, Bruno. 2002. Author interview with jefe, Proyecto 2000, Ministerio de Salud and USAID. Lima: 5 July.

Bendezú, Carlos. 2002. Author interview with former reform team member, Comités Locales de Administración de Salud, Ministerio de Salud. Lima: 15 July.

Bendor, Jonathan. 2003. Herbert A. Simon: Political Scientist. *Annual Review of Political Science* 6: 433–71.

Bengoa, Rafael. 1996. Perú—Reforma del Sector Salud. Proyecto MINSA-ODA. N.p.

Bergesen, Albert, ed. 1980. *Studies of the Modern World System*. New York: Academic Press.

Berlinguer, Giovanni. 1989. Reforma Sanitária Brasil–Itália. *Saúde em Debate* 24 (March): 43–47.

———. 1978. *Medicina e Política*. São Paulo: CEBES–HUCITEC.

Berlinguer, Giovanni, Sonia Fleury Teixeira, and Gastão Wagner de Souza Campos. 1988. *Reforma Sanitária: Itália e Brasil*. São Paulo: HUCITEC.

Berry, Frances. 1994. Sizing Up State Policy Innovation Research. *Policy Studies Journal* 22:3 (Autumn): 442–56.

Berstein, Solange, and José Luis Ruiz. 2005. Sensibilidad de la Demanda con Consumidores Desinformados. Santiago de Chile: Superintendencia de AFP.

Betancourt, Herbert. 2004. Author interview with former vice-minister and minister of health (1999–2004). San Salvador: 6 July.

Blay, Eva. 1993. *Proposta Revisional, N° 13869 a 13936*. Brasília: Congresso Nacional, Revisão da Constituição Federal.

Blyth, Mark. 2002. *Great Transformations: Economic Ideas and Institutional Change in the Twentieth Century*. Cambridge: Cambridge University Press.

Böhrt Arana, Roberto, and Oscar Larraín Sánchez. 2002. *La Revolución Silenciosa: El Seguro Básico de Salud*. La Paz: Ministerio de Salud y Previsión Social.

Boloña, Carlos. 1997. Testimony: Pension Reform in Peru. N.p.: International Center for Pension Reform. http://www.pensionreform.org/articles/carlos_bolona.html.

———. 1996. Author interview with former economy and finance minister (1991–93). Lima: 14 August.

———. 1995. *¿Dueño de tu Jubilación?* Lima: Instituto de Economía de Libre Mercado (IELM).

———. 1994. La Privatización de los Servicios de Salud en el Marco de las Reformas Estructurales. In José Carlos Vera la Torre et al. *La Privatización de la Salud: Rumbo a la Modernidad*, 149–63. Lima: IELM.

———. 1993. *Cambio de Rumbo*. Lima: IELM.

Bonadona, Alberto. 2002. Author interview with core member of pension reform team (1991–97). La Paz: 9 August.

———. 1998. *Marco Regulador, Privatización y Reforma de Pensiones*. La Paz: Ediciones ABC.

Bonilla, Alejandro. 2005. Author telephone interview with chief of Studies and Operations Branch, International Social Security Association: 25 January.

Bornhausen, Roberto Konder. 2003. Author interview with former president, Federação Brasileira de Bancos. São Paulo: 17 July.

Bossert, Thomas, et al. 2000. *Applied Research on Decentralization of Health Systems in Latin America: Bolivia Case Study*. Cambridge: Harvard School of Public Health. LAC-HSR Health Sector Reform Initiative No. 34.

Brady, Henry, and David Collier, eds. 2004. *Rethinking Social Inquiry*. Lanham, MD: Rowman & Littlefield.

Brevé, Francia. 2004. Author interview with political leader of pension reform team (1995–98). San Salvador: 7 July.

Britto, Antonio. 1992. Author interview with federal deputy (PMDB—RS). Brasília: 26 June.

Brooks, Sarah. N.d. Social Protection and the Market: The Making of Latin American Pension Reform. Ms. Department of Political Science, Ohio State University.

———. 2005. Interdependent and Domestic Foundations of Policy Change: The Diffusion of Pension Privatization around the World. *International Studies Quarterly* 49:2 (June): 273–94.

———. 2004. International Financial Institutions and the Diffusion of Foreign Models of Social Security Reform in Latin America. In Kurt Weyland, ed. *Learning from Foreign Models in Latin American Policy Reform*, 53–80. Washington, DC: Woodrow Wilson Center Press.

———. 2002. Social Protection and Economic Integration. *Comparative Political Studies* 35:5 (June): 491–523.

Brooks, Sarah, and Kent Weaver. 2005. *Lashed to the Mast? The Politics of Notional Defined Contribution Pension Reforms*. Chestnut Hill, MA: Center for Retirement Research. Boston College.

Büchi, Hernán. 1994. La Privatización de los Servicios de Salud en el Marco de las Reformas Estructurales. In José Carlos Vera la Torre, Margarita Petrera,

Jorge Ruiz, et al. *La Privatización de la Salud: Rumbo a la Modernidad,* 131–48. Lima: Instituto de Economía de Libre Mercado.

Bustamante, Julio. 1995. *Agenda para el Desarrollo de una Propuesta de Reforma del Sistema Nacional de Pensiones (Borrador para Comentarios).* San José: N.p.

Bustamante, Julio, and Jorge Tarziján. 1993. Estudio Referido a Creación y Organización de Superintendencia de Sociedades Administradoras de Pensiones para Bolivia. Santiago de Chile: N.p.

Calderón, Victor. 2002. Author interview with director de cooperación externa y relaciones internacionales, Ministerio de Salud y Deportes. La Paz: 16 August.

Calderón Fournier, Rafael Angel. 1993. Carta de Declaración de Política del Gobierno de La República a la Presidencia del Banco Mundial, Respecto a la Reforma del Sector Salud. In Caja Costarricense de Seguro Social (CCSS). *Proyecto Reforma Sector Salud—CCSS. Resumen Ejecutivo.* San José: CCSS.

Camargo, Carlos. 2002. Author interview with former secretario de seguridad social, Central Obrera Boliviana (COB) (1986–97). La Paz: 30 July.

Campbell, John. 2004. *Institutional Change and Globalization.* Princeton: Princeton University Press.

Campbell, John, and Ove Pedersen, eds. 2001. *The Rise of Neoliberalism and Institutional Analysis.* Princeton: Princeton University Press.

Campos, Gastão Wagner de Souza. 2003. Author interview with leading member of sanitary movement and secretário executivo, Ministério da Saúde. Brasília: 4 August.

———. 1997. Análise Crítica das Contribuições da Saúde Coletiva à Organização das Práticas de Saúde no SUS. In Sonia Fleury, ed. *Saúde e Democracia: A Luta do CEBES,* 113–24. São Paulo: Lemos Editorial.

Capote Mir, Roberto. 1982. La Evolución de los Servicios de Salud y la Estructura Socioeconómica en Cuba. *Saúde em Debate* 14: 51–68.

Capra, Katherina, et al. 1998. *Estudio de Costos del Paquete Materno–Neonatal en Salud.* La Paz: MotherCare Bolivia.

Cárdenas, Marina. 2002. Author interview with former health specialist, Unidad de Análisis de Políticas Sociales (1993–97), and gerente del Proyecto Abrir-Salud. La Paz: 5 August.

———. 2000. *Cuentas Nacionales de Financiamiento y Gasto en Salud: Bolivia.* La Paz: Data for Decision Making, Harvard University.

Cárdenas, Marina, Mukesh Chawla, and Jorge Muñoz. 1997. *Movilización de Recursos para el Sector Salud en Bolivia.* La Paz: UDAPSO. Documento de Trabajo 58/97.

Cárdenas, Marina, Jeanine Madden, and Sonia Contreras Gómez. 1997. *Análisis Costo-Efectividad de Intervenciones de Salud en Bolivia.* La Paz: UDAPSO. Documento de Trabajo 56/97.

Carpenter, Daniel. 2000. What Is the Marginal Value of *Analytic Narratives? Social Science History* 24:4 (Winter): 653–67.

Carrillo, Ubaldo. 2004. Author interview with director de pensiones, Gerencia de Pensiones, Caja Costarricense de Seguro Social. San José: 23 June.

———. 2000. Costa Rica: Así Será el Nuevo Sistema de Pensiones. San José: CCSS, Gerencia de Pensiones.

Carvajal, Juan Carlos, and Pedro Francke. 2000. *La Seguridad Social en Salud.* Lima: Pontificia Universidad Católica del Perú, Departamento de Economía. Documento de Trabajo 187.

Carvalho, Celecino de. 2003. Author interview with chefe de gabinete, Secretaria Executiva, Ministério da Previdência e Assistência Social. Brasília: 8 August.

———. 1999. Author interview with Assessor Especial, MPAS. Brasília: 11 June.

———. 1993. Propostas de Reforma da Seguridade Social: Uma Visão Crítica. *Planejamento e Políticas Públicas* 9 (June): 101–43.

———. 1992. Author interview with diretor de previdência social, Ministério da Previdência Social. Brasília: 22 June.

———. 1989. Author interview with secretário de estudos especiais, Ministério da Previdência e Assistência Social. Brasília: 12 July.

Castro, Mauricio. 2004. Author interview with labor observer of Concertación Nacional (1998). San José: 21 June.

———. 2001. Reforma de Pensiones y Transformación del Auxilio de Cesantía en Costa Rica. San José: N.p.

Castro, Paulo Rabello de, and Paulo Carlos de Brito. 1992. *Brasil: Este País Tem Jeito?* Rio de Janeiro: Riofundo.

Castro Valverde, Carlos, and Luis Bernardo Sáenz. 1998. *La Reforma del Sistema Nacional de Salud.* San José: Ministerio de Planificación y Política Económica.

CCSS (Caja Costarricense de Seguro Social). 1998. *Articulación del Sistema de Pensiones de la Seguridad Social: Resumen Ejecutivo.* San José: CCSS.

———. 1996. *Hacia un Nuevo Sistema de Asignación de Recursos.* San José: CCSS.

———. 1993. *El Proyecto de Reforma del Sector Salud: Resumen.* San José: CCSS.

———. 1986. *Desarrollo de un Nuevo Modelo de Atención Ambulatoria en Costa Rica.* San José: CCSS.

———. 1985. *Visita del Dr. Brian Abel-Smith a Costa Rica.* San José: CCSS.

———. Comisión Proyecto de Barva. 1986. *Desarrollo de un Nuevo Modelo de Atención Ambulatoria: Anteproyecto de Barva de Heredia. Propuesta Inicial.* San José: CCSS.

———. DAPE (Dirección Actuarial y de Planificación Económica). 1995. *Una Evaluación Económica y Financiera de las Modalidades de Gestión de Servicios Ambulatorios de Salud mediante Cooperativas.* San José: CCSS.

———. DTSS (Dirección Técnica Servicios de Salud). 1990. *Estudio acerca de la Administración y la Utilización de Servicios de Salud en la Clínica de Pavas 1990.* San José: CCSS.

———. Gerencia de División Pensiones. 1996. *Proyecto de Reforma del Sistema de Pensiones: Bases, Estrategias, Principios y Objetivos. Agenda para 1996.* San José: CCSS.

————. PM (Proyecto Modernización). 1997. El Compromiso de Gestión. *Gestión 5* (extraordinary issue): 25–30.

————. UCPM (Unidad Coordinadora del Proyecto de Modernización). 1995. *Reporte de Avance del Proyecto de Modernización de la C.C.S.S., PR.CR-3654 Banco Mundial.* San José: CCSS.

CCSS and Banco Mundial. 2002. *Fortalecimiento y Modernización del Sector Salud de Costa Rica. Informe Ejecutivo.* San José: CCSS.

CEPB (Confederación de Empresarios Privados de Bolivia). Unidad de Análisis. 1991a. La Atención de la Salud Previsional en Bolivia: Necesidad de una Cirugía. La Paz: CEPB.

————. 1991b. La Crisis de los Fondos de Pensiones. La Paz: CEPB.

Cercone, James. 2005. Email communication from former health reform consultant of the Salvadoran government. 12 January.

————. 2004. Author interview with former World Bank consultant and member of Proyecto de Modernización, Caja Costarricense de Seguro Social. San José: 14 June.

————. 1996. Alternativas en la Organización, Financiamiento y Prestación de Servicios. *Gestión* 4:1 (first semester): 20–27.

Cercone, James, and Rodrigo Briceño. 2004. La Cooperación Pública y Privada en Acción: El Caso de las Cooperativas de Servicios de Salud en Costa Rica, 1988–2000. In Claudio Arce, ed. *La Reforma de Salud.* San José: Caja Costarricense de Seguro Social (ms.).

Céspedes, Víctor Hugo. 2004. Author interview with asesor de la presidencia ejecutiva, Caja Costarricense de Seguro Social. San José: 24 June.

Chalmers, Douglas. 1977. The Politicized State in Latin America. In James Malloy, ed. *Authoritarianism and Corporatism in Latin America,* 23–45. Pittsburgh: University of Pittsburgh Press.

Chamley, Christophe. 2004. *Rational Herds. Economic Models of Social Learning.* Cambridge: Cambridge University Press.

Chaves Marín, Ronald. 1999. *Reforma al Sistema de Pensiones: La Experiencia de Costa Rica.* San José: Superintendencia de Pensiones. DI-1999–01.

Chávez, Hector. 1993. Programa Integrado de Servicios Básicos de Salud y Fortalecimiento Institucional (PSF). In Instituto Latinoamericano de Investigaciones Sociales, ed., *Hacia un Sistema de Salud Descentralizado,* 155–65. La Paz: ILDIS.

Chong, Dennis. 2000. *Rational Lives: Norms and Values in Politics and Society.* Chicago: University of Chicago Press.

Cichon, Michael. 1999. Notional Defined-Contribution Schemes. *International Social Security Review* 52:4 (October–December): 87–105.

Cifuentes, Mercedes. 2000. *Revisión Propuesta de Reforma del Sector Salud de FUSADES.* Santiago de Chile: Instituto Libertad y Desarrollo.

CINDE (Centro Internacional para el Desarrollo Económico), ed. 1994. *Soluciones Descentralizadas/Privadas a Problemas Públicos.* San Salvador: CINDE.

Clark, Mary. 2005. The Medical Profession, the State, and Health Reform in Costa Rica. Paper prepared for 46th annual convention, International Studies Association, Honolulu, Hawaii, 1–5 March.

————. 2004. Reinforcing a Public System: Health Sector Reform in Costa Rica.

In Robert Kaufman and Joan Nelson, eds. *Crucial Needs, Weak Incentives,* 189–216. Washington, DC: Woodrow Wilson Center Press.

———. 2001. *Gradual Economic Reform in Latin America: The Costa Rican Experience.* Albany: State University of New York Press.

Claro y Asociados. 1994. Comentarios al Anteproyecto de Ley del Sistema de Fondos de Pensiones de Capitalización Individual. Santiago de Chile: Claro y Asociados.

———. 1991. Reforma del Sistema del Seguro Social. Componente Pensiones. Santiago de Chile: Claro y Asociados.

Clemens, Elisabeth, and James Cook. 1999. Politics and Institutionalism: Explaining Durability and Change. *Annual Review of Sociology* 25: 441–66.

Coelho, Vera Schattan. 1999. A Reforma da Previdência e o Jogo Político no Interior do Executivo. *Novos Estudos CEBRAP* 55 (November): 121–42.

Cohn, Amélia. 2003. Author interview with leading member of sanitary movement and director of Centro de Estudos de Cultura Contemporânea. São Paulo: 21 July.

———. 1989. Caminhos da Reforma Sanitária. *Lua Nova* 19 (November): 123–40.

Colegio Médico de El Salvador. 2002. Opinión del Colegio Médico de El Salvador en Relación a la Imposición por el Presidente Flores, de una Reforma de Mercado de la Salud. San Salvador: Colegio Médico.

Colegio Médico del Perú. N.d. Anteproyecto de Ley Sustitutorio de la Ley Nº 26790 "Modernización de la Seguridad Social en Salud." Lima: Colegio Médico.

Collier, David, Henry Brady, and Jason Seawright. 2004. Sources of Leverage in Causal Inference. In Henry Brady and David Collier, eds. *Rethinking Social Inquiry,* 229–66. Lanham, MD: Rowman & Littlefield.

Collier, David, and Richard Messick. 1975. Prerequisites Versus Diffusion. *American Political Science Review* 69:4 (December): 1299–1315.

Collor, Fernando. 1995. Author interview with ex-president (1990–92). Brasília: 9 June.

———. 1991. *Brasil: Um Projeto de Reconstrução Nacional.* Brasília: Presidência.

Comisión para la Reforma al Sistema de Pensiones. 1996. Propuesta de Reforma al Actual Sistema de Pensiones. San Salvador: Comisión para la Reforma.

Comisión Técnica de Pensiones. 1990. *Sistema de Pensiones en Chile: Informe de la Visita Efectuada a Chile.* San José: Caja Costarricense de Seguro Social.

CONASA (Comisión Nacional de Salud). 1999. *Propuesta de Lineamientos para la Reforma del Sistema de Salud de El Salvador.* San Salvador: CONASA.

Conferência Nacional de Saúde. 1987. *Anais da 8ª Conferência Nacional de Saúde, 1986.* Brasília: Ministério da Saúde.

Contreras, Manuel. 1997. Capacity Building in the Bolivian Social Policy Analysis Unit. In Merilee Grindle, ed. *Getting Good Government,* 199–228. Cambridge: Harvard Institute for International Development.

Cook, Karen, and Margaret Levi, eds. 1990. *The Limits of Rationality.* Chicago: University of Chicago Press.

Cordero Vásquez, Miguel Angel. 1988. *Nuevo Modelo de Atención Ambulatoria "Capitación."* San José: Ministerio de Salud and Caja Costarricense de Seguro Social.

Córdoba Herrera, Anayansy. 1995. *Regímenes de Pensiones de Capitalización Individual.* San José: Comisión Nacional de Valores. Departamento de Proyectos.

Córdova, Ricardo. 1999. *El Proceso de Gestación de la Reforma Educativa.* San Salvador: Fundación Dr. Guillermo Manuel Ungo. Documento de Trabajo. Serie Análisis de la Realidad Nacional 99–2.

———. 1993. *La Reforma a la Seguridad Social en El Salvador.* San Salvador: FundaUngo. Documento de Trabajo. Serie Seguridad Social 93–4.

Corrales, Javier. 2003. Market Reforms. In Jorge Domínguez and Michael Shifter, eds. *Constructing Democratic Governance in Latin America,* 2nd ed., 74–99. Baltimore: Johns Hopkins University Press.

———. 2002. ¿Cuánto Duran los Ministros de Educación en América Latina? *Formas & Reformas de la Educación: Serie Políticas* 4:12 (July): 1–4.

———. 1999. *The Politics of Education Reform.* Washington, DC: World Bank. Education Reform and Management Series, vol. 2, no. 1.

Cortez, Jorge. 2002. Author interview with former assessor of Economy Minister Carlos Boloña (1991–92). Lima: 17 July.

Costa Bauer, Marino. 2002. Author interview with former health minister (1996–98). Lima: 1 July.

Cotlear, Daniel. 2000. *Peru: Reforming Health Care for the Poor.* Washington, DC: World Bank. Latin America and the Caribbean Regional Office. Human Development Department. LCSHD Paper No. 57.

Cox, Gary, and Scott Morgenstern. 2001. Latin America's Reactive Assemblies and Proactive Presidents. *Comparative Politics* 33:2 (January): 171–89.

Cox, Robert. 1986. Social Forces, States, and World Orders. In Robert Keohane, ed. *Neorealism and Its Critics,* 204–54. New York: Columbia University Press.

Crean el Sistema Privado de Salud el cual tendrá Carácter de complementario al Sistema administrado por el IPSS. Decreto Legislativo N° 718. 1991. *El Peruano* (10 November): 101589–92.

Créase Sistema Privado de Pensiones complementario al Sistema Nacional de Pensiones a cargo del IPSS. 1991. Decreto Legislativo N° 724. 1991. *El Peruano* (11 November): 101613–18.

CRSS (Consejo de Reforma del Sector Salud). 2000. *Propuesta de Reforma Integral de Salud.* San Salvador: CRSS. http://www.mspas.gob.sv/avance_reforma.asp (accessed 30 June 2004).

Cruz, Carlos, and Elena Carrera. 2004. The Role of Foreign Models in Mexican Healthcare Reforms of the 1990s. In Kurt Weyland, ed. *Learning from Foreign Models in Latin American Policy Reform,* 219–40. Washington, DC: Woodrow Wilson Center Press.

Cruz, Miguel, Patricia Craig, and Luis Ventosa. 1999. *Visión de la Población sobre el Sistema Nacional de Salud.* N.p. Instituto Universitario de Opinión Pública and Harvard Institute for International Development. Report for USAID, El Salvador.

Cruz Saco, María Amparo. 2001a. Public Policy and New Approaches for the Expansion of Social Protection: The Case of Peru. Paper for 23rd International Congress, Latin American Studies Association. Washington, DC: 6–8 September.

———. 2001b. *Sistema de Salud en El Salvador.* San Salvador: Fundación Friedrich Ebert.

———. 1998. The Pension System Reform in Peru. In María Amparo Cruz Saco and Carmelo Mesa-Lago, eds. *Do Options Exist?* 165–85. Pittsburgh: University of Pittsburgh Press.

Cuentas Yáñez, Guillermo. 2002. Author interview with former vice-minister and minister of health (1989–93, 1997–2001). La Paz: 9 August.

Cueto Arteaga, José Luis, ed. 2002. Reforma del Sector Salud. *Temas en la Crisis* 60 (May): 1–56.

Cueto, Marcos. 2004. The Origins of Primary Health Care and Selective Primary Health Care. *American Journal of Public Health* 94:11 (November): 1864–74.

Cuevas Argote, Javier. 2002. Author interview with director de investigación y análisis, Confederación de Empresarios Privados de Bolivia. La Paz: 13 August.

Cyert, Richard, and James March. 1963. *A Behavioral Theory of the Firm.* Englewood Cliffs, NJ: Prentice-Hall.

Daboub, Juan José. 2004a. Author interview with former finance minister. San Salvador: 9 July.

———. 2004b. Email communication from former finance minister. 16 December.

Da Cunha, João Paulo, José Machado, and Maria José Brant. 1994. Niterói: Relato de Experiência. *Espaço para a Saúde* 3:3 (May): 25–29.

Dahl, Robert. 1984. Political Influence. Chap. in *Modern Political Analysis,* 4th ed., 19–35. Englewood Cliffs, NJ: Prentice-Hall.

DDM (Data for Decision Making. Harvard University). 1995. *Cost and Cost-Effectiveness of Health Services. Workshop Proceedings, May 9–11.* La Paz: DDM.

De Groote, Tony, Pierre de Paepe, and Jean-Pierre Unger. 2005. Colombia: In Vivo Test of Health Sector Privatization in the Developing World. *International Journal of Health Services* 35:1 (January): 125–41.

De Habich, Midori. 2002. Author interview with health economist, Proyecto 2000, Ministerio de Salud and USAID. Lima: 27 June.

De los Heros, Alfonso. 2002 Author interview with former labor minister (1991–92). Lima: 8 July.

Demarco, Gustavo. 2004. The Argentine Pension System Reform and International Lessons. In Kurt Weyland, ed. *Learning from Foreign Models in Latin American Policy Reform,* 81–109. Washington, DC: Woodrow Wilson Center Press.

Demirgüç-Kunt, Asli, and Anita Schwarz. 1995. *Costa Rican Pension System: Options for Reform.* Washington, DC: World Bank. Policy Research Working Paper 1483.

Departamento de Ciencias Jurídicas. Universidad Centroamericana "José Simeón

Cañas" (UCA). 1997. Inconstitucionalidad de la Ley del Sistema de Ahorro para Pensiones. *Estudios Centroamericanos* 52:585–86 (July–August): 711–25.

De Soto, Hernando. 1996. Author interview with former special adviser to President Fujimori (1990–92). Lima: 20 August.

Dezalay, Yves, and Bryant Garth. 2002. *The Internationalization of Palace Wars: Lawyers, Economists, and the Contest to Transform Latin American States.* Chicago: University of Chicago Press.

Díaz Ortega, Enrique. 1996. Desarrollo y Experiencies del Sistema Privado de Pensiones en el Perú. Paper for seminario regional "Situación Actual de las Reformas a los Sistemas de Pensiones en América Latina y el Caribe," Comisión Económica para América Latina y el Caribe, Santiago de Chile, 7–8 October.

DIES-CENITEC (Dirección de Investigaciones Económicas y Sociales. Centro de Investigaciones Técnicas y Científicas). 1993. La Crisis del Sistema Previsional de El Salvador. *Política Económica* 20 (September-October): 1–34.

DiMaggio, Paul, and Walter Powell. 1983. The Iron Cage Revisited. *American Sociological Review* 48:2 (April): 147–60.

Dmytraczenko, Tania, et al. 1998. *Evaluación del Seguro Nacional de Maternidad y Niñez en Bolivia.* Bethesda, MD: Partnerships for Health Reform. Informe Técnico No. 28.

Domínguez, Jorge. 1998. Free Politics and Free Markets in Latin America. *Journal of Democracy* 9:4 (October 1998): 70–84.

———, ed. 1997. *Technopols: Freeing Politics and Markets in Latin America in the 1990s.* University Park: Pennsylvania State University Press.

Downs, Anthony. 1957. *An Economic Theory of Democracy.* New York: Harper.

Drummond, Carlos. 1998. Aposentadoria em Risco. *Carta Capital* (15 April): 32–41.

Du Bois, Fritz. 2002. Author interview with former adviser to economy ministers Carlos Boloña (1991–92) and Jorge Camet (1993–97). Lima: 2 July.

Durán, Fabio. 2004. Author interview with former director actuarial y de planificación económica, Caja Costarricense de Seguro Social. San José: 25 June.

———. 1995. *Plan de Estabilización Financiera del Seguro de Invalidez, Vejez y Muerte, 1995–2020.* San José: CCSS, Dirección Actuarial.

Echeverri, Oscar. 1989. El Banco Mundial: Políticas, Instrumentos, Procedimientos y Experiencias en el Sector Salud. N.p.: Banco Mundial.

Eckstein, Harry. 1975. Case Study and Theory in Political Science. In Fred Greenstein and Nelson Polsby, eds. *Handbook of Political Science,* vol. 7: *Strategies of Inquiry,* 79–137. Reading, MA: Addison-Wesley.

Edwards, Sebastián. 1995. *Crisis and Reform in Latin America.* Washington, DC: World Bank and Oxford University Press.

Eiseman, Ellen. 2002. Author interview with jefa adjunta de la asistencia técnica, Proyecto 2000, Ministerio de Salud and USAID. Lima: 24 June.

Elkins, Zachary, and Beth Simmons. 2005. On Waves, Clusters, and Diffusion. *Annals of the American Academy of Political and Social Science* 598 (March): 33–51.

Elster, Jon. 2000. Rational Choice History: A Case of Excessive Ambition. *American Political Science Review* 94:3 (September): 685–95.

Enríquez, Octavio, and Juan Carlos Bow. 2004. Réquiem a nueva Ley de Pensiones. *El Nuevo Diario* (22 July).

Epley, Nicholas, and Thomas Gilovich. 2002. Putting Adjustment Back in the Anchoring and Adjustment Heuristic. In Thomas Gilovich, Dale Griffin, and Daniel Kahneman, eds. *Heuristics and Biases: The Psychology of Intuitive Judgment,* 139–49. Cambridge: Cambridge University Press.

Eróstegui, Rodolfo. 1996. Die bolivianischen Gewerkschaften. *Lateinamerika: Analysen, Daten, Dokumentation* 13:31: 37–42.

ESAN/IDE (Escuela de Administración de Negocios. Instituto de Desarrollo Económico), ed. 1994. *Foro Internacional. Administración de la Salud: Enfoques, Tendencias, Propuestas.* Lima: ESAN/IDE.

Escobar, Federico, and Osvaldo Nina. 2004. *Pension Reform in Bolivia.* La Paz: Grupo Integral. Study No. GI-E6.

Escorel, Sarah. 1999. *Reviravolta na Saúde: Origem e Articulação do Movimento Sanitário.* Rio de Janeiro: Editora FIOCRUZ.

Espinoza, Rubén. 2002. Author interview with former coordinador de equipos de reforma, Programa de Fortalecimiento de Servicios de Salud (PFSS), Ministerio de Salud. Lima: 10 July.

———. 1998a. *Análisis del Proceso de Reforma en el Perú: Informe del Coordinador del Componente de Reestructuración Sectorial del Programa de Fortalecimiento de Servicios de Salud.* Lima: Ministerio de Salud. PFSS.

———. 1998b. *Cronología de Hechos de Reforma en el Perú.* Lima: Ministerio de Salud. PFSS.

Esquivel, Douglas. 1998. Perspectiva Empresarial sobre Reforma del Régimen de Pensiones en el Marco de la Seguridad Social en Costa Rica. San José: Unión Costarricense de Cámaras y Asociaciones de la Empresa Privada.

Esser, James. 1998. Alive and Well after 25 Years: A Review of Groupthink Research. *Organizational Behavior and Human Decision Processes* 73:2/3 (February–March): 116–41.

Evia Viscarra, José, and Miguel Fernández Moscoso. 2004. *Reforma de Pensiones y Valoración del Seguro Social de Largo Plazo en Bolivia.* La Paz: Universidad Católica Boliviana, Instituto de Investigaciones Socio Económicas.

Ewig, Christina. 2004. Piecemeal but Innovative: Health Sector Reform in Peru. In Robert Kaufman and Joan Nelson, eds. *Crucial Needs, Weak Incentives,* 217–46. Washington, DC: Woodrow Wilson Center Press.

———. 2000. Democracia Diferida: Un Análisis del Proceso de Reformas en el Sector Salud. In Felipe Portocarrero, ed. *Políticas Sociales en el Perú,* 481–518. Lima: Red para el Desarrollo de las Ciencias Sociales en el Perú.

Exposición de Motivos: Ley del Sistema de Ahorro para Pensiones. 1996. San Salvador: N.p.

Exposición de Motivos y Proyecto de Ley de Pensiones. Sistema Previsional de Capitalización Individual. 1993. La Paz: N.p.

Faro, Clovis de, ed. 1993. *Previdência Social no Brasil.* Rio de Janeiro: Editora da Fundação Getúlio Vargas.

Felipe, Saraiva. 2003. Author interview with leading member of health reform movement and Deputado Federal (PMDB-MG). Brasília: 13 August.

Fernández Fagalde, Luis. 2002. Author interview with former president, Comisión de Política Social, Cámara de Diputados. La Paz: 25 July.

Fiedler, John. 1996. The Privatization of Health Care in Three Latin American Social Security Systems. *Health Policy and Planning* 11:4 (December): 406–17.

Fiedler, John, and John Rigoli. 1991. *The Costa Rican Social Security Fund's Alternative Models*. Washington, DC: International Science and Technology Institute.

FIESP/CIESP (Federação e Centro das Indústrias do Estado de São Paulo). 1993. Uma Proposta de Reforma Tributária e de Seguridade Social. *Conjuntura Social* 4:1 (January): 5–20.

Filgueira, Fernando, and Juan Andrés Moraes. 1999. *Political Environments, Sector Specific Configurations, and Strategic Devices: Understanding Institutional Reform in Uruguay*. Washington, DC: Inter-American Development Bank. Office of the Chief Economist. Working Paper R-351.

Finkelman, Jacobo. 2003. Author interview with representative of Pan-American Health Organization in Brazil. Brasília: 6 August.

Finnemore, Martha. 1996a. *National Interests in International Society*. Ithaca: Cornell University Press.

———. 1996b. Norms, Culture, and World Politics. *International Organization* 50:2 (Spring): 325–47.

Finnemore, Martha, and Kathryn Sikkink. 1998. International Norm Dynamics and Political Change. *International Organization* 52:4 (Autumn): 887–917.

Fiorina, Morris. 1996. Rational Choice, Empirical Contributions, and the Scientific Enterprise. In Jeffrey Friedman, ed. *The Rational Choice Controversy*, 85–94. New Haven: Yale University Press.

FIPE (Fundação Instituto de Pesquisas Econômicas). 1994. *Proposta FIPE/PROSEG para a Reforma da Seguridade Social. Versão para Debate*. São Paulo: FIPE.

Fleury, Sonia, ed. 1997. *Saúde e Democracia: A Luta do CEBES*. São Paulo: Lemos Editorial.

Fleury Teixeira, Sonia, and Maria Helena Mendonça. 1989. Reformas Sanitárias na Itália e no Brasil: Comparações. In Sonia Fleury Teixeira, ed. *Reforma Sanitária: Em Busca de uma Teoria*, 2nd ed., 193–232. São Paulo: Cortez.

Flores, Francisco. 2002. Mensaje del Presidente de la República Licenciado Francisco Flores. *El Diario de Hoy* (15 October).

Flores, Hugo. 2002. Author interview with task manager for health, Inter-American Development Bank. La Paz: 12 August.

FMI (Fondo Monetario Internacional). 1992. Bolivia: Reforma del Sistema de Pensiones Públicas. Ayuda Memoria. N.p.

Força Sindical. 1993. *Um Projeto para o Brasil*. São Paulo: Geração Editorial.

Francke, Pedro. 2002. *El Financiamiento de la Salud en Bolivia*. La Paz: Ministerio de Salud y Previsión Social. Dirección General de Servicios de Salud.

———. 1998. *Focalización del Gasto Público en Salud en el Perú*. Lima: Pontificia Universidad Católica del Perú (PUCP), Departamento de Economía. Documento de Trabajo Nº 155.

Francke, Pedro, et al. 2002. Análisis Independiente del Presupuesto Público 2003 en el Sector Salud. Lima: PUCP, Proyecto Análisis Independiente del Presupuesto Público 2003.

Freundt Thurne, Jaime. 2002 Author interview with former congressman (1993) and health minister (1993–94). Lima: 27 June.

Friedman, Jeffrey, ed. 1996. *The Rational Choice Controversy*. New Haven: Yale University Press.

Fundación Milenio. 1994. *Reforma del Sistema de Pensiones*. Diálogos de Milenio No.12. La Paz: Fundación Milenio.

Gabriel, Almir. 1992. Author interview with federal senator (PSDB—PA). Brasília: 17 June.

Galindo, Mario. 2002. Author interview with former official of Ministerio de Finanzas and vice-ministro de microempresa. La Paz: 2 August.

Garita Bonilla, Nora, and Jorge González Varela. 1992. *Estructuras de la Opinión Pública y la Seguridad Social. Informe presentado a la Caja Costarricense de Seguro Social*. San José: Universidad de Costa Rica. Vicerrectoría de Investigación.

Garrett, Geoffrey. 1998. *Partisan Politics in the Global Economy*. Cambridge: Cambridge University Press.

Gauri, Varun, James Cercone, and Rodrigo Briceño. 2004. Separating Financing from Provision: Evidence from 10 Years of Partnership with Health Cooperatives in Costa Rica. *Health Policy and Planning* 19:5 (September): 292–301.

Geddes, Barbara. 1994. *Politician's Dilemma*. Berkeley: University of California Press.

———. 1990. How the Cases You Choose Affect the Answers You Get. *Political Analysis* 2: 131–52.

George, Alexander, and Andrew Bennett. 2005. *Case Studies and Theory Development in the Social Sciences*. Cambridge, MA: MIT Press.

Giambiagi, Fabio, and Lavinia Barros de Castro. 2003. Previdência Social: Diagnóstico e Propostas de Reforma. *Revista do BNDES* 10:19 (June): 265–92.

Giambiagi, Fabio, Francisco de Oliveira, and Kaizô Beltrão. 1996. Alternativas de Reforma da Previdência Social. *Revista do BNDES* 3:6 (December): 63–78.

Gigerenzer, Gerd, and Reinhard Selten, eds. 2001. *Bounded Rationality*. Cambridge, MA: MIT Press.

Gilbert, Alan. 2004. Learning from Others: The Spread of Capital Housing Subsidies. *International Planning Studies* 9:23 (May–August): 197–216.

Gill, Indermit, Truman Packard, and Juan Yermo. 2004. *Keeping the Promise of Social Security in Latin America*. Washington, DC: World Bank.

Gilovich, Thomas, Dale Griffin, and Daniel Kahneman, eds. 2002. *Heuristics and Biases: The Psychology of Intuitive Judgment*. Cambridge: Cambridge University Press.

Girade, Halim. 2003. Author interview with leader of primary health care movement and UNICEF expert. Brasília: 29 July.

Goedeking, Ulrich. 2003. *Politische Eliten und demokratische Entwicklung in Bolivien 1985–1996*. Münster: LIT Verlag.

Goldenberg, Efraín, and Germán Suárez. 2000. Letter to Stanley Fischer, Fondo

Monetario Internacional. Lima: Ministerio de Economía y Finanzas (13 March). http://www.mef.gob.pe/misc/cfmi2000.htm, accessed 2/21/2005.

Goldstein, Judith, and Robert Keohane. 1993. Ideas and Foreign Policy. In Goldstein and Keohane, eds. *Ideas and Foreign Policy*, 3–30. Ithaca: Cornell University Press.

González, Luis Armando. 2002. Absurda Politización de la Crisis del Sistema Nacional de Salud. *Estudios Centroamericanos* 57:648 (October): 952–57.

Goodman, Carey. 2004. The *Bolsa Escola* in Latin America and Africa: An Example of International Diffusion. M.A. thesis, University of Texas at Austin.

Gottret, Pablo. 2002. Author interview with superintendente de pensiones, valores y seguros and ex-director of World Bank pension reform project. La Paz: 30 July.

———. 1999. Bolivia: Capitalisation, Pension Reform and their Impact on Capital Markets. Paper for Organisation for Economic Co-operation and Development. Advisory Group on Privatisation, Paris, 21–22 September.

Gowda, Rajeev, and Jeffrey Fox, eds. 2002. *Judgments, Decisions, and Public Policy*. Cambridge: Cambridge University Press.

Graham, Carol. 1998. *Private Markets for Public Goods*. Washington, DC: Brookings Institution.

Grandi, Evelyn. 2002. Author interview with former subsecretaria nacional de pensiones (1995–97). La Paz: 2 August.

Gray-Molina, George, Ernesto Pérez de Rada, and Ernesto Yañez. 1999. *La Economía Política de Reformas Institucionales en Bolivia*. Washington, DC: Inter-American Development Bank. Office of the Chief Economist. Working Paper R-350.

Green, Donald, and Ian Shapiro. 1994. *Pathologies of Rational Choice Theory*. New Haven: Yale University Press.

Greif, Avner, and David Laitin. 2004. A Theory of Endogenous Institutional Change. *American Political Science Review* 98:4 (November): 633–52.

Grindle, Merilee. 2004. *Despite the Odds: The Contentious Politics of Education Reform*. Princeton: Princeton University Press.

———. 2000. *Audacious Reforms: Institutional Invention and Democracy in Latin America*. Baltimore: Johns Hopkins University Press.

———. 1991. The New Political Economy. In Gerald Meier, ed. *Politics and Policy Making in Developing Countries*, 41–67. San Francisco: ICS Press.

Grindle, Merilee, and John Thomas. 1991. *Public Choices and Policy Change*. Baltimore: Johns Hopkins University Press.

Grupo Consultivo. 2000. *Evaluación del Seguro Básico de Salud (Versión final para Discusión)*. La Paz: N.p.

Grupo Técnico. 2005. Propuesta para la Sostenibilidad del Régimen de Invalidez, Vejez y Muerte de la CCSS. San José: N.p.

GTI (Grupo de Trabalho Interministerial). 1994. Conclusões do Grupo de Trabalho Interministerial para Racionalização dos Gastos com Saúde e Melhoria do Atendimento a População: Relatório Final. N.p.

Güendel, Ludwig, and Juan Diego Trejos. 1992. Reformas recientes en el Sector Salud de Costa Rica. San José: N.p. Documento de trabajo para el Proyecto Regional sobre Reformas de Política Pública para aumentar la Efectividad del Estado, Comisión Económica para América Latina y el Caribe.

Guérard, Yves, and Martha Kelly. 1997. Bolivia's Pension Reform. In Bernardo Requena et al. *The Deepening of Market Based Reform*, 81–131. Washington, DC: Woodrow Wilson Center. Latin American Program. Working Paper No. 231.

Guevara, Carlos. 2002. Author interview with former member of pension reform team (1993–96). La Paz: 31 July.

Guimarães, Luisa. 2003. Author interview with assessora, Secretaria de Políticas de Saúde, Ministério da Saúde. Brasília: 29 July.

Guisinger, Alexandra. 2003. Patterns of Trade Protection and Liberalization. Paper for conference on "The International Diffusion of Political and Economic Liberalization," Harvard University, 3–4 October.

Guzmán, Ana. 2004. Author interview with directora de compra de servicios de salud, Caja Costarricense de Seguro Social. San José: 30 June.

Haas, Peter. 1992. Epistemic Communities and International Policy Coordination. *International Organization* 46:1 (Winter): 1–35.

Haggard, Stephan, and Robert Kaufman. 1995. *The Political Economy of Democratic Transitions*. Princeton: Princeton University Press.

Haggard, Stephan, and Mathew McCubbins, eds. 2001. *Presidents, Parliaments, and Policy*. Cambridge: Cambridge University Press.

Hall, Peter. 2003. Aligning Ontology and Methodology in Comparative Research. In James Mahoney and Dietrich Rueschemeyer, eds. *Comparative Historical Analysis in the Social Sciences*, 373–404. Cambridge: Cambridge University Press.

Hall, Peter, and David Soskice, eds. 2001. *Varieties of Capitalism*. Oxford: Oxford University Press.

Hawkins, Darren. 2002. *International Human Rights and Authoritarian Rule in Chile*. Lincoln: University of Nebraska Press.

Heclo, Hugh. 1974. *Modern Social Policies in Britain and Sweden*. New Haven: Yale University Press.

Hedström, Peter, and Richard Swedberg, eds. 1998. *Social Mechanisms*. Cambridge: Cambridge University Press.

Henisz, Witold, Bennet Zelner, and Mauro Guillén. 2003. International Coercion, Emulation and Policy Diffusion. Wharton School, University of Pennsylvania.

Hidalgo Capitán, Antonio Luis. 2003. *Costa Rica en Evolución*. San José: Editorial de la Universidad de Costa Rica.

Hochman, Gilberto. 1992. Os Cardeais da Previdência Social. *Dados* 35:3: 371–401.

Holzmann, Robert, and Richard Hinz. 2005. *Old-Age Income Support in the 21st Century*. Washington, DC: World Bank.

Holzmann, Robert, Landis MacKellar, and Michal Rutkowski. 2003. Accelerating the European Pension Reform Agenda. In Robert Holzmann, Mitchell Orenstein, and Michal Rutkowski, eds. *Pension Reform in Europe*, 1–45. Washington, DC: World Bank.

Homedes, Núria. 2001. Managing Externally Financed Projects: Integrated Primary Health Care in Bolivia. *Health Policy and Planning* 16:4 (December): 386–94.

Homedes, Núria, et al. 2000. Health Reform: Theory and Practice in El Salvador. In Peter Lloyd-Sherlock, ed. *Healthcare Reform and Poverty in Latin America*, 57–77. London: University of London, Institute of Latin American Studies.

Huber, Evelyne, ed. 2002. *Models of Capitalism: Lessons for Latin America.* University Park: Pennsylvania State University Press.

Huber, Evelyne, and John Stephens. 2001. *Development and Crisis of the Welfare State.* Chicago: University of Chicago Press.

———. 2000. *The Political Economy of Pension Reform.* Geneva: United Nations Research Institute for Social Development.

Hunter, Wendy, and David Brown. 2000. World Bank Directives, Domestic Interests, and the Politics of Human Capital Investment in Latin America. *Comparative Political Studies* 33:1 (February): 113–43.

IBSS (Instituto Boliviano de Seguridad Social). 1992. *Reforma de la Seguridad Social (Opciones).* La Paz: IBSS.

IDB (Inter-American Development Bank). 2004a. *Argentina: Apoyo al Plan Familias. Documento Conceptual de Proyecto.* Washington, DC: IDB.

———. 2004b. *The Bank's Country Strategy with Bolivia (2004–2007).* Washington, DC: IDB.

———. 2004c. *Perú: Reforma de Programas de Superación de la Pobreza y Desarrollo de Capital Humano (PE-0247): Propuesta de Préstamo.* Washington, DC: IDB.

———. 2001. Perfil de Proyecto de Innovación: Programa de Apoyo a la Reforma de la Seguridad Social de Salud, BO-0198. La Paz: IDB.

———. 2000. *Programa de Apoyo para la Transformación Institucional del Instituto Salvadoreño del Seguro Social (ISSS) (ES-0134).* Washington, DC: IDB.

———. 1999a. *Escudo Epidemiológico Boliviano y Apoyo a la Reforma del Sector Salud (BO-0115).* Washington, DC: IDB.

———. 1999b. *Programa de Desarrollo del Sector Salud: Seguro Materno-Infantil (PE-0146).* Washington, DC: IDB.

———. 1998. El Salvador: Project to Support Modernization of the Ministry of Public Health and Social Assistance (ES-0053). Loan Proposal. Executive Summary. http://www.iadb.org/EXR/doc98/apr/es1092e.htm.

———. 1996. *Economic and Social Progress in Latin America: 1996 Report.* Washington, DC: IDB.

———. 1992. *Costa Rica: Programa de Mejoramiento de Servicios de Salud (CR-0120). Propuesta de Préstamo.* Washington, DC: IDB.

Iglesias, Augusto. 1996. Interview by Raúl Madrid with founder of pension reform consulting company Primerica. Santiago de Chile: 23 December.

Ikenberry, John. 1990. The International Spread of Privatization Policies. In Ezra Suleiman and John Waterbury, eds. *The Political Economy of Public Sector Reform and Privatization*, 88–110. Boulder: Westview.

IL (Instituto Liberal). 1994. *Políticas Alternativas: Saúde.* Rio de Janeiro: IL.

———. 1991. *Previdência Social no Brasil: Uma Proposta de Reforma.* Rio de Janeiro: IL.

ILDIS (Instituto Latinoamericano de Investigaciones Sociales). 1996. *La Administración Privada de los Fondos de Pensiones.* La Paz: ILDIS.

IMF (International Monetary Fund). 1998. IMF Concludes Article IV Consultation with Brazil. Press Information Notice No. 98/18. Washington, DC: IMF.

Inglés, Dorys. 2002. Arranca Labor de Equipos Técnicos: Inicia Discusión de Temas de ENADE. *El Diario de Hoy* (13 August).

IPE (Instituto Peruano de Economía). 1997. *Reforma del Régimen Previsional Peruano. Informe No. 97032-IPE*. Lima: IPE.

Isasi, Felipe. 1998. El Modelo Peruano de Seguridad Social en Salud Comparado. Lima: Ministerio de Salud, Programa de Fortalecimiento de Servicios de Salud.

Iunes, Roberto. 2001. Health Sector Organization/Reorganization in Latin America and the Caribbean. In Carlos Molina and José Núñez del Arco, eds. *Health Services in Latin America and Asia*, 203–21. Washington, DC: Inter-American Development Bank.

Jacoby, Wade. 2000. *Imitation and Politics*. Ithaca: Cornell University Press.

James, Estelle. 2006. Email communication from former lead author of the World Bank's pension reform study (21 March).

———. 1998. Pension Reform: An Equity-Efficiency Tradeoff? In Nancy Birdsall, Carol Graham, and Richard Sabot, eds. *Beyond Tradeoffs*, 253–72. Washington, DC: Inter-American Development Bank.

Jara, Osvaldo, and Marcos Vergara. 1995a. Informe Final de Consultoría. Consultoría para la Reforma del Sector Salud en el Perú. N.p.

———. 1995b. La Reforma del Sector Salud en el Perú. N.p.

Jaramillo, Miguel, and Sandro Parodi. 2004. *El Seguro Escolar Gratuito y el Seguro Materno Infantil*. Lima: GRADE. Documento de Trabajo 46.

Jennings, Dennis, Teresa Amabile, and Lee Ross. 1982. Informal Covariation Assessment. In Daniel Kahneman, Paul Slovic, and Amos Tversky, eds. *Judgment under Uncertainty: Heuristics and Biases*, 211–30. Cambridge: Cambridge University Press.

Jiménez, Mirna. 2005. Piden al ISSS ampliar la Cobertura para el Sector Informal. *Diario CoLatino* (11 March).

Jiménez, Ronulfo. 2004. Author interview with director, Consejo Económico, Presidencia de la República, and former leader of pension reform project (1998–2000). San José: 17 June.

———. 2000. El Proceso de la Aprobación de la Ley de Protección al Trabajador. In Ronulfo Jiménez, ed. *Los Retos Políticos de la Reforma Económica en Costa Rica*, 247–72. San José: Academia de Centroamérica.

Jobim, Nelson. 1994. Seguridade Social: Parecer N° 78. *Conjuntura Social* 5:9 (September): 11–42.

John Snow Inc./Banco Mundial. 2000. Mejoramiento de la Atención a la Mujer debido a la Reforma en Salud en Bolivia. La Paz: N.p.

Johnson, Jaime. 2001. Reestructuración Institucional del Sector Salud. In Pedro Francke et al., *Políticas de Salud, 2001–2006*. Lima: Consorcio de Investigación Económica y Social.

———. 1998. La Reforma del Sector Salud. *Socialismo y Participación* 83 (December): 45–61.

Jones, Bryan. 2001. *Politics and the Architecture of Choice: Bounded Rationality and Governance*. Chicago: University of Chicago Press.

———. 1999. Bounded Rationality. *Annual Review of Political Science* 2: 297–321.

Jones, Bryan, and Frank Baumgartner. 2005. *The Politics of Attention.* Chicago: University of Chicago Press.

Kahler, Miles. 1992. External Influence, Conditionality, and the Politics of Adjustment. In Stephan Haggard and Robert Kaufman, eds. *The Politics of Economic Adjustment,* 89–136. Princeton: Princeton University Press.

Kahneman, Daniel. 2003. Maps of Bounded Rationality. *American Economic Review* 93:5 (December): 1449–75.

Kahneman, Daniel, Jack Knetsch, and Richard Thaler. 1986. Fairness as a Constraint on Profit Seeking. *American Economic Review* 76:4 (September): 728–41.

Kahneman, Daniel, Paul Slovic, and Amos Tversky, eds. 1982. *Judgment under Uncertainty: Heuristics and Biases.* Cambridge: Cambridge University Press.

Kahneman, Daniel, and Amos Tversky. 1982. On the Study of Statistical Intuitions. In Daniel Kahneman, Paul Slovic, and Amos Tversky, eds., *Judgment under Uncertainty,* 493–508. Cambridge: Cambridge University Press.

Kandir, Antonio. 1992. Author interview with former secretário de política econômica, Ministério de Economia, Finanças e Planejamento (1990–91). São Paulo: 8 June.

Kane, Cheikh. 1995. Policy Note. Peru: Reforming the Pension System. Washington, DC: World Bank, Human Resources Development and Operations Policy.

Kaufman, Robert, and Joan Nelson. 2004a. Conclusions: The Political Dynamics of Reform. In Kaufman and Nelson, eds. *Crucial Needs, Weak Incentives,* 473–519. Washington, DC: Woodrow Wilson Center Press.

———. 2004b. Introduction: The Political Challenges of Social Sector Reform. In Kaufman and Nelson, eds. *Crucial Needs, Weak Incentives,* 1–19. Washington, DC: Woodrow Wilson Center Press.

Kay, Stephen. 2001. Brazil's Social Security Reform in Comparative Perspective. Paper for 23rd International Congress, Latin American Studies Association, Washington, DC, 6–8 September.

———. 1999. Unexpected Privatizations. *Comparative Politics* 31:4 (July): 403–22.

———. 1998. Politics and Social Security Reform in the Southern Cone and Brazil. Ph.D. Dissertation, University of California, Los Angeles.

Kay, Stephen, and Barbara Kritzer. 2001. Social Security in Latin America. *Economic Review* (Federal Reserve Bank of Atlanta) 86:1 (first quarter): 41–52.

King, Gary, Robert Keohane, and Sidney Verba. 1994. *Designing Social Inquiry.* Princeton: Princeton University Press.

Kingdon, John. 1984. *Agendas, Alternatives, and Public Policy.* Boston: Little, Brown.

Kingstone, Peter. 2003. Democratic Governance and the Dilemma of Social Security Reform in Brazil. In Ana Margheritis, ed. *Latin American Democracies in the New Global Economy,* 221–40. Miami: North-South Center Press.

Kitschelt, Herbert, et al., eds. 1999. *Continuity and Change in Contemporary Capitalism.* Cambridge: Cambridge University Press.

Klugman, Mark. 1993. Author interview with leading advisor to pension re-former José Piñera. Santiago de Chile: 19 August.

Kogut, Bruce, and J. Muir Macpherson. 2003. The Decision to Privatize as an Economic Policy Idea. McCombs School of Business, University of Texas at Austin.

Kohl, Ben. 2004. Privatization Bolivian Style. *International Journal of Urban and Regional Research* 28:4 (December): 893–908.

Kolodin, Susan. 2002. Author interview with task manager for health, Inter-American Development Bank. Lima: 19 July.

Kopstein, Jeffrey, and David Reilly. 2000. Geographic Diffusion and the Trans-formation of the Postcommunist World. *World Politics* 53:1 (October): 1–37.

Kotlikoff, Laurence. 1994. Letter to The Honorable Gonzalo Sachez de Losada [*sic*]. Boston University, Department of Economics (21 November).

Kuran, Timur, and Cass Sunstein. 1999. Availability Cascades and Risk Regula-tion. *Stanford Law Review* 51 (April): 683–768.

Labra, Maria Eliana. 1988. Chile: A Contra-Reforma sanitária do Regime au-toritário. *Saúde em Debate* 23 (December): 19–24.

La Forgia, Gerard. 2004. Interview by Natasha Sugiyama with program officer for health programming, World Bank. Brasília: 4 May.

Lagos, Ricardo. 1993. Author interview with former education minister and leader of Partido por la Democracia. Santiago de Chile: 26 July.

Laínez, Luis. 2005. Se disponen de $310 Millones para la Reforma. *El Diario de Hoy* (10 March).

Larraín, Luis. 1997. Interview by Raúl Madrid with pension consultant and former Labor Ministry official. Santiago de Chile: 10 January.

Laserna, Roberto. 2003. Bolivia: Entre Populismo y Democracia. *Nueva Socie-dad* 188 (November–December): 4–14.

Lavadenz, Fernando. 1993. Proyecto Integrado de los Servicios de Salud (PRO-ISS). In Instituto Latinoamericano de Investigaciones Sociales, ed. *Hacia un Sistema de Salud Descentralizado*, 145–54. La Paz: ILDIS.

———. 2001. Basic Health Insurance in Bolivia. In Carlos Molina and José Núñez del Arco, eds. *Health Services in Latin America and Asia,* 53–67. Washington, DC: Inter-American Development Bank.

Lazer, David. 1999. The Free Trade Epidemic of the 1860s and Other Out-breaks of Economic Discrimination. *World Politics* 51:4 (July): 447–83.

Leal, David. 2004. 75% de las Pensiones se invierten en Sector público. *La Na-ción* (San José), *Economía* (21 June): 3.

Lehoucq, Fabrice. 1997. *Lucha Electoral y Sistema Político en Costa Rica 1948–1998.* San José: Porvenir.

Leite, Celso Barroso. 1990. Author interview with former secretário de previdên-cia social, Ministério da Previdência e Assistência Social. Rio de Janeiro: 19 March.

Leiteritz, Ralf. 2003. Capital Account Liberalisation in Latin America in the 1990s—The Role of the International Financial Institutions and Professional Training. Paper for 3rd annual CSI Conference "Global Development and Poverty Reduction," Innsbruck, 19–21 November.

León, Alberto. 2002. Author interview with pension reform team member and gerente general, Asociación de Administradoras Privadas de Fondos de Pensiones. Lima: 2 July.

León Barth, Mario. 2004. Author interview with former member of health reform team, Caja Costarricense de Seguro Social. San José: 2 July.

Levi, Margaret. 1988. *Of Rule and Revenue.* Berkeley: University of California Press.

Levi-Faur, David. 2005. The Global Diffusion of Regulatory Capitalism. *Annals of the American Academy of Political and Social Science* 598 (March): 12–32.

Levitt, Barbara, and James March. 1988. Organizational Learning. *Annual Review of Sociology* 14: 319–40.

Lewis, Maureen, Gunnar Eskeland, and Ximena Traa-Valerezo. 1999. *Challenging El Salvador's Rural Health Care Strategy.* Washington, DC: World Bank. Policy Research Working Paper 2164.

Ley de Modernización de la Seguridad Social en Salud. Decreto Legislativo Nº 887. 1996. *El Peruano* (11 November): 144233–36.

Ley del Sistema de Salud Previsional. 2002. San Salvador: N.p.

Li, Richard, and William Thompson. 1975. The "Coup Contagion" Hypothesis. *Journal of Conflict Resolution* 19:1 (March): 63–88.

Lichbach, Mark. 2003. *Is Rational Choice Theory All of Social Science?* Ann Arbor: University of Michigan Press.

Lieberson, Stanley. 2000. *A Matter of Taste.* New Haven: Yale University Press.

Lindblom, Charles. 1965. *The Intelligence of Democracy.* New York: Free Press.

Lineamientos Básicos de la Política Social. 1993. Lima: Presidencia del Consejo de Ministros (23 November).

Lloyd-Sherlock, Peter. 2004. Ambitious Plans, Modest Outcomes: The Politics of Health Care Reform in Argentina. In Robert Kaufman and Joan Nelson, eds. *Crucial Needs, Weak Incentives,* 93–123. Washington, DC: Woodrow Wilson Center Press.

Loaiza, Hugo. 1997. Debate. In Loaiza, ed. *El Seguro Nacional de Maternidad y Niñez. Temas sobre Reforma de Salud 1,* 43–46. La Paz: Ministerio de Desarrollo Humano, Secretaría Nacional de Salud.

Londoño, Juan Luis, and Julio Frenk. 2000. Structured Pluralism. In Peter Lloyd-Sherlock, ed. *Healthcare Reform and Poverty in Latin America,* 21–56. London: University of London, Institute of Latin American Studies.

Lowi, Theodore. 1964. American Business, Public Policy, Case-Studies, and Political Theory. *World Politics* 16:4 (July): 677–715.

Lugo, Orlando. Author interview with coordinador de programas, UNICEF. La Paz: 12 August.

Lugo, Orlando, and Mario Gutiérrez. 2002. *El Seguro Básico de Salud.* La Paz: Ministerio de Salud y Previsión Social, Dirección General de Servicios de Salud.

Lupia, Arthur, and Mathew McCubbins. 1998. *The Democratic Dilemma.* Cambridge: Cambridge University Press.

Lupia, Arthur, Mathew McCubbins, and Samuel Popkin, eds. 2001. *Elements of Reason.* Cambridge: Cambridge University Press.

Lutz, Ellen, and Kathryn Sikkink. 2000. International Human Rights Law and

Practice in Latin America. *International Organization* 54:3 (Summer): 633–59.

Machado de Souza, Heloiza. 2003. Author interview with former diretora, Departamento de Atenção Básica, Ministério da Saúde. Brasília: 11 August.

McAdam, Doug, Sidney Tarrow, and Charles Tilly. 2001. *Dynamics of Contention*. Cambridge: Cambridge University Press.

McDermott, Rose. 2004. *Political Psychology in International Relations*. Ann Arbor: University of Michigan Press.

McFadden, Daniel. 1999. Rationality for Economists? *Journal of Risk and Uncertainty* 19:1–3 (December): 73–105.

McGuire, James. 2006. Politics, Policy, and Mortality Decline in Costa Rica. In Politics, Policy, and Mortality Decline in East Asia and Latin America. Book ms., Department of Government, Wesleyan University.

McNamara, Kathleen. 1998. *The Currency of Ideas*. Ithaca: Cornell University Press.

Madrid, Raúl. 2003a. Labouring against Neoliberalism. *Journal of Latin American Studies* 35:1 (February): 53–88.

———. 2003b. *Retiring the State: Pension Privatization in Latin America and Beyond*. Stanford: Stanford University Press.

Mahoney, James. 2003. Tentative Answers to Questions about Causal Mechanisms. Paper for 99th annual meeting, American Political Science Association, Philadelphia, 28–31 August.

———. 2000. Path Dependence in Historical Sociology. *Theory and Society* 29:4 (August): 507–48.

Mainwaring, Scott. 1999. *Rethinking Party Systems in the Third Wave of Democratization*. Stanford: Stanford University Press.

Mallaby, Sebastian. 2004. *The World's Banker*. New York: Penguin Press.

Malloy, James. 1979. *The Politics of Social Security in Brazil*. Pittsburgh: University of Pittsburgh Press.

Manrique, Luis. 2002. Author interview with former superintendente de entidades prestadoras de salud (1998). Lima: 4 July.

Manz, Thomas. 1996. Die Rentenreform in Bolivien. *Lateinamerika: Analysen, Daten, Dokumentation* 13:31: 74–83.

March, James. 1966. The Power of Power. In David Easton, ed. *Varieties of Political Theory*, 39–70. Englewood Cliffs, NJ: Prentice-Hall.

March, James, and Johan Olsen. 1976. *Ambiguity and Choice in Organizations*. Bergen: Universitetsforlaget.

March, James, and Herbert Simon. 1958. *Organizations*. New York: Wiley.

Marín, Fernando. 2004. Author interview with former vice-minister of health (1994–98) and architect of Costa Rican health reform. San José: 24 June.

———. 1986. *Desarrollo de un Modelo de Atención familiar y comunitaria: "Proyecto Barrio la Peregrina" (Tercera Propuesta)*. San José: CCSS. Dirección Técnica de Servicios de Salud.

Marín, Fernando, and Mauricio Vargas. 1990. Plan para la Reestructuración del Sistema Nacional de Salud con la Participación activa del Sector privado. Conferencia presentada el 6 de junio de 1990 ante el Colegio de Médicos y Cirujanos. San José: N.p.

Martínez Franzoni, Juliana. 2005. Reformas recientes de las pensiones en Costa Rica. San José: N.p.

———. 2004. Author interview with participant in pension reform commission (2004–05). San José: 15 June.

———. 1999. Poder y Alternativas: Las Agendas Internacionales en las Reformas del Sector Salud en Costa Rica, 1988–1998. *Anuario de Estudios Centroamericanos* 25:1 (first semester): 159–82.

———. 1998. Policy Environments and Selective Emulation in the Making of Health Policies: The Case of Costa Rica, 1920–1997. Ph.D. dissertation, University of Pittsburgh.

Martínez Franzoni, Juliana, and Carmelo Mesa-Lago. 2003. *Las Reformas Inconclusas: Pensiones y Salud en Costa Rica.* San José: Friedrich Ebert Stiftung.

Martínez Orellana, Orlando. 2004. Author interview with former Central Bank official and pension reform consultant. San Salvador: 6 July.

———. 1998. Comentarios al Estudio "Evaluación de la Reforma de Pensiones en El Salvador." In *La Polémica Reforma del Sistema de Pensiones en El Salvador,* 1–27. San Salvador: Friedrich Ebert Stiftung.

Martone, Celso, et al. 1994. *Uma Proposta de Reforma Fiscal para o Brasil.* São Paulo: Fundação Instituto de Pesquisas Econômicas.

Mattos Filho, Ary Oswaldo. 2003. Author interview with former president of Comissão Executiva de Reforma Fiscal. São Paulo: 15 July.

———. 1992. Author interview with president of Comissão Executiva de Reforma Fiscal. Brasília: 1 July.

Mayntz, Renate. 2004. Mechanisms in the Analysis of Social Macro-Phenomena. *Philosophy of the Social Sciences* 34:2 (June): 237–59.

MDH (Ministerio de Desarrollo Humano). 1995. *Programa de Acciones Estratégicas de Desarrollo Humano en Favor del Niño y la Mujer (1995–1997).* Draft of 30 September. La Paz: N.p.

———. SNS (Secretaría Nacional de Salud). 1997a. *Evaluación Nacional del Seguro de Maternidad y Niñez.* La Paz: MDH, SNS (27 June).

———. 1997b. *Resultados de Gestión: Secretaría Nacional de Salud. Bolivia 1993–1997.* La Paz: MDH, SNS.

———. 1994. *Plan Vida: Plan Nacional para la Reducción Acelerada de la Mortalidad Materna, Perinatal y del Menor, 1994–1997.* La Paz: MDH, SNS.

———. SE-GRSS (Secretariado Ejecutivo–Grupo de Reforma del Sector Salud). 1994. *Documento de Propuesta: Lineamientos para un Proyecto de Reforma del Sector Salud y la Constitución de un Sistema Nacional de Salud.* La Paz: MDH, SNS, SE-GRSS.

Médici, André, Francisco de Oliveira, and Kaizô Beltrão. 1993a. Subsídios para a Reforma Constitucional no Campo da Seguridade Social. *Planejamento e Políticas Públicas* 9 (June): 1–67.

———. 1993b. *Universalização com Qualidade: Uma Proposta de Reorganização do Sistema de Saúde no Brasil.* Rio de Janeiro: Instituto Brasileiro de Geografia e Estatística, Escola Nacional de Ciências Estatísticas. Relatório Técnico Nº 03/93.

MEF (Ministerio de Economía y Finanzas) and BCRP (Banco Central de Reserva del Perú). 1999. Memorándum de Políticas Económicas y Financieras del Gobierno del Perú para el Período 1 Abril 1999 al 31 Marzo 2002. Lima: MEF and BCRP.

———. 1993. Carta de Intención de Perú ante FMI. Lima: MEF and BCRP.

MEF (Ministerio de Economía y Finanzas). DGAES (Dirección General de Asuntos Económicos y Sociales). 2001. Informe: Bases para la Reforma de la Salud. *Boletín Fiscal* 1:2 (31 August): 26–32.

MEFP (Ministério de Economia, Finanças e Planejamento). Comissão Executiva de Reforma Fiscal. 1992. *A Reforma Fiscal: Delineamento Básico (Versão atual – 26/06/92)*. Brasília: MEFP.

Meloni, Augusto. 2005. Email communication from former director general, Oficina de Financiamiento, Inversiones y Cooperación Externa, Ministerio de Salud (1993–2000). Peru: 22 February.

———. 2002. Author interview with former director general, Oficina de Financiamiento, Inversiones y Cooperación Externa, Ministerio de Salud (1993–2000). Lima: 12 July.

Mendes, Eugênio Vilaça. 1999. *Uma Agenda para a Saúde*, 2nd ed. São Paulo: HUCITEC.

Mendonça, Jacy. 2003. Author interview with member of Instituto Liberal and former president of Associação dos Fabricantes de Veículos Automotores. São Paulo: 11 July.

Mercado, Marcelo. 2002. Author interview with former secretario nacional de pensiones (1993–1995). La Paz: 26 July.

———. 1998. La Reforma del Sistema de Pensiones de la Seguridad Social. In Juan Carlos Chávez Corrales, ed. *Las Reformas Estructurales en Bolivia*, 125–80. La Paz: Fundación Milenio.

———. 1994. La Transformación del Sistema de Pensiones en Bolivia. Presentación al CIEDESS. Santiago de Chile: N.p.

———. 1991. El Sistema de Pensiones en Bolivia. Santiago de Chile: Comisión Económica para América Latina y el Caribe.

Mercer, Jonathan. 2005. Rationality and Psychology in International Politics. *International Organization* 59:1 (Winter): 77–106.

Mesa-Lago, Carmelo. 2003. El Sistema de Pensiones de El Salvador después de cinco Años. San Salvador: Fundación Friedrich Ebert.

———. 1997. Social Welfare Reform in the Context of Economic-Political Liberalization. *World Development* 25:4 (April): 497–517.

———. 1996. La Reforma del Sistema de Salud en Perú. Lima: Programa de Fortalecimiento de Servicios de Salud.

———. 1991. Social Security in Latin America. In Inter-American Development Bank. *Economic and Social Progress in Latin America: 1991 Report*, 179–216. Washington, DC: IDB.

———. 1989. *Ascent to Bankruptcy*. Pittsburgh: University of Pittsburgh Press.

———. 1978. *Social Security in Latin America*. Pittsburgh: University of Pittsburgh Press.

Mesa-Lago, Carmelo, with Alberto Arenas de Mesa et al. 2000. *Market, Socialist, and Mixed Economies: Chile, Cuba, and Costa Rica*. Baltimore: Johns Hopkins University Press.

Mesa-Lago, Carmelo, and Ricardo Córdova. 1998. Social Security Reform in El

Salvador. In María Amparo Cruz Saco and Carmelo Mesa-Lago, eds. *Do Options Exist?* 109–29. Pittsburgh: University of Pittsburgh Press.

Mesa-Lago, Carmelo, Ricardo Córdova, and Carlos López. 1994. *El Salvador: Diagnóstico y Propuesta de Reforma de la Seguridad Social.* San Salvador: Centro Internacional para el Desarrollo Económico.

Mesa-Lago, Carmelo, and Fabio Durán. 1998. *Evaluación de la Reforma de Pensiones en El Salvador.* San Salvador: Fundación Friedrich Ebert.

Mesa-Lago, Carmelo, and Katharina Müller. 2002. The Politics of Pension Reform in Latin America. *Journal of Latin American Studies* 34:3 (August): 687–715.

Meseguer, Covadonga. 2005. Policy Learning, Policy Diffusion, and the Making of a New Order. *Annals of the American Academy of Political and Social Science* 598 (March): 67–82.

———. 2002. *Bayesian Learning about Policies.* Madrid: Instituto Juan March.

Meseguer, Covadonga, and Fabrizio Gilardi. 2005. What is New in the Study of Policy Diffusion? Mexico City: Centro de Investigación y Docencia Económicas.

Meyer, John, and Brian Rowan. 1977. Institutionalized Organizations. *American Journal of Sociology* 83:2 (September): 340–63.

MIDEPLAN (Ministerio de Planificación Nacional). 1998a. *Documento sobre Pensiones: Propuesta del Gobierno para el Proceso Concertación Nacional.* San José: MIDEPLAN (14 July).

———. 1998b. *Foro de Concertación Nacional. Comisión sobre Pensiones: Informe Final.* San José: MIDEPLAN.

———. 1998c. *Gobernando en Tiempos de Cambio: La Administración Figueres Olsen.* San José: MIDEPLAN.

———. 1998d. *Proceso de Concertación. Participantes en la Comisión de Pensiones.* San José: MIDEPLAN.

———. 1992. *Programa de Reforma del Estado. Programa Nacional de Reforma del Sector Salud.* San José: MIDEPLAN.

MINSA (Ministerio de Salud), ed. 1997. *Seminario Internacional: Reforma del Sector Salud.* Lima: MINSA.

———. DGSP (Dirección General de Salud de las Personas). 2003. *Análisis y Tendencias en la Utilización de Servicios de Salud: Perú 1985–2002.* Lima: MINSA, DGSP.

———. PAC (Programa de Administración Compartida). 1996. *Los Comités Locales de Administración de Salud (CLAS).* Lima: MINSA and UNICEF.

———. PSBPT (Programa Salud Básica para Todos). 1998. *Memoria 1994–1997.* Lima: MINSA, PSBPT.

———. 1997. Programa Salud Básica para Todos. Lima: MINSA.

Mintrom, Michael. 1997. Policy Entrepreneurs and the Diffusion of Innovation. *American Journal of Political Science* 41:3 (July): 738–70.

Mintrom, Michael, and Sandra Vergari. 1998. Policy Networks and Innovation Diffusion. *Journal of Politics* 60:1 (February): 126–48.

Miranda, Guido. 2004. Author interview with former executive director of Caja Costarricense de Seguro Social (1982–90). San José: 21 June.

———. 2003. *La Seguridad Social y el Desarrollo en Costa Rica*, 3rd ed. San José: Editorial Universidad Estatal a Distancia.

Monasterios, Guido. 2002. Author interview with director general de planificación y proyectos, Ministerio de Salud y Previsión Social. La Paz: 2 August.

Monteiro Neto, Armando de Queiroz. 2003. A Reforma da Previdência como Instrumento de Desenvolvimento Econômico. In Lauro Morhy, ed. 2003. *Reforma da Previdência em Questão*, 215–33. Brasília: Editora Universidade de Brasília.

Mooney, Christopher. 2001. Modeling Regional Effects on State Policy Diffusion. *Political Research Quarterly* 54:1 (March): 103–24.

Moraes, Marcelo Viana Estevão de. 2003. Author interview with former secretário de previdência social, Ministério da Previdência e Assistência Social. Brasília: 4 August.

———. 1999. Author interview with former secretário de previdência social, MPAS. Brasília: 12 June.

———. 1995. Reforma da Previdência. In João Paulo dos Reis Velloso and Roberto Cavalcanti de Albuquerque, eds. *Governabilidade e Reformas*, 219–42. Rio de Janeiro: José Olympio.

———. 1995. Author interview with secretário de previdência social, MPAS. Brasília: 12 June.

Morales, Juan Antonio. 2006. Author interview with former Central Bank president (1996–2006). La Paz: 26 June.

Morales, Luis. 2004. A Day in the Life of . . . a District Secretary of Health. *Health Policy and Planning* 19:5 (September): 346–47.

Moreira, Marcílio Marques. 1995. Author interview with former minister of economy, finance, and planning. Rio de Janeiro: 7 July.

Morhy, Lauro, ed. 2003. *Reforma da Previdência em Questão*. Brasília: Editora Universidade de Brasília.

Morón, Eduardo, and Eliana Carranza. 2003. *Diez Años del Sistema Privado de Pensiones (1993–2003)*. Lima: Universidad del Pacífico, Centro de Investigación.

Morón, Eduardo, and Cynthia Sanborn. 2004. The Pitfalls of Policymaking in Peru: Actors, Institutions and Rules of the Game. Lima: Universidad del Pacífico.

Mortalidad infantil con descenso histórico en Costa Rica. *La Nación* (3 March).

Movimiento Libertad. 1988. *Libertad. Primer Ciclo de Conferencias*. Lima: Pro-Desarrollo.

MPAS (Ministério da Previdência e Assistência Social). 2001. *A Economia Política da Reforma da Previdência*. Brasília: MPAS.

———. 1995a. Exposição de Motivos N° 12 (10 March). N.p.

———. 1995b. *Reforma da Previdência*. Brasília: MPAS.

———. SPS (Secretaria de Previdência Social). 1999. A Reforma da Previdência na Suécia—Um Novo Paradigma. *Informe de Previdência Social* 11:3 (March): 1–3.

———. 1998. Custos de Transição para um Sistema de Capitalização Individual. *Informe de Previdência Social* 10:2 (February): 1–2.

MPS (Ministério da Previdência Social). 2003. *Mudar a Previdência: Uma Questão de Justiça*. Brasília: MPS.

———. 1993–94. *A Previdência Social e a Revisão Constitucional*, 7 vols. Brasília: MPS/Comissão Econômica para América Latina e Caribe.

MS (Ministério da Saúde). 2002. Desafios e Conquistas do PSF. *Revista Brasileira de Saúde da Família* 2:5 (May): 7–24.

———. 1999. *I Seminário de Experiências Internacionais em Saúde da Família: Relatório Final*. Brasília: MS.

———. 1997. *Saúde da Família: Uma Estratégia para a Reorientação do Modelo Assistencial*. Brasília: MS.

———. DAB (Departamento de Atenção Básica). 2002. *Relatório de Gestão, 1998–2002*. Brasília: MS, DAB.

———. FUNASA (Fundação Nacional de Saúde). 1994. *Programa de Saúde da Família: Saúde dentro da Casa*. Brasília: MS, FUNASA.

———. SAS (Secretaria de Assistência à Saúde). 2002. *Experiências Inovadoras no SUS*. Brasília: MS, SAS.

MSD (Ministerio de Salud y Deportes). 2006. Propuesta: Seguro Universal de Salud (Primera Fase). La Paz: MSD.

MSPAS (Ministerio de Salud Pública y Asistencia Social). N.d. *Marco Conceptual y Operativo para el Desarrollo del Sistema Básico de Salud Integral (SIBASI)*. San Salvador: MSPAS. http://www.mspas.gob.sv/sibasi1.asp (accessed 10 January 2005).

———. 1999. *Modernización Institucional y Reforma del Sector Salud*, vol. 4: *Organización de los Sistemas Sanitarios*. MSPAS. Dirección Nacional de Modernización.

———. 1996. *La Salud de El Salvador: Visión de Futuro. Documento Marco, Primera Versión*. San Salvador: MSPAS.

———. 1994. *Plan Nacional de Salud 1994–1999*. San Salvador: MSPAS.

———. GRSS (Grupo de Reforma del Sector Salud). 1995. *Documento Guía para la Reforma del Sector Salud en El Salvador (Borrador para Discusión)*. San Salvador: MPSAS, GRSS.

MSPS (Ministerio de Salud y Previsión Social). DGSS (Dirección General de Servicios de Salud). 2000. *Evaluación del Seguro Básico de Salud (a junio de 2000)*. La Paz: MSPS, DGSS.

———. URS (Unidad de Reforma de Salud), and Banco Mundial. 2000. *Evaluación del Seguro Básico de Salud*. La Paz: MSPS, URS.

MTPS (Ministério do Trabalho e da Previdência Social). 1991. *Palestra do Ministro de Estado Antonio Rogério Magri na Escola Superior de Guerra (ESG)*. Brasília: MTPS.

MTSS (Ministerio de Trabajo y Seguridad Social—Argentina). Secretaría de Seguridad Social. 1991–92. La Situación actual de la Previsión social nacional. *Previsión Social* 5 (November-March): 6–16.

Müller, Katharina. 2004. Non-Contributory Pensions in Latin America: The Case of Bolivia's BONOSOL. Paper for 25th International Congress, Latin American Studies Association, Las Vegas, 7–9 October.

———. 2003. *Privatising Old-Age Security*. Cheltenham: Edward Elgar.

Muñoz, Italo. 2000. La Reforma del Sistema Privado de Pensiones. In Roberto

Abusada et al., eds. *La Reforma Incompleta,* 49–82. Lima: Universidad del Pacífico. Centro de Investigación, and Instituto Peruano de Economía.

Muñoz Reyes, Álvaro. 1993. Proyecto de Salud Infantil y Comunitaria (CCH). In Instituto Latinoamericano de Investigaciones Sociales, ed. *Hacia un Sistema de Salud Descentralizado,* 167–74. La Paz: ILDIS.

Murillo, María Victoria. 2002. Political Bias in Policy Convergence: Privatization Choices in Latin America. *World Politics* 54:4 (July): 462–93.

———. 2001. *Labor Unions, Partisan Coalitions, and Market Reforms in Latin America.* Cambridge: Cambridge University Press.

Myers, Charles. 1997. Policy Research Institutes in Developing Countries. In Merilee Grindle, ed. *Getting Good Government,* 177–98. Cambridge: Harvard Institute for International Development.

Naím, Moisés. 2000. Author interview with Venezuela's former ministro de fomento (1989–90). Washington, DC: 30 March.

———. 1995. *Latin America's Journey to the Market.* San Francisco: Institute for Contemporary Studies.

Najberg, Sheila, and Marcelo Ikeda. 1999. Previdência no Brasil. In Fabio Giambiagi and Maurício Moreira, eds. *A Economia Brasileira nos Anos 90,* 261–90. Rio de Janeiro: Banco Nacional de Desenvolvimento Econômico e Social.

Negri, Barjas. 2003. Author interview with former vice-minister and minister of health (1998–2002). São Paulo: 23 July.

Negri, Barjas, and Ana Luiza d'Ávila Viana, eds. 2002. *O Sistema Único de Saúde em dez Anos de Desafio.* São Paulo: Sociedade Brasileira de Vigilância de Medicamentos.

Nelson, Joan. 2004. The Politics of Health Sector Reform. In Robert Kaufman and Joan Nelson, eds. *Crucial Needs, Weak Incentives,* 23–64. Washington, DC: Woodrow Wilson Center Press.

———. 1999. *Reforming Health and Education.* Washington, DC: Overseas Development Council.

———. 1997. Reforming Social Sector Governance. Paper for conference on "Governance, Poverty Eradication, and Social Policy," Harvard University, 12–14 November.

———. 1996. Promoting Policy Reforms. *World Development* 24:9 (September): 1551–59.

Nisbett, Richard. 2003. *The Geography of Thought.* New York: Free Press.

Nitsch, Manfred, and Helmut Schwarzer. 1998. De Paradigmas e Mitos. *Revista de Economia Política* 18:2 (April-June): 96–105.

North, Douglass. 1990. *Institutions, Institutional Change and Economic Performance.* Cambridge: Cambridge University Press.

Novak, Kathleen. 2004. Ensuring that Peruvian Public Health Insurance Reaches the Poor. *Partners for Health Reform*Plus *Highlights* (April): 3.

Olano, Gerardo. 2003. *La Privatización del ISSS, ¿Solución o Problema?* San Salvador: Friedrich Ebert Stiftung.

Oliveira, Francisco de. 2001. *Previdência Social e Assistência Social.* In Fátima Bayma and Istvan Kasznar, eds. *Saúde e Previdência Social,* 111–25. São Paulo: Makron.

Oliveira, Francisco de, Kaizô Beltrão, and Mônica Guerra Ferreira. 1998. Reforma da Previdência. In Instituto de Pesquisa Econômica Aplicada, ed. *A Economia Brasileira em Perspectiva 1998*, vol. 1, 337–413. Rio de Janeiro: IPEA.

Oliveira, Francisco de, Kaizô Beltrão, and André Medici. 1992. Proposta de um Modelo de Seguridade Social. N.p.

Oliveira, Francisco de, Kaizô Beltrão, and Maria Marsillac. 1996. *Reforma da Previdência: Modelo de Opções*. Rio de Janeiro: Instituto de Pesquisa Econômica Aplicada (IPEA). Texto para Discussão N° 436.

Oliveira, Francisco de, Kaizô Beltrão, and Maria Marsillac Pasinato. 1999. *Reforma Estrutural da Previdência*. Rio de Janeiro: IPEA. Texto para Discussão N° 690.

Oliveira, Jaime. 1989. Reformas e Reformismos. In Nilson do Rosário Costa et al., eds. *Demandas Populares, Políticas Públicas e Saúde*. Vol. 1: *Ciências Sociais e Saúde Coletiva*, 13–44. Petrópolis: Vozes & ABRASCO.

Oliveira, Ribamar. 1991. Previdência beneficia minoria e exclui necessitados. *Jornal do Brasil* (24 March): 3.

OPS (Organización Panamericana de la Salud). 2001. *El Salvador: Perfil del Sistema de Servicios de Salud*. San Salvador: OPS, Serie Aportes para la Reforma del Sector Salud en El Salvador No. 13.

Ordóñez, Cosme. 1989. El Sistema nacional de Salud en Cuba. *Saúde em Debate* 24 (March): 78–83.

Orenstein, Mitchell. 2005. The New Pension Reform: Global Policy and Democratic Deliberation. Maxwell School, Syracuse University.

———. 2003. Mapping the Diffusion of Pension Innovation. In Robert Holzmann, Mitchell Orenstein, and Michal Rutkowski, eds. *Pension Reform in Europe*, 171–93. Washington, DC: World Bank.

———. 2000. *How Politics and Institutions Affect Pension Reform in Three Postcommunist Countries*. Washington, DC: World Bank. Policy Research Working Paper 2310.

Organismo Andino de la Salud. 2003. Estudio de Reformas y Financiamiento de Sistemas y Servicios de Salud en la Subregión Andina. Resumen Ejecutivo. Caracas: Organismo Andino de la Salud.

Ornélas, Waldeck, and Solange Vieira. 1999. Novo Rumo para a Previdência Brasileira. *Revista do BNDES* 6:12 (December): 31–48.

Orszag, Peter, and Joseph Stiglitz. 1999. Rethinking Pension Reform. Paper for conference on "New Ideas about Old Age Security," World Bank, Washington, DC, 14–15 September.

Ortiz de Zevallos, Gabriel, et al. 1999. *La Economía Política de las Reformas Institucionales en el Perú*. Washington, DC: Inter-American Development Bank, Office of the Chief Economist. Working Paper R-348.

Oyarzo, César. 1994. La Administración de la Salud en el Contexto de Reforma y Privatización del Sector. In Escuela de Administración de Negocios, Instituto de Desarrollo Económico, ed. *Foro Internacional. Administración de la Salud: Enfoques, Tendencias, Propuestas*, 123–44. Lima: ESAN/IDE.

Page, Benjamin, and Robert Shapiro. 1992. *The Rational Public*. Chicago: University of Chicago Press.

Panadeiros, Mónica. 2000. La Organización del Sistema de Salud en El Salvador. In Fundación Salvadoreña para el Desarrollo Económico y Social, ed. *Crecimiento con Participación: Una Estrategia de Desarrollo para el Siglo XXI*, vol. 2: *El Desafío Social en El Salvador*, 204–31. San Salvador: FU-SADES.

Pantoja, Isabel. 2002. Author interview with former member of pension reform team. La Paz: 31 July.

Parandekar, Suhas. 2002. Democratic Decentralization and People's Participation. In Louise Haagh and Camilla Helgø, eds. *Social Policy Reform and Market Governance in Latin America*, 165–79. Houndmills: Palgrave Macmillan.

Paredes, Víctor. 2002. Personal communication from former Peruvian health minister (1991–93). Lima: 25 July.

Parikh, Sunita. 2000. The Strategic Value of *Analytic Narratives*. *Social Science History* 24:4 (Winter): 677–84.

Pastor, Manuel, and Carol Wise. 1999. The Politics of Second-Generation Reform. *Journal of Democracy* 10:3 (July): 34–48.

Pawlowski, Vinícius. 2003. Author interview with assessor, Projeto REFORSUS, World Bank and Ministério da Saúde. Brasilia: 5 August.

Payet, José Antonio. 2002. Autor interview with former reform team member, Entidades Prestadoras de Salud, Ministerio de Salud. Lima: 19 July.

Paz Panizo, Jorge, and Rafael Ugaz Vallenas. 2003. *Análisis del Sistema Privado de Pensiones desde un Enfoque de Costos Hundidos Endógenos*. Lima: Consorcio de Investigación Económica y Social.

Pêgo, Raquel Abrantes, and Célia Almeida. 2002. *Ámbito y Papel de los Especialistas en las Reformas en los Sistemas de Salud: Brasil y México*. Notre Dame: Kellogg Institute, University of Notre Dame. Working Paper 299.

Peña Rueda, Alfonso. 2002. Author interview with former secretario nacional de pensiones (1995–97). La Paz: 24 July.

Peñaranda, César. 2002. Author interview with former jefe de asesores, Ministerio de Economía y Finanzas. Lima: 12 July.

Pereira, Cristián. 2002. Author interview with gerente general, Proyecto Reforma de Salud, Ministerio de Salud y Previsión Social. La Paz: 1 August.

Pérez B., Martín. 2000. Circúito Político de una Política Pública: Reforma al Sistema de Pensiones en Bolivia. La Paz: Centro Boliviano de Estudios Multi-disciplinarios.

Pérez Montás, Hernando. 1994. Determinantes y Agenda para la Reforma del Sistema de Pensiones. San José: N.p.

Perry, Guillermo. 2005. The Structural Reform Agenda: Revisiting the Role of the State. Presentation for conference on "Latin America in the Global Economy," Kellogg Institute, University of Notre Dame, 19 April.

Phang Romero, Carmen. 2002. Reforma del Sector Salud y la Política Farmacéutica en Perú. *Cadernos de Saúde Pública* 18:4 (July–August): 1121–38.

Pichihua, Juan. 2005. Email communication from former coordinador, Seguro Materno Infantil, Ministerio de Salud, Peru: 6 March.

———. 1998. Informe de Visita de Observación del Seguro de Maternidad y Niñez en Bolivia. Lima: Ministerio de Salud. Programa de Fortalecimiento de Servicios de Salud.

Pierson, Paul. 2004. *Politics in Time*. Princeton: Princeton University Press.

———. 1994. *Dismantling the Welfare State?* Cambridge: Cambridge University Press.

Pincus, Jonathan, and Jeffrey Winters. 2002. Reinventing the World Bank. In Pincus and Winters, eds. *Reinventing the World Bank,* 1–25. Ithaca: Cornell University Press.

Pinheiro, Vinícius. 2004. The Politics of Social Security Reform in Brazil. In Kurt Weyland, ed. *Learning from Foreign Models in Latin American Policy Reform,* 110–38. Washington, DC: Woodrow Wilson Center Press.

———. 1999. Author interview with secretário de previdência social, Ministério da Previdência e Assistência Social. Brasília: 11 June.

Pinheiro, Vinícius, and Solange Paiva Vieira. 2000a. Capitalização, Repartição e o Fator Previdenciário. *Investidor Institucional* (14 February): 30–31.

———. 2000b. *Reforma Previsional en Brasil.* Santiago de Chile: Comisión Económica para América Latina y el Caribe. Serie Financiamiento del Desarrollo 97.

Piola, Sérgio, Solon Magalhães Vianna, and David Vivas Consuelo. 2001. *Tendências do Sistema de Saúde Brasileiro.* Brasília: Instituto de Pesquisa Econômica Aplicada.

(El) Plan de Todos. 1993. La Paz: N.p. (May).

PNUD (Programa de las Naciones Unidas para el Desarrollo). 2002. *Informe de Desarrollo Humano en Bolivia 2002.* La Paz: PNUD.

Poltronieri, Jorge. 2003. *Estructuras de la Opinión Pública. Informe presentado a la Caja Costarricense de Seguro Social.* San José: Universidad de Costa Rica. Vicerrectoría de Investigación.

Pooley, Bertha. 2002. Author interview with former health specialist, Unidad de Análisis de Políticas Sociales (1993–97). La Paz: 14 August.

Popkin, Samuel. 1991. *The Reasoning Voter.* Chicago: University of Chicago Press.

Presidencia de la República. Programa Reforma del Estado. 1993. *Plan Nacional de Reforma del Sector Salud: Lineamientos Fundamentales.* San José: Presidencia.

Price Waterhouse. 1993. *Proyecto de Reforma del Sistema Previsional Boliviano: Proyecciones Financieras del Sistema Vigente de Seguridad Social y del Sistema de Capitalización Individual.* N.p. (27 January).

Principales Lineamientos de la Reforma de Pensiones. Seminario Político. 1994. N.p. (Bolivia).

Proceso de Implementación de la Reforma al Sistema de Pensiones de El Salvador. N.d. N.p.

Programa Reforma Integral de Pensiones. 1998a. *Historia de las Pensiones en Costa Rica.* San José: Segunda Vicepresidencia.

———. 1998b. *Reforma de Pensiones del Magisterio Nacional.* San José: Segunda Vicepresidencia.

Proyecto de Ley: "Ley de Protección al Trabajador," Agosto 1999. Exposición de Motivos. San José: N.p. http://www.nacion.co.cr/ln_ee/ESPECIALES/pensiones/leyprol.html.

Proyecto de Ley del Sistema Boliviano del Seguro Universal de Salud. 2002. In Nazario Tirado Cuenca, ed. *El Libro Blanco de la Salud: Memorias del Con-*

greso Boliviano de Salud, 277–305. La Paz: Ministerio de Salud y Previsión Social.

Queisser, Monika. 1998. *The Second-Generation Pension Reforms in Latin America*. Paris: Organisation for Economic Co-operation and Development.

Quiroga Stöllger, Yesko. 2002. Author interview with director, Fundación Friedrich Ebert en Bolivia. La Paz: 23 July.

Ragin, Charles. 2000. *Fuzzy-Set Social Science*. Chicago: University of Chicago Press.

Ramírez, Víctor. 2004. Author interview with intendente del sistema de pensiones público and leading reform team member. San Salvador: 8 July.

———. 1994a. El Sistema de Pensiones de El Salvador. In Víctor Ramírez and Mauricio Chavarría. *Diagnósticos sobre la Seguridad Social en El Salvador*, 1–17. San Salvador: Fundación Dr. Guillermo Manuel Ungo. Documento de Trabajo. Serie Seguridad Social 94–1.

———. 1994b. El Sistema de Pensiones de El Salvador. In Centro Internacional para el Desarrollo Económico, ed. *Soluciones Descentralizadas/Privadas a Problemas Públicos*, 92–103. San Salvador: CINDE.

Rauch, James, and Peter Evans. 2000. Bureaucratic Structure and Bureaucratic Performance in Less Developed Countries. *Journal of Public Economics* 75:1 (January): 49–71.

Reforma da Previdência. 1992. N.p. (Brazil).

Remmer, Karen. 2003. Elections and Economics in Contemporary Latin America. In Carol Wise and Riordan Roett, eds. *Post-Stabilization Politics in Latin America*, 31–55. Washington, DC: Brookings.

Resende, André Lara. 1998. Todos Vão Pagar (Interview with Ricardo Galuppo). *Veja* (29 October): 11–13.

Ribas, Oswaldo. 2003. Bomba-Relógio. *Problemas Brasileiros* 356 (March–April): 4–11.

Ricse Cataño, Carlos. 1999. *Evaluación Preliminar del Funcionamiento Operativo de los Pilotos de Moyobamba y Tacna: Informe*. Lima: Ministerio de Salud, Seguro Materno Infantil.

Risse-Kappen, Thomas. 1994. Ideas Do Not Float Freely. *International Organization* 48:2 (Spring): 185–214.

Rodríguez, Adolfo. 2004. Author interview with superintendente general de valores and former secretario técnico, Programa Reforma Integral de Pensiones (1995–98). San José: 21 June.

———. 2001. A Experiência da Costa Rica. In Ministério da Previdência e Assistência Social, ed. *Reformas dos Sistemas de Pensão na América Latina*, 79–87. Brasília: MPAS.

———. 1998a. El Gran Desafío de la Seguridad Social. In Adolfo Rodríguez, ed. *América Latina: Seguridad Social y Exclusión*, 15–22. San José: Segunda Vicepresidencia.

———, ed. 1998b. *América Latina: Seguridad Social y Exclusión*. San José: Segunda Vicepresidencia, Programa Reforma Integral de Pensiones.

———. 1996. Ventajas, Peligros y Desafíos de la Reforma de Pensiones en Costa Rica. San José: N.p.

Rodríguez, Adolfo, and Fabio Durán. 1998. *Reforma de Pensiones: Los Desafíos de la Vejez*. San José: Segunda Vicepresidencia.

Rodríguez, Rodolfo. 1995. La Reforma del Sector Salud en el Perú: Viabilidad y Factibilidad. Lima: Ministerio de Salud, Programa de Fortalecimiento de Servicios de Salud.

Rodriguez Neto, Eleutério. 1988. Saúde: Promessas e Limites da Constituição. Doctoral thesis, Departamento de Medicina Preventiva, Faculdade de Medicina, Universidade de São Paulo.

Rogers, Everett. 1995. *Diffusion of Innovations*, 4th ed. New York: Free Press.

Roggero, Mario. 2002. Author interview with former diputado (FREDEMO). Lima: 11 July.

———. 1993. *Escoja Usted*. Lima: N.p.

Romero, Alfredo. 2002. Author interview with former leader of pension reform team (1992). Lima: 17 July.

Rosas, Eric Jenner. 1988. Alguns Comentários sobre a nova Proposta de Saúde em Cuba. *Saúde em Debate* 23 (December): 104–5.

Rose, Richard. 1991. What Is Lesson-Drawing? *Journal of Public Policy* 11:1 (January): 3–30.

Rosenau, James. 2003. *Distant Proximities: Dynamics beyond Globalization*. Princeton: Princeton University Press.

Rosero-Bixby, Luis. 2004. Spatial Access to Health Care in Costa Rica and its Equity. *Social Science and Medicine* 58:7 (April): 1271–84.

Ross, Lee, and Craig Anderson. 1982. Shortcomings in the Attribution Process. In Daniel Kahneman, Paul Slovic, and Amos Tversky, eds. *Judgment under Uncertainty: Heuristics and Biases*, 129–52. Cambridge: Cambridge University Press.

Rossi, José Arnaldo. 1992. Author interview with former president of Instituto Nacional da Seguridade Social. Rio de Janeiro: 30 July.

Sáenz, Luis Bernardo. 2004. Author interview with former director, Proyecto de Modernización, Caja Costarricense de Seguro Social. San José: 28 June.

Sáenz, Luis Bernardo, and Carlos Zamora. 1988. *Evaluación del Programa de Atención Médica Ambulatoria por Capitación en el Cantón de Barva durante 1987*. San José: CCSS, Dirección Técnica de Servicios de Salud.

SAFP (Superintendencia de Administradoras de Fondos de Pensiones). 2004. Rentabilidad Real Anual del Fondo de Pensiones. Santiago de Chile: SAFP. http://www.safp.cl/inf_estadistica/index.html.

Salas Chaves, Álvaro. 2004. Author interview with former director técnico de servicios médicos (1990–94) and executive president (1994–98) of Caja Costarricense de Seguro Social. San José: 17 June.

Saldain, Rodolfo. 2006. Author interview with former consultant to Costa Rica's pension reform team (1996–97). Montevideo: 8 May.

———. 1996. Sistema Nacional de Pensiones—Costa Rica: Principios y Objetivos. San José: N.p.

Salinas, Helga. 2002. Author interview with intendente de pensiones and former leader of pension reform team (1991–93). La Paz: 26 July.

———. N.d. La Reforma Previsional en Bolivia. Santiago de Chile: International

Center for Pension Reform. http://www.josepinera.com/icpr/pag/pag_tex_boliviapensionreform.htm.

Samwick, Andrew. 2000. Is Pension Reform Conducive to Higher Saving? *Review of Economics and Statistics* 82:2 (May): 264–72.

Sánchez, Héctor. 1997. Evaluación del Desarrollo de la Reforma del Sistema de Seguridad Social en Salud y sus Efectos. In Ministerio de Salud, ed. 1997. *Seminario Internacional: Reforma del Sector Salud,* 109–20. Lima: MINSA.

———. 1993. Author interview with former superintendente de ISAPRE and international health consultant. Santiago de Chile: 5 August.

Sandoval, Oscar. 2002. Author interview with former secretario nacional de salud (1995–97) and leader of Movimiento Nacionalista Revolucionario. La Paz: 16 August.

Santiso, Javier. 2006. *Latin America's Political Economy of the Possible.* Cambridge: MIT Press.

Sassen, Saskia. 1996. *Losing Control: Sovereignty in an Age of Globalization.* New York: Columbia University Press.

Satz, Debra, and John Ferejohn. 1994. Rational Choice and Social Theory. *Journal of Philosophy* 91:2 (February): 71–87.

Schattschneider, Elmer. 1975. *The Semisovereign People.* Hinsdale, IL: Dryden.

Schofield, Norman. 1996. Rational Choice and Political Economy. In Jeffrey Frieden, ed. *The Rational Choice Controversy,* 189–211. New Haven: Yale University Press.

Schulthess, Walter E. 1988. El Sistema Boliviano de Seguridad Social: Pautas para su Reforma. N.p.

Schwarzer, Helmut. 2003a. Author interview with secretário de previdência social, Ministério da Previdência Social. Brasília: 11 August.

———. 2003b. *Sozialstaatliche Rentenreformen in Lateinamerika? Der Fall Brasilien.* Frankfurt am Main: Peter Lang.

Segovia, Alexander. 2002. *Transformación Estructural y Reforma Económica en El Salvador.* Guatemala City: Democracia y Desarrollo, Consultores.

Segura, Edwin. 2002. No se puede dar todo a todos. *La Prensa Gráfica* (San Salvador) (21 October).

Seguro de Salud ha atendido a 46 millones. 2005. *La República* (Lima) (31 January).

Seiber, Eric. 2002. *Baseline and Best Practice Assessment of Seven SIBASI in El Salvador: Phase I and II.* Bethesda, MD: Partners for Health Reform*plus.*

Selva Sutter, Ernesto. 2000. Al Oído de Aquellos Interesados en la Reforma de Salud. *Estudios Centroamericanos* 55:619–20 (May-June): 573–98.

Senna, Mônica de Castro, and Mirian Cohen. 2002. Modelo Assistencial e Estratégia Saúde da Família no Nível Local. *Ciência & Saúde Coletiva* 7:3 (July–September): 523–35.

Seoane, Guillermo. 2002. Author interview with former subsecretario de salud (1993–94). La Paz: 16 August.

———. 1994. *Principio y Pilares de la Transformación en Salud.* La Paz: N.p.

SEPS (Superintendencia de Entidades Prestadoras de Salud). 2004. *Memoria Institucional: Año 2003.* Lima: SEPS.

———. 2002. *Participación del Sector Privado en la Seguridad Social en Salud–En Busca de Nuevas Oportunidades.* Lima: Apoyo Consultoría.

———. 2000. *Encuesta de Opinión a los Componentes del Sistema de Entidades Prestadoras de Salud.* Lima: SEPS.

Serra, José. 2000. *Ampliando o Possível: A Política de Saúde do Brasil.* São Paulo: HUCITEC.

Serra, José, and Regina Faria. 2004. Reforma de la Salud en Brasil, 1995–2002. In Clarisa Hardy, ed. *Equidad y Protección Social,* 153–78. Santiago de Chile: LOM.

Shapiro, Ian, Rogers Smith, and Tarek Masoud, eds. 2004. *Problems and Methods in the Study of Politics.* Cambridge: Cambridge University Press.

Shiffman, Jeremy. 2003. Generating Political Will for Safe Motherhood in Indonesia. *Social Science & Medicine* 56:6 (March): 1197–1207.

Shiffman, Jeremy, Cynthia Stanton, and Ana Patricia Salazar. 2004. The Emergence of Political Priority for Safe Motherhood in Honduras. *Health Policy and Planning* 19:6 (November): 380–90.

Shugart, Matthew, and Scott Mainwaring. 1997. Presidentialism and Democracy in Latin America. In Mainwaring and Shugart, eds. *Presidentialism and Democracy in Latin America,* 12–54. Cambridge: Cambridge University Press.

Silva, Hector. 2004. Author interview with former FMLN leader and jefe de fracción, CDU, Asamblea Legislativa. San Salvador: 6 July.

———. 1998. Salud y Política Sanitaria. Chap. in *¿Existe una Política Social en El Salvador?* 29–63. San Salvador: Konrad Adenauer Stiftung.

Simmons, Beth. 2001. The International Politics of Harmonization. *International Organization* 55:3 (Summer): 589–620.

Simmons, Beth, Frank Dobbin, and Geoffrey Garrett. 2006. The International Diffusion of Liberalism. *International Organization* 60:4 (Fall): 781–810.

Simmons, Beth, and Zachary Elkins. 2004. The Globalization of Liberalization. *American Political Science Review* 98:1 (February): 171–89.

Simon, Herbert. 1985. Human Nature in Politics. *American Political Science Review* 79:2 (June): 293–304.

———. 1957. *Models of Man.* New York: Wiley.

Slaughter, Anne-Marie. 2004. *A New World Order.* Princeton: Princeton University Press.

Sobrevilla, Alfredo. 2002. Author interview with former reform team member, Comités Locales de Administración de Salud, Ministerio de Salud. Lima: 15 July.

———. 2000. Informe Final de Consultoría. Lima: Ministerio de Salud, Programa de Fortalecimiento de Servicios de Salud.

Socimer International Bank. 1993. *Reforma Estructural al Sistema Previsional Salvadoreño. Anexo Propuesta Técnica. Revisión Plan de Trabajo.* N.p.: Socimer International Bank.

Sojo, Ana. 1998. *Hacia unas nuevas Reglas del Juego: Los Compromisos de Gestión en Salud de Costa Rica.* Santiago de Chile: CEPAL. Serie Políticas Sociales 27.

Solari, Alfredo. 1994. Reforma del Sector Salud. In Centro Internacional para el

Desarrollo Económico, ed. *Soluciones Descentralizadas/Privadas a Problemas Públicos*, 104–35. San Salvador: CINDE.

Solimano, Giorgio. 1997. Perspectiva sobre la Reforma de Salud en Chile. In Ministerio de Salud, ed. *Seminario Internacional: Reforma del Sector Salud*, 37–44. Lima: MINSA.

Solimeo, Marcel Domingos. 2003. Author interview with director, Instituto de Economia Gastão Vidigal, Associação Comercial de São Paulo. São Paulo: 7 July.

Solórzano, Ruth del Castillo de. 2004. Author interview with leading pension reform team member and directora ejecutiva, Asociación Salvadoreña de Administradoras de Fondos de Pensiones. San Salvador: 7 July.

Sousa, Arlindo Gómez de. 1987. Author interview with coordenador, Secretaria Técnica, Comissão Nacional da Reforma Sanitária. Manguinhos, RJ: 2 September.

Sousa, Maria Fátima de. 2003. Author interview with leader of primary health care movement. Brasília: 13 August.

———. 2001. *Agentes Comunitários de Saúde*. São Paulo: HUCITEC.

Stallings, Barbara. 1992. International Influence on Economic Policy. In Stephan Haggard and Robert Kaufman, eds. *The Politics of Economic Adjustment*, 41–88. Princeton: Princeton University Press.

Starr, Harvey. 1991. Democratic Dominoes. *Journal of Conflict Resolution* 35: 2 (June): 356–81.

Stephanes, Reinhold. 1992. Author interview with Ministro da Previdência Social. Brasília: 29 June.

Stiglitz, Joseph. 1999. Scan Globally, Reinvent Locally. Keynote Address, First Global Development Network Conference. Bonn, Germany: December.

Stokes, Susan. 2001. *Mandates and Democracy*. Cambridge: Cambridge University Press.

Stone, Randall. 2002. *Lending Credibility: The International Monetary Fund and the Post-Communist Transition*. Princeton: Princeton University Press.

Strang, David, and Michael Macy. 2001. In Search of Excellence. *American Journal of Sociology* 107:1 (July): 147–82.

Strang, David, and Sarah Soule. 1998. Diffusion in Organizations and Social Movements. *Annual Review of Sociology* 24: 265–90.

Strange, Susan. 1996. *The Retreat of the State*. Cambridge: Cambridge University Press.

Sugiyama, Natasha Borges. 2008. Theories of Policy Diffusion: Social Sector Reform in Brazil. *Comparative Political Studies* 41:4 (April): forthcoming.

Swank, Duane. 2002. *Global Capital, Political Institutions, and Policy Change in Developed Welfare States*. Cambridge: Cambridge University Press.

Synthesis. 2000. *El Proceso de Reforma Previsional en El Salvador*. San Salvador: Synthesis Consultores Internacionales. Estudio Especial de Synthesis No. 8.

Tamayo, Sergio. 2004. Author interview with pension reform team member and asesor, Intendencia del Sistema de Pensiones Público. San Salvador: 6 July.

Tamburi, Giovanni. 1994. Objetivos y Opciones para el Diseño del Segundo Pilar en el Sistema Nacional de Pensiones de Costa Rica. San José: N.p.

Tank, Matthew. 2004. Author interview with loan officer, Inter-American Development Bank. San José: 29 June.

Taylor, Shelley. 1982. The Availability Bias in Social Perception and Interaction. In Daniel Kahneman, Paul Slovic, and Amos Tversky, eds. *Judgment under Uncertainty: Heuristics and Biases,* 190–200. Cambridge: Cambridge University Press.

Teichman, Judith. 2001. *The Politics of Freeing Markets in Latin America.* Chapel Hill: University of North Carolina Press.

Teixeira, Carmen Fontes, and Cristina Melo, eds. 1995. *Construindo Distritos Sanitários: A Experiência da Cooperação Italiana no Município de São Paulo.* São Paulo: HUCITEC.

Teixeira, Suely, Valéria Monteiro, and Verônica Miranda. 1999. Programa Médico da Família no Município de Niterói. *Estudos Avançados* 13:35 (January): 147–55.

Temporão, José Gomes. 1988. Alguns Comentários sobre o Documento "Brasil Public Speding (sic) on Social Programs: Issues and Options"–Banco Mundial–Janeiro de 1988. *Saúde em Debate* 22 (October): 30–35.

Tendler, Judith. 1997. *Good Government in the Tropics.* Baltimore: Johns Hopkins University Press.

Tetlock, Philip. 2005. *Expert Political Judgment.* Princeton: Princeton University Press.

Thaler, Richard. 2000. From Homo Economicus to Homo Sapiens. *Journal of Economic Perspectives* 14:1 (Winter): 133–41.

Thelen, Kathleen. 2004. *How Institutions Evolve.* Cambridge: Cambridge University Press.

———. 1999. Historical Institutionalism in Comparative Politics. *Annual Review of Political Science* 2: 369–404.

Toledo, Alejandro. 2001. "Una Guerra frontal contra la Pobreza será el Eje Central de mi Gobierno." Discurso del Presidente del Perú en el Acto de Juramentación de su Mandato en el Congreso de la República, 30 de Julio. http://www.analitica.com/va/hispanica/documentos/9360837.asp.

Torres Goitia Caballero, Javier. 2006. Author interview with former health minister (2002–03). La Paz: 19 June.

———. 2002. Hacia la Participación Social en la Salud. In Nazario Tirado Cuenca, ed. *El Libro Blanco de la Salud: Memorias del Congreso Boliviano de Salud,* 116–23. La Paz: Ministerio de Salud y Previsión Social.

———. 2000. La Reforma de Salud en Bolivia. In José Luis Evia et al. *Las Reformas Estructurales en Bolivia,* vol. 2, 301–61. La Paz: Fundación Milenio.

Torres Goitia Torres, Javier. 2006. Author interview with former health minister (1983–85). La Paz: 20 June.

———. 1987. *Salud y Democracia: La Experiencia de Bolivia (1982–1985).* Santiago de Chile: Editorial Universitaria.

Torres y Torres Lara, Carlos. 1999. Author interview with former prime minister (1991) and leader of Cambio 90/Nueva Mayoría. Lima: 8 July.

Trejos, Juan Diego, et al. 1994. Enhancing Social Services in Costa Rica. In Cristián Aedo and Osvaldo Larrañaga, eds. *Social Service Delivery Systems,* 51–90. Washington, DC: Inter-American Development Bank.

Tsebelis, George. 1995. Decision Making in Political Systems. *British Journal of Political Science* 25:3 (July): 289–325.

———. 1990. *Nested Games*. Berkeley: University of California Press.

Turner, Marlene, and Anthony Pratkanis. 1998. Twenty-Five Years of Group-think Theory and Research. *Organizational Behavior and Human Decision Processes* 73:2–3 (February–March): 105–15.

Tversky, Amos, and Daniel Kahneman. 1982. Judgments of and by Representa-tiveness. In Daniel Kahneman, Paul Slovic, and Amos Tversky, eds. *Judgment under Uncertainty*, 84–98. Cambridge: Cambridge University Press.

UDAPE (Unidad de Análisis de Políticas Sociales y Económicas). 2004. *Evalua-ción de la Economía al Primer Semestre 2004*. La Paz: UDAPE.

UDAPE (Unidad de Análisis de Políticas Sociales y Económicas) and OPS Orga-nización Panamericana de la Salud. 2004. *Caracterización de la Exclusión en Salud en Bolivia*. La Paz: UDAPE.

UDAPSO (Unidad de Análisis de Políticas Sociales). 1993. *Diagnóstico Social*. La Paz: UDAPSO.

UPC (Unidad Preparatoria de Proyectos). 1993. *Proyecto Reforma Sector Salud. Componente Readecuación del Modelo de Atención*. San José: N.p.

Uribe, Juan Pablo. 2004. The Influence of Foreign Models on Health Reform in Colombia. In Kurt Weyland, ed. *Learning from Foreign Models in Latin Ameri-can Policy Reform*, 196–218. Washington, DC: Woodrow Wilson Center Press.

Urroz, Ernesto. N.d. El Sistema Previsional de El Salvador y su Reforma. San Salvador: Superintendencia de Pensiones de El Salvador.

Valenzuela, Gustavo. 2002. Author interview with former IDB-consultant on Reforma de los Seguros de Salud. La Paz: 14 August.

———. 2001a. Informe Final de Consultoría. Programa: Préstamo BID 1031/SF-BO. La Paz: N.p.

———. 2001b. *Propuesta de Reingeniería de la Caja Nacional de Salud*. La Paz: Ministerio de Salud y Previsión Social (4 April).

Valiente, Bernardo. 2004. "Mesa" de Concertación Define Agenda. *La Prensa Gráfica* (San Salvador) (7 July): 25.

Valverde, Jorge. 2004. Author interview with jefe del Departamento de Pensi-ones, Gerencia de Pensiones, Caja Costarricense de Seguro Social. San José: 30 June.

Vargas, Mauricio. 2004. Author interview with former member of health reform team (1987–94) and president of association of health cooperatives. San José: 3 July.

Vargas, Teresa. 2002. Author interview with former core member of pension reform team and directora de prestaciones, Intendencia de Pensiones. La Paz: 31 July.

Vásquez, Enrique. 2002. Author interview with former director, Programa Naci-onal de Asistencia Alimentaria (1996). Lima: 17 July.

Velit Granda, Ernesto. 1997. Incoherencias en el Sector Salud. *El Comercio* (Lima) (18 April).

Vera del Carpio, Juan José. 2002. Author interview with former project leader, Comités Locales de Administración de Salud, Ministerio de Salud (1994–98). Lima: 26 June.

Vera la Torre, José Carlos. 2003a. *Cobertura y Financiamiento del Seguro Integral de Salud en el Perú.* Lima: ForoSalud. Cuaderno de Trabajo N⁰ 2.

———. 2003b. *Economía Social de Mercado en los Sectores Sociales.* Lima: ESAN Ediciones.

———. 2002. Author interview with former economy ministry consultant (1991) and chief adviser to health minister Jaime Freundt (1993–94). Lima: 28 June.

———. 1994a. Modernización y Apertura de los Servicios de Salud a la Participación del Sector Privado. In José Carlos Vera la Torre et al. *La Privatización de la Salud: Rumbo a la Modernidad,* 1–22. Lima: Instituto de Economía de Libre Mercado.

———. 1994b. Propuesta de Ley sobre el Sistema Privado de Seguridad Social en Salud. In Escuela de Administración de Negocios, Instituto de Desarrollo Económico, ed. *Foro Internacional. Administración de la Salud: Enfoques, Tendencias, Propuestas,* 173–97. Lima: ESAN/IDE.

Vera la Torre, José Carlos, et al. 1994. *La Privatización de la Salud: Rumbo a la Modernidad.* Lima: IELM.

Viana, Ana D'Ávila, and Mario dal Poz. 1998. A Reforma do Sistema de Saúde no Brasil e o Programa de Saúde da Família. *Physis—Revista de Saúde Coletiva* 8:2 (December): 11–48.

Vittas, Dimitri, and Augusto Iglesias. 1992. The Rationale and Performance of Personal Pension Plans in Chile. Washington, DC: World Bank.

Von Gersdorff, Hermann. 1997. The Bolivian Pension Reform. Washington, DC: World Bank.

Vreeland, James. 2003. *The IMF and Economic Development.* Cambridge: Cambridge University Press.

Walt, Stephen. 2000. Fads, Fevers, and Firestorms. *Foreign Policy* 121 (November–December): 34–42.

Way, Christopher. 2005. Political Insecurity and the Diffusion of Financial Market Integration. *Annals of the American Academy of Political and Social Science* 598 (March): 125–44.

WB (World Bank). 2004a. Asistencia del Banco Mundial en El Salvador. Hoja Informativa. N.p.: WB.

———. 2004b. *El Salvador: Evaluación del Gasto Público. Resumen Ejecutivo.* N.p.: WB.

———. 2004c. *Health Sector Reform in Bolivia: A Decentralization Case Study.* Washington, DC: WB.

———. 2004d. *Implementation Completion Report on a Health Sector Reform Project (APL-I).* Report No. 28270-BO. Washington, DC: WB.

———. 2004e. *Implementation Completion Report on a Health Sector Reform Project—REFORSUS.* Report No. 29325-BR. Washington, DC: WB.

———. 2004f. *Republic of Bolivia: Country Assistance Strategy.* Report No. 26838-BO. Washington, DC: WB.

———. 2004g. *Republic of Peru: Fourth Programmatic Social Reform Loan.* Report No. 30113-PE. Washington, DC: WB.

———. 2003a. *Argentina: Provincial Maternal-Child Health Sector Adjustment Loan.* Report No. 26527-AR. Washington, DC: WB.

———. 2003b. *Brazil—Equitable, Competitive, Sustainable: Contributions for Debate.* Washington, DC: WB.

———. 2003c. *Costa Rica: El Gasto Social y la Pobreza.* Washington, DC: WB.

———. 2003d. *Peru: Programmatic Social Reform Loan II. Implementation Completion Report (SCL-46780). Report No. 25864-PE.* Washington, DC: WB.

———. 2002. *El Salvador: Country Assistance Evaluation. Report No. 23626.* Washington, DC: WB.

———. 2001a. *Bolivia: Second Phase of the Health Sector Reform Program. Report No. 22301-BO.* Washington, DC: WB.

———. 2001b. *Brazil: Critical Issues in Social Security.* Washington, DC: WB.

———. 2001c. *El Salvador: Country Assistance Strategy. Report No. 22932-ES.* Washington, DC: WB.

———. 2001d. *El Salvador: Earthquake Emergency Reconstruction and Health Services Extension Project. Report No. 22626-ES.* Washington, DC: WB.

———. 2001e. *Peru: Programmatic Social Reform Loan (PSRL). Report No. PID10052.* Washington, DC: WB.

———. 2000a. *Bolivia: From Patronage to a Professional State. Report No. 20115-BO. Vol. 1.* Washington, DC: WB.

———. 2000b. *Costa Rica: Country Assistance Evaluation. Report No. 21391.* Washington, DC: WB.

———. 1999a. *Bolivia: Health Sector Reform Project. Report No. 18980-BO.* Washington, DC: WB.

———. 1999b. *Bolivia: Public Expenditure Review. Report No. 19232-BO.* Washington, DC: WB.

———. 1999c. *Peru: First Phase of the Health Reform Program (Mother and Child Insurance and Decentralization of Health Services). Report No. 19901-PE.* Washington, DC: WB.

———. 1999d. *Peru: Improving Health Care for the Poor.* Washington, DC: WB.

———. 1998a. *Brazil. The Brazil Health System: Impact Evaluation Report. Report No. 18142.* Washington, DC: WB.

———. 1998b. *Costa Rica: A Pension Reform Strategy. Draft Report No. 17766-CR.* Washington, DC: WB.

———. 1996a. *Brazil: Health Sector Reform Project—REFORSUS. Report No. 15522-BR.* Washington, DC: WB.

———. 1996b. *El Salvador: Public Sector Modernization Technical Assistance Loan (PSM-TAL). Technical Annex. Report No. T-6839-ES.* Washington, DC: WB.

———. 1995. *Brazil: Social Insurance and Private Pensions. Report No. 12336-BR.* Washington, DC: WB.

———. 1994a. *Averting the Old Age Crisis.* Washington, DC: Oxford University Press.

———. 1994b. *Brazil. The Organization, Delivery and Financing of Health Care in Brazil: Agenda for the 90s. Report No. 12655-BR.* Washington, DC: WB.

———. 1994c. *El Salvador: The Challenge of Poverty Alleviation. Report No. 12315-ES.* Washington, DC: WB.

———. 1994d. *Peru: Basic Health and Nutrition Project. Report No. 11801-PE.* Washington, DC: WB.

———. 1993a. *Costa Rica: Health Sector Reform—Social Security System Project. Report No. 11986-CR.* Washington, DC: WB.

———. 1993b. *World Development Report 1993: Investing in Health.* Washington, DC: Oxford University Press.

———. 1991. *Brasil: Novo Desafio à Saúde do Adulto. PUB-7807.* Washington, DC: WB.

———. 1989. *Brazil: The Macroeconomics of Social Security: Fiscal and Financial Issues. Report No. 7800-BR.* Washington, DC: WB.

WB IEG (World Bank Independent Evaluation Group). 2006. *Pension Reform and the Development of Pension Systems: An Evaluation of World Bank Assistance.* Washington, DC: WB.

Weinberg, Stephanie. 1998. Banco Mundial y BID en El Salvador. *Alternativas para el Desarrollo* 52 (March). http://ladb.unm.edu/econ/content/sad/1998/march/banco.html.

Weyland, Kurt. 2005a. The Diffusion of Innovations: How Cognitive Heuristics Shaped Bolivia's Pension Reform. *Comparative Politics* 38:1 (October): 21–42.

———. 2005b. Theories of Policy Diffusion: Lessons from Latin American Pension Reform. *World Politics* 57:2 (January): 264–98.

———. 2004a. Learning from Foreign Models in Latin American Policy Reform: An Introduction. In Weyland, ed. *Learning from Foreign Models in Latin American Policy Reform,* 1–34. Washington, DC: Woodrow Wilson Center Press.

———. 2004b. Lessons about Learning in Latin American Policy Reform. In Weyland, ed. *Learning from Foreign Models in Latin American Policy Reform,* 241–83. Washington, DC: Woodrow Wilson Center Press.

———. 2002a. Limitations of Rational-Choice Institutionalism for the Study of Latin American Politics. *Studies in Comparative International Development* 37:1 (Spring): 57–85.

———. 2002b. *The Politics of Market Reform in Fragile Democracies.* Princeton: Princeton University Press.

———. 1996a. *Democracy without Equity: Failures of Reform in Brazil.* Pittsburgh: University of Pittsburgh Press.

———. 1996b. How Much Political Power Do Economic Forces Have? Conflicts over Social Insurance Reform in Brazil. *Journal of Public Policy* 16:1 (April): 59–84.

White, Joseph. 2000. Why Chile Provides No Evidence for Social Security Privatization. *Public Budgeting & Finance* 20:4 (Winter): 52–62.

Wibbels, Erik, and Moisés Arce. 2003. Globalization, Taxation, and Burden-Shifting in Latin America. *International Organization* 57:1 (Winter): 111–36.

Wildavsky, Aaron. 1964. *The Politics of the Budgetary Process.* Boston: Little, Brown.

Wise, Carol. 2003a. Introduction: Latin American Politics in the Era of Market Reform. In Carol Wise and Riordan Roett, eds. *Post-Stabilization Politics in Latin America,* 1–28. Washington, DC: Brookings.

————. 2003b. *Reinventing the State: Economic Strategy and Institutional Change in Peru.* Ann Arbor: University of Michigan Press.

Yamamoto, Víctor. 2002. Author interview with former health minister (1991). Lima: 4 July.

Yong Motta, Eduardo. 2002. Author interview with former health minister (1994–96). Lima: 3 July.

Zaller, John. 1992. *The Nature and Origins of Mass Opinion.* Cambridge: Cambridge University Press.

Zockun, Maria Helena. 2003. Author interview with former assessora, Departamento Econômico, Federação de Indústrias do Estado de São Paulo. São Paulo: 8 July.

Zylberstajn, Hélio. 2003. Author interview with former secretário nacional do trabalho, Ministério do Trabalho e Administração (1992). São Paulo: 15 July.

Index

Walt, Stephen, 19
Way, Christopher, 19
Weingast, Barry, 227
Weyland, Kurt, viii, 224; diffusion issues and, 13, 44; health care reform and, 159, 187, 215n1; pension reform and, 74, 80–81, 124, 129
White, Joseph, 112
Wibbels, Erik, 237
Wildavsky, Aaron, 36
Winters, Jeffrey, 2, 53, 217
Wise, Carol, 22, 38, 114n12
Woodrow Wilson Center, vii
World Bank, 1–2, 4, 104, 142, 237; Brazil and, 129–31; Costa Rica and, 135, 138; external pressures and, 37–39, 69–91; health care reform and, 144–58; international norms and, 69–70; as knowledge bank, 217; limited success of, 71–79; model diffusion and, 37–43; normative appeal and, 39–43; notional defined-contribution (NDC) scheme and, 98–

99, 107–8; PAYG systems and, 89; Peru and, 158–63; policy issues and, 10, 17, 19, 47, 51, 53; quasi-market mechanisms and, 145; rational learning and, 43; reform and, 69–91; representativeness and, 110–11, 113. *See also* international financial institutions (IFIs)
World Development Report, 37–38, 154, 166–67, 177, 179
World Health Organization (WHO), 9, 145, 171, 175, 177, 217

Yamamoto, Victor, 159, 187
Yañez, Ernesto, 113–14
Yermo, Juan, 43n5, 113, 122
Yong Motta, Eduardo, 187

Zaller, John, 54
Zelner, Bennet, 33
Zimbabwe, 38
Zockun, Maria Helena, 126
Zylberstajn, Hélio, 126